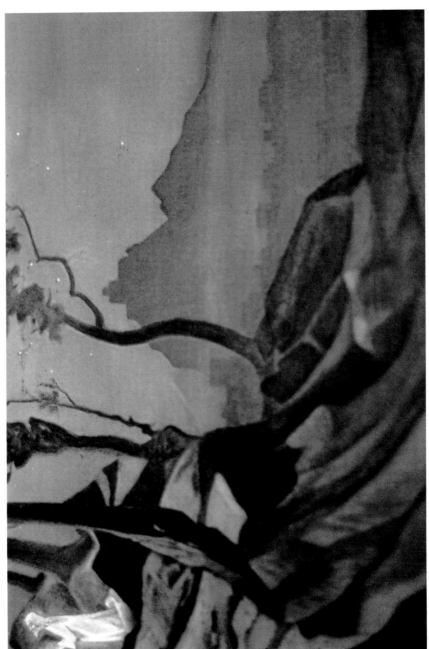

CHALICE OF CHRIST

Mark L. Prophet

THE LOST TEACHINGS OF JESUS

I

ELIZABETH CLARE PROPHET

THE LOST TEACHINGS OF JESUS

I

MARK L. PROPHET
ELIZABETH CLARE PROPHET

SUMMIT UNIVERSITY ✦ PRESS®

THE LOST TEACHINGS OF JESUS I
Mark L. Prophet • Elizabeth Clare Prophet

Copyright © 1986 Summit University Press
All rights reserved.

Library of Congress Catalog Card Number: 81-52784
International Standard Book Number: 0-916766-71-3

For information on the magnificent art of Nicholas Roerich
reproduced in this volume, write Nicholas Roerich Museum,
319 West 107th St., New York, N.Y. 10025.

This book is set in 12 point Times Roman with 1 point lead.
Printed in the United States of America
First Printing: August 1986. Second Printing: August 1987

Cover: Taken from a painting
by Nicholas Roerich, *Treasure in the Mountain*

To our beloved friends
throughout the world
who have endured with us
through our trials and triumphs
in Jesus Christ.
Without you
his Lost Teachings
could not have been preached
and published in every nation.

THE LOST TEACHINGS OF JESUS
VOLUME ONE *Contents*

VOLUME ONE *Illustrations*

THE LOST TEACHINGS OF JESUS
VOLUME TWO *Contents*

491   CHAPTER FOURTEEN

YOU WILL BECOME ONE WITH GOD!

VOLUME TWO *Illustrations*

THE PAST IS PROLOGUE

The Past Is Prologue

IMAGINE you are a detective. It's night. You close the file on *The Lost Years of Jesus* and lean back in the old swivel chair.

Cases like this one are hard to find. Harder still to crack. The hole in your shoe tells it all.

But then, that's what this is all about. Getting to the bottom of things. Making the pieces fit. Putting it all together. And then. . . the quiet glow of satisfaction. After all, who would've ever expected Jesus to have gone to the Himalayas?

Now you can tend to all those things that have been stacking up for weeks, such as. . .

But wait. There. Under some unopened mail. Another file?

You see the words *Lost* and *Jesus* scrawled across the top. I'll look at it tomorrow, you tell yourself.

That's right, tomorrow. But that only lasts two seconds. Curiosity starts to gnaw at your sense of professionalism. Suppose it's another case? You're seized by the inescapable feeling that mystery awaits.

Just when you thought things were slowing down. You sigh. Haven't you had your fill of mysteries lately? You struggle with the thought for a moment, muttering something about no rest for the weary. But you've made your mark doing things the right way. So, hiding the thrill of a new adventure under a here-we-go-again sigh of resignation, you reach for the file.

You open it and read a few pages. You look cool on the outside. That comes from years of practice. But your heart starts to pound and the fatigue melts like a snowman in the Texas sun. Who would have thought there would be anything else missing about Jesus after the so-called lost years had been found? But if this file is correct, there's something even more remarkable—lost *teachings.*

Lost teachings? Remarkable? Maybe. But when you think of it, seventeen years in the Orient should have produced more than a travelogue. Especially from the mind of so perceptive and persistent a student of life as Jesus must have been!

Lost teachings? All along it should have been the ineluctable conclusion. They had to exist. But where are they now?

A few memories flicker in your mind. You remember having heard that the New Testament is supposed to contain everything of import that Jesus said.

You scratch your head. You recall a priest here and a minister there saying something about Jesus having a brief ministry and the good book containing all that is needful. Not much to go on. But to tell the truth, you weren't always as attentive as you might have been. And with all due respect, some of those men of the cloth weren't as inspiring as *they* might have been. Anyway, you deal with facts.

But this file. It's electric.

Some ministers, you say to yourself, ought to get a hold of it. Do them a world of good.

The phone rings. It's that old gang of yours wanting to get together for maybe the zillionth time. You can tell by the ring.

You stick the phone in a drawer and let it ring. The file is addictive.

The phone starts up again. You take the receiver off the hook and lay it on last month's light bill.

"Hello? Hello?"

You've got to read. They'll get the point in a minute.

"Listen. We know you're there. We weren't born yesterday, you know."

Yes. This file says as much. But then, it would probably shock them to find out just when they *were* born.

A few minutes pass and slowly, half-consciously you realize they're wrong on the first point. You're not really there. You're lost in the midst of an ancient panorama as the words come to life off the page.

A minute more and you've had enough. You grab your coat and head out into the night looking for clues.

————————————

Clues, yes. But you won't find a file with the lost parables, sayings, and teachings of Jesus neatly recorded, categorized, indexed and available word-for-word in a concordance. Nor will you find a complete chronology of his unrecorded acts—healings, exorcisms, miracles, confrontations with friend and foe, and the myriad other interactions Jesus had with men and angels that, if we only knew them, could be so edifying to our souls. Nor any of the countless other things Jesus did that, if they should be written, John supposes, the world itself could not contain the books.[1]

Yet there is little question that there *are* lost teachings of Jesus, many of them given in secret, that are vitally important to each of us. Clues as to their existence abound, many in plain sight (for those who have eyes to see), starting right under our noses in the New Testament!

Now, Jesus was a teacher. He was also a healer, miracle worker and Messiah, but *teaching* occupied much of his mission—in the cities and villages in Galilee, in the synagogues, in the lands beyond the Jordan and, later, daily in the temple at Jerusalem. The people were astonished at his doctrine and at the authority with which he taught, the more so because he was presumed to be unlettered.

Yet in proportion to the number of occasions on which Jesus is said to have taught, a surprisingly small number of verses record just what those teachings were. Some accounts show Jesus teaching for several hours or more without including one word of what he said. For example, at the feeding of the five thousand the people were clearly present long enough to get hungry. Jesus seems to have begun early, continuing until the day was "far spent."[2]

He must have been saying something of note, for the multitudes were spellbound and did not leave as evening drew on, not even to find food. Moved with compassion, he multiplied the five loaves and two fishes and fed them. But none of the four Gospels, which all tell of the episode, record what Jesus said, with the exception of Luke's single comment that Jesus "spake unto them of the kingdom of God."[3]

Luke also relates the story of Jesus' walk with the disciples on the road to Emmaus where, "starting with Moses and going through all the prophets, he explained to them the passages throughout the scriptures that were about himself."[4] Neither the passages nor their attendant explanation is given.

Matthew, Mark, and Luke all report that Jesus "sat at meat" with many publicans and sinners for the purpose of calling them to repentance.[5] In Luke we read that Martha's sister, Mary, "sat at Jesus' feet and heard his word."[6] But, again, the Gospels are silent on what the Master specifically taught on those occasions.

At least twelve more passages throughout the Gospels show Jesus teaching but do not record his words.[7] Still other passages—at least ten—recount some of Jesus' words but imply that not all of what he said is recorded.[8] For instance, John 7 tells us that Jesus traveled to Jerusalem for the Feast of Tabernacles (a seven-day event) and "about the midst of the feast" he "went up into the temple and taught."[9] Just fourteen verses contain Jesus' words from that moment until the end of the feast—and most of the content is his answers to the queries of the Jews who marveled as he taught.

Surely he said more. For the people argued amongst themselves whether or not he was the Christ and the officers of the temple, when called to task for failing to arrest Jesus, defended their actions, saying, "Never man spake like this man!"

Matthew gives us a vivid description of Jesus' charge to his disciples prior to sending them forth to preach to the lost sheep of the house of Israel. His instructions to them were specific: "What I tell you in the dark, utter in the light; and what you hear whispered, proclaim upon the housetops."[10] Yet beyond "the kingdom of heaven is at hand,"[11] it is not clear in this context what he whispered or what they were to proclaim.

By inference, other teaching seems to be missing as well. Jesus has a number of disciples in his inner circle other than the twelve apostles—Mary, Martha and Lazarus of Bethany, Joseph of Arimathea, and Nicodemus, a Pharisee of considerable stature, are mentioned by name. All of these are close friends and followers of the Master, yet we have no record of how they became his intimates.

The first time we meet Martha of Bethany in John she clearly knows Jesus well, for she greets him with a chastisement born of this familiarity: "Lord, if thou hadst been here, my brother had not died!" Then a bare six verses later, in John 11:27, she declares, "Yea, Lord: I believe that thou art the Christ, the Son of God, which should come into the world!"

Can we really believe that we possess all the teaching which the Master gave Martha—the true understanding whereby she could have made that momentous declaration concerning Jesus' divine reality?

A well-known gap in the Gospels and Church history is the childhood chronology and the seventeen missing years of Jesus: Luke moves quickly from his birth, circumcision, and presentation in the temple, to age twelve in Jerusalem sitting midst the doctors of the law ("both hearing them and asking them questions"), to his baptism by John in Jordan at age thirty, while Matthew supplies the detail of the holy family's flight into Egypt, following the visitation of the Magi, and their return after the death of Herod. [12]

Where was he from childhood to age twelve and then between the ages of twelve and thirty?

My research on Jesus' journey to the East during the seventeen unaccounted-for years is presented in *The Lost Years of Jesus,* published in 1984. Numerous travelers to Ladakh have reported hearing of the Buddhist texts and legends which say that Jesus was teaching as well as studying in India, Nepal, Tibet, Ladakh and Persia. Nicolas Notovitch, Swami Abhedananda and Nicholas Roerich came upon and translated these texts, now reproduced in my book. Apart from the teaching they contain, whatever else the Messiah gave to the people of the lands through which he traveled has so far not come to light.

Jesus' post-resurrection teaching also deserves closer scrutiny. Much of what he said to his apostles after Easter morn is missing—for example, during the 'forty days' [13] when Acts says Jesus was seen by his disciples "speaking of the things pertaining to the kingdom of God." [14]

But another important facet of his teaching was still to come. After he has apparently finished his mission, after Luke says in Acts 1 that in the presence of witnesses he was "taken up and a cloud received him out of their sight," [15] within a year he reappears to raise up and tutor the apostle Paul, and sixty years later he gives to John his Book of Revelation, "sent and signified" by his angel. [16]

It is to these two instances of progressive revelation that we should pay close attention. That the Lord desired to add a new dimension to the already established teaching and that, in the case of Paul, he needed a messenger schooled well enough and empowered by himself to address the Gentiles is evident.

If we take Paul's words literally, we must consider the possibility that Jesus was in constant communion with his apostle for a period of years and personally taught him his entire message, bringing him to a level of understanding equal to or even greater than that of the chosen twelve. I believe examination of the scriptures shows that the full story of Paul's journey to apostleship, and consequently what Christ taught him along the way, is recorded neither in Acts nor in his epistles.

Paul's contact with Jesus began with the blinding light of conversion on the road to Damascus. But that was only the beginning. He says twice in I Corinthians that he saw the Lord. [17] In II Corinthians, he speaks of "visions and revelations" he has had from him; [18] then, later in the passage, he tells of pleading with the Lord three times regarding a "thorn in the flesh" and being answered, "My grace is enough for you: my power is at its best in weakness." [19]

Acts 18 records that one night the Master spoke to Paul in a vision. [20] Another time, in Acts 22, Paul fell into a trance while praying and "saw him." They have a brief conversation. [21] In Acts 16, the "Spirit of Jesus" will not allow Paul to cross the frontier of Mysia.[22] Paul also mentions twice in I Corinthians having received a certain teaching "from the Lord."[23]

Some scholars insist that Paul's sole contact with the Lord was at his conversion; although they admit he had later revelations, they say any factual knowledge he had of Christ and his mission must have come either from that single encounter or from other Christians. While Paul's teaching may have been supplemented by traditions of the Jerusalem Church or from written accounts, I believe that Paul's gospel was taught him directly by the Lord and not by flesh and blood. As he says in Galatians: "I want you to realize this, the Good News I preached is not a human message that I was given by men, it is something I learned only through a revelation of Jesus Christ. . . . Before God, I lie not."[24]

Some have suggested that the three years after his conversion when he "went off to Arabia at once and later went straight back from there to Damascus"[25] were spent in meditation—to prepare his message. I believe this was a period of daily intercourse with Jesus who gave to him initiations of the Spirit, a message to preach for the two-thousand-year dispensation, and mysteries of God that, as he said, were "not lawful for a man to utter."[26]

Even though the Book of Acts, which devotes a good amount of space to Paul, together with Paul's letters make up a large part of the New Testament, they still give a sketchy picture of the man, his message and his thirty-year ministry. Paul's letters do not illumine his gospel as much as they might since they focus on specific doctrinal points rather than undertake to systematically set forth his Good News. Furthermore, we do not even possess all of his letters.[27]

Aside from the unrecorded acts and preachments of Paul, we are faced with another area of loss: the first written accounts of Jesus' life and ministry. Scholars have concluded that the Gospelers wrote sometime between thirty and seventy years after the crucifixion (c. A.D. 60–100) and compiled their books from a diverse body of oral sources and a series of source documents containing the actions, sayings and teachings of Jesus upon which they relied heavily.

They have postulated a number of documents the Evangelists may have used, including Q (for *Quelle*, "source" in German); the Little Apocalypse used by Mark; M and L (sources used by Matthew and Luke); a Proto-Mark and Proto-Luke; sources for the infancy narratives in Matthew and Luke; an early Aramaic gospel upon which both Mark and John drew; and other documents as well.[28]

Trying to determine precisely what source materials were used is a complex and, to some degree, theoretical venture; scholarly study and debate about just what was used is ongoing. But there is little question that such sources once did exist. "Collections of the sayings [of Jesus] underlie all four of our gospels," point out biblical scholars Robert M. Grant and David Noel Freedman.[29] This is evidenced by the fact that Matthew, Mark and Luke, the synoptic Gospels,[30] use much of the same material but arrange it in different sequence.

For instance, in Matthew the Lord's Sermon on the Mount is 111 verses long. Luke's Sermon on the Plain, in approximately the same chronological position, is only 30. Both sermons contain the Beatitudes but Luke sprinkles much of Matthew's other 81 verses in different contexts further on in his Gospel. In Matthew the Lord's Prayer is within the sermon, but Luke puts it several chapters after the sermon and in a different setting.[31]

Thus, scholars have concluded from a combination of evidence that the writers were working from

source documents as they were weaving existing sayings and parables into an outline of Jesus' ministry.

This process may have contributed to the loss of
teaching since it is highly unlikely that the Evangelists
(or even Paul) used every saying, act, parable, sermon,
teaching, etc., available to them from source documents or the oral tradition. There is no reason why the
Gospel writers would have felt it necessary to include
all of their material; each Gospeler had a particular
theological, hence literary, goal in mind which man-
dated his selection.

Nonfiction writers of our time may use only 10
percent of the hard information at hand in their
works; whether the Gospel writers used more or less
than 10 percent of the material they had, we have no
way of knowing. But whatever was in the source documents used by the Gospelers and Paul that did not
find its way into the canon[32] has probably been dis-
counted as noncanonical, legendary, apocryphal or
anathema—hence ignored, suppressed, even destroyed.

Oral tradition was a parallel vehicle for the transmission of Jesus' teaching, and Christians continued
to use it long after the four canonical Gospels were
in circulation. As Grant and Freedman observe: "In
Christian writings of the early second century there are
a good many sayings of Jesus which seem to be derived
not from written gospels but from oral tradition."[33]

Papias, bishop of Hierapolis in Asia Minor who
lived c. A.D. 70–155, bore witness to the vitality of
the oral tradition in the second century. The prelate
collected verbal accounts from those who knew the
apostles and, according to Church Father Irenaeus,
was a companion of Polycarp, disciple of John the
Evangelist. Papias wrote in his five-volume opus
(c. A.D. 140), *Explanation of the Sayings of the Lord,*
that "whenever anyone came who had been a follower

of the presbyters, I inquired into the words of the presbyters, what Andrew or Peter had said, or Philip or Thomas or James or John or Matthew, or any other disciple of the Lord, and what Aristion [34] and the presbyter John, disciples of the Lord, were still saying." [35]

These eyewitness reports included, as the fourth-century historian Eusebius tells us, "a wonderful story from the lips of Philip's daughters," an account of "the resurrection of a dead person" and another of one Justus, surnamed Barsabus, who drank poison and "by the grace of the Lord was none the worse." Eusebius also says that "in his own book Papias gives us accounts of the Lord's sayings obtained from Aristion or learnt direct from the presbyter John" as well as "some otherwise unknown parables and teachings of the Saviour." [36]

From Eusebius' description it is certain that Papias' treatise would do much to increase our knowledge of the lost teachings of Jesus conveyed by oral tradition. But except for a few fragments recorded principally by Eusebius and Irenaeus, Papias' work has been lost.

In addition to the loss of the source documents and the oral tradition upon which the Gospel writers and possibly Paul relied, we are confronted by yet another missing piece in the puzzle of Jesus' teaching: the lack of literature produced by Jesus' disciples, close friends such as Martha, Mary and Lazarus, and "the other seventy"—and even by Jesus himself.

The age that initiated the Christian dispensation was one of a high degree of literacy; the literary works of the Hebrews, Greeks, and Romans were part of the cultural tradition of the time. As biblical scholar Morton Smith writes, "It is most unlikely that they [Jesus and his disciples] were all illiterate; literacy was common even among the lower classes in the Roman world."[37]

It is therefore difficult to believe that only two of the twelve, Matthew and John, would have written at length about their Master. Moreover, few scholars today believe that they wrote the Gospels attributed to them. The only other writings in the New Testament attributed to the apostles are brief letters by Peter, James, and John, and the Book of Revelation.[38]

What about the other apostles—a gospel, a letter, a polemic, a memoir, a prayer? "The fact that Jesus and his followers founded a surviving sect," says Smith, "makes the loss of *all* their writings surprising indeed."[39]

Luke does open his Gospel with the words: "Forasmuch as *many* have taken in hand to set forth in order a declaration of those things which are most surely believed among us, even as they delivered them unto us, which from the beginning were eyewitnesses, and ministers of the word..." This decidedly suggests other gospels similar in scope to Luke.

Who wrote them? No one knows who these many compilers were. Scholars speculate Mark and perhaps Matthew were among them. *Among* them but not *all* of them. These gospels or "declarations," together with whatever else the apostles may have written, are also lost—unless, of course, they are to be found amongst the apocrypha.

And what about communications to and from the Church at Jerusalem, which served as the headquarters for a growing Christian community? "The Epistles of Paul clearly attest the position of the Church at Jerusalem as the Mother Church of the Christian Faith," says Professor S. G. F. Brandon. "The position of the Jerusalem Church then being such, it is certainly remarkable that, except for a few minor documents of more than doubtful authorship, there has survived no important authentic writing of the leaders of this Church. That these leaders should have written letters as Paul did, dealing with various matters of faith and practice which must inevitably have required authoritative direction from time to time, would seem to be a reasonable assumption to make."[40]

If the disciples, eyewitnesses of Jesus' mission, and leaders of the early Church wrote more than we now possess, what about their Master?

It is widely assumed by scholars and laymen alike that throughout the course of his life Jesus wrote nothing. Based on their understanding of Jewish eschatology, some scholars believe that Jesus would have thought it unnecessary to write down his teaching, for the world was coming to an end.[41] Curiously—with the exception of a mysterious message he wrote in the sand in the scene of the woman taken in adultery[42]— the Gospels do not mention him writing anything at all.

Yet there is no question that Jesus was literate. And we do not have to rely on hieroglyphs in the sand for proof. Luke 4:16–19 records the dramatic moment in the synagogue at Nazareth when, reading from the first and second verses of Isaiah 61, stopping in the middle of verse 2, Jesus articulates these telling words:

> The Spirit of the Lord GOD is upon me; because the LORD hath anointed me to preach good tidings unto the meek; he hath sent me to bind up the brokenhearted, to proclaim liberty to the captives, and the opening of the prison to them that are bound;
> To proclaim the acceptable year of the LORD . . .

And he began to say to them, "This day is this scripture fulfilled in your ears."[43] In this act surely he acclaimed himself the fulfillment of Isaiah's prophecy.[44] Luke says that "all bare him witness and wondered at the gracious words which proceeded out of his mouth."[45] Are we, then, to believe that those crucial words spoken by the Saviour concerning his Advent were not preserved? How is it that so much of that which is so precious to us could have been lost?

That Jesus could read and write does not prove that he *did* write something. Yet there is no reason why he should not have written *something*. And considering the state of affairs in which he found himself, there are some good reasons why he should have.

Could the task of recording an accurate account of his life and teaching reasonably be entrusted to his disciples? All four Gospels insist that the chosen twelve frequently did not understand his teachings—especially the all-important statements about his death and resurrection. It was only after the resurrection—after the Lord had upbraided them for their "unbelief and hardness of heart" and after he had "opened their understanding" that they might understand the scriptures[46] and after the Holy Ghost had illumined them—that they were able to take the mantle of the Lord and run with it.

Jesus, however, *did* have a very clear understanding of Old Testament scripture and the role he was to play in fulfilling it. If, as we shall see, the scriptures were such an essential part of his teaching and mission, and only he had the fullness of that understanding, would not the Master have felt compelled to preserve that message for posterity?

The Gospels tell us of the Master's reverence for the word of God written in the Old Testament and of his versatility in applying it to many different situations—echoing the style of the prophets of old as he taught. [47] "All four Gospels depict Jesus as a literary genius," *The Bible Almanac* notes. "His teaching reflects the style and standpoint of both the prophets and the Old Testament wisdom literature." [48]

This is evident in many scenes, from Jesus' rebuke of the tempter Satan, in which he quotes passages from Deuteronomy, [49] to his confrontations with Pharisees, Sadducees, and scribes—the learned men of the day—whom he adeptly engages in debate. In one case, when the Pharisees and scribes complain that his disciples are not acting "according to the tradition of the elders," Jesus goes beyond their reasoning, refers directly to the words of Moses, and reproves his accusers for having made God's word "null and void for the sake of your tradition." [50] When the Sadducees try to back him into a corner on a certain point of the law, he replies, "Ye do err, not knowing the scriptures, nor the power of God," then proceeds to quote from Exodus. [51]

On another occasion, as the Jews are about to stone Jesus, "because that thou, being a man, makest thyself God," he counters with the words of Psalms: "Is it not written in your law, I said, Ye are gods?" [52] And when the rich young ruler asks Jesus what he should do to obtain eternal life, the Master directs him to keep certain of the ten commandments given in Exodus and to obey the injunction of Leviticus to "love thy neighbor as thyself." [53]

His prophecy in Matthew 24 of the destruction of Jerusalem and of his Second Coming is replete with language from the Old Testament. [54] Even the Saviour's final words on the cross, "My God, my God, why hast thou forsaken me?" are from Psalm 22:1. [55]

Jesus may have also quoted passages from sacred writings which are now lost. In his strong denunciation of the lawyers in Luke, Jesus says, "Therefore also said the wisdom of God, I will send them prophets and apostles, and some of them they shall slay and persecute."[56] Some scholars have conjectured that "the wisdom of God" is a lost apocryphal book.[57] The work referred to in Mark 9:13 may also point to a missing text: "Elias is indeed come, and they have done unto him whatsoever they listed, *as it is written of him.*"[58]

In addition to appealing to the scriptures in his teachings and in confrontations with opponents, Jesus often refers to biblical passages to establish that he and the events surrounding his mission are the fulfillment of Old Testament prophecies. Early in his ministry Jesus emphatically states that he has come not to destroy the law or the prophets "but to fulfill."[59] In Luke 18:31–33, he foretells his death and resurrection, beginning with the words "All things that are written by the prophets concerning the Son of man shall be accomplished," and later warns the disciples that "this that is written must yet be accomplished in me, 'And he was reckoned among the transgressors,'"[60] referring to Isaiah 53:12.

In John 13:18, Jesus predicts the betrayal of Judas as a fulfillment of Psalm 41:9 and in Matthew 11:10 he tells the multitudes that John the Baptist "is he of whom it is written, Behold, I send my messenger before thy face, which shall prepare thy way before thee."[61] Jesus' statement "It is written of the Son of man that he must suffer many things and be set at nought"[62] is generally taken to be a reference to Psalm 22 and Isaiah 53, and his ringing message before arriving at Gethsemane that the world has "seen and hated both me and my Father. . . . This cometh to pass that the word might be fulfilled that is written in their law, They hated me without a cause" refers to two verses in Psalms.[63]

As we noted earlier, Luke tells us that as the Master walked with the disciples on the road to Emmaus following his resurrection, "he expounded unto them in all the scriptures the things concerning himself." [64] And in the last chapter of Luke, just before his ascension, Jesus explains to the apostles, "These are the words which I spake unto you, while I was yet with you, that all things must be fulfilled, which were written in the law of Moses and in the prophets and in the psalms concerning me." [65]

All of this evidence forces us to ask: Would not Jesus—who knew, based on his own keen understanding of the Old Testament, that his mission was ordained to be the fulfillment of scripture—document this fact for all time, even as he spoke it? Dare we, therefore, venture the hypothesis that the Lord himself in his will to preserve the living Word for us, though "heaven and earth shall pass away," [66] did write down for us *his* Gospel?

Should we not reexamine our attitude about Jesus and *his* message? We are conditioned to accept without question what we were told in Sunday school—that Jesus just didn't write down his sermons. And today we still take for granted that he who said, "The words I say to you I do not speak as from myself: it is the Father, living in me, who is doing this work. . . . And my word is not my own: it is the word of the one who sent me," [67] never saw to it by his own diligent hand that the Father's words—entrusted to him for us, mind you, to be unto us a lamp, lo these two thousand years—were carefully copied and preserved.

Jesus was sent to deliver the most important message ever vouchsafed by the Father to the Son—the message of our salvation. His was a solemn commission before the altar of God. And I for one cannot believe that our beloved Brother did not write down his message for our heart's keeping and consolation. In view of the foregoing, why not assume, if only for the sake of discussion, that Jesus did in fact write something and then proceed to ask what?

Although it is, in some respects, a moot point, one candidate is the Epistle to the Hebrews. In style, arrangement and thought, this stirring, elegantly phrased work is in a class by itself. Volumes could be written about the theological implications of some of its verses.

But scholars do not know who wrote it. It has sometimes been attributed to Paul and there are certain similarities in theme between Paul's writings and Hebrews. The differences, however, are greater. And the style of Hebrews, as Origen, the Church's first great theologian (c. A.D. 185–c. 254), wrote, "is not rude like the language of the apostle, who acknowledged himself 'rude in speech', that is, in expression; but that its diction is purer Greek, any one who has the power to discern differences of phraseology will acknowledge." [68]

Origen nevertheless understands why some may think Paul wrote Hebrews and says they are to be commended—but he has his reservations. Modern scholars agree. "The author of Hebrews is an independent thinker," asserts New Testament scholar Alexander C. Purdy. "His name is not Paul, nor is he a Paulinist. The evidence for this conclusion is cumulative, including style—which the Alexandrian scholars saw and acknowledged." [69] Origen, aware of the difficulty of the problem, finally concluded that "who wrote the epistle is known to God alone." [70]

Many authors besides Paul have been suggested: Clement, Timothy, Barnabas, Apollos, Aquila and Priscilla, Silas, Aristion, Luke, and Philip the deacon among them. The fact that he is so hard to identify should in itself provoke our suspicion. "He must have been a person of great ability and originality," observes scholar Hugh Montefiore. "It is almost inconceivable that such a person should have left no mark (other than this Epistle) on the records of the primitive church."[71]

Nevertheless, two thousand years after Hebrews was written, a giant question mark still hangs over it. Who wrote it? Perhaps Jesus—at least in part. For who else but the Son of God could have known that Melchizedek was "made like unto the Son of God" or that Jesus himself was "made an high priest forever after the Order of Melchizedek"?[72] Unless, of course, the Master Jesus Christ dictated the epistle either to his messenger Paul or to another.

We are now faced with the problem of determining how any further writings of the disciples—and even Jesus himself—conspicuous today by their absence, were lost. One answer is that they were destroyed in the sack of Jerusalem around A.D. 70 or they perished in the unsettled times that followed. But it is not likely the twelve would have entrusted all of their treasure to temples made with hands.

Morton Smith offers another possibility: that their writings were suppressed.[73] How, when, and by whom? We may never know the whole of it, but it is clear that certain teachings were withheld *deliberately* by Jesus and his apostles themselves. For, as we shall see, they did have a mystery teaching and they did intend to keep it secret.

Mark, the earliest and least ornamented of the synoptic Gospels, tells us unambiguously that the parable of the sower was designed to conceal rather than to reveal the true meaning of Jesus' message—a technique so thoroughly successful that later Jesus, somewhat to his dismay, had to explain the parable to his own disciples.

And when he was alone, they that were about him with the twelve asked of him the parable.

And he said unto them, Unto you it is given to know the mystery of the kingdom of God: But unto them that are without, all these things are done in parables:

That seeing they may see, and not perceive; and hearing they may hear, and not understand; lest at any time they should be converted, and their sins should be forgiven them. [74]

Matthew and Luke repeat the same passage, with some subtractions and additions and variations in style, then proceed to give the interpretation. [75] One of Matthew's additional verses explains Jesus' secrecy as the will of God observable from ancient times:

For verily I say unto you, That many prophets and righteous men have desired to see those things which ye see, and have not seen them; and to hear those things which ye hear, and have not heard them. [76]

Another verse from Mark further delineates Jesus' mystery teaching:

But without a parable spake he not unto them: and when they were alone, he expounded *all things* to his disciples. [77]

Some scholars studying these and other passages of the New Testament have recognized that Jesus had an "esoteric," or "inner," teaching restricted to the circle of initiates. Others have difficulty accepting the message of the Gospel writers at face value: that for the anointed the parables were explained and as for the multitudes, it was up to the individual how he would respond to the initiations of the Word—"He that hath ears to hear, let him hear."[78]

Let us consider for a moment Mark's statement, "But without a parable spake he not unto them." Was Mark exaggerating? The Gospels do contain public instruction not in parable style. The Sermon on the Mount is one such example. Perhaps he was generalizing when he said the Master spoke to the multitudes only in parable (the Greek and Latin root of the word is "to compare" or "comparison") and meant that the public teachings of Jesus were largely given in story or simile and those that weren't were closer to the parable form than the secret teachings he gave to his students in private.

The Gospels do not record many teachings Jesus gave his disciples in confidence. Of the thirty or so parables, few of the Lord's interpretations are there. And even if we take everything Jesus said to his disciples when they were alone to be secret teaching, it falls short of Mark's "expounded all things."

Indeed, the large majority of Jesus' words recorded in the Gospels are either his repartee with the scribes (lawyers) and Pharisees or his preaching to the multitudes. Neither qualifies as inner teaching. Furthermore, some of what the Gospels show Jesus saying to his disciples "when they were alone" is rebuke for their misunderstanding of him, such as when he tells them to "beware of the leaven of the Pharisees and of the Sadducees" and they reason, "It is because we didn't bring any bread that he is saying this to us."[79]

If, as some Christians would have us believe, everything Jesus ever taught to our need or benefit is recorded in the Bible, then why does it not include more of Jesus' expounding "all things"? Where are the missing links which would tell us of the real work entailed in *the process* of salvation, as Paul said, "*Work out** your own salvation with fear and trembling"?[80]

Well, Mark, whose Gospel is acknowledged as the earliest—the one upon which Matthew and Luke were based (they use his outline and borrow 90 percent of his verses)—contains, verse for verse, the least amount of private teaching. Presumably, Mark should have more of Jesus' inner teaching since he was the one who said the Lord expounded all things to his disciples when they were alone.

Can we conclude that he did not consider the secret teaching valuable to future generations? Hardly. Perhaps this withholding of the "strong meat"[81] of the Word was part of the tradition of Christ and his apostles. Origen, whom the learned Church Father Jerome called "the greatest teacher of the Church after the apostles," said that the apostles taught some doctrines and not others, even though they knew their meaning, in order "to supply the more diligent of those who came after them, such as should prove to be lovers of wisdom, with an exercise on which to display the fruit of their ability."[82]

But it was not always to leave an exercise sufficiently challenging to "lovers of wisdom" that prompted the disciples to keep certain teachings under wraps. "Origen," says scholar Johannes Munck, "in his commentary on Mt. by his treatment of the parable, Mt. 20:1–16 [the laborers in the vineyard], showed himself convinced that Matthew knew the secrets (or mysteries) of this parable as well as those of the parables of the sower and of the tares, but kept silent about them. He did not make known everything which was revealed because he was aware of the danger."[83]

Was this because of his fear of reprisals from the tares, "the children of the wicked one,"[84] who, as also

*"Work for," Jerusalem Bible.

noted by Jude, were the enemies of Jesus and the disciples?

Then again, apart from it being his style and the means by which he conveyed the Holy Ghost to the "pure in heart," Jesus spoke in parables according to the discernment of his hearers, who as Mark says, received the word "as they were able to hear it." [85]

In a similar vein, Paul speaks of veiled truths reserved for those who are "perfect," or "mature," that is, among those who are initiated [86] into the deeper mysteries Jesus taught, which, as far as the canon goes, are simply not there.

In his first epistle to the Corinthians, Paul declares, "We speak wisdom among them that are perfect: yet not the wisdom of this world, nor of the princes of this world, that come to nought: But we speak the wisdom of God in a mystery, even the hidden wisdom, which God ordained before the world unto our glory [but we impart a secret and hidden wisdom of God, which God decreed before the ages for our glorification (RSV)]." [87]

Clearly Paul, like Jesus, possesses from his Lord an esoteric teaching that is not for everyone. He thinks of himself as one of the "stewards of the mysteries of God," [88] writes to the converts at Ephesus of "the mystery, which from the beginning of the world hath been hid in God," [89] and to the church at Colossae of "the mystery which hath been hid from ages and from generations, but now is made manifest to his saints." [90] Paul's choice of words emphasizes that the Master's most precious teachings have been hidden from those not spiritually prepared to receive them.

The word *mystery,* which Paul uses so frequently, comes from "the same root as the verb 'to initiate,'" New Testament scholar Francis W. Beare points out, "and its first sense appears to be 'a rite of initiation' or 'a secret to which initiation is the key.' In the common language of the time it is sometimes weakened to mean 'a secret' in the most general sense; but in the vocabulary of religion it stands for the whole complex of initiation, cult, and secret doctrine on which the numerous private religious brotherhoods of the time were based."[91]

It would not have been unusual for Jesus, his immediate disciples and Paul to have had an esoteric tradition. People in many walks of life had secrets and/or secret doctrines—members of mystery cults, philosophical schools, and Jewish sects such as the Pharisees and Essenes, temple priests at Jerusalem, Samaritan priests, physicians taking the Hippocratic oath, political factions, women, slaves, craftsmen. It was a veritable world of secrets. Moreover, the practice of giving an outer teaching to the multitudes and an inner teaching to disciples was well established in rabbinical circles.[92]

Teaching is only one of a number of acts Jesus did in secret which the Gospels portray but do not illumine. "The reports of Jesus' secret practices are not limited to [a] few stories," writes Morton Smith. "They are all over the Gospels. We are often told that before performing a cure he took the sick man aside, privately. Or, if he went in where the patient was, he shut out everyone and took with him only his closest disciples. After his miracles he repeatedly ordered the persons concerned to keep the event secret. . . . Important men came to see him by night; some were said to be his disciples, but in secret."[93]

Naturally Jesus' secret practices influenced the Gospel writers, seeped into their Gospels and left indelible traces. "John swarms with contradictions that look like deliberate riddles," writes Smith. "John and Luke hint at secret teaching to be given by the resurrected Jesus or by the spirit, after Jesus' death."[94] In fact, in his *Outlines* Clement of Alexandria mentions that "James the Righteous, John, and Peter were entrusted by the Lord after his resurrection with the higher knowledge."[95]

In sum, the evidence in the New Testament that Jesus and Paul had a secret teaching which Christianity today knows little or nothing of is certainly considerable enough to bear further investigation.

Yet another clue points to the existence of a large body of secret teaching never intended for the masses— a find as important as any of the Dead Sea Scrolls or the Nag Hammadi texts: the 1958 discovery by Morton Smith of a "secret Gospel of Mark" at Mar Saba, a Greek Orthodox monastery in the Judean desert.

A secret Gospel of Mark!

Actually what he discovered was a portion of the Gospel quoted by Clement of Alexandria in a fragment of a letter to a certain Theodore. Clement, who was an influential early Church Father living around A.D. 200, was trying to set Theodore straight about the evil Carpocrations and in the cross talk revealed that

> Mark, then, during Peter's stay in Rome... wrote [an account of] the Lord's doings, not, however, declaring all [of them], nor yet hinting at the secret [ones], but selecting those he thought most useful for increasing the faith of those who were being instructed. But when Peter died as a martyr, Mark came over to Alexandria, bringing both his own notes and those of Peter, from which he transferred to his former book the things suitable to whatever makes for progress toward knowledge [gnosis]. [*Thus*] *he composed a more spiritual Gospel for the use of those who were being perfected.* Nevertheless, he yet did not divulge the things not to be uttered, nor

did he write down the hierophantic[96] teaching of
the Lord, but to the stories already written he
added yet others and, moreover, brought in certain sayings of which he knew the interpretation
would, as a mystagogue, lead the hearers into
the innermost sanctuary of that truth hidden by
seven [veils]. Thus, in sum, he prearranged matters, neither grudgingly nor incautiously, in my
opinion, and, dying, he left his composition to
the church in Alexandria, where it even yet is
most carefully guarded, *being read only to those
who are being initiated into the great mysteries.*
[emphasis added][97]

This is indeed an astonishing letter. In it, Clement
writes of "a more spiritual Gospel" which was given
only to initiates of "the great mysteries"!

Smith and other scholars analyzed the fragment
of Clement's letter and the majority agreed it had
in fact been written by the Church Father. Smith then
concluded from stylistic study that secret Mark
(further discussed in Volume II, Chapter 10) did not
belong to the family of New Testament apocrypha
composed during and after the late second century,
but that it had been written at least as early as
A.D. 100–120.[98] Furthermore, from other clues Smith
makes a good case for it having been written even
earlier—around the same time as the Gospel of Mark.[99]

Most significantly, the fragment reveals more
about Jesus' secret practices. It contains a variant of
the Lazarus story, which theretofore was found only
in the Book of John.[100] Secret Mark says that after the
resurrection of the Lazarus figure (Clement's fragment leaves him nameless), the youth,

looking upon him [Jesus], loved him, and began
to beseech him that he might be with him. And
going out of the tomb they came into the house

of the youth, for he was rich. And after six days
Jesus told him what to do and in the evening the
youth comes to him, wearing a linen cloth over
[his] naked [body]. And he remained with him
that night, for Jesus taught him the mystery of
the kingdom of God. [101]

This story, coupled with the very existence of
a secret Gospel, strengthens the evidence for secret
teachings and initiatic rites. [102] Clement's reference to
Mark having combined his notes with "those of Peter"
supports the theory that the immediate followers of
Jesus were literate and kept a record of their Lord's
teachings—if not a historical diary.

Secret Mark casts the official canon in another
light. Could the Gospels themselves be the "exoteric"
teachings, for those who were "without," so intended
by their authors from the start? Clement tells us that
Mark's secret Gospel was for those "who were being
perfected," i.e., in the language of Paul—"we speak
wisdom among them that are perfect"—initiated.

The existence of secret Mark brings up another
question: If Mark wrote "a more spiritual Gospel,"
was he the only one who did? Or were there others?

Yet even if all the secret texts, however many or
few they may be, were to be discovered, we still would
not have access to all of Jesus' secret teachings. For in
the same fragment, Clement tells Theodore that Mark
"did not divulge the things not to be uttered, nor did
he write down the hierophantic teaching of the Lord."

Thus, there were teachings that could not be
committed to writing. The best Mark could do was to
put the seeker on the right track and trust in the Holy
Spirit to quicken his heart in the Lord. But if Mark
excluded the Lazarus story from his canonical Gospel
for secrecy's sake, it raises the question as to what else
he, or someone, omitted.

Apart from intentional deletions by the authors, we know that the Gospels have been edited, interpolated, subjected to scribal errors, garnished by additions and plagued by subtractions. As Professor James H. Charlesworth tells us, "All the gospel manuscripts contain errors: some mistakes were caused by a scribe's faulty hearing or eyesight; others occurred because of poor spelling or inattentiveness; others were deliberate alterations due to changes in doctrinal or theological beliefs." [103]

This can be seen in the thousands of New Testament manuscripts we possess—and thousands of Bible quotes preserved in ancient writings—which differ from each other in over 250,000 ways. "The texts have been extensively worked and reworked," explains Marvin Meyer, professor of religion and New Testament studies. "One scribe after another has gone through the texts commonly making mistakes, commonly correcting what are perceived to be mistakes, so that the end result is outstanding differences from one manuscript to another." [104] In fact, says Professor Merrill M. Parvis, "it is safe to say that there is not one sentence in the New Testament in which the manuscript tradition is wholly uniform." [105]

One of the most important manuscripts, and a telling piece of evidence for doctrinal editing, is Codex Sinaiticus. [106] Written in Greek, it is one of the oldest Bibles in the world. Dated around A.D. 340, it was discovered in 1859 in the Greek Orthodox monastery of St. Catherine of Alexandria at the foot of Mount Sinai by German scholar Constantin Tischendorf. The codex seems to be one of the most authentic of all New Testament manuscripts we possess and has been corroborated by earlier fragments of some books of the Bible. It shows unequivocally that the New Testament we hold in our hands today was edited and embellished for doctrinal reasons.

Although many of the passages in which Codex Sinaiticus differs from our New Testament can be explained as mere scribal or copyists' errors, some can be explained only as deliberate edits. As James Bentley, author of *Secrets of Mount Sinai*, says:

> Codex Sinaiticus...contains many texts which later scribes were theologically motivated to delete or change.
>
> For example, in the first chapter of Mark's Gospel we are told of a leper who says to Jesus, "If you will, you can make me clean." Codex Sinaiticus continues, Jesus, "angry, stretched out his hand and touched him, and said, 'I will; be clean.'" Later manuscripts, perceiving that to attribute anger to Jesus at this point made him appear, perhaps, too human, alter the word "angry" to "moved with compassion."
>
> In Matthew's Gospel Codex Sinaiticus contains another suggestion about Jesus which conflicted with the theological views of later Christians and was therefore suppressed. Speaking (in Matthew chapter 24) of the day of judgment, Jesus, according to Codex Sinaiticus, observes that "of that day and hour knoweth no-one, not even the angels of heaven, neither the Son, but the Father only."
>
> Other ancient manuscripts also contain the words "neither the Son." But the suggestion here that Jesus might not be on the same level of knowledge as God was unacceptable to later generations of Christians, and the phrase was suppressed.[107]

Therefore, today the King James Version of Matt. 24:36 reads: "But of that day and hour knoweth no man, no, not the angels of heaven, but my Father only." However, the phrase "nor the Son" does appear in the Jerusalem Bible and Revised Standard Version after "the angels of heaven." These were translated within the last forty years from early manuscripts, such as Codex Sinaiticus, which were not available to the translators of the King James Version. [108]

And so it seems that many of the changes that were doctrinally oriented move in the same direction—to make Jesus less human and more unapproachably divine.

One of the most striking discrepancies is that the codex contains no reference to Jesus' ascension as recorded in Mark and Luke. The scribe who copied the Book of Mark ended the Gospel at chapter 16, verse 8. He drew a decorative line beneath the verse, signifying "the end." The last twelve verses of Mark absent from the codex describe Jesus' ascension as well as his appearances after his resurrection.

"Luke chapter 24, verse 51, tells how Jesus left his disciples after his resurrection," says Bentley. "He blessed them, was parted from them, 'and was carried up into heaven.' Sinaiticus omits the final clause. Textual critic C. S. C. Williams observes that if this omission is correct, 'there is no reference at all to the Ascension in the original text of the Gospels.'" [109] Since Matthew and John do not include the ascension passages, the only mention of it in Sinaiticus is in the Book of Acts, which was also written by Luke.

Astoundingly, another ancient Bible, Codex Vaticanus, also written in Greek, likewise omits the last twelve verses of Mark. This codex, about as old as or slightly older than Sinaiticus, was also first brought into the public eye by Tischendorf. But the method of its discovery was far different.

Vaticanus had been in the Vatican since at least 1475. When in the nineteenth century the world began to take interest in it, the Church did not publish its treasure but showed an interesting, if not curious, reticence. "For some reason which has never been fully explained," writes New Testament scholar Bruce M. Metzger, "during a large part of the nineteenth century the authorities of the library put continual obstacles in the way of scholars who wished to study it in detail."[110]

Some scholars were allowed to look at it—but not to copy a single word. One of them circumvented this interdict by taking notes on his fingernails. In response to increasing clamor, the Church announced it was preparing a soon-to-be-published edition of the manuscript. In 1866, Tischendorf came on the scene. He managed, as Bentley writes,

> to obtain permission to consult such parts of [the] ancient manuscript as might bear on passages of special interest or difficulty in Holy Scripture. Once inside the Vatican, he instantly started to copy out the whole codex. After eight days he was discovered. By now he had copied nineteen pages of the New Testament and ten of the Old. For this flagrant breach of his agreement, Tischendorf's permission to see Codex Vaticanus was withdrawn. With his customary resourcefulness under difficulty, he now persuaded Carlo Vercellone, the Roman Catholic scholar who was actually preparing the official edition of Codex Vaticanus, to let him examine the manuscript for a further six days. This enabled Tischendorf to bring out his own edition the following year, anteceding Vercellone's.[111]

Was Tischendorf's discovery of Sinaiticus the catalyst for the Roman publication of their Vaticanus? Did they withhold it from the people for centuries because it would have cast doubt on their 'infallible' doctrine?

Vaticanus agreed with Sinaiticus in several other crucial passages that differed from our New Testament, also indicating that the Bible was edited.

But these two codices were probably not the beginning or the end of scribal editing. They may be two of the fifty manuscripts of the Bible which Constantine the Great ordered produced in A.D. 331. If so, then they incorporate any changes which had been introduced up to that date and cannot illumine any editing that took place before 331.

Sinaiticus itself reveals the doctrinal controversy that raged in the centuries following its creation. 14,800 alterations and notes, still readable, were written onto the codex over a period of time by nine "correctors" who were indicating, Bentley says, "what they believed was the true text."[112] Additional edits of the ancient book, not perceivable to the naked eye, were only recently discovered through the use of ultraviolet light—for instance, the last verse of the Gospel of John had been added in by a later hand.

Another clue pointing to the possible editing of the Gospels is the absence of any mention of the Essenes. Whether or not Jesus was an Essene, he could not have escaped knowing *of* the Essenes. They were, along with the Pharisees and Sadducees, one of the three most influential Jewish sects of the time.

"It is extraordinary that the Essenes are not named in the New Testament," declares Frank Moore Cross, Jr., Hancock Professor of Hebrew and other Oriental languages at Harvard University Divinity School. "I know of no fully adequate explanation of this circumstance. Certainly it is not to be attributed to ignorance."[113]

If Jesus was an Essene, as some have suggested, why do we find no mention of this influential group? If he was opposed to their doctrine, why do we find no record of his challenging them? Possibly references pro, or con, were expunged.

In addition, some of Jesus' teaching may have been lost during the setting of the canon—the process by which, Professor Robert M. Grant tells us, "the books regarded as authoritative, inspired, and apostolic were selected out of a much larger body of literature"[114] that had been preserved by the many early Christian churches.

The process of fixing the canon went on for centuries and the earliest authoritative list containing all of our modern New Testament appeared around A.D. 367. Significantly excluded from the canon were the Gnostic writings—often allegorical or symbolical and designed to lead the aspirant to a higher knowledge (gnosis), or truth.

Truly they are a "mixed bag" and it is not the purpose of this writing to bless or curse them or to equate them with the canon. Nevertheless, the mere fact that a text was excluded from the canon is not the final test of whether or not it actually contained Jesus' teachings. The discovery of a large body of Gnostic writings at Nag Hammadi, Egypt, in 1945 made this abundantly clear.

It is evident that those who collected the Nag Hammadi Library manuscripts were Christians, as James M. Robinson, general editor of *The Nag Hammadi Library*, points out, and "many of the essays were originally composed by Christian authors."[115]

The Gnostic *Gospel of Thomas*, which opens with the words "These are the secret sayings which the living Jesus spoke,"[116] repeats some of Jesus' sayings in a form older than they appear in the synoptics. It was composed, writes scholar Helmut Koester in *The Nag Hammadi Library*, "as early as the second half of the first century."[117]

"The *Gospel of Thomas* resembles the synoptic sayings source, often called 'Q,' . . . which was the common source of sayings used by Matthew and Luke," notes Koester. "Hence, the *Gospel of Thomas* and its sources are collections of sayings and parables which are closely related to the sources of the New Testament gospels."[118]

That the Gnostics ran afoul of other Christians in a period of time when Christianity was a good deal more heterodox than it is today has been documented by scholar Elaine Pagels in her popular work *The Gnostic Gospels.*

After orthodox Christians gained the power of the state following Constantine's conversion to Christianity, it was only a matter of time, she says, before the works they had condemned were suppressed and largely lost for nearly sixteen centuries.

> When Christianity became an officially approved religion in the fourth century, Christian bishops, previously victimized by the police, now commanded them. Possession of books denounced as heretical was made a criminal offense. Copies of such books were burned and destroyed. . . .
>
> It is the winners who write history—their way. No wonder, then, that the viewpoint of the successful majority has dominated all traditional accounts of the origin of Christianity. Ecclesiastical Christians first defined the terms (naming themselves "orthodox" and their opponents "heretics"); then they proceeded to demonstrate—at least to their own satisfaction—that their triumph was historically inevitable, or, in religious terms, "guided by the Holy Spirit."[119]

But it was not only Gnostic works that fell by the way. The *Epistle of Barnabas* and the *Shepherd of Hermas,* works contained in Codex Sinaiticus with no indication that they were regarded as less authentic than the other books of the New Testament, were also not included in the canon. Date was not always the decisive factor, for some of the excluded works had been written *before* others that were included.

"We cannot say that the gnostic gospels, revelations, and other books which were definitely rejected toward the end of the second century were necessarily written at a late date," says Grant in *The Cambridge History of the Bible*. "They may well have been written early even though they came to be viewed as unorthodox and non-canonical only later."[120]

While many of the rejected books *were* spurious (a number of gospels written between the second and fifth centuries contained wild and outlandish stories), some books were rejected not necessarily for want of authenticity but, as Grant says, "because they seemed to conflict with what the accepted books taught."[121]

Thus, Christianity has been missing for two thousand years whatever authentic material was excluded from the canon and subsequently banned as heretical or destroyed. The conflict between orthodoxy and Gnosticism may have obscured for all time the complete teachings of Jesus.

Will we ever know which of Jesus' teachings were lost to us merely because they did not conform to the doctrine of the then most powerful Church?

Will we ever know Christianity as Jesus taught it?

Will we ever recover *all* of the lost teaching?

Maybe our detective knows. . .

One thing is sure: he's onto something and he's out looking for more clues.

The night, like so many others on this case, is wearing away. You sigh and lean back in your chair. All right, you say. You've managed to prove that there are lost teachings. You've even managed to uncover what *kinds* of lost teaching: recorded, unrecorded, secret and more or less open, parable and mystery, gospel and saying.

But where to find them? You look up and run your fingers through your hair. Even Sherlock Holmes would have had a problem with this one. You hate to think of giving up. Of having to tuck this case away in that small, embarrassing file marked "UNSOLVED," waiting for another Qumran or Nag Hammadi to shed a glimmer of light on the matter.

The only thing that could help me now, you say to yourself, is a time machine. If only you could go back and listen to Jesus' words yourself. . .

But wait. Even after his resurrection, you recall, many reported hearing and even talking to the Master. Beginning with his disciples, Magdalene and the holy women, and the five hundred, followed by Paul and John the Revelator and then the saints, from the earliest Christians throughout the last two thousand years, 'numberless numbers' have witnessed to his personal intercession in their lives.

Paul said that he received his gospel by "a revelation of Jesus Christ" but that it was nevertheless acceptable to the leaders of the Christian community in Jerusalem, so much so that "James, Cephus [Peter] and John, these leaders, these pillars, shook hands with Barnabas and me as a sign of partnership."[122]

The very fact that Jesus felt it necessary to give revelations to Paul and John raises the question: When did he stop revealing himself and his mysteries to his chosen?

How can any man give the date and draw the line and say to him, "That's it, Lord, the Bible is a closed book"?

You recall Saint Catherine of Siena—the unlettered girl who said she was taught to read by Jesus himself, who carried on a noteworthy correspondence with the pope and who for five consecutive days dictated to her secretaries revelations she was receiving from the Father in ecstasy.

If Jesus found a way to unveil his mysteries to saints throughout the ages, you reason, why not now? Why not the whole Lost Teaching? Today.

After a hypothesis like that, some of that old gang of yours might shake their heads and tell you to take a rest—or, better yet, a vacation to some tropical isle. But then, Jesus didn't seem like the kind of guy to let his teaching be lost forever just because of a couple disciples who didn't quite understand him, a few monks with overeager quill pens, or some self-righteous document burners. That was elementary.

But a new revelation of Christ today?

That's quite a tall order, but you sense you're onto something. After all, didn't Christ tell his disciples he would send the Holy Spirit to bring all things to their remembrance?[123] Surely he didn't think they would forget everything he said in a few short years!

So he must have known all along that his teaching would be tampered with; that's probably why he sealed the Book of Revelation with the warning that if any man added to or took away from the book, God would add to him the plagues described therein and strike his name from the book of life.[124]

But the Holy Spirit? Doesn't just about every TV preacher and Bible thumper claim to have it? There must be someone who has the real thing. What you need are facts.

Indeed, as a wise detective once told you, "the past is prologue to the mystery unveiled."

You slip on your shoes, pick up your overcoat and head out once more into the night.

Verily, verily, I say unto you,
He that believeth on me,
the works that I do shall he do also;
and greater works than these shall he do
. . . because I go unto my Father.

Jesus

Foreword

BLESSED readers, bear with us as we unfold the mysteries of God. Be patient with our effort as together we walk and talk with Jesus and the servant-sons in heaven whose revelations we bear. For as emissaries of their teaching, we must attempt to make plain according to twentieth-century thinking and theological modality a vast gnosis of the Lord that does and does not necessarily fit the mind-sets and mind-traps of the very ones for whom his Lost Teaching is sent.

Above all, have patience with yourself, endure to the end of our treatise and pray fervently and without fear to the Holy Spirit to enlighten you—both through and beyond the written word. These pages are a garden path where you meet the Lord Jesus and the masterful beings and intelligences who comprise the "cloud of witnesses" to the Universal Christ, whose point of Light is also in ourselves.

In these two volumes we bring you the most precious instruction we have received for lifetimes from our Good Friend and the Shepherd of our souls. While the words and images may not be those Christ used two thousand years ago, you will find the heart of the message he imparted on the road to Emmaus; at Bethany with Mary, Martha and Lazarus; at meat with sinners and publicans; to the multitudes on the desert, by the sea, and in the mountains; in the synagogue at Nazareth; in the Temple at Jerusalem; and on the Mount of Transfiguration with Peter, James and John—as well as the message he whispered in the ear of Paul.

You won't find two dozen lost parables with a cast of sowers, servants, rich men, virgins and mustard seeds. But you will learn from our cast of Fords, Chevys, homegrown philosophers, our Pierre and our parrot and from the many portraits of life from which Jesus has drawn to teach us the fine points of the Law.

You won't find verbatim the words and phrases expunged from the Gospels, but you will find the essential truths they contained as well as some of the Lord's most precious secrets which we herein transcribe—some plain for all to see, some hidden in enigma for riddle lovers and detectives to sleuth and solve. You may find yourself rereading these volumes as you carefully choose the missing pieces to fill in the mosaic of your inner life as you commune with the Master in the cloisters of your soul.

The chapters we set forth for you in the name of Jesus Christ and in defense of every seeker for his Truth contain the fundamentals of his Lost Teachings which he himself has taught us. Profound in their simplicity, when understood they lead to the complexities of the Law of every man's true nature in God.

This book consists of fourteen lectures delivered by Mark between 1965 and 1973, illuminated by the lessons Jesus has given us in dictations, sermons and letters over the past thirty years. The message that unfolds as the rose of Sharon is compiled from these as well as private conversations with the Master. It is the Lord's gift to your soul, that you might keep his flame and not lose the way when the darkness of personal and planetary karma covers the land and all else fails of human institutions and nations and their armies and armaments.

As he said to us, "Though heaven and earth pass away, my Word shall live forever—in the hearts of those who are the spiritual survivors of earth's schoolroom. Go and find them and show them the Way!"

Especially do we urge those who have never contacted the heart of Jesus' teachings as we have presented them in our ministry to read with new hope these chapters of the Saviour's wisdom. They are gathered together for the dissolving of schism in the body politic, for the furtherance of the spirit of ecumenism—and for the healing of the diseases of the flesh and the mind, and of the soul's anguish in its aloneness in time of trouble and mourning.

O world, you need this Teaching more than you know for that which is coming upon your soul and the souls of your people in the days ahead. May you take the little book and eat it up, enjoying the sweetness in the mouth, resisting not the bitterness in the belly, but understanding the necessity for the full alchemy of the Word to work his work in you.

We are the two witnesses standing now, one on either bank of Life's great river. We preach his Everlasting Gospel and the hidden wisdom: for the Lamb is come—and the mystery of God which was not to be finished till the days of the voice of the seventh angel.

The prophecy is fulfilled. That which was spoken to the disciples in the upper room is being shouted from the housetops. At last the path of discipleship to which Jesus called his chosen does appear for all to see and know and enter in these end times of the Piscean age—for the Light of Aquarius dawns.

With our life we have given the Saviour's discourses to your hearts' keeping, fully assured by Jesus himself that through these pages and your oneness with his sacred heart, you may seek and find the keys to the kingdom.

The Lord is waiting. Please take his gift, entrusted to us for you, before it is too late.

Faithfully,

Mark L. Prophet

Elizabeth Clare Prophet

Servants of God in Jesus Christ

These are the very things that God has revealed to us through the Spirit, for the Spirit reaches the depths of everything, even the depths of God. After all, the depths of a man can only be known by his own spirit, not by any other man, and in the same way the depths of God can only be known by the Spirit of God. Now instead of the spirit of the world, we have received the Spirit that comes from God, to teach us to understand the gifts that he has given us. Therefore we teach, not in the way in which philosophy is taught, but in the way that the Spirit teaches us: we teach spiritual things spiritually. [1]

The Apostle Paul

Chapter One

REMOVING THE MASK

Removing the Mask

IT doesn't take long on Halloween or at a masquerade ball to pull the mask off, does it? Everybody says, "Surprise!"

First of all, if we're going to take a mask off, we have to take the mask off of something. Now, what are we going to unmask? In this case we must perceive that there is something real about us. There is also something that is unreal about us. And the quicker we discover it and acknowledge it and learn to distinguish the difference, the quicker we will make progress in the Light.

Why is it important that we know the difference? It is important that we know the difference because otherwise we are going to be feeding the mask and starving the real man.

We do a great deal to the mask, as we find out when we travel around and notice the fortunes that are amassed by people like Helena Rubinstein, Max Factor, Elizabeth Arden, and other famous beauticians who make a comfortable living on the idea of creating shimmering glamour for the feminine sex.

They seem to have neglected us men, and about all that we have to put on, as far as glamour goes, is scented shaving lotion. But we have our masks, ladies, I assure you! Both men and women have the mask of the human consciousness and we spend a great deal of time and a great deal of energy in creating these masks which we are now deciding we're going to remove.

Someone may say, "Why should I? I've been pampering my ego all these years. Why in the world should I now decide that I'm going to quit pampering it?"

Well, there are many good reasons why we should. The main thing is that we must learn to overcome illusion because it has the word *i-l-l* in the front of it. You know what *i-l-l* means? It means ill! The mask is sick! That's why people are sick. Because it's a *phony* creation!

THE MASQUERADE HUMAN BEINGS INDULGE IN

You and I may look a little bit askance sometimes at the bearded rebels that are sprouting out in California and all over the country—men who resent the times. They rebel against the type of life that we call conformism and they go into what we call nonconformism.

We must understand these people. They're not all as bad as they look. They have a mask and they're sick and tired of the phoniness of the world, so they put another mask on! Some of them look like Santy Claus and some look like the prophet Amos. But whatever the case may be (and we may laugh at them if we want to), it's all part of the masquerade that human beings indulge in. And we do a lot of it. We do an awful lot of it. In fact, we even sometimes fool ourselves.

I remember the American Express man in my hometown. He said to me one time, "You'd better behave yourself or you'll meet yourself coming out the door." Well, this is very true!

Sooner or later you're going to bump into the very same mask you've created—only it'll be on someone else's face. It's the way the law works: Like attracts like and so in the caricature masks of others you begin to recognize a few of your own eccentricities. Because, you know, you can't ever see yourself in the mirror as you really are.

Now let's take a look at the Chart of Your Real Self (page 203). This will tell you who you are if you learn how to read it. This is the area of the mask (the lower figure) down here in the human level. There's no masquerade up here at all (at the level of your I AM Presence). And there's no masquerade here in the Holy Christ Self (the middle figure). The unrealities of life are all centered down in the human.

You'll never find any unreality in your Real Self and you'll never find anything phony in God. But we do deceive ourselves. We go easy on ourselves and we're pretty hard on our neighbor sometimes.

Did I ever tell you about the time in New York City, when I was speaking in one of the finer old homes there, that a lady came up to me and she said, "I want to talk to you in private. May I?"

And I wanted to be obliging, so I said, "Certainly."

So we went over to a corner of the room and she took her finger out and she pointed it at another woman and she said, "You see that woman over there?"

I said, "Yes."

She said, "Well, that woman is a *terrible* woman!"

And I said, "Why?"

She said, "Why, she wears mascara!"

Mascara! And this lady who said it had her eyes plastered with it!

Now, this actually happened to me. I couldn't believe it! I didn't know whether to laugh or cry.

The Scotsman has an old saying for that. He says, "Oh, wad some Power the giftie gie us, to see oursels as ithers see us!"* We are always able to remove other people's masks but we want to keep our own firmly fixed on our faces.

So the mask is made of mascara and paint and papier-mâché and even plastic surgery—and the masqueraders go prancing down Fifth Avenue in all their costumes, just like a Halloween parade at midnight. Except it's high noon on Broadway, and they're dead serious.

WILL ROGERS—FRIEND OF THE REAL MAN

Nevertheless, I think the world is becoming increasingly more honest, speaking of people in general. I think it goes back to the time of Will Rogers (of "I-never-met-a-man-I-didn't-like" fame) because Will Rogers practiced honesty and he was a very popular figure and he unmasked many of the stilted situations in life with his very clever wit.

He had the knack of putting into words what a lot of us are thinking. Like, "There is nothing as stupid as an educated man if you get him off the thing he was educated in."

Now, our home in Colorado Springs was located just below Will Rogers Shrine of the Sun. And one time when we were up there we noticed some of the memorable pictures of him and Wiley Post which hang on the walls of the shrine.

And if you ever visit Colorado Springs and the Broadmoor Hotel, we want you to go up there and look the shrine over because it does bring out the character of a man who was quite unique in his day— one who showed the phoniness and the sham of society. And he got away with it!

---

*"Oh would that some Power would give us the gift / To see ourselves as others see us!" Robert Burns, "To a Louse," stanza 8, lines 1–2.

You know what he once said as the opening line of his speech before a bankers' convention? He said, "Loan sharks and interest hounds! I have addressed every form of organized graft in the U.S. excepting Congress. So it's naturally a pleasure for me to appear before the biggest!"

And the bankers and the millionaires laughed at themselves just like they did in the days of Molière. They laughed at themselves—and they liked it! And they made friends with Will Rogers. This shows that deep in their hearts people really like to laugh at themselves, because when they laugh at themselves and don't take themselves too seriously, they're unmasking this human ego and putting it in its place.

Summing up us humans, he said, "There ain't but one word wrong with every one of us in the world, and that's selfishness."

And then one day the original unmasker, Will Rogers, left Fairbanks with Wiley Post in his Lockheed "spare parts" plane heading north. They crashed in the Alaskan barrens and didn't survive. But he had lived his life as he once said all of us should—"so if you lose you are still ahead."[1]

The one thing Will Rogers had that he would keep forever was his sublime ability to remove the mask with the persistent love of the true friend. Will Rogers was everybody's friend because he was the friend of the real man.

MOCKING THE MASK

Martin Luther—he was pretty serious about removing the mask, too. As the story goes, he picked up a bottle of ink and threw it at the devil when the devil appeared to him in his study. And he hit the wall with his bottle of ink. And they tell me the ink blot is still there. (I wonder if a Rorschach test would reveal a devil's face!) Well, you see, the mask of the devil was a very serious thing with him. He knew it wouldn't go away unless he cast it out.

Even though the mask is unreal, you can't just say, "Oh, it's not real," and turn your back on it and ignore it. 'Cause if you do, the goblin'll getch'a every time! No, you can't ignore the mask. But there is one thing you *can* do. You can mock it!

Therefore, in a sense, if we can learn to laugh at ourselves, we can actually break the ice of this frozen energy veil that prevents us from seeing our Real Self. And this laughter is very valuable. I recall in one of the early Pearls of Wisdom that the Master El Morya, our beloved Teacher and Founder of The Summit Lighthouse, said, "A twinkle of mirth is needed on earth."[2]

When he was embodied as Thomas More he made a statement about the devil that I thought was very interesting. He said, "The devill. . . , the prowd spirite, can not endure to be mokqued [mocked]."[3] (You see, the 'devil' is a mask worn by the one who has chosen to *de*ify *evil* and has therefore become the 'embodied' delusion of the deified energy veil which the Hindus call maya.)

Nor did his mirth or his mockery of that devil mask abate. Moments before he was beheaded on Tower Hill by the edict of King Henry VIII, both he and his wit were in fine spirits. Going up the scaffold, which was so weak that it was ready to fall, he said merrily to one of the Sheriff's officers, "I pray you, see me safe up, and for my coming down let me shift for myself."

His prayers said, he turned to the executioner, gave him a gold coin, and with a cheerful countenance spake thus to him, "Pluck up thy spirits, man, and be not afraid to do thine office; my neck is very short; take heed therefore thou strike not awry for the saving of thine honesty."[4]

When it came time for him to lay down his head on the block, he, having a great gray beard, striked out his beard and said to the hangman, "I pray you, let me lay my beard over the block lest ye should cut it—for it hath never offended his Highness." Thus, with a mock of the mask he ended his life—"the King's good servant, but God's first."[5]

IT'S THE REAL SELF WE'RE UNMASKING

Now, there is a serious side to this business of removing the mask, as Morya will also tell you. And the serious side is that the divine creation, the wholly perfect creation of God, needs to be revealed by the unmasking.

It is not just a matter of ridiculing our human ego—which in many cases has served us well and has helped us to discover many beautiful things about ourselves—because the ego is not all bad. In the initial stages of identity development, the ego represents the will to be. And the ego must have some sense of self-worth to maintain that will until the soul itself attains the strength and the desire for self-transcendence. At this point the divine ego, magnetized by the soul's very will to be, supersedes the lesser ego—the lesser sense of selfhood no longer being needed to sustain the finite awareness.

It is when the human ego becomes too rigid, too centered upon its own doings, that it becomes frozen in time. It doesn't move to the right or to the left. And this rigidity will be its ultimate undoing. In fact, its only chance for survival at that point will be its displacement by the divine filament of being.

You see, eternity is circular. It is fulfilled in laws of cycles. I once read that in days of old the vestal virgins climbed the stairs of the cycles. Thus, it is possible for us to utilize the laws of God to bypass our present era and do what the mystics have done in another time and space: climb the stairs of the cycles.

We can also descend those stairs backward in time and make historical comparisons of the then and the now. But this requires a great deal of spiritual advancement. Nevertheless, it is possible for you to do it. And it is valuable because it makes man to be untethered to the present moment and it brings him into the Eternal Now where the past, the present, and the future blend in one grand, noble concept. We see an entire unit, rather than just increments.

We may reach a point in this life, however, where everything becomes very brittle, and this is easy to do. And in the maturing process, which is intended to be an ennobling process, we sometimes lose sight of the goal—that is, we lose our balance and our perspective, and thus we lose our way.

It's unfortunate that many times as people mature, they think, "Well, I'm getting older now and I don't have much time left." How do you know? In Los Angeles we have a member in the Summit who is ninety-seven and she gets around mighty well.

You don't know! You may have a lot of time left. And this is one thing that you should unmask in yourself—this silly idea of saying you don't have any time left.

It isn't how long you live that counts anyway. It's how well you live. And some people have crowded more living into just a few short years than others have managed to chalk up in ten lifetimes. A lot of people drink the froth but very few understand what there is in the full-bodied measure of life.

It's so important for us to learn that in removing the mask from the self, it's the Self we're uncovering—the *Real* Self. What we have to do is take the mask off of the Divine Presence and show the Divine—that which is shining through the mask. It's so powerful, so radiant that it shines through the mask! Now I'll give you an illustration.

I drove to this conference almost nonstop from Colorado Springs, got hardly a drop of sunlight and was as white as could be. But did you know that I tan from the radiation? I tan when the Master Jesus speaks through me. I've been known to get a tan so deep that I looked as if I'd been down in Mexico! (That's putting on the mask, I guess!)

But this is true! I actually get a tan from the Light released in a dictation or in my meditations with the Holy Spirit. And some of the students who have traveled with me have also gotten a tan as the Master's radiation poured through them also. And it's perfectly natural. Spiritual radiation will tan you, just as the sun will tan you.

People Think the Divine Is Part of the Mask

You see, it's the sun of the Master's presence coming through. The sun of the Real Self is the reality that shines through *and even colors the mask!*

But people still don't recognize the Divine—they think it's part of the mask, so they see no reason to remove a mask that appears buoyant and energetic and full of life. This confusion about what is real and what is unreal leads to procrastination in removing the mask. As long as God is shining through, they say, why get in there and mess up your life and everyone else's by peeling off the human disguise? Besides, people will call you a cultist!

So there is a *real* you and there is a *false* you. But I think that words are sometimes very inadequate tools to convey ideas, because the false you is really the mask that itself will be discarded. And we hang on to that mask!

One of the great fallacies in this whole process of removing the mask is that we keep thinking that we are going to change the mask and make the mask look like the Divine Presence. But this isn't true at all. The mask is that *false* creation which we have *thought* to be our True Self—the creation that we are not only going to discard but never pick up again!

How Much of Life Would You Retain for Eternity?

How much of life, as you have lived it up till now, would you like to retain for all eternity? Ask yourself the question. Of what part of your living, as you have lived it in this life alone, would you want to say, "This is so valuable, I want to keep it forever"? That's a pretty good test of who's who in your book of life. Who's the masked and the unmasked you?

Every virtuous act that you have ever done that has helped someone or brought a little ray of sunshine into someone's life is a thing of worth, and you could say, "Well, I'd like to keep the memory of that." Well, you will!

I don't mean that you'll keep that memory in the sense that you're going to say, "Oh, I was good to somebody once, so somebody should be good to me." I mean that you will rejoice more in the things that you have done that have assisted the unfoldment of Good in the world than you will in anything else—and it will be the sheer joy of rejoicing in the Good and being a part of it. And therefore, this should clue you in to the worthwhile things in life that will unmask what is of value and what is not of value.

When you pull the mask off, you should see shining through a splendid, radiant divine being—the real you! And that real you cannot be concentrated upon too much.

WHAT WE CONTEMPLATE WE BECOME

Because of the density of our own human creation, the Masters continue to stress the same teaching again and again. They tell us to place our attention on the Presence and, keeping it there, to look up into the face of our guardian angel and adore the Light who sent this winged messenger to our side. For, what we contemplate—especially with deep thoughts and feelings of cherishment—we become.

We have lived so long and we've thought so hard upon externals that internals have almost been ignored. Yet internal values and internal beauty are the greatest things in the world, because they're real.

A lot of ladies wear costume jewelry simply because they can't afford to buy the real thing, but you show me the lady today who wouldn't be happy and proud to wear genuine diamonds if she could find the money to buy them! The phoniness in the world is the result, in some cases, of economic necessity; and in other cases, it's just because people don't know the value of things.

Elizabeth was speaking on color. We don't wish to be fanatics on color. We don't wish to be fanatics on anything. We have found that there are people and there are religions that stress externals and they try to create the idea that in removing the mask we have to destroy beauty. So they say, "Don't wear lipstick. Don't wear powder. Don't wear rouge. Be natural."

Fine! This is a good idea if you have a naturally beautiful complexion. Some ladies are blessed with it. Some men are blessed with it. Some have a poor complexion. Some require powder because their skin is oily. These are cosmetic values.

I do not see that religion should invade the privacy of men's lives. That which makes people look a little better seems to me to be wholly justified until such a time as one can attain enough God-control over his form to make the form respond to the impetus of the Divine within.

I'd find no fault in someone dyeing their hair and being a student of the Ascended Masters. If it helps you in some way to feel younger, this is perfectly alright. We don't feel that religion should invade these matters at all. We don't feel that the Masters are going to stress this. This is not the phoniness we wish to take off.

THE PHONINESS WE WISH TO TAKE OFF

The phoniness we wish to take off is more our pseudoideas that have no real value to us—ideas of self-importance, when we're not any less important than any other human being upon earth but we're not any more important either.

It's just as wrong in my opinion (if you're a person who wants to remove the mask) for you to belittle yourself as it is for you to exalt yourself. And please remember this! I don't think much of a person's cutting himself down or coming up to me and saying, "Oh, I'm so nothing. I hate to bother you or take up your time." I am here to serve everyone! And I feel that every human being should remember that every other human being is entitled to respect for the God flame that is within him.

And therefore, what we seek to unmask is the God flame within so that the Light that's within people can shine forth. And then there will be nothing phony about anything. Not a thing! Everything will *be* real because it *is* real! It will not only *seem* real but it will *be* real! Then the jewels that we will wear will be the spiritual jewels of light substance that are within our minds and beings. And, after all, what's real in me and in you—that's the important thing in life!

So when you come to a point where you desire to unmask yourself, this is not to belittle yourself. It's to get rid of the shell of illusion about anything—yourself or someone else. If you're round-shouldered because you're stooping over all the time, well then, straighten your spine! That's what it means.

If there's something wrong with your thinking and every once in a while you begin to doubt your own capacity, then remember that God is within. And remind yourself, as many times as you need to, that you're alive. Pinch yourself if you have to—but don't bruise yourself!

These ideas are simple, but they are vital to the realization pattern of God-identity. As long as we keep on fooling ourselves by wearing a mask of un-reality, we are going to suffer the ill effects of our own wrong thinking. This is not mere metaphysics—Christian Science, Unity—call it what you will. This is actually practical Ascended Master law!

THE ASCENDED MASTERS ARE PRACTITIONERS OF TRUTH

The Ascended Masters are practitioners of Truth. And the Truth that they export into our octave is strictly for our benefit and for the benefit of humanity. But if we're going to be beneficiaries of their wisdom, we have to use it.

I catch myself every once in a while doing or saying something that I feel is not compatible with the Masters' principles. And when I see it happening,

I don't let it go by—and neither does anyone else! (This is one of the prices you have to pay for being in the public eye.)

But all of us can open our own eyes to see ourselves as we really are. And as I said before, put away from your consciousness the idea that you're a tiny little idiot of some kind. Now, some people don't think they're idiots. They think they're very wise. Put that idea away, too!

Realize that your God Presence has all the qualities of wisdom, all the qualities of compassion, all the qualities of peace, all the qualities of Christ-victory—every quality you need to make your ascension. If you will remind yourself that these qualities exist within the God flame, if you'll fix that in your mind, this human person, the mask you see that is not real, will do like old General MacArthur—it won't die, it'll just simply fade away.[6]

You won't even have to take the mask off because the mask will fade away. It'll perish! But in its place the spiritual flowers will grow in the garden of your heart.

And it isn't important that your neighbor see them. If your neighbor has spiritual vision, your neighbor will see them and rejoice with you, and you will rejoice with your neighbor when you see the flowers of spiritual expansion coming to life in him as well as in yourself.

AVOID PHONINESS IN ANYTHING YOU DO

This is the thing: Avoid phoniness in anything you do because you pay a terrible price for it.

Every time you create an illusion and consciously know that you're creating it, every time that you deceive yourself or others knowingly, you are weaving a veil that one day the Great Law will require you to fight through. Therefore, learn to look within with the purity of a child. Learn to value the flame that God has placed within you as being the be-all and end-all of existence. It is! It's the endless circle—the endless cycles of your life.

The outer self, you know, comes to an end. Yet haven't we all "died daily," as Saint Paul says?[7] Every time we lay our body down to rest at night, we go out of that body temple and maybe we're up there playing hide-and-seek with the stars. Or maybe we're swimming with the undines somewhere down here in the ocean. Or maybe we're leaping from cloud to cloud with the sylphs. Or maybe we're over at an Ascended Master temple. But wherever we are, there God is! So learn to enjoy this universe. You're going to be in it for a long, long time!

You know, the suicide entity works overtime in all the cities. The suicide entity has worked a lot in San Francisco and people have jumped off of the Golden Gate Bridge because they felt that they were tired of the phoniness of life.

Well, in reality there is no phoniness! People have created it. They've wrapped it around themselves. It's the mask that they wear and they're tired of that mask. There's only one way to remove it, and that's to tear it off and throw it away!

Look at yourself as you really are in the eyes of God. Don't see yourself through your own eyes. See yourself through God's eyes, and God will hold a vision for you that you can live up to. And he will believe with you that you can live up to it. And actually, this is the way to happiness—not only happiness today but perpetual happiness.

EXTERNALIZE YOUR DIVINE SELF BY DETERMINATION

But remember one thing, and this is a solemn warning: No one who begins to externalize the Divine Self, through love of that Self, will ever find that his faith will not be tested. It will be—and I don't mean maybe.

Do not expect, simply because you do these things *one day* that they will remain with you forever. Your Divine Self is a permanent gift, but you have to externalize that gift daily by renewing your determination to do it.

The mask is thrown away and discarded. Yet, it can be picked up again and you can keep on tricking yourself, if you want to. A lot of people do it.

But when you determine that you're going to renew your covenant with your Divine Self *every day,* that you're going to see behind the mask and let that Light shine through, and you do it day after day— then life will begin to smile upon you with a greater and greater measure of kindness because you are harmonizing yourself with the Life principle of Almighty God.

This is what beloved Jesus has taught us. He has taught us to relax, to be calm, to trust in God, to adore cosmic law and cosmic principles, and to feel joy that we are free from the world's matrix.

Wouldn't it be a frightful thing if you had to live in your homes with some of the world's matrices all around you, if you had to live with their dissonance and have it dinging into your ears all the time, if you had to look at the pictures that they want you to look at? Well, it wouldn't take very long before you'd find yourself falling into decay.

It's the mental furniture that you have that is very important to you because that is what you furnish your home with—not the sofas you buy, not the beds you lie on, not the chairs you sit on; it's the spiritual furnishings of your house of light that determine just how happy or how sad you'll be.

We hope that as you continue to unmask your Self (not necessarily to discover that you're a phony but to discover that you're real) ever-new joy will wing its way into your world here, now, always and forever!

I hope these little thoughts have been of some benefit to you. That's my desire.

Chapter Two

THE POINT OF ORIGIN

The Point of Origin

ETERNAL Creator of Cosmos, Unfolder of the Destiny of Man, Creator of the Flame of Life and the divine matrices within man—we come before thee in the name of the living Christ, asking for the mental, emotional, and spiritual release into our consciousness of a chalice of thy thoughts for our advancement, for our admonishment and for our instruction. In the name of Jesus Christ, we thank thee.

The point of origin is the Beginning of every man, woman and child of God upon this planetary home and all systems of worlds. It is the moment of the creation of all his Sons—"male and female created he them"[1]—and the heavenly/earthly hierarchies of angels and nature spirits who occupy the vast ranges of our Spirit/Matter cosmos—and beyond.

Of this we are certain: that the point of origin is in the Light-emanation of First Cause and that the Light, referred to as the Word, from the Greek *Logos,* is "the only begotten Son of the Father, full of grace and truth."[2]

The Word as *the* founding principle of Life is the instrument of creation by which the Creator formed and fashioned all things. This Light is the point of our soul's origin both in Spirit and in Matter.

From a scientific standpoint, all Matter in manifestation and all Intelligence by which the living Word engraved itself in the beginning upon all substance is Light. All things spiritually substantive and physically apparent were made by this Light, and without the Light was not any thing made that was made[3]—not in the whole of the universe nor in the farthest reaches of the Universal Sound.

This thought is a propulsive thought because it propels us to the first moment of creation with God—Elohim. And we behold that if all things were made by the Universal Word, or Christ, then we were also made by this Christ. And our souls are comforted. For through this Holy One of God we find an affinity *(a fine tie),* a beautiful tie between ourselves and the Father; and beyond the form of the Trinity we are bound by this Logos to the formless, pure Spirit, the point of origin of the All, called in the ancient tradition BRAHMAN.

Yes, by the Word our ties reach out through the latticework of cosmos as it trembles the veil of the Cosmic Virgin with the soundless sound which we may approach as we intone the sacred OM.

This Word resounding through all planes and light molecules of our Being is the origin of the Spirit/Matter creation. Out of the origin sprang forth the Alpha and the Omega, the "beginning and the ending" of our comings and our goings in these worlds within worlds.

We are one with the Word as the Word is one with us. We can be separated neither from the creative Sound nor from the creative Source. So we contain all our beginnings and our endings—and even the Origin of our origin, to which we are about to return through the Lost Teachings of Jesus.

THE PATH: CO-CREATORS WITH GOD

Now, in the ticking of a Swiss watch we see only mechanical precision. In the creation of the universe we see the heart of flesh involved with the manifestation. And we ourselves are involved. It is possible—through our union with God, who made the sun to stand still at the command of Joshua[4]—for the Light to bring us back (no matter how far we have traveled on the belt of time) to the point of origin in the Universal Word.

Through our identification with God in the timeless, spaceless, infinite realm, we become co-creators with the God of the universe, even though we now abide in finite form in the schoolroom of the Matter cosmos where our souls are tried and whitened, beautified and perfected.[5]

As Christ declared this very purpose to be his and ours when he was threatened by King Herod, "Go and tell that fox that today and tomorrow I cast out devils and heal the sick, and the third day *I shall be perfected,*"[6] so we declare it to you today:

The path of the perfecting of the self by the Great God Self—the ritual of the soul's absolution through the dear Father—is the way of return to the point of origin. The student's consummate attainment on this path, as Jesus pointed out to his disciples, is achieved through the Word, believing on the "One Sent,"[7] as he engages all of his forces in the LORD's Work.

This Work consists of casting out the devils of the mind and devouring by sacred fire the corruptible consciousness of the lower self. It is the restoring of the Light of the chakras and their alignment with the seven planes of Being. It is the transfer of Light to the components of the Body of God.

Sons and daughters of God awakened by the memory of your point of origin: this is your joy in the LORD as you take up the purpose of your origination in the Word—to wear the mantle of your divine office as co-creator with God and to exercise the powers of that office to re-create yourself after the Divine Image and Likeness.

To submit yourself unto the Holy Spirit in order to be formed and re-formed in the Perfect Design, the original blueprint of yourself as the mirror image of the God Self—this is the co-creative Work of Father and Son together by which the Light-emanation of the Word is released unto its fulfillment in you.

THE LIGHT OF NON-CONDEMNATION

In contradistinction to this path of discipleship made plain by the true Masters of East and West as "the mighty work of the ages," those false pastors who spend their time in condemnation of humanity, with intolerance toward any but their own and in complete contradiction of the word of our Lord—"For God sent not his Son into the world to condemn the world, but that the world through him might be saved"[8]—will rue the day they spread the doctrine of condemnation upon the world.

As a result of this pernicious habit that is contrary to God's purposes—which have been defined for us and by us from the beginning—men bear a heavy yoke of condemnation upon their shoulders. And it does not cease in the midst of religious fanaticism and political strife.

Even great sinners—murderers and thieves of all kinds say in their dying moments, "I really wasn't a bad person. I've always had a heart that wanted to do right." It's true, that's what they say. That's the amazing part of it—people go wrong without really understanding what it is that makes them go wrong. You see, they are resisting the curse of world condemnation at the same time they are trapped by it.

Though some who are their own worst enemies suffer ultimate self-humiliations, self-denials and defeats—the healing, beautifying apparatus of heaven is still functional. *"I AM come* not to call the righteous but sinners to repentance,"[9] he said. *I AM the One Sent* "unto the lost[10] sheep of the house of Israel."[11]

We see the figure of the Master Jesus appearing to Saint Paul on the Damascus way—"a light from heaven, above the brightness of the sun, shining round about me," as he described his experience to Agrippa. And he heard the voice of the Master saying, "Saul, Saul, why persecutest thou me? It is hard for thee to kick against the pricks."[12]

Like Saul of Tarsus prior to his conversion, we find people today who were made in the image of God not understanding that it is so. And this is because our religious terminology in its orthodoxy, in its catechism, has failed to convey to contemporary man the great burnishment possible to the soul that can shine in the divine light and receive succor from the living God.

It was a blinding light and a purging light that descended on Paul. It was for the rebuke of his human consciousness that had persecuted the true servants of God. It was for the purification of his sight that he might behold the Son of God. It was the light of conversion that turned him around and set him on the path of his own personal walk with the Master Jesus Christ. But it was not the light of condemnation.

Quite the contrary, by the power of the Logos Jesus bore, the Master was calling and recalling Saul to his point of origin in the I AM Presence.

The Saviour is the same today as he was when he

appeared to his disciples both before and after his resurrection and he will always be the same. We must therefore relate to him not out of the concept of time and space but in the concept of the Eternal Now. The question is not whether the Ascended Master Jesus Christ can appear to you today just as he did then; the question is, Are you ready for the change in your life that his Light will produce?

Whatever else Paul was outwardly, inwardly his soul was ready!

As he had been prepared of the Spirit, so he had readied himself through diligent application to his studies in this and previous lives. You will remember that Paul was a citizen of Cilicia, a learned Jew brought up at Jerusalem at the feet of Gamaliel, who was a Pharisee of the council and doctor of the law.

Familiar with the path of learning and the learned, the soul within, quite apart from the outer mentality, was no stranger to its spiritualization by the Word. Though the mind of Saul was prejudiced against Christ (by hereditary and environmental factors that cannot permanently alter the soul's direction except it give consent), the image of the apostle Paul, his fiery destiny, was already etched within his spirit.

So it is with you, beloved. And the choice is yours: to allow yourself, or not, to be converted *when*—not if but *when*—Christ comes knocking at your door.

The grasp of cosmos is to be captured in the *Now*—that very nexus where "as Above, so below" the grain of sand in the hourglass sounds the moment of opportunity. Looking down from above, the nexus is the past—it's already passed you by; looking up from below, the nexus is the future—it's about to descend. But in both cases, action (or the activating force—i.e., the movement of time) is the key to the Now.

What is happening in your life *now?* What are

you today? For in the now we not only form our tomorrows but we also transform our yesterdays.

And that is the point of Origen—of Alexandria, that is. Following the apostles, he was the first great theologian of the Church, whose doctrines were later anathematized, he himself suffering torture and imprisonment for Christ Truth in the Decian persecution (A.D. 250–251). Fragments of his extraordinary writings reveal many of the Lost Teachings of Jesus that our Lord gave to him through his meditation on the scriptures.

One of the things he said, which is completely opposite to the condemnation that today's religions put upon people, is that perfection is achieved in stages. Increases in virtues are sought one by one, he explained, and therefore our salvation is in the eternal now, not in the past or in the future.

He believed that all rational creatures began at some higher point and fell to their present position, necessitating the creation of the material world, but that no matter how far a rational being has fallen, it is *always possible* for him to reascend to his former state of unity with God.[13]

After its conversion, Origen wrote, the soul dwells in the spiritual wilderness where it is trained and tested. "And when it conquers one temptation . . . it comes to another one; and it passes, as it were, from one stage to another . . . until the soul arrives at its goal, namely the highest summit of virtues, and crosses the river of God and receives the heritage promised it."[14]

Therefore, you see, just because you make one mistake doesn't mean you're going to burn forever, and just because you've experienced your conversion, doesn't mean you've achieved your divine inheritance. People are so condemned by the idea that if they make one mistake, they've had it.

The world has not understood the power of forgiveness. Forgiveness is not a mere toleration of us by the Deity, as though God were to say, "Well, I'll just put up with them for a while. Either they'll learn or they'll burn!" This is the statement of an anthropomorphic god—a god made in the image of man. God is not built that way!

The living God we worship through the Person of the Father whom we adore says that instead of burning we're going to be earning—and learning our lessons as we go. And if we burn at all, it will be in our conscience and in our realization that there are higher standards to be reckoned with. These were pointed out to us by the Master. We may resist them if we will. Heaven is not going to do anything to change your mind, nor am I.

As one of the servants of God—perhaps the least of the brethren [15]—I am not going to struggle with anyone, either in this room or outside of this room. But no matter what perversity may occupy the human mind, I will serve those who come with an open mind, a pure heart, and the willingness to experiment with the techniques that have been proven by the Ascended Masters throughout many lifetimes of our joint service with them as well as throughout humanity's existence on this planet.

Although the significance of the Brotherhood's cooperation with unascended man is not apprehended by some people, this does not change the outworking of cosmic law—nor does any man's assessment of what is or is not significant make any difference to the holy angels or to the Law.

I will not entice anyone to listen to my sermons against his will. And therefore, beware of me, because I'm not going to do anything to you—nothing! I'm just going to talk about the Father's purposes. And if you find agreement with me, I won't even be concerned. If you find disagreement with me, I may know it, but I won't even let you know that I know it.

So, all we are really interested in doing is to act as the instrument of beloved Jesus—that our hands may be his hands, that our feet be his feet, that our tongue be his tongue, that our eyes be his eyes seeing the perfection that God sees for us. So graced by the Lord are we, that we are also willing to pay the price. Because God is a God of Love, far greater than most of us have realized. And we trust in that Love. We follow and obey. For Love has called and we have answered.

But the world has not always captured in its sights that which God really is. People have talked about divine love. In fact, people talk about divine love all the time, but as long as they are trapped in their limited, possessive loves, even toward God, there is very little practice upon this planet of the true meaning of divine love. Our loves just don't seem to get beyond the emotional, the sensual or the sympathetic.

But we must be very careful with this two-edged sword that we sometimes carry. And I'm speaking of the whole human race. The sword of condemnation is a dangerous sword. Especially when assessing our fellow human beings. Because, in their minds and in their hearts, so many people really love to do well and they sincerely mean to do well. And their loves, though perhaps not fully freed by the Spirit, do well up from deep within the psyche. They're just up against hidebound tradition and human habit patterns which are probably the root cause of most of the world's problems today.

But for every root cause there is a root solution—dissolution by the Holy Spirit! And when the baptism by sacred fire comes to you in the descent of violet flame day by day in answer to your call, you will know Love's power of transmutation in Love's all-suffusing glow and "glow-ry," as our Baptist friend Ruthie from North Carolina used to say it.

What a strange tragedy we see before us, that while all religion has had but one purpose—the brotherhood of man under the Fatherhood of God—it has actually achieved the opposite by attempting to reduce the Spirit of Love to a doctrine of do's and don'ts. But even this will respond to the Holy Spirit's all-consuming violet flame.

The violet flame is the universal solvent and the universal panacea sought by alchemists, physicians, and philosophers alike, yet found only by the few. But until you master the art and science of the spoken Word[16] and learn to call forth its seventh-ray action into your mind and soul and body, you won't know what the violet flame can do for you.

The violet flame is one of the greatest mysteries ever taught by Jesus Christ and we will unfold it to you in due course. Meanwhile, as we consider first principles, watch and pray for the descent of the Paraclete[17] as you enter the garden of our Lord's heart.

RELIGION AND MAN'S STRUGGLE TO REACH GOD

We see that in the very earliest primitive cultures there arose the shaman, the priest, the witch doctor. Whatever he was, he was a focalization of the tribal consciousness of the people who recognized the impermanence of physical life and sought to find some contact with the macrocosmic universe (in contrast to the microcosmic universe that we see around us—for we see only a little glimpse of the world).

This was the beginning of a religion that sought to meet the needs of the people both in the control of the immediate environment and for the assurance of self-preservation beyond this mortal life span.

We live in a very rigid world—our own personal world, that is. It is a world that revolves around our living room rug and our kitchen table and then an occasional trip here and there. And we say we know about the world.

From the encyclopedias we may glean a little knowledge of what the world is like. We learn about the psychological world of man, the astral world and the subconscious realm. And this is where man experiences strange and horrid tortures—and he gets emotionally out of control, "all bent out of shape," as they say.

You and I both know that people are not really satisfied with what our modern priests and ministers and rabbis and psychoanalysts are telling them about the world. People know that there is a missing link. We know—and we've known from childhood—that we are not being told the Truth that we know to be true inside of ourselves.

And so, we should begin to understand something about ourselves and the self that relates back to man's earliest struggle in his attempt to find out God.

Well, if you want to have some fun sometime, you get a chart of all the religions that have ever been practiced on earth. And once you've examined it, you are going to know that there will be no Summit Lighthouse people in heaven, there will be no Presbyterians in heaven, there will be no Roman Catholics in heaven, there will be no Methodists in heaven, and there will be no Pentecostals in heaven, because there'll only be the universal people who will have forgotten all about who they were or what they belonged to, who will have recognized that they belong to God first—and forgotten about the rest! You see, you've got to leave the bag and baggage of religion behind if you're going to reach the summit and the summation of Love!

Jesus once remarked to us, "Many would be astounded to know that I personally answer the prayers of the Moslem, the Jew, the Hindu, the Buddhist, and those who simply cry out without the understanding of me in my person. Beloved ones, there is a smugness, a self-righteousness and a spiritual pride among those who have thought that [in their doctrine] they held the keys to the kingdom, and yet they have betrayed the very Light and the very Mysteries of my Body." [18]

Don't you see? Paul said, "Above all these things [i.e., the religions] put on charity, which is the bond of perfectness." [19]

So here we are searching for our Maker and all of these religions stand before us. And they're all supposed to be ways to God. You know these signposts that lead from Belgium over to Paris? They'll be going every way. One will be pointing to Paris this way, another will be pointing to Paris that way, and still another points to Paris a third way. And sometimes I think they even point straight up!

And you become seized with the idea that you can get to Paris just about any way you want to.

And I quite agree, except that some of these ways are more circuitous than others. You see what I mean. They go around Robin Hood's barn. And I do believe that the shortest distance between any two points is a straight line—not a devious line or a circle or a zigzag.

And so we need to understand what the Teachings of the Ascended Masters are all about. Well, the first thing they teach you is that you have free will; and the next thing they tell you is that within the bounds of man's habitation set by God [20] you can have anything you want in this lifetime or the next.

And then they'll tell you that maybe after many lifetimes of struggle and senseless detours—always on your way to see the Master of Paris but never quite getting there—you'll find yourself going the same way the Masters are going today. You're going to be going the same way because toward the end of your circuitous route, you'll come back onto the straight line.

But it usually takes place in the next embodiment—not in this one—because most people are born in one religion and they die in it. And they're usually buried in it, too!

You know about pews? Some churches rent out pews to their parishioners and sometimes they even rent out grave sites. Yes! You can rent your family pews and your family plots and the whole works. And I suspect one of these days it'll be all done by computer. You just punch a few buttons and you'll have everything from the cradle to the grave all taken care of—except your soul!

Most of the time in this competitive world the soul is sort of gently overlooked. And that's the most important part. We take care of our teeth—we get Water Piks and toothbrushes and dental floss. And we really look good, you know, with all these things. And some people get false eyelashes and wigs and everything you can think of to put on.

It's alright. It doesn't hurt the soul at all. But the problem is, it doesn't help it!

If we'd only pay as much attention to that soul within, why then we just *might* decide to proceed in a direct line. Knowing where the real me really wants to go and how to get there, why, of course, we'd take the shortest route, wouldn't we? Or would we.

Now, you think about that for a while. The question is, given the Truth and almost unlimited opportunity within our sphere, do we opt for the highest and the best Life can afford?

While we busy ourselves about making life's short-term and long-term decisions, the Creator has given us his footstool kingdom[21] as a platform for our evolution.

And so, we live in a beautiful world, really. It's

not an ugly world, though in certain corners man has
made it appear that way. Nature has endowed us and
enrichened us with beautiful, mellow, golden sunshine. Probably Colorado has one of the best sun-
shines in the whole country. But everybody who lives
anywhere in this country, even in Boston, manages to
have some days of rich sunshine and beauty for walking out in the fresh air. And, of course, while some of
them don't have as nice a fresh air as they have in
Colorado, still, anytime you get outdoors where you
can breathe that fresh air and take it into your lungs, it
goes to work for you and it makes you feel better.

But we also live in a time of bromides, where all
of the little sayings, the clichés, and the comfortable
feelings of our consciousness tend to put us to sleep
and make us feel that we are secure and that there is
no insecurity. Yet there's another side of ourselves
that tells us that uncertainty itself is an insecurity. And
we are not quite sure.

And so one man said that he joined about
eighteen different churches. Somebody asked him
why he was a member of so many churches. And he
said, "Well, just in case." In case one wasn't working,
why, he wanted to be with the one that would work,
you see.

THE QUESTION OF REEMBODIMENT

Our religion is simply our belief in the immortality of Life. Whereas the flowers fade in autumn and
the leaves of the trees tumble earthward in their season, and the grass in a temperate climate turns brown
and dries up and new grass comes to life again in the
spring, we observe an eternal process of renewal sig-
naling that we just might be around here for a lot
longer than we think.

Some people say, "Well, do you believe in reembodiment?"

Well, of course I do!

"But," they say, "what's the value of reembodiment? I can't remember who *I was* ten thousand years ago. And because I can't remember, I don't really believe it happened."

Well, experiences have happened all over the world that ought to convince us of our existence in the past. One very interesting story is that of Shanti Devi; it's a known occurrence because it was verified by a number of investigators. [22]

Shanti Devi was a little girl who at three years of age began speaking about her husband and children from her past life. Eventually she told her new family her husband's name, where he lived, described the house and said she had died after giving birth to her second child.

A relative of her husband was sent to investigate and Shanti recognized him on arrival, threw her arms about him and then recounted her previous life exactly as he had witnessed it. Next her husband and son came to see her unannounced and she recognized them both immediately. Shanti finally led a committee of investigators to her previous home. She used idioms of speech familiar in that town, though she had never been there before, and even told the observers where she had buried some money before her death!

Her profound emotion in each encounter with loved ones is a touching tribute to the soul's undying faithfulness to its own. But the pain of living two lives at once was very difficult for her to bear. Thus, for most of us the Great Law in its mercy veils the past so that we may live each episode of the present without the sharp delineations of past involvements.

And so it was attested in the annals of Indian

psychologists as being a true case of reembodiment. And it was widely publicized and accepted throughout India, where reincarnation is almost universally believed.

In fact, did you know that in 1930 Spencer Lewis made the remark that over three-quarters of the world's thinking and analyzing minds have accepted reincarnation?[23] Of course, with the increased population, the takeovers of World Communism, and atheism a common malignancy of the mind, there's no telling what that figure is today.

In the third century, Origen of Alexandria taught reincarnation by the logic of his theory on the preexistence of souls, and this was one of the chief causes for the anathemas decreed against his pure doctrine.

He taught that we are responsible for what we are—that the good things that happen to us are because we have done good things in the past, and vice versa. The conclusion he reached was "that the position of every created being is the result of his own work and his own motives."[24]

Origen points out the case of Jacob and Esau, of whom God said before they were even born, "Jacob have I loved, but Esau have I hated."[25] Origen wondered about this, because, he thought, this would mean either that God was capricious and not good and righteous and fair as everyone knew him to be, or else that the souls of the two brothers already struggling in the womb had made choices and committed deeds in some previous existence.

Origen noticed that Paul had wondered the same thing, that he had asked how God could say such a thing about infants "not yet born, neither having done any good or evil, . . . What shall we say then? Is there unrighteousness with God? God forbid."[26]

The question of Jacob and Esau can be applied to

us: How can we be born in a lesser situation than our neighbor? Origen wrote in *On First Principles,* "The same question which faces us in connection with Esau and Jacob may also be raised in regard to all the heavenly beings and all creatures on earth and in the lower regions."

From his study of the situation of the twins, the first red and hairy, the other taking hold of his heel, Origen elicited this proof of reincarnation:

"When the scriptures are examined with much diligence in regard to Esau and Jacob," he said, "it is found that there is 'no unrighteousness with God' in its being said of them, before they were born or had done anything, in this life of course, that 'the elder should serve the younger', and as it is found that there is no unrighteousness in the fact that Jacob supplanted his brother even in the womb, provided we believe that by reason of his *merits in some previous life* Jacob had deserved to be loved by God to such an extent as to be worthy of being preferred to his brother." (emphasis added)

And the people loved him and his teaching, but the powers that be were incensed. They couldn't argue with Origen, so they burned his books.

We see emerging from the fragments that remain of his teachings principles that lead us to the conclusion of reincarnation and the inevitable law of karma. He said if you believe that God is righteous (something that they couldn't disagree with), then each person, "whether of heaven or earth or below the earth, may be said to possess within himself the causes of diversity antecedent to his birth in the body."

And then Origen said something that incited them even more. He said that this preexistence of the soul was the explanation for the inequality of circumstance.

"In this way it is possible," he said, "for us to

understand that even before the present life there
were rational vessels [souls], either wholly purged or
less so, that is, vessels which had purged themselves or
had not, and that from this circumstance each vessel
received, according to the measure of its purity or
impurity, its place or region or condition in which to
be born or to fulfil some duty in this world. All these,
down to the very least, God supervises by the power of
his wisdom and distinguishes by the controlling hand
of his judgment; and thus he has arranged the universe on the principle of a most impartial retribution,
according as each one deserves for his merit to be
assisted or cared for.

"Herein is displayed in its completeness the principle of impartiality, when the inequality of circumstances preserves an equality of reward for merit."

This principle of the law of retribution, or the law
of karma, was the pivot of Origen's proof of God's
impartiality in the face of man's inequities. Having
agreed with his premise, his critics were obliged to
admit his conclusion—that man is solely responsible
for who and what he is. Whether or not they did, or
wanted to, is another matter entirely.

But Christ's chosen didn't derive from all of this
that we should go around looking down on people
who are poorer than we are. The one whom Jesus
anointed doctor of his divine doctrine was very careful about that. He said that "the grounds of merit in
each individual are known with truth and clearness
only to God, together with his only-begotten Word
and Wisdom and his Holy Spirit." [27]

You may be way ahead of those who are richer
than you. After all, riches are a burden too. So reincarnation is the means by which we have the opportunity to regain our point of origin—oneness with
God. Submitting upon the altar of Christianity the

true Teachings of Jesus, Origen taught that it was this oneness, which we had lost so long ago, which we should find in the future—if we diligently seek Him.

Reincarnation is not just some philosophical postulation or the outcome of an exercise in logic. There are all sorts of examples besides the one of Shanti Devi.

In England a couple by the name of Pollock had two children, Joanna and Jacqueline, who were run over by a car on their way to church.[28] A year after their tragic death their mother gave birth to twin girls. Many similarities between them and their deceased sisters were noted, from an identical birthmark to personality traits and temperaments. Though no one had told them of the accident, one remembered the coat her mother had worn on the fatal day. She became noticeably agitated upon seeing it again and identified it as the one "Mother used to wear to school."

The mysteries of childhood! Except ye become as a little child, ye cannot enter in.[29] We pay too much attention to our old-age rigidity—the age of twenty-one!—and not enough to the ageless aeons of our soul evolution.

THE MYSTERIES OF CHILDHOOD—ANGELS AND FAIRIES

I remember that when I was four I could see angels. Have you ever seen an angel, any of you? Any of you people dare to put your hand up and say you've seen an angel? One. Two. Two people have seen angels!

We have a book that tells the story of a teacher who taught in a Christian school.[30] One year she decided to include in the regular devotional exercises songs to Mother Mary and the angels. And she had quite an experience with pupils reporting visitations of the angels to her classroom.

My heavens, what didn't happen! Why, one child had a learning problem. He couldn't learn. And so one of the other children went up to an angel that had appeared to her in the classroom and she said, "Bobby has a learning problem." The angel answered, "Well, we'll help him with it." The angel then promised Bobby that from that time on he would be able to learn more rapidly—and he did!

One day Mother Mary visited a little girl in the class and told her that she was the one who had wiped the tears from Mary's eyes on Golgotha. On another day letters floated down to several of the children with the message "I love you!" on them. All kinds of wonderful things happened. And these experiences were written up at the instigation of Dr. Helen MacDonald, who knew the teacher, Mrs. Marguerite Baker, personally. This was a true story.

Several years later, I met one of the boys who had attended this school. And I will have to admit that he was an unusual child. There was something about him that was out of this world. Really! Mrs. Baker remarked to me that they were a very special group, extremely intelligent and responsive to the ministrations of our unseen helpers.

This is an example of how God's helpers bypass the pulpits and preachments and go directly to the pure in heart for whom the promise still stands: *They shall see God.* [31]

We ought to ask ourselves why there is no room in the edifices of men for the religion of God. We ought to be asking questions like: Why is the communion of souls with saints and angels and our immortal teachers not encouraged, sought and taught by pastors as the means God provided for heavenly intercession? Where are the true evangels of the Comforter, the Teacher? [32]

Well, I think this extraordinary event that took place in a first-grade classroom does indicate that there are differences between people.

Some see fairies and angels and some don't, and those who don't, say they don't exist. And this is how arguments about doctrine all got started. It was based on every man's perception of himself and his universe. Then someone said there should be no private interpretation of scripture.[33] But then, how else is anyone supposed to find out God—except God reveal himself to his heart by his Spirit!

If you go out into the streets of a city and you are observant, you are going to see all types of human emotions written on the faces of people. I believe with everything they go through, people are basically searching for God, even though they may not think of it as such. And do you know what? God is searching for them, too—which does pose quite a problem to our understanding: If God is searching for them and they're searching for God, why don't they get together?

It's the blasted religions! That's why they don't get together.

MESSENGERS OF CHRIST REJECTED

Mahatma Gandhi put it very succinctly: He said the reason he didn't become a Christian—he wanted to be, you know, he loved that "Lead, Kindly Light"—was because most of the Christians took a little inoculation of religion as proof against the real thing. He didn't observe that Christians were truly Christlike. They said, "I'll go this far: I'll join the church, I'll go to church, I'll be good"—but they never really had an internal revolution where God came out on top. The human will prevailed all the way.

Louis Fischer writes in his anthology on Gandhi:

Gandhi's Christian friends taught him the essence of Christianity. They said if he believed in Jesus he would find redemption.

"If this be the Christianity acknowledged by all Christians, I cannot accept it," [Gandhi told them]. "I do not seek redemption from the consequences of my sin. I seek to be redeemed from sin itself. . . . Until I have attained that end, I shall be content to be restless."

Gandhi liked the sweet Christian hymns and many of the Christians he met. But he could not regard Christianity as the perfect religion or the greatest religion.

". . . It was impossible for me to believe that I could go to heaven or attain salvation only by becoming a Christian. . . .

". . . I could accept Jesus as a martyr, an embodiment of sacrifice and a divine teacher, but not as the most perfect man ever born. . . . The pious lives of Christians did not give me anything that the lives of men of other faiths had failed to give. I had seen in other lives just the same reformation that I had heard of among Christians. Philosophically there was nothing extraordinary in Christian principles. . . .

"Thus, if I could not accept Christianity either as a perfect or the greatest religion, neither was I then convinced of Hinduism's being such. Hindu defects were pressingly visible to me. If untouchability could be a part of Hinduism, it could be but a rotten part or an excrescence."[34]

That's exactly why Jesus said, "Woe unto you, lawyers! for ye have taken away the key of knowledge: ye entered not in yourselves, and them that were entering in ye hindered."[35]

He didn't mince words. He kicked the merchants out of the temple and he kicked over the tables of the moneychangers.[36] Isn't that interesting? Now, if he didn't approve of what was going on in his time, why should we be so sure that he would approve of what is going on in our time?

Maybe Gandhi hit upon something. Maybe he was just as dissatisfied as Jesus would be with the merchandising in men's souls that goes on in so-called religious organizations today. Maybe this "little man" who by the force of Love liberated the whole of India— whose few worldly possessions upon his death included his dhoti and shawl, eyeglasses, watch, sandals and spinning wheel—was speaking out of the depths of the Universal Christ who would surely rebuke the churches today as he did in his messages to the seven churches recorded in the Lord's Revelation to John on Patmos.[37]

Gandhi is not well liked by certain Christian sects today. What a pity. So often we scorn as beggars and scoundrels the very ones God sends for our edification. Gandhi wasn't perfect. So what! Neither are we.

We love him because he fought for Truth, lived it as best he could, wrestled with the snake of politics, as he put it,[38] freed a great nation to pursue its spiritual and political destiny, and dedicated his life upon the altar of Love and its nonviolent resistance to every evil. Members of all religions can learn much from such a soul whose living, practical faith embodied the ideals and lessons taught in the parables of Jesus and the sermons of the Buddha—and in the example of every other saint who has contacted the Light as the point of his origin.

El Morya once wrote: "If the messenger be an ant, heed him." Thus judge the message by its inherent Truth, always consistent with the Law of Love. And do not make the fatal mistake of rejecting Truth because you think the messenger beneath your rank—morally, economically or academically. For the one sent is always the tester of our humility before God, as Naaman, captain of the hosts of the king of Syria, found out before Elisha and the prophet's messenger.[39]

If the messenger be an ant, heed him! Because it's your response to the message that counts in the courts of heaven. And you will be richly rewarded for your graces shown to the one who cometh in the name of the Lord.

Note well, if the messenger were to tell you only what you already know and accept and believe, it would be pointless for the Lord to send him. Messengers bear good and bad tidings of fateful events. Prophecy of that which can and cannot be—of that which is and is not to be. Warnings of things to come unforeseen.

Jesus has told us that some of his best servants have rejected the messages he has sent them through various messengers, and even when he himself has spoken directly to their hearts. His own have rejected him—as it is written, "he came unto his own and his own received him not"[40]—because of preconceived notions and dangerous doctrines not of the Saviour but handed down as such. Thus you see the quandary of the Lord and his angels who would save us if they could. But the followers of Christ today, so accustomed to the sorry state of their ignorance, instead of reading the vibration of the message, shun it, preferring the rule of repetitious ignorance.

Though it may be a frightening process, the one who desires truly to know the Lost Teachings and the Christian Mysteries must set aside his favorite concepts with which he has clothed his mind and feelings, even as Jesus set aside his garment and took a towel and girded himself to wash the disciples' feet.

Today's disciple must wash his own feet (which symbolize our understanding under the Piscean Master) in order that he might be clean and clear-headed to walk in the Master's footsteps, and to put on his sandals.

Yes, Gandhi himself was a revolutionary for the Universal Christ. Like so many others, Christians and non, he took his stand outside the frozen orthodoxy of the Church because he found no room on the inside for interior self-correction. And we also who count ourselves revolutionaries of the Spirit have knocked upon her doors and still knock. . . and wait.

So we have to go deeper than that, deeper than the churchmen of our time would allow us. We have to go deeper than the fleeting surface ideas of an emotional religion. We have to get down to the bedrock of Jesus' own Christ-I-AM-ity—his way of life, his doctrine, his religion based on his scientific affirmation of Being in the Word.

We have to understand that it is not up to us to speak out in condemnation of the world, for the world has already manifested its gamut of action. Its actions speak so loud, we can't hear its words anymore. We can't hear its words! There are books written galore. They fill the libraries of the world. They tell us of the meaning of love. But in practice, it's only a theory.

What, then, can we do? Well, we can begin to *heal* the world of its hypocrisy by first healing ourselves of our own hypocrisies.

I don't believe in esoteric societies. I don't believe in the "inner circle." Yet it exists. And I participate, yes. But I don't believe in it in the phony sense that so many people do—that affiliation with the so-called spiritual elite makes them better than someone else. We are all in the same role: the role of trying humbly to find God.

FINDING OURSELVES IN THE IDENTITY OF GOD

And, my friends, unless we find God, we have missed the greatest opportunity of our lives. He cannot be intellectualized. Do you understand that? I mean, you can't just sit down and theorize on what God is. We cannot intellectualize God. And that's one of the things that people really get hung up on. A lot of people want to intellectualize God. They want to take a crack at defining him!

Well, the word that comes closest to defining God is that he is Spirit. As Jesus said before me, "God is a Spirit and they that worship him must worship him in Spirit and in Truth."[41]

I like to think that God is a Spirit—like a great big ocean. And I like to think of all of us as being like drops of water in a vast sea of Light.

Reciting the great mysteries of the universe, the Hindu sage used to say: "God is the ocean..."—it was his favorite similitude, and he would hold up his finger with one little drop of water glistening on the end of it as he continued—"and this drop is the soul. This is a part of the ocean of God. It lacks only the quantity of God, but none of the quality."

Put your finger down into the ocean sometime when you're at the beach. Then hold it up in the sunlight. You see a single drop of water sparkling jewel-like. Do you know that all of the elements of the whole ocean are to be found in that drop of water?

So you see, you have all of the shining qualities of God, of the Creator of a living soul which has the real potential—the *real*izable potential—of the Spirit. *Qualitatively* you can become God. But *quantitatively* you will always be the all within the All. And this monadic self is made in the *real* Christ image, in whose name it, too, has been slain from the foundation of the world.

And that means that you have within yourself a glisteringly beautiful spark of the Son of God, of the Christ consciousness—of Reality. It's right there in front of you. That's you! You're a drop in an infinite ocean of God. Isn't that something to think about, to contemplate!

And then our thoughts flow into that ancient Buddhist mantra *Om Mani Padme Hum*—"O thou jewel in the heart of the lotus!" And we realize that in the eyes of God, every one of us is a jewel of light.

People are inclined to think of themselves as the patine. So here we have a bright, golden image of the Son of God, a miniature babe born in the manger of the divine identity. With the passing of the years, the real image becomes tarnished and scarcely recognizable. And we identify with the patine that has formed over the image, and even though it may seem to become more beautiful with age (like the green oxide that forms on copper), it's still not the real thing. We identify with *that,* when we are no part of it!

We're no part of what *appears* to be, but every whit a part of what *is*. And now we must learn to love Reality even more than we love our attachment to our sense of what is beautiful. And it is indeed a matter of relearning the ABCs of spiritual discernment because our conditioned sensual preferences are still for the patine.

And so we begin to realize that it's the way we focus the eyes of consciousness upon ourselves and our identity—or what we think it is—that steers us wrong. When we look at the patine instead of looking at the golden image—the vibrant image that is within—we are the losers, because in time, through the gradual and subtle process of association, we can get so identified with the glamour, so enmeshed with the aura of the patine that for entire embodiments we lose touch with our Reality.

Our psychologists talk about the *id*—the "it" or the "idiot"—you know, the *id-y-it?* When they speak of the id they mean the undifferentiated momentum of desire that can impel creation without the control of conscience or the restraint of a real sense of right and wrong. Mindless actions prompted by the id may have to do with the brute channeling of the libido into sadistic or masochistic diversions harmful to life. So, in this sense, we may consider the id the idiot, because it is the 'raw self', mindless without the Mind of Christ.

Well, we're not going to talk about the idiot anymore. We're going to talk about the ego.

You see, it's hard for people to realize that we all have one Identity. Now, you heard me say we all have one Identity. Did that startle you? If it did, you need to refamiliarize yourself with the Law of the One—which you knew all about when you served the Light on Atlantis[42] fifty thousand years ago.

You are children of the One and God is that One. In his oneness he created all of us as a part of himself. Simply stated, we are all cells in the Universal Body of God and in him we live and move and have our being.[43] In him we have our Identity. Outside of him we have none.

And that God Identity is one, the same One for you and for me. But we're all very different expressions of that One and by our individual expressions we define his Oneness, even as he defines our own.

Now, when the Law of the One gets interpreted as an exclusivity instead of as the all-inclusive Light, that's when you get into the consciousness of the insiders and the outsiders—like in Boston, where we find the old aristocratic families like the Lowells and the Cabots. They say that the Lowells speak only to the Cabots, and the Cabots speak only to God![44]

That's probably the way Will Rogers would have

said it, you know, because he really cut right to the heart of what was going on. He knew! We were all born the same way and when you come right down to it (the flesh), we all get shoved into the same hole, into Mother Earth, don't we? But, as Will said, "Nobody wants to be called common people, especially common people."

Why identify with the flesh? The flesh is nothing but the clay vessel that contains for a season the fires of the immortal soul. And the immortal soul is that which gives us intelligence and gives us our feelings about God and about the universe.

PROJECTING BACKWARDS/FORWARDS IN TIME AND SPACE

The ancient memories are stirring within us. We ourselves go back to the foundation of the world. Why, life is utterly meaningless if we're going to be segmented into an era of time and a slice of space—and that's all there is to it.

In order to have real depth of being, in order to have a flow of consciousness, to become a vital person, to become a *real* person, you have to open up those frozen sluice gates that are in your own brain and being and let the water of Life flow!

By observing the process of flow, you begin to recognize that you can flow backwards in time. This backflow will enable you to identify with events that took place in your soul long before your physical body was born.

And if you can't do this, your consciousness is even worse than a horse with blinders on it. He can only see where he's going, unless you pull his halter a little bit to one side, and then he'll turn his head—and that's the only way that he'll see where he's been.

But we human beings, we have, if we will exercise

it, peripheral vision. Like the proverbial teacher, we have eyes in the back of our head—if we want to use them. We can see ahead, we can see behind, we can see to the right, we can see to the left, above, and below. We can see if we wish to see. And we can close our eyes, if we so choose.

Seeing or not seeing is an act of free will. And "there are none so blind as those who will not see." And I'm speaking of the activation by man of his spiritual senses. Many people don't have them because they don't want them. Because there's a lot of responsibility that comes with inner sight. Some people used to have it in former lives, but they've let it atrophy. They're shortsighted. They haven't exercised their long-distance vision and other soul faculties that bridge the planes and can probe other dimensions.

How many of you can close your eyes and immediately be in the heart of London, in Piccadilly Circus? How many of you can be there and hear the roar of the traffic, see the whirl of the lights, and know whether it's day or night? How many of you can see what's going on right now, just as though you were looking into a television screen? Not very many, I'm sure. Yet it's possible.

It's one of the powers of man, a power that Jesus had, that the great avatars have, that the Masters have, and that many people on earth have, I'm sorry to say— because some of them who have it aren't very good people. You see, the possession of psychic powers doesn't necessarily mean that you are a good person; it merely means that you've awakened certain psychic centers.

Yet the very possession of these qualities, when properly used, can be a blessing to you and to others. You can see without eyes. You can hear without ears. You can speak without a tongue. You can bilocate. Some people who are living in this world today—the

saints and the unascended Masters of the Far East—
can do these things. Sometimes it's really startling.

People can heal at a distance. Jesus had the power
and did it. Do you remember the incident?

It was a Roman centurion who came to him and
said, "Lord, my servant is home sick of the palsy, griev-
ously tormented." Jesus' immediate reply was "I'll
come and heal him." But the centurion said, "Lord,
I'm not worthy to have you come under my roof. Just
speak the word and my servant shall be healed."

What did the Master say? He said, "Verily, I have
not found so great a faith, no, not in Israel. Go thy way
and as thou hast believed, so be it done unto thee."
And his servant was healed in the selfsame hour. [45]

Here was a Roman centurion, not a Jew, but
nevertheless one humbly aware of his soul's need for a
correct relationship with Christ. This was not a false
humility but a true understanding of who he was and
who Christ was. His faith was the sole agency of Jesus'
healing. This shows that God is the God of all nations,
the God of both Jew and Gentile, the God of the
whole earth. [46]

There isn't anything that Jesus did that can't be
duplicated today. He said, "Verily, verily, I say unto
you, He that believeth on me, the works that I do shall
he do also; and greater works than these shall he do,
because I go unto my Father." [47]

If Christians believe this promise, they ought to
seek a path and a teaching that show them *how* to live
a life of discipleship in imitation of Christ. And this is
precisely what the Ascended Masters of the Great
White Brotherhood offer. They take the hand of the
devotee of Christ and lead him from faith to the
science of Being.

From the belt of time we move into the lap of
infinity where we see that the power of God can reach
out and—from the records of our earliest beginnings—

pull together in our consciousness the necessary harvest of understanding and the gifts of divine intelligence for our use today. There is no time limit on this promise. "The works that I do shall he do also; and greater works. . ." It is infinite.

The Mysteries of God Revealed to the Prophets

Then who will condemn us for trying to be Christlike, for following the saints who followed him, for communing with the Body of God in heaven and on earth, for seeking to find out and apply the mystery of God which he has declared to his servants the prophets?[48]

For are we not also prophets—all of us, when we are endued with the Holy Ghost? Are we not also heirs of the promise, the handiwork of Love destined to return to his throne of grace?

Will our Father exclude any of us from the secrets of Enoch or the hidden wisdom which Paul says God ordained before the world *unto our glory?* Nay, he will not! For the deep things of God *are* revealed to us by his Spirit.[49] The Teachings which Jesus kept secret from the masses, the Teachings which were never recorded—for these our souls do hunger. For these, too, are a part of our ancient soul memories.

We know that Jesus spoke in parable to the people, and to his disciples he gave a fuller teaching. In the fourth chapter of Mark, following the parable of the mustard seed, it is written, "And with many such parables spake he the word unto them, as they were able to hear it. But without a parable spake he not unto them: and when they were alone, he expounded all things to his disciples."[50]

Jesus told them why he spoke in parable to the multitudes—"that seeing they may see, and not perceive; and hearing they may hear, and not understand;

lest at any time they should be converted, and their sins should be forgiven them."⁵¹ His disciples would ask him privately what he had meant, as in the comparison of the tares and the wheat, and he would explain to them the mysteries hidden in parable.

But he didn't tell all. Or all that he told was not recorded. Or, was it originally recorded and later expurgated? For throughout the Bible, there is a tradition of Jesus' secrecy.

As biblical scholar Morton Smith observed,

> Actually the reports of Jesus' secret practices. . . are all over the Gospels. We are often told that before performing a cure he took the sick man aside, privately. Or, if he went in where the patient was, he shut out everyone and took with him only his closest disciples. After his miracles he repeatedly ordered the persons concerned to keep the event secret. He also kept his movements secret, so that even the people following him did not know where he had gone, or where he came from, when he reappeared. He would go off by himself or with his closest disciples, and nobody knew what happened. It was said that his disciples sometimes saw him in a different form, talking with supernatural beings, but this, too, he told them to keep secret. Important men came to see him by night; some were said to be his disciples, but in secret.⁵²

It becomes more and more apparent that the Bible does not contain all of the Teachings of Jesus, secret or not. This is further evidenced by the last verse of the Book of John, "And there are also many other things which Jesus did, the which, if they should be written every one, I suppose that even the world itself could not contain the books that should be written. Amen."

We want to know and Jesus wants us to know what precisely is the Truth we need in order to get from here to there—from where we are to where Jesus is in consciousness. Let us then continue the Emmaus walk all the way to the Upper Room. (All the way to the plane of the superconscious mind, to the memory of God.) For these things we speak of here are a preparation of the heart for "the deep things of God" which shall be revealed.

We can see through the gateway of the future and the years beyond, because the soul that abides within us is a burning and a living fire. It is a flame that is vital, that can never be extinguished by the water of our human emotions.

But yes, with all of our aspirations toward God, we are also creatures of emotion. As such, one of the greatest problems from which we suffer is the problem of identifying with a certain pattern. And that's all it is, now mark you well. There is a pattern that we create from birth. We create it and it is involved in *me, mine, and I*, you see. *This is mine! I! Me!* That's the way we think.

And what is this creature that we call *I, me, and mine?* Actually it's the I AM Presence, the Gentle Presence of God that's always with you, but people don't know this. They say *I, me, mine,* meaning themselves. And the problem of human pride is triggered by our identification with our human patterns which we say "are mine."

Do you know about human pride? People *love* to talk about themselves. They love to think about themselves in their co-relationships with others. Almost every single person has a motive that involves the ego. "How can I improve the ego?" they say. "Show me." They marry because of the ego. They want a wife that does them justice. Everything they do is motivated around the ego—practically nothing around God.

Once we were creatures of Elohim founded upon the Rock of our true identity in the Universal Christ. Now we have become creatures of emotion and human pride. And this is the very element within ourselves that keeps from us the Lost Teachings.

We've talked about the enemy without who has stolen the Bread of Life, which the Lord was and which he left for us in the tradition of the living Word. But now we must talk about the enemy within—the emotions and the pride that engage us and that we ourselves engage. For these, too, keep us from the deep things of God and his Christ, which must be sought in quietude and aloneness with the Lord. We must have regular study time and prayer time if we are going to inherit the promises, beginning with the Lost Teachings.

So sometimes it is we ourselves who deprive ourselves of the Holy Grail, and no one else is to blame for our failures in the lists and the quest.

Thus, let us pursue the mysteries that lead to the communion and the dominion of our Christ both with us and in us. And let us set aside all these things of the ego and the momentums of the subconscious that tie up our energy and have stood in the way of our spiritual progress all these centuries.

As we joyfully, wholeheartedly go about our Father's business, offering Christ's Lost Teaching "without money and without price,"[53] we shall return to our God-estate of divine Being—just being creatures reborn in Christ returning unto Elohim.

KING OF SALEM AND PRIEST OF THE MOST HIGH GOD

Why, then, did Christ, Buddha, and all the avatars put everything around God? It goes right back to Melchizedek, King of Salem (Jeru*salem*[54]) and Priest of the Most High God.

Melchizedek met Abraham returning from the slaughter of Chedorlaomer and the kings who were with him in the valley of Shaveh. (He'd gone to rescue his nephew Lot, who was being held captive with his family by the wicked kings.) And the Priest of the Most High God brought forth bread and wine (the earliest record of the serving of Communion) and blessed Abram and praised God for delivering his enemies into his hand. And Abram gave his obeisance and paid tithes to Melchizedek—a tenth of all the treasures he had captured.[55]

It says in the Bible that Melchizedek was "without father, without mother, without descent, having neither beginning of days nor end of life but *made like unto the Son of God...*" Thus abideth a priest continually.[56] And of Jesus Christ it was said that he was made "a priest forever after the order of Melchizedek."[57]

When we talk about Melchizedek and Jesus Christ we're talking about the Masters who hold their divine offices by the power and ordination of Almighty God and have attained their self-mastery through their *internalization* of the Word of God. They are the co-creators with God in whose shoes we must learn to walk. They have gone before us to re-create themselves after the Divine Image, as we must also do.

This is a most amazing teaching from the author of Hebrews, because only Jesus could have told him that there was another who, like himself, was "made like unto the Son of God." This is one of the imponderable mysteries of the Bible, or it should be seen as such by those who preach the doctrine of "only one Son of God."

The mystery of the Son of God as the chief cornerstone of every man's divinity is the very crux of Jesus' own teaching both before and after his resurrection.

Hebrews 7:3 is a crack in the stone wall of an

adamant doctrine. And through that crack all the Ascended Masters of the Great White Brotherhood step through the veil to deliver humanity from the stone-walling of a false theology!

The Ascended Masters and their path are the witness and the example of what the Christ of the son of man taught beloved Paul and all of the saints of East and West both before and since the advent of Jesus.

He taught him that by following his example each one of us could be a joint-heir with Christ[58] by putting on our own individual Christhood—"till Christ be formed in you."[59] He taught his unascended disciple that his hope was in that Christ who lived in himself—"Christ *in you,* the hope of glory."[60] These statements set forth the Master's teaching to Paul concerning the Christ Self—the realizable Real Self of us all!

Now, when the point of one's true origin in the Universal Word is realized as the goal of Life, when the footsteps have been victoriously taken, then the soul, satisfied because it has awakened to the likeness of the Son of God,[61] is truly 'born again'—"like unto the Son of God" in whose image the soul was made in the beginning.

Melchizedek and Jesus Christ, both priests of the Most High God, had come full circle back to the point of origin. They both walked the earth in the full God consciousness that they were in the presence of the Son of God—Christ in them and they in Christ. They wore his mantle, wielded his sword, served bread and wine in communion with and commemoration of his Universal Light Body. Each knew that he was his representative and his messenger. Burdenbearers of the LORD's Light were they—and everyone who saw them knew it also.

These two "kings and priests unto God,"[62] accountable unto no man, set the example of the path of attainment as taught and demonstrated by the Great White Brotherhood.

As the Master told Nicodemus he must be 'born again' to enter the kingdom of God,[63] so these two messengers from God's kingdom walked the earth as strangers in a strange land proving before us that Law which you and I must also prove.

We're talking about the power of the Masters when they were on earth. And we're talking about their power after they 'ascended' (i.e., took their ascension as Jesus, Enoch and Elijah did) and became known as *Ascended* Masters. We're talking about a power that involves other planets as well as our own. We're talking about a power that involves the whole of cosmos!

We're talking about the three 'men'[64] who 'came down' and talked to Abraham and told him his wife, Sarah, would have a son. These so-called men were emissaries of other worlds. And then we're talking about the LORD who spoke to Abraham face to face and told him he would destroy Sodom and Gomorrah for their grievous sin and wayward evolution.[65]

The problem with our age is that we get infatuated with material scientists. We make *them* our gods, but we fail to take into account the spiritual scientists who have been the masters of time and space for tens of thousands of years, as Melchizedek was. Of him Hebrews says, "Now consider how great this man was, unto whom even the patriarch Abraham gave the tenth of the spoils."[66]

Indeed, consider just who might have had no father, mother or ancestry, his life without beginning or ending like the Son of God, who remains a priest *forever.*[67] First of all, to be anything *forever* he must needs be immortal. So what kind of a soul was he? There is not another like him in the whole of scripture.

Well, he himself was born again of the Spirit—he was the equivalent of an Ascended Master at the time he met Abraham. And by the lineage of his priesthood was Jesus ordained.

As only one who had passed through the initiation of the ascension could have had the authority to baptize Jesus (which, as we shall soon see, was the case with John the Baptist[68]), so only an initiate of the highest order could have been the predecessor of his everlasting priesthood. *Now* consider just how great this man was. For you see, no man is great save God is in him, for his greatness is God's.

THE VIOLET FLAME AND THE KEYS TO THE KINGDOM

The violet flame is the sacred fire of the Melchizedekian priesthood. Both Melchizedek and Jesus, Enoch, Elijah, and Elisha as well as the initiates of the Great White Brotherhood of all ages have used the alchemy of this flame to accomplish the healings and miracles, prophecies and judgments which were the signs of their coming.

The saturation of their auras by the violet flame was and is the means whereby the avatars have held the balance of world karma. By the amplification of the violet flame through the seat-of-the-soul chakra, they have engaged in planetary transmutation of Darkness by Light and they have survived as pillars of fire midst the planetary weight of Evil.

The power of the spoken Word taught by Saint Germain is a stepped-up version of the ancient science of mantra. This holy brother, who is the sponsor of the United States of America and the great exponent of world and individual freedom, teaches the use of this seventh-ray aspect of the sacred fire to the people of earth in the Aquarian age.

Whereas formerly the scientific use of the violet flame was given only to those who made their way by the severest tests to the retreats of the Brotherhood, today the Ascended Masters, as true shepherds in Jesus' name, have gone forth to find the souls of Light who have lost their way, in order to initiate them in the yoga of the seventh ray and the dynamic decree to the violet flame.

Now, mathematically the violet flame is the zero—one, two, three, four, five, six, seven, eight, nine, zero. And so it goes to the next series of cycles, up to the twenty and thirty and forty, ad infinitum. You'll always find your zero.

In this case, your zero is very important, because we're talking about the whole complex of rainbow colors. When you come up through the rainbow rays to the seventh, continuing beyond the physical spectrum to the ninth, you get into the beautiful gradations of purples and violets.

The violet flame is the alchemist's power of the three-times-three and is used by the adepts in all alchemical experiments. And this you must study under the Master Saint Germain himself.[69] And what is the purpose of this spiritual alchemy? It's the zeroing of the computer, putting it back to zero when the nonproductive programs of the human consciousness are seized and bound by violet-flame angels in order that they may be erased.

As Saint Paul declares, "If any man build upon this foundation gold, silver, precious stones, wood, hay, stubble," or any creation that is not according to the pattern of the Christ, "every man's work shall be made manifest: for the day shall declare it." Because the fire is going to come along and try his work to see of what sort it is. If it's the wrong kind of work, he says it'll be burned. The man will suffer loss, "but," he continues, "he himself shall be saved; yet so as by fire."[70]

And this fire is the violet flame of the Holy Spirit. It is the specific antidote for our humanly imperfect creations. And it is called the "all-consuming fire"[71] or the "violet transmuting flame" for the very reason that it erases the cause, effect, record, and memory of sin—our unrighteous words and works.

And so the violet transmuting flame is a wonderful thing from the divine standpoint, because if it burns our lesser creation and 'destroys' it—or 'transmutes' it, as we understand it (for in one sense, energy is neither created nor destroyed but only changes its form)—it gives us the opportunity of re-creating a greater work. It zeroes in and reduces your miscreation to zero, so you can start multiplying true sums of Light all over again.

Saint Paul said, "I die daily."[72] Do you understand the importance of this dying daily? It means dying unto the ego-self. It means living unto God. The whole pattern was brought out by John the Baptist when he said of Jesus Christ, "He must increase, but I must decrease."[73] The human qualities have to go down (into the violet flame) and the divine have to go up (into the causal body). Christ's reign on earth must wax strong, but the era of the ego-self must wane. And that is the only way we can ever get to God. (And we'll have more to say about John's statement later.)

"Well," somebody says, "what really happens if I get to God?" Just wonderful things! When you get to God, you're going to find that God is more than happy to turn over to you the keys to the kingdom. A lot of people think that this is something figurative. But it's not. The genuine keys to God's kingdom are very, very important—and they're real!

Back in the forties, Gregory Peck starred in a movie called *The Keys to the Kingdom.* Some of you may have seen it. It was centered in China and it contrasted a proud and "successful" ecclesiastic, who was really after the keys to an earthly kingdom, with a poor priest who served long and hard as a missionary to gain the keys to the heavenly kingdom.

There are mysteries in this universe that are described in the Book of Revelation. And the alchemical keys are given in the description of the "white stone, and in the stone a new name written which no man knoweth saving he that receiveth it."[74]

Then in the mystery of the New Jerusalem John speaks of the alchemical stones garnishing the foundation walls of the city. He talks about the jasper and the sardonyx and other precious jewels, such as the sapphire, the emerald, the topaz—the twelfth being the amethyst,[75] the sign of the seventh angel,[76] Saint Germain, and the fulfillment of the seventh (the Aquarian) cycle of planetary initiation. Their crystalline structure and chemical composition have meaning.

And these are mysteries which the average person does not perceive. They're formulated according to mathematical law. And in reality they are keys to the kingdom. And the man that possesses them is given the white stone.

Don't get the idea that God doesn't have lots of mysteries in the universe. But he would never enjoy these mysteries if he didn't enjoy watching people solve them. You know, it's the idea of the father giving to his son the little puzzle. And he says, "Son, now you figure it out. And when you figure that out, you're going to be as wise as I am."

That gets you right back to what the devil told Eve—which was a direct counterfeit of the Father/Son or Master/disciple relationship. He said to her, "You'll be as wise as the gods,"[77] you see. But he described it as the taking of the pill—that little instantaneous pill, "knowing good and evil."

We live in a time of instant coffee, instant love, instant everything. And we want instant religion, instant salvation. You won't get it. You never will get it! It's impossible! Your heavenly Father will give you his wisdom if you earn it, but the serpent will sell you the knowledge of the things of this world—cheap.

Now, I'm going to tell every one of you that the pathway to spiritual initiation is the hardest pathway that you will ever find anywhere. It's hard and mean and cruel. In your mouth it will be a little book of sweetness—sweet as honey. But in your belly, it'll be as bitter as gall. [78]

And if you don't seek it now, someday you're going to have to seek it, whether you want to or not. Because if you decide not to seek it, you'll just be tilted and turned around in this world and tumbled upside down, life after life, and you're never going to achieve anything more than supposedly three square meals a day (if you're lucky) and three score and ten years (if you're lucky). This is the norm. You get your norm, *maybe*.

I said you're going to be tumbled and turned and tilted around. And no one is going to do it to you, because you'll do it to yourself. It'll be your karma. And some of you are going to come right back to the place you're at today. You're going to have to decide whether or not you want to seek God with all your heart. Because when you seek God with all your heart, when you put your soul and everything into it, *he will be found.* And you will be the one who finds him. And when you find him, you will be so happy inside.

But as long as you live in this world, you're going to find that you're not going to be able to make everybody do what you want them to do. They have a will of their own. You're going to have to live with people and try to be as Christ was, a Teacher of Righteousness.

You're going to have to be humble and recognize your reality in God.

Do you see my point? It's really very simple. But believe me, there *are* mysteries and there *are* keys and there *are* initiations and there *are* tests. And nobody is going to make it on this pathway unless he has the guts to stick it out with God, to go forward in the Light and to be oblivious of all attempts of the devil to detour him from the spiritual path.

CLAIM YOUR INHERITANCE!

I can promise you one thing on the path of discipleship—and it's guaranteed: As you sow, so shall you reap.[79] So says the Law. And when you have enough good karma, when the law of the circle returns to you the good you're sending out—why, you're going to have your whole body full of light.

Jesus said it. He spoke about the double-eyed vision where people see with their two eyes. And then he talked about the spiritual eye and he said, "If thine eye be single, thy whole body shall be full of light." But "if the light that is in thee be darkness, *how great is that darkness!*"[80]

In other words, if we allow our consciousness to imagine that we have light, to think we're very good when we're not, then we have all the filters to draw darkness into our world.

And when you draw darkness in—and it'll come in if you don't watch out—nothing is really accomplished of Good. Darkness won't do a thing for you. But light will. So draw in light. Be a child of the Light.

I want you to claim your inheritance. I don't care where you came from or where you're going. I want you to claim your inheritance from God. This is what's meaningful. You are a child of the Light. That means you're the seed of Christ.[81] Sing it to each other. Hold the vision of perfection for each other:

> You are a child of the Light
> You were created in the Image Divine
> You are a child of Infinity
> You dwell in the veils of time
> You are a son of the Most High![82]

And when you come to that part that says "You are a son of the Most High," see the blazing sun of the I AM Presence enveloping one another. "You are a child of the Light. You were created in the Image Divine"—that's the Christ. You were created in his Image. That's why he said it.

Churches have changed it all around. They think of Jesus Christ as the only begotten Son of God without understanding that this is the matrix from which we were all made. Christ is the Universal Reality from which we all sprang. This is our point of origin.

We are joint-heirs with Jesus of this Light. For Jesus attained the epitome of that Christhood to which we, therefore, can aspire. We forget that sometimes.

"You are a child of Infinity. You dwell in the veils of time. You are a son (sun). . .," and just see that blazing sun expanding as you realize: "You are a 'sun' of the Most High."

As Paul wrote from Rome to the early followers of Christ at Ephesus:

> Be ye therefore followers of God, as dear children;
> And walk in Love, as Christ also hath loved us. . . .
> Let no man deceive you with vain words: for because of these things cometh the wrath of God upon the children of disobedience.

Be not ye therefore partakers with them.

For ye were sometimes Darkness, but now are ye Light in the Lord: walk as children of Light. . . .

Giving thanks always for all things unto God and the Father in the name of our Lord Jesus Christ.[83]

KEEPERS OF THE FLAME
Portraits by Nicholas Roerich

Among Russian artist Nicholas Roerich's many talents was the ability to capture the mysteries of God on canvas. His vast landscapes, Oriental in scale, somewhat impressionistic in style, and in a class all their own, are the distillation of man's highest aspirations. Free of dogma or creed, he sought in his writings and in his art to draw his world audience toward a higher goal.

From 1924 to 1928 Roerich, his wife, Helena, son George and five other Europeans embarked on an expedition which encircled the heart of Asia. He found, among other discoveries, documents and legends to corroborate the mounting evidence that Jesus had spent his seventeen lost years in the East.

The expedition's purpose was a religious and anthropological study of the region, but one of Roerich's chief projects was to paint the rugged terrain he passed through and to depict the legends and religious teachers of the Heart of Asia. During the journey he executed over five hundred paintings, which he shipped back to New York at various stopping points. *The Lost Years of Jesus,* which chronicles the Roerichs' trek, preserves sixteen of his awe-inspiring landscapes that ensoul the mysticism of the artist and the region.

Roerich's masterpieces are inherently spiritual. As one art critic wrote, "In the midst of our modern society, so positive and so limited, he gives to his fellow-artists a prophetic example of the goal they must reach—the expression of the Inner Life."[1]

And with his unique talent, he not only painted the places where Christ walked during his lost years, but he also traced the lines of his Lost Teachings.

In Roerich, we see the universality of religion which the anointed youth Jesus—known in the East as Issa—

embodied as he compassionately taught the Hindus, studied with the white priests of Brahma, pored over the Sutras and expounded upon these sacred Buddhist writings, championed the cause of the lower castes, persuaded the pagans to give up their idols, prophesied and healed by prayer, extolled womanhood and roused the Zoroastrians out of the erroneous doctrine and religious ceremony into which their faith had fallen.

The paintings we reproduce here, most of which were executed on Roerich's epic journey, illustrate against the backdrop of their native lands fourteen World Teachers and Keepers of the Flame. In so doing, the Russian master has captured something of the Eastern chalice, something of the universal penetration of that Mind which was in Christ Jesus and of the Lost Teachings of a prophet who—as the sacred scriptures discovered by Roerich, Nicolas Notovitch and Swami Abhedananda show—did not come to tear down, destroy or supplant the world's religions, but to reinfuse them with the vital fires of their founders, sent by God to also illumine a world—for His Coming.

Yes, Saint Issa came to root out dead doctrine and dogma whereby first principles had been corrupted. He came to return the lost sheep, turned aside by hirelings, to the heart of the Good Shepherd, and to the worship of the one God whence the Lightbearers had descended in the beginning. Truly we bear one common Light—as Roerich wrote:

"In the cults of Zoroaster there is represented the chalice with a flame. The same flaming chalice is engraved upon the Hebrew silver shekels of the time of Solomon and of an even remoter antiquity. In the Hindu excavations of the periods from Chandragupta Maurya, we observe the same powerfully stylized image. Upon Tibetan images, the Bodhisattvas are holding the chalice blossoming with tongues of flame. One may also remember the Druid chalice of life. Aflame, too, was the Holy Grail. Not in imagination but in realities are being interwoven the great teachings of all ages; the language of pure fire!"[2]

1. *Nicholas Roerich* (New York: Nicholas Roerich Museum, 1974), pp. 7, 8.
2. Frances R. Grant et al., *Himalaya* (New York: Brentano's, 1926), p. 79.

KUAN YIN, MOTHER OF MERCY

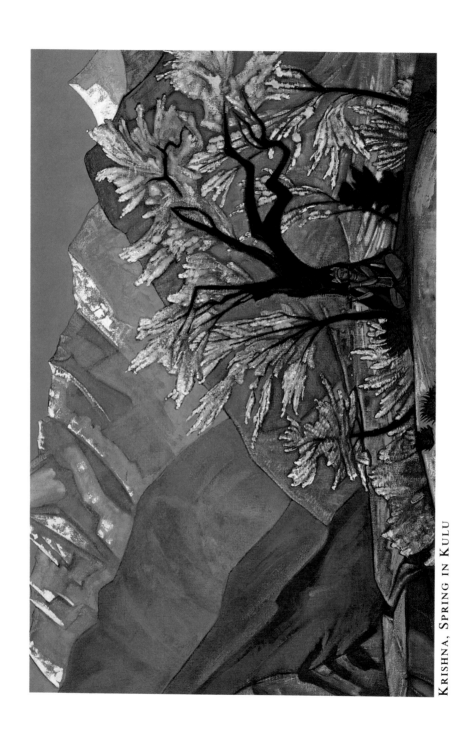

KRISHNA, SPRING IN KULU

BUDDHA THE CONQUEROR *at the Spring of Life*

MOSES THE LEADER

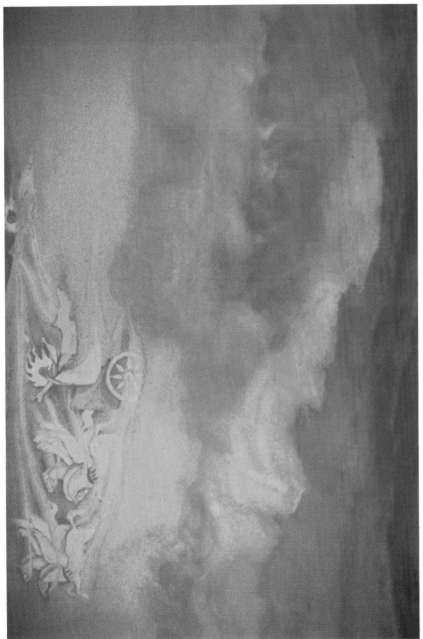

ELIJAH THE PROPHET

MOHAMMED *upon Mount Hira*

CONFUCIUS THE JUST *Traveler in Exile*

LAO-TZU *As We Remember Him*

MILAREPA *The One Who Hearkened*

PADMA SAMBHAVA *The Taming of the Giant*

DORJE THE DARING *Who Faced Mahakala Himself*

MOTHER OF THE WORLD

Keeper of the Flame

SAINT SERGIUS THE BUILDER

Chapter Three

A PERFECT DESIGN

A Perfect Design

FROM the beginning—from the very, very beginning, God designed perfection and designed perfectly. We, as his handiwork, were given a Perfect Design—a design geometrically and spiritually perfect, a design that could not possibly reflect aught else save the Light from whence it came.

CHRIST THE LIGHT OF THE WORLD FROM THE BEGINNING

The Divine Image of the Universal Christ has been seen in many forms and called by many names: the most memorable, of course, being Wonderful, Counsellor, The Mighty God, The Everlasting Father, The Prince of Peace.

We hear of the Rose of Sharon and the chiefest among ten thousand, while Mary Magdalene, fairest rose of his heart, hailed him "Rabboni!" Whereas John knew him intimately as the Logos, the people sought him as Saviour, Healer, Burden-Bearer, and fiery Baptizer by the Holy Spirit. And the chosen and faithful acclaimed him King of kings and Lord of lords.

Jesus himself knew him in the tradition of Moses as the I AM THAT I AM, the universal and ever-flowing stream of the Christ consciousness who had been with the son of man from the beginning. The

World Mother cherished him as the Lamb slain from the foundation of the world (slain because the world does not behold the things of the Spirit). And to this very hour armies of saints follow him as the Faithful and True, The Word of God.[1]

In contrast to the original Light of the Elect One, the Light-emanation of First Cause foreknown by Enoch of old[2]—somewhere in time and space we have a finite world of limited cause and effect. Now, if you were asked to create such a world, it would require more than the mere mastery of computer technology and the physical sciences. Yes, you would be required to learn a great deal more in order to be able to create even a heart of flesh. But to be able to create by Light, as God does, you must discover the key to heart contact with the Creator.

And so, as we are thinking about God and his most wonderful creation, we think about the perfection of our High Priest—the beloved Christ, the Light "like unto the Son of God"[3] that from the beginning was the Perfect Design for each of us, the Word by whom all things were made and without whom was not any thing made that was made.[4]

We ourselves descended from great causal spheres of rainbowed light—souls are we who once surveyed worlds within worlds in the Being of God. Spirits trailing clouds of glory, now veiled in flesh, how easily we became lost in the morass of the human personality—and lost the memory of the origin of our twin flames,[5] lost the meaning and the worth of our individuality in the cosmic consciousness of Alpha and Omega.

Once again we would approach the throne of grace. Too long we have wandered in a far country without the honor and privilege once accorded us as heralds of this Beloved, the High Priest who officiates before the Court of Sacred Fire. Now we

look to our First Love and long to be called once
more in the service of that Universal One—the LORD's
Emmanuel.

Our absence has made our hearts grow fonder all
the more for the simple, straightforward, resplendent
beauty of his face. Therefore, as servants restored and
sons surrendered to the High Priest before the Ancient
of Days, we come boldly unto the throne of grace—
our divine right, our inheritance—that we may obtain
mercy—his right and inheritance to bestow—and find
in the beloved Christ grace to help in time of need.⁶

Who's Who in Cosmic Consciousness is a book
that ought to be written. It should be a compilation
of those who know who they are—who I AM—in the
procession of the disciples of the Lamb. It's the High
Priest's book of life of the lost who have returned for
grace, by his grace.

It reminds me of when we were on tour in Egypt
with our staff and students, and our guide proudly announced: "This is the house where Nasser was born."
(He was referring to Gamal Abdel Nasser, former
president of Egypt.) Our group was nonplussed; so he
repeated his announcement twice more, each time
louder and with greater fanfare. Still no response.
They did not know enough to know they should be
impressed.

Well, we could say this about everyone living on
the planet: "This is where so and so was born." But are
we really so concerned with the emphasis on the physical side of life? Do we actually think that the mere
reproduction of the human embryo and the manifestation of a body in which the soul can dwell is in itself
the allness of man, the allness of his most purposeful
design?

Or, are we willing to admit that the gift of consciousness itself can hold something near and dear for

us and something near and dear for the Creator himself—if we will allow him to utter through us the divine
fiat of the Word that was from the beginning?

The Word that was from the beginning is lucid
and beautiful. Yet we ask ourselves this question:
How did it come about that we today manifest states
of relative imperfection? And why is it that the consciousness of some is, vibrationally speaking, so far
removed from the thoughts of the Creator and from
his actions?

Why do people today dwell in a realm where they
say, "Peace and safety"—only to have the "sudden
destruction" of the carnal mind take them away from
that apparent peace and safety into another domain
that God did not create but that we did?

To know the answer to our quandary we must
consult the Logos. For the Law, incomplete in scripture, is written in akasha: *And they shall not escape
their karma!*[7]

How quickly our little children begin to learn in
the sandbox of life how to radiate patterns of imperfection. It doesn't take very long before they learn the
art of possessiveness—if it can be called an art. "That
is mine. You can't have it! That is mine." And the ref-
utation is quickly learned, "No, that isn't yours! That
is mine."

It is as though our first little war of the worlds was
created in a thimble or a teacup. This actually happens to people. It happens to children. Multiplying
people's personal wars all over the world in every race
and every tongue, we find a great babel of voices rising up which are the strident voices of struggle.

Thus the condition of our microcosm reminds us
that we contain the memory of other wars—of cycles and
choices we have made in the macrocosm: the seduction

of our souls by reprobate angels—the alienation of our affections from first principles and our Father. This record is traumatic. We have blocked out the inner conflict, the seemingly irretrievable loss and the spiritual pain. Yes, the world is as it is, beloved, because something inside of all of us requires resolution: cosmic resolution at the crossroads of time and eternity where the confrontation between Light and Darkness took place.

God has mercifully sealed the memory until the time at hand when he should send his holy angels to unveil the veils of layered illusion (maya) till we should no longer be afraid to face the Truth and the accuser of the brethren in Christ "which accused them before our God day and night."[8]

Today is the accepted time. Today is the day of salvation.[9] In the lost Word found again in Mighty Love, we stand, face and conquer every latter self and selfhood that has ever been apart from Him.

"Come now, and let us reason together, saith the LORD: though your sins be as scarlet, they shall be as white as snow; though they be red like crimson, they shall be as wool."[10]

We unfold the skeins of light as spirals of the LORD's Teaching—not linear or logical though straight and reasonable they be, but according to the cycles of the soul's assimilation of the most brilliant Light contrasted by the darkest Night. Since neither extreme is tolerable to the disciple gaining mastery over self, as he is positioned midpoint on the spectrum, let us let the Master, who is the Great Mediator between the highest and the lowest vibrations in ourselves, speak from his heart to our own in his most gracious way. Let us listen as he unfolds Life's mysteries, comforting our souls with his Truth.

Jesus Christ said, "I AM come that they might have Life, and that they might have it more abundantly."[11]

The abundant Life is not merely a physical life of buttons and bows and diamond safety pins and Cadillacs and all the things that people hold dear. It is something greater: a treasure of the heart and a treasure of the soul. It is a treasure of Universal Reality. It is the love of harmony and the perfection of first spheres, whence man first came forth in Christ.

For as Abraham paid tithes to Melchizedek when he met Abraham returning from the slaughter of the kings, so we, too, as the seed of *Christos* nestled in the loins of Abraham,[12] paid homage to the High Priest and to the Sun behind the sun—the Lamb of God slain from the foundation of the world.

We are not Johnny-come-latelies. We are not new to the ideas of God, to the idea of a Father who cares. We are not new to a vast universe we have called home for aeons; but perhaps we are a little new to our own outer personality consciousness. We don't quite know how to handle ourselves. We don't know who we are or where we came from or where we are going—outwardly. Nor are we acquainted with the true science of man's raison d'être.

From time to time, people in the midst of the miasma of world thought ask themselves questions like "Where did I come from?" And "I wonder who is going to speak Truth to me today?"—because we live in a world of great hypocrisy.

Let's face it, whether or not we will it so, whether or not God wills it so, our world is filled with people who seem to feel that the practice of deceit toward one another and even toward themselves is the order of the day. It is permissible. We don't even bother to chastise ourselves for it anymore. We just say, "Why, everyone's doing it."

This is not true, of course, because everyone is not doing it. Nevertheless, all people have the right to maintain their own state of vibration. And, in effect, they are doing just that. They simply need to be reminded that they will pay the price—not only for their deceptions but also for the minutest digression from the path of personal Christhood.

What, then, are the causative factors of the rate of man's vibration? of the light quotient of his aura? of the equivalency of his chakras? How does man create or re-create himself in or out of the Perfect Design? When and how is the Light that is in him turned to Darkness?

Why do people in the marketplaces feel the need for fearsome competition, which starts out so early in the sandbox of life? And why must they do it to the hurt of themselves and others? How does the collective consciousness of success without scruples lower the rate of the planetary vibration? How do mankind without knowledge violate the world chalice of the Universal Christ?

We read on the front page of the *Rocky Mountain News* of a group of young people who murdered a family of five in Denver by burning them to death. We hear of the Los Angeles Hillside Strangler and the nude bodies of twelve young women found mercilessly strangled to death. And we cry out from within ourselves, "O God, how can these things be!"

"Am I my brother's keeper?"[13] someone shrugs.

"Do I have any real interest in helping my fellowmen and women or am I concerned just with myself?"

"Why should I be concerned with others? Is it my responsibility?"

These questions can be heard in the streets of the big cities—even as the answers resound from the universe itself. And both question and answer are inherent within man the microcosm, your very own cosmos. These we shall unfold from the Tree of Life in the leaves of the Lost Teaching.

For Christ *is* the Light of your world from the beginning.

Cancer: The Last Plague of Human Selfishness

One of the quandaries most burdensome to people everywhere is the devastation of the last plagues and sudden cataclysm upon their nations, homes and families. As these are the signs of the end times and of the time of trouble,[14] we shall address them—for the consolation of the Divine Mother's children and for their illumination, that calamity may be foreseen and averted by the Holy Spirit and our call to his violet flame.

We see that the generation of hatred in human thought and feeling is that which produces what we have called cancer, one of the last plagues that so many people, tragically, are passing on with these days.

For some it is old karma falling due; for others, it is their soul's sacrifice on the altar of the world community: They have made a vow to God to take unto themselves—even into their very flesh and blood, their brain cells and the marrow of their bones—the karma of world hatred, bearing the sins of the world as Christ did, both in order to stay the hand of descending world karma and to obtain for themselves "a better resurrection," as it is written in Hebrews.[15]

And so, in the acceptance of personal and psychological accountability for our words and deeds— the very first step on the path of discipleship—we seek to understand the laws governing personal and planetary rates of vibration and we ask ourselves, case in point, this question: "What, then, is a cancer?"

And we soon find out that cancer cells are rebel cells that turn against healthy cells and 'devour' them in order that they may take of their substance but not give. [16]

But we seldom realize that a cancer, or a cancerous person, can be something or someone that is selfish. Because you can have a spiritual cancer, too. You can have in your world and be broadcasting from your aura the cancerous type of feeling that you don't really want to give of yourself either to the universe or to your fellowman.

Then you become the Dead Sea, in effect, with an inlet but no outlet. You do not have the channels for giving in order that you may receive. You do not understand the basic laws of the universe which clearly and beautifully illustrate that every single one of us always receives by giving.

So, then, if we cease to give and we become that cancer that demands and demands and eats of the substance of others—either through covetousness or greed or a failure to recognize the meaning of true love—this is the condition that will manifest in us mentally, emotionally and, finally, physically. And the case is pronounced terminal. And in many cases it is too late to turn back the cycles of karma.

It starts out in the psyche of man. It starts out as a state of mind that does not care for anyone else but oneself—and we say, "That person is selfish." And this word vibrates with *shellfish*—a parallel hard-shell psychology.

This type of personality builds a wall of self-defense and holes up inside. It's a scavenger. Skillfully appropriating the light of others, such people always appear to give, but they never really do give of themselves. Just when you need them, they withdraw into that shell of 'shellfishness', clam up and retreat into the anonymity of the sands and seas of life, camouflaged by anemones and stones of prehistoric hardness—unmovable symbols of themselves.

They rarely come through in plans and projects that require the giving of the last full measure of the heart. Though sure to warm themselves by the heat of another's labor, they will not be counted among the bearers of the votive candle to the altar of community; and if you're looking for them, you can always find them up front in food lines, scarcity or not.

The systems of this personality are always go when it comes to self-feeding. They never let an opportunity pass to help themselves to anything at all that's available for consumption—especially the light in the chakras of the lightbearer. (They also make good garbage collectors and entrepreneurs of junk yards, collecting and selling and growing rich on other people's discards!)

Instead of sharing what they so carefully amass, they are possessive to the extreme, thus stopping the flow of the water of Life, becoming prey to the very vibrations of shellfishness which cause to rot and bring to naught what they have so carefully accumulated. And the astral vibrations of their hoarded goods begin to pollute their cells, and the cancer chemistry begins to run its course. Then this all-pervasive decay of mind, soul, and body—the thing they feared most—comes upon them as disease, disintegration and death.

Looking upon the remains of such types, people invariably remark, "There is no spirit there, only the shell remains." And this is the sign most often noted of those whose terminal cancer is the conclusion of a long self-devouring process—the last mark of the shellfish type after they have devoured the light-energy-consciousness-creativity of everyone else around them.

They cannot stop the inevitable karma of this self-consuming 'virus' that consumes them from within. Thus, despite all desperate attempts to build the impenetrable shell, the malignancy could not be screened out because all the while the enemy gainst which they built their fortress was within.

But remember this: every day seemingly ordinary people, self-sacrificing people who have given of themselves all their lives expecting no reward, pass from the screen of life—victims of the cancer of world selfishness outplayed in their physical bodies (perhaps from cancer-causing chemicals in the environment, selfishness' pollution syndrome of corporations who take care of profits, not people).

Lovers of life are these, often in the very midst of selfless service to family and community; yet deep within their souls, they have seen the greater need of atonement for world sin and they have given themselves willingly. Others, also saints in this lifetime, have chosen at inner levels to pay the last farthing of an ancient karma of a forgotten past by thus transmuting the woes of planetary karma.

Oh, the seeming injustice of it all! We who stand by helplessly before the physical or psychological metamorphosis of souls whose temples have become the microcosmic battleground for the war waged between cells of Light and Darkness simply cannot comprehend (until we understand the Great Law) the sacrifice of the one who lays down his life for his friends[17] nor the outworking of personal and planetary karma relentless on the world scene.

Thinking back, we can see that at first the cancerous state of mind is not apparent. Just as the detection of a physical cancer is often too late, so this

malady of the soul can devour one's spiritual energies
at the subconscious level even before it is diagnosed.
You see, by definition the beast of human selfishness
is rarely self-disclosed, because it is self-serving. Most
of the time we're so busy having just plain fun that we
fail to recognize that we are all too self-centered, and
dangerously so.

Even our loves can be selfish, excluding others,
nonsharing. In this state, alas, we also fail to recognize
that inherent within the universe are the most exciting
discoveries that man could ever make about himself—
discoveries that show him his own spiritual potential,
that suddenly cause man to realize that he is not just a
body vegetating in a hospitable environment:

Now he realizes that he is a soul—and a soul is an
exciting thing!

Above all, let us learn that while one part of life
suffers in pain, or is in a state of sinful selfishness,
none of us can be free from the burden of either.
In this sense, the planetary evolution is one—partak-
ing of and contributing to the same pea-soup rate of
vibration. Therefore, we must watch and pray for
world transmutation of world karma (by the Holy
Spirit's violet flame) as well as the records of our own
past misdeeds, which do come full circle for redemption in order that we may fulfill every jot and tittle [18] of
the law of our personal Christhood—both here and
hereafter.

Thus, let Higher Consciousness and Love accelerate universally in the Perfect Design that all may
thrive and bask in a planetary renewal based on the
scientific raising of the rate of personal vibration!

For the universe above and below is one. And the
Body of God is one. And his Love makes us one, bearing one another's burdens unto the end of world
karma in this dark cycle of the Kali Yuga [19] that is

waiting, yea, as the Woman in travail,[20] waiting to give birth to the universal age of peace, enlightenment, and freedom.

CHRIST THE PERFECT DESIGN

The Designer of the soul's perfection that is repeated out of the original matrix in rhythmic redundancy is not a God requiring propitiation through human sacrifice, that one soul passing through the crucifixion may bear for another the burden that is solely his own.

No, the Grand Architect of our individuality is a God that from the beginning designed the salvation of man through spiritual sacrifice unto the attainment of the original Christ image—the perfect man, the man that Jesus spoke of when he said, "Before Abraham was, I AM."[21]

Certainly the flesh-and-blood Jesus did not exist before his birth in Bethlehem. Therefore, you see, by this very scientific affirmation of his being, Jesus is showing us that he knows who he is—who "I AM," who is the I AM THAT I AM and who is the "One Sent" into the world as the messenger of that God Presence.

He who is become the Sun of Righteousness that has arisen with healing in his wings[22] wants you to know that this selfsame Sun is also destined to rise within you—bearing the matrix of your Perfect Design.

Jesus is the bearer of the Light of God, hence the Son of God (the 'Sun', the shining One showing forth the glory of the I AM). And this Light is manifest through the Word—the Word that is the pronouncement of all Being and *Be-ness*—I AM THAT I AM.

Jesus knows his True Self to be the Light-emanation of this Christ that always was, is, and ever shall be.

And he wants you to know that your Real Self is also that selfsame Light. He—the son of David, the Sun of my soul and your soul, *who fastened himself to that Christ* and made that Christ his own identity through the ultimate sacrifice of the lesser self for the Greater Self—lives today to teach you how to do the same.

In those days many were crucified, but only one self-transcended the ordeal to prove the life everlasting. Only one became the Saviour. Thus, the crucifixion in and of itself could not automatically make this son of man the Son of God. Nor was the shedding of his essential Light for the transmutation of the sins of the whole world—nor his Sonship, his resurrection or his everlasting glory—dependent upon this torture by the seed of the Wicked One.

Something more—something much more—had to be involved.

Something which had been going on inside the soul of Jesus for aeons brought him to that moment of the divine interchange where the infinite Light that was in him displaced the finite expression and the Son of God declared:

Behold *I AM* alive forevermore!
The *I AM* in me is my Life.
Because I am *that I AM,*
I, too, shall live like God, with God.
Only God can live forever.
I AM that God in manifestation.
This is the grand equation of Life—
And of life becoming Life.
Behold! because I AM alive forevermore,
You, too, can enter the Central Sun of Being
And know yourself as I AM—the Sun of God.

This *something* more that was involved in Jesus' crucifixion, and everything there is to know about it,

the Lord is come to teach us today. He is here to tell us
the story of his lost years and his lost words—because
no one of us could tell it quite like our Jesus.

Come, let us together take his hand and in his
name and by his God-direction, let us walk through
these chapters unveiling the mysteries of Christ. For
the Lord will show us how to remove the mask of the
pseudo-image, how to discover the Real Self, how to
reestablish our point of origin in him and how to outpicture our Perfect Design.

With the Master Mason, by his Word and Love,
let us build the pyramid of our Christhood by the
momentum of our loving words and works. Thus we
shall come to appreciate the beauty of time and space,
kal/desh, suspended in the Infinite, which gives us the
perception of God's kingdom within us through the
Chart of the Divine Self and the integration of the
chakras. Truly, these are the eternal verities we seek.

As the ancient fiat went forth before the descent
into Matter by our spiritual forbears: "Establish thou
It!" so we shall establish our continuing opportunity
to self-realize God through the initiatic ladder of life,
re-creating the God-man by the mirror of His consciousness. So shall we renew our relationship to God,
vowing "I *will* become one with God!" by the fiat of
the violet flame.

And so our Lord begins by telling us that because
long, long ago he laid down his human identity pattern and took up his divine *id-entity,* he is become
Christ the Saviour—through whose Light (attainment)
you may also gain your own victory.

Not human sacrifice or the mere human shedding
of blood, but the divine integration of the Son with the
Father and the shedding of the glorious light rays of
the Shekinah glory—where God and Man meet on the
cosmic cross of white fire—this is the Open Door, this

is the Way, the Truth, and the Life[23] of our soul's devotion through the Word made flesh.

And the Word is made flesh over and over again, because his Light Body, the universal Corpus Christi, was fragmented—like the infinite drops of the infinite ocean—so that you could experience the Person of Christ in your very own being.

Behold, the Bridegroom cometh![24]

We have to recognize, then, that *Be-ness,* the beginning, the foundation of each of us, had its creation in a realm far, far removed from our present levels of human evolution and society.

Shall we condemn the Creator because it is so?

Shall we say to the Creator, "You did not make a perfect man," when he did? When he made that perfect man to be a joint-heir of the Christ *Light,* or the Christ *consciousness,* with all other parts of Life?

Contemplating the mystery of the Great Pyramid of Egypt at Giza, we think about the fact that on earth life begins in the cornerstone of matter. But the chief cornerstone of this great pyramid of Self is a living Christ, a lively stone which the builders rejected—but it became the *true* head of every *true* man-ifestation of God.[25]

This chief cornerstone of our true identity in God, without whom we have no identity, is the beloved Christ Self. Yes, beloved, the same, the One, for you and for me.

The Truth is that the beloved Christ Self is the Perfect Design. Your Christ Self is your Real Self whom ye have sought, all the while thinking he was someone somewhere else but in thy God Self!

Because this chief cornerstone of our being is rejected by the counterfeit creators, we have not known neither have we been taught the simple realities of our God Reality within!

Well, let them clone the human animal and create human life in a test tube and genetically engineer the 'perfect' human brain and body if they will! They can never in all eternity create an immortal being who shall escape the enslavement of mortality and death! (Nor shall they ultimately escape accountability for their counterfeit creation.)

If it's human perfection they want, let them have it! But we know mere flesh and blood cannot inherit the kingdom of God[26]—neither will the corruption of the fallen ones inherit the incorruptible lifeblood of the Logos.

Therefore let us seek the perfection of the heart through the path of the sacred heart—the sacred fire that burns in the heart of Jesus Christ for you and for me. This is the path of the Ascended Masters and the avatars who also knew themselves as the One Sent. For the Light was in them, and the Light was God and they became the Light.

And when they did, they could not deny their Light. For to do so would have been blasphemous. Even so, you, too, though now a babe in Christ, will one day proclaim him as thyself, else forfeit Reality ere you thrice deny your LORD. This crossroad—where the self, having passed through the nexus to the Great God Self, must proclaim its God Reality—awaits every courageous soul whose assimilation by the Spirit will know the bliss of heavenly company and the pain of world condemnation.

Now, we are not thinking of anyone's personality per se, but of the Universal Reality of the living Christ who appeared so magnificently in Christ Jesus, the Great Exemplar, and can appear in Christ right where you are. Because, unless Christ can appear in you as you partake of his consciousness—or as Saint Paul declared, "until Christ be formed in you"[27] (not referring just to the personal knowledge of this magnificent God-man Christ Jesus, but referring to the Universal Christ who is the Light of every man)—*verily you have no Life in you!* [28]

—Of whom the scriptures speak plainly, saying of the name of Jesus, every knee shall bow and every tongue shall confess that Jesus Christ is LORD (the Incarnation of the I AM THAT I AM) to the glory of God the Father. [29] "And when all things shall be subdued unto him, then shall the Son also himself be subject unto him that put all things under him, that God may be all in all" [30]—that God may *be the All, and in all.* [31]

In this Teaching from his heart the Master Jesus reveals to us that the great and vast common denominator of the Universal God is far more important than any one personality in God. For anyone's personality is a single cup, and it takes many, many cups to contain the All. Then when God is become in us the All-in-all (the All in all of our cups of consciousness)—and this takes place through our assimilation of Christ's 'Blood' and his 'Body' (the Alpha and Omega of the Godhead which Jesus, the son of man, embodied)— we see that God himself as the Divine Whole is the only way in which true access to his Allness can be afforded to any of us.

Only through God can we have the Allness of God. There is no other way.

In no other way could we be integrated into the Whole of the universe. In no other way could the spiral nebulae—enfolding the domain of perfection peopled by Ascended Masters, cosmic beings, archangels, cherubim and seraphim, and those great intelligences that assisted in the very act of our creation by Elohim—be gathered around the polestar of Being but by our own realization of God as the All-in-all.

Shut the door when Jesus knocks, if you will, and behold no Reality at all, neither his nor yours—except that meager portion you parsimoniously admit because of your impoverished sense of self, because of your own tradition-bound concepts.

But if instead you are willing to heed the universality of the universe, to submit yourself unto this very Wonderful One who is the Author and Finisher of our faith and of our creation [32]—if you're willing to submit to his Universal Consciousness, if that's what you really want, you can have it. It's available to you. It's potential. It's possibility right here and now today!

"Lo, I AM Come to Do Thy Will, O God!"

Now, we could speak to those who perhaps have never heard of the Masters of Wisdom and say, "These are the Masters. Let me introduce you to the Masters."

We could speak to you of some of the hidden gifts that you don't even know that you have. We could speak to you of the potential that you have (which Jesus also had) to lay your body down upon your bed at night and rise from your physical body in that soul potential, clothed with your etheric garment, to navigate out into the universe—fully conscious, now, mind you—and journey anywhere upon the planet.

But then we could not be responsible for what you would see. Because you would see exactly what is happening in the world today. You might just as well take a jet or a magic carpet and travel to India or Paris or Portugal or darkest Africa or to the polar regions or wherever you want to—it doesn't matter because, after all, what you would see is what is actually going on, if you see correctly.

And what would you say to yourself if you were to see only the mass consciousness? Well, if you really saw the mass consciousness of the planet for what it is, you would say: "I cannot learn from that! I must turn to the strait and narrow gate of Christ-perfection.[33] I must turn within myself to the point where I can realize the treasure of heaven that God has put all inside of me. I must seek the kingdom to come—which I now know to be his Universal Consciousness—*within me!*"[34]

Unless you are able to realize this treasure of heaven, although all the world may be waiting for the Sun to rise, although all the world may sing songs of praise to the Lamb of God—if you are out of step with the universe, if you are out of step with harmony, if you are out of step with the creation, if you have not found the universal kingdom as God's consciousness within you—you do not realize that the world is already perfect.

And you will never realize, given all material evidence to the contrary, that in the octaves of Light right within the inner planes of your being *the world is perfect.* And you'll still be mouthing these insipid statements: "But the world is not perfect. And there was only one man that was perfect, and they crucified him"—while the stellar world and the hosts of the LORD and the glories of the Endless Day are all around you, and the saints are immortalized, and the sheep are coming Home.

Surely, as the LORD liveth, this was not the intention of God—that we should be left behind while the cosmic cycles go marching in, simply because we look at the world today and judge it as imperfect. Rather is it the divine intent that we judge it as the creation of God, behold its giant potential, see the means of moving (even from a legalistic standpoint) from the fragments of the code of Hammurabi to English common law to the domain of American jurisprudence into a realm where we can truly understand that the laws were made for man, not man for the laws.[35]

It is the divine intent that we understand that God has created in us a masterful creator and endowed us with the means of taking dominion over the earth,[36] not as mere puppets, even of the will of God, but as those who willingly submit and call forth the will of God, as Jesus Christ did when his soul was descending over the plains of Bethlehem two thousand years ago.

For he uttered *the Word* as he descended—words of Light and Will in his thrust for a cosmic purpose, which was greater by far than man ever realizes in connection with the Christmas story. It was a story for the new year and a story for all years to come—that Word he uttered with a resounding cry into the cold night sky: *"Lo, I AM come to do thy will, O God!"*[37] And he felt this because he saw the greater will, he saw the more magnificent will, he saw the tremendous impact of the will of spirituality in relation to himself.

He did not come down just with the concept of "Yes, I'm going to minister unto mankind. I'm going to do all these great things." But he held that one and only aspect of divine "selfishness" which is approved of God—and that is "This above all: to thine own self be true, and it must follow, as the night the day, thou canst not then be false to any man."[38]

And so, he recognized that sometimes you have to be selfish in order to later be generous. When he came he was selfish to the extent that he coveted for himself his oneness with the Father, because he knew that that was the only way that he could ever satisfy human needs and bring to mankind the right spirit, the right vibration, the right quality of life, which he did. And which now we must do.

But in many cases people do not understand this. They seem to think of this as just an altruistic gesture of a giant humility, without realizing that in order that we may be generous, all of us have a need to be spiritually selfish for a moment—spiritually selfish to the extent that we at least take care of our own spiritual affairs and conduct ourselves accordingly. You see, you must zealously guard your oneness with the Father, lest someone slink in in the night and take it from you.

You cannot give away your oneness with the Father; for each one must get that for himself, and the Father chooseth his own and you may not choose them for him. But you can give away the by-products of that oneness—patient kindness, long-sufferingness, care for the sick and the needy, the orphan and the widow. You can bind up the brokenhearted,[39] but you must not let them steal into your tryst with Christ in the bridal chamber.

There is only room for you and God in the secret chamber of your heart. And yes, you must selfishly guard this union. For he has prepared the same marriage feast for all who love him and obey his commandments.[40]

People do not always understand this. Sometimes it seems to be a stumbling block. People say, "I shouldn't be selfish." No, of course not—you shouldn't be worldly selfish. While others are in want, you shouldn't be selfish for the material things that you covet or the human happiness you desire.

But when it comes to being spiritual, you should definitely entertain the enlightened self-interest of the wise Sons of God who have something to give because they first garnered the gifts of Life in their hearts. They first tended their own flame so that they could be chosen to ignite the flames of others.

Having thus set thyself to the gettingness of understanding,[41] see to it thou failest not to fulfill the promised givingness that will seal thy heart forever in Christ's.

You should not deny yourselves, as many people do. So many people deny themselves spiritual gifts and treasures. But they don't understand that by getting these gifts and treasures, they could very shortly attain to a relative state of soul mastery and thus serve in some capacity to assist their fellowmen.

And this is not, then, a gift wherein they simply say, "Oh, look at me. Behold, I'm so wonderful now!" Not at all. But instead of that, they say:

O God, let me do thy will! I love your will. I want to do your will. I want to be as you want me to be. I can't consider, O God, that being the way you want me to be is in any way imperfect. But, rather, I see it as a perfect manifestation of thy intent. And if it is thy intent, then it must be Christ's intent. And if it is Christ's intent, and I believe with all my heart that it is, it must be the intent of the saints, the sages and all who work together in thy Work on earth.

O God, let me be with them, thy servant in Christ.

All of us must recognize that in the long night of man's outreach for Light, there have been levels and degrees on the ladder of attainment. The same is true from a social standpoint and from the standpoint of human evolution. There have been levels and degrees marking the progress of pilgrims in the religious quest. On the path of scientific discovery, some have excelled beyond others. In every area of life there is a race, and at a given point in time and space the cosmic moment of the victory belongs to one and one alone.

Yes, there is a moment when the Christ Light shines more brightly for the one, that the many may applaud that one's overcoming of the obstacles to pure Selfhood. And not only applaud but recognize that the glory of God shining in the winner can also shine forth from their own heart and being if they will put forth the same effort and self-discipline. This is that cosmic thrust for a purpose which vows with the son of man descending in the night of the Kali Yuga:

"Lo, I AM come to do thy will, O God!"

Yes, the purposes of God are great in every department of life. As in a race, all run but one receiveth the prize.[42] Paul knew it. He taught it. And he won—for himself, for Christ, and for all of us. And you must realize that inherent within this universe, within this great ticking, perfect little watch, there is perfection—in its movement, in its timing, in its scheduling. . . in its magnificence.

And this speaks to us. And what does it tell us? It tells us there is a vast and noble purpose in us and that this purpose must be realized. It tells us that by realizing it, we are fulfilling the will of God and the will of Christ, and that we are coming into a state of consciousness, a rate of vibration that is at the level of the Christ consciousness, and that it can be measured by the Masters.

WHAT IS THE CHRIST CONSCIOUSNESS?

Therefore you ask, "What is the Christ consciousness?" Well, after careful thought I would say it is a state of Love which, once having attained to it, and not before, you will know it is Christ's own.

I would say it is a rate of vibration, a quotient of Light, an auric emanation and an equivalency of the chakras that can be measured and is known by the holy angels and intelligences who guide the precious feet of earth's children.

I would say that any effort toward the goal of attainment of the Christ consciousness that is made without application of the violet flame, without the priority of balancing the threefold flame along with the real resolution of karma, and without the fulfillment of one's dharma as the duty to be oneself and to do one's work and not another's—any such effort will not, can not avail the desired end.

Therefore we are about to teach you how to do these things as Jesus has taught us—to be faithful over these few things in order that he might make us rulers over many other things[43] pertaining to the planes of consciousness we occupy—our four lower bodies and the kingdom of nature.

Additional help and in-depth study on the ways and means of attainment of the Christ consciousness may be found in the Keepers of the Flame Fraternity lessons written by the Ascended Masters. Embodying the Lost Teachings of Jesus, these lessons are directed specifically to those who sense their calling to be their brother's keeper by keeping the flame of Life on earth with the Goddess of Liberty. This cosmic being sponsors the Mother flame in America—the golden flame of illumination and the book of the law—as she focuses freedom and the self-mastery of golden-age woman through her statue in New York harbor.

I think Dr. Richard Maurice Bucke very wisely pointed out in his book *Cosmic Consciousness*[44] many elements that reveal to man the fact that spiritual attainment is within his grasp. Yes, you can grasp the torch of Liberty—her knowledge and her wisdom—and her love adjudicating personal karma and the seeming injustices of life. Yes, you can grasp the science of the violet flame and know freedom from want, from fear and self-doubt. By your call to God for his sacred fire to penetrate your subconscious with the all-consuming violet fire of Freedom's love, you can begin right now to erase the records of the past—

the very ones which have heretofore blocked your attainment of Higher Consciousness.

Truly this is Love in its most blessed role of transmutation—forgiveness of sin by sacred-fire resolution of the cause, effect, record and memory of sin, and that of all parties thereto.

So this is the grace of God in the Aquarian age dispensation of the Universal Christ!

Believe you me, we do not have to feel neglected insofar as the abundant Life goes. We can have the abundant Life and it can provide the stimulus for every single vestige of cosmic attainment that we want, here and now. *Here and now!*

We do not have to wait for a far-distant heaven in time or in space to finally catch up with us, because the hound of heaven[45] is breathing down our necks—right now, today! The gifts of God are ours, and heaven is anxious to bestow them upon us.

Why is it, then, that we ourselves have lack? It is because we all too easily submit to what we find in the streets of life. Men or women of the streets are we, because we do not recognize that the passions and desires and the dreams and the goals of humanity are not cosmic goal-fitting at all; but rather are they goals for a very short life upon a very, very small planet—a span of relative indecision and disunity in a world of war and internal struggle.

How many times have you gone somewhere in your car and remarked to yourself, as you drove along the streets, how easily you could be goaded into a drag race? Well, this is one of the signs of the competitiveness of life. It's the idea that we don't want anyone to get ahead of us. And how is this? Is it not in a materialistic sense that we want this? And why do we want it? Let's look at the cause behind the effect.

It's because we feel so small. We look at the universe

in awe and we say, "Ho, this great vast universe! I don't understand it. And what is important is that I brighten the corner where I am with my own personal glory." And we say this because we feel so small. We cheat ourselves. We defraud ourselves constantly. And we see others defrauding themselves and we say, "Well, they do it too"—and we find solace in that. And is it really something that brings any degree of comfort to our hearts? Of course not.

So let's master a few first principles as we now take up those elements of the Lost Teaching which Jesus deems most essential for our soul growth. Jesus' greatest concern while in embodiment, and it remains so today, was that men would worship him instead of mastering the same Word he demonstrated. You see, it affords you and him nothing if you advance on his coattails without fulfilling the Law in all your members.

In this book, the Master calls us to set forth the missing links caused by doctrinal error and omissions as well as the neglect of emphasis on certain virtues and rituals needed for the daily mastery of intellect and emotions. His Teaching is for our greater mastery of all limiting factors of heredity and environmental conditions and the key karmic ties one has with people, which may become major stones of stumbling on our spiritual path and with our twin flame if we don't master these rudiments of the Law.

Jesus cautions that you pursue the embodiment of his Truth in action and not by mere intellectual word knowledge. He says you do not really know the Truth by way of inner comprehension until the Truth has made you free.[46] Experiencing the self-mastery Truth brings in the most difficult tests of life is the only surety that you truly know the Truth.

So don't skip the 'simple' Teaching. For anything

in this book may be the missing link that has held up
your progress for lifetimes. Then be a doer of that
Truth, doing it again and again like a piano exercise,
until you know the Law is satisfied within you and you
rejoice with the Father in your victory and take the
next step on the ascending scale of Truth's testing of
your soul.

THE STAR OF YOUR CAUSAL BODY

If we only knew the meaning of the apostle Paul's
observation: "One star differeth from another star in
glory. So also is the resurrection of the dead."[47] He saw
that the effulgence of each one's spirit was different.
He observed the degrees and levels of attainment, won
not by the drag races of life but by self-discipline and
a sacred labor for the love of Christ in every son and
daughter of God.

Each one's star is his causal body (see page 247).
Surrounding and enfolding the Almighty I AM Presence (the Great God Being of First Cause depicted in
the Chart of Your Real Self), your causal body consists of the rainbow "spheres within spheres" which
comprise your individual heaven world, or cosmic
consciousness. You actually experience this higher
awareness at inner levels when your soul takes flight to
the Father's house during sleep or deep meditation.

The I AM Presence is the First Cause in your life
who sent forth your soul (in answer to its demand for
free will)[48] from this causal body of God into the
planes of Matter to demonstrate the Law of Life. In
your experiences on this and other systems of worlds,
you have added to these original spheres the qualities
and the momentums of your good works and words.

Because this process is one of freewill choice, each
soul choosing to glorify God in a different occupation,

each one's individual causal body takes on unique characteristics of Christly beauty and expertise. Thus, Paul called a man's causal body his star; he observed the differences and noted that these are keenly apparent in the resurrection when each one's glorying in the Lord shines resplendently, a rare jewel in the heart of the cosmic lotus, complementing all others in the Mystical Body of God.

In his *Confessions,* Jakob Boehme, German cobbler and mystic of the sixteenth century, also described the sight of his causal body:

> For the Being of God is like a wheel, wherein many wheels are made one in another, upwards, downwards, crossways, and yet continually turn all of them together.
>
> At which indeed, when a man beholds the wheel, he highly marvels, and cannot at once in its turning learn to conceive and apprehend it. But the more he beholds the wheel the more he learns its form; and the more he learns the greater longing he has towards the wheel, for he continually sees something that is more and more wonderful, so that a man can neither behold nor learn it enough. . . .
>
> Though the spirit sees the wheel and would fain comprehend its form in every place, yet it cannot do it exactly enough because of the turning of the wheel. But when it comes about that the spirit can see the first apprehended form again, then continually it learns more and more, and always loves and delights in the wheel, and longs after it still more and more. . . .
>
> The universal God is that one only body. But sin is the cause that thou doest not wholly see and know him. With and by sin thou, within this great divine body, liest shut up in the mortal

flesh; and the power and virtue of God is hidden from thee, even as the marrow in the bones is hidden from the flesh.

But if thou in the spirit breakest through the death of the flesh, then thou seest the hidden God. For the mortal flesh belongs not to the moving of life, so it cannot receive or conceive the Life of the Light as proper to itself; but the Life of the Light in God rises up in the flesh and generates to itself, from out of it, another, a heavenly and living, body, which knows and understands the Light.[49]

You see, the so-called 'sin' that Jakob Boehme was talking about as hiding God was the vibrational patterns of misqualified energy: Light-substance densified and calcified from man's misuse of the laws of God and of the true science of spiritual alchemy. This karmic condition obscures his perception of the glory of the I AM THAT I AM and the great wheel of the Lawgiver—the causal body.

So, let's try to realize what the Master Jesus and the Master Saint Germain are talking about when they talk about changing our vibrations—changing the vibrational aspects of our thoughts and feelings. They want us to transmute by the violet flame the records of so-called sin, or *karma*—to use the Sanskrit term for the causes and effects of actions we have set in motion. They want us to magnetize more Light from the spheres of our causal bodies into the planes of Matter so that we can benefit ourselves and others with the momentum of our First Cause and all that we have added thereto in many lifetimes.

But you can't draw it down if you let your vibrations drag. And this is one drag race you simply can't afford not to win! Acceleration is the key to the control of your vibrational rate and its maintenance at the electronic rate of your unique Perfect Design. And Light is the way to do it—by your dynamic decrees.

In the case of Philip, he came right out and said to Jesus, "Lord, shew us the Father, and it sufficeth us." In response, the Master asked his disciple the same provocative question which he is asking us today: "Have I been so long time with you, and yet hast thou not known me, Philip?" He wanted his disciples to know something about themselves:

Were they unable to measure the depth and the degree of his spirituality? Were they unable to understand what he could do and what he did not always do? Were they unable to read the vibrational rate, that he was the vessel of the Father's Light, hence of the Father?

Then he said, "He that hath seen me hath seen the Father; and how sayest thou then, Shew us the Father?"

The Master wanted them to know that they didn't really understand as much as they thought they did—because they hadn't reached for the vibrational rate of his Christ consciousness that would enable them to commune with *Who* he was and *What* he was.

"Believest thou not that I am in the Father, and the Father in me? The words that I speak unto you I speak not of myself: but the Father that dwelleth in me, he doeth the works. Believe me that I am in the Father, and the Father in me: or else believe me for the very works' sake." [50]

Nowhere else in scripture do we find such a succinct statement by the Master of his integration with the Law of the One—his identity with the Father gained through his instrumentation of the *Word* and the *Work*, the *Alpha* and the *Omega* of His Spirit. This is the "I AM He" [51] consciousness of the Son of God fully self-realized in the son of man, Jesus.

In the face of this so great a Saviour, his disciples hadn't necessarily seen their discipleship as a path of *self*-discipline under the Law of the One of their I AM Presence, persevering until such time as they should, like Peter, receive the keys[52] to their causal body ("the kingdom") that would unlock the gifts and graces stored there as their treasure in heaven.

They hadn't yet perceived Christ as the instrument of the Great Initiator, teaching, trying, testing their souls until they should become worthy of (capable of bearing in their members) the secrets of the causal body held in store by the Father for each one through his I AM Presence with them. And so it is true of many Christians today. But yesterday, today and forever, Jesus would freely give this comfort of the Teaching to all who love him and desire to follow him *all the way* in the Resurrection and the Life.

"I AM the Resurrection and the Life: he that believeth in me, though he were dead, yet shall he live: And whosoever liveth and believeth in me shall never die. Believest thou this?"

If you believe, then you must submit your human self to the Rock of the Universal Christ as Martha of Bethany did when she said, "Yea, Lord: I believe that thou art the Christ, the Son of God, which should come into the world."[53]

You must know that you can trust this Christ to lead you on the most scientific and personal path of initiation—the one that is the best for *you,* the one that can take you all the way to your soul's resurrection unto eternal Life through the ritual of the ascension. No man or woman can do this save through the Great Initiator—step by step through glories won and Light's mastery.

You know the Master did not always heal everyone. Nor did he necessarily heal their understanding.

This is because he came in the role of Initiator, choosing, rather than being chosen by, his followers—as he said:

"Ye have not chosen me, but I have chosen you, and ordained you, that ye should go and bring forth fruit, and that your fruit should remain: that whatsoever ye shall ask of the Father in my name, he may give it you.

"These things I command you, that ye love one another."[54]

We read in Mark that at Nazareth "he could there do no mighty work" because of their lack of faith—showing to us that he whom we consider to be the incarnation of the LORD of the universe could not, in effect, bring down "many mighty works" of his I AM Presence and causal body *because of the unbelief of the people.* By their free will—manifest as their lack of faith—they disallowed the Master his mission there, "save that he laid his hands upon a few sick folk and healed them," as Mark notes.[55]

Don't you see how you play an important role in what is accomplished for you? Don't you see how it's necessary for you to have faith, and if you don't have faith, how by free will you ought to ask God for it?

Jesus concluded his admonishment to the disciples, spoken in the Passover chamber only hours before his betrayal, with this promise which, as we have stressed in our sermons, must become the chief cornerstone of his Christhood in our discipleship today:

"Verily, verily, I say unto you, He that believeth on me, the works that I do shall he do also; and greater works than these shall he do, because I go unto my Father.

"And whatsoever ye shall ask in my name, that will I do, that the Father may be glorified in the Son. If ye shall ask any thing in my name, I will do it.

"If ye love me, keep my commandments."[56]

You see, in the magnificent Love of Jesus unto us, we are able to keep his commandments *because* we love him in the LORD, the I AM THAT I AM. Therefore do we love one another through the same Word and vessel who is Christ in us as He is in Jesus. In this Love which we share through the Lord's Universal Light Body, you need to ask the Father in Jesus' name to release the heavenly quality of faith to you from your causal body.

For in the beginning, beloved, the Father (individualized in the Mighty I AM Presence) did endow you with all the faith you will ever need to regain his lost Word. It is only lost to you down here in the human, you see, but what's up here in your causal body is available to you through your beloved Christ Self in answer to your call.

Not to believe is an act of will which closes the door to the healing hands of Christ in your life. But if you have a momentum on unbelief and you can no longer overthrow it by an act of will, because you've reinforced it so long, then you need to take the hand of the Master. You need to let his healing currents flow through you to restore your belief in the universal availability of Christ to raise you from a dead faith to an enlivened ministry of good works which prove the constancy of your faith.

These are priceless gifts. We're not talking about outer accomplishments, we're talking about the inner accomplishments of the Spirit. We're talking about your spirit working with the Lord's to assist him in accomplishing both his mission and yours—through you—in this life.

Let's not be like Philip who couldn't see the forest for the trees, who couldn't see the Father in his beloved, or the LORD in his messenger. And let's not be like the people of Nazareth and not allow the Master to do his mighty work through us. Let's let him marvel at our belief (not our unbelief) and reward us according to divine justice, not human justice.

Now, you've heard about those so-called success-motivation courses on commercial airlines. You put on the headphones, and they tell you about this wonderful course that will stimulate you and provide the motivation that you require in order to be a success in life. "Isn't that wonderful," you say to yourself— "I pay so much money, and I receive this wonderful course. Then I become a success in life."

But what standard of success are we talking about? I am not belittling the idea that right attitudes will assist people in greater realizations, even in the physical sense. But now we're talking about who is going to give us our course in spiritual success for the long journey into eternity.

Like Philip, man has an image of God, and that image represents God to him—but that image may be merely the mirror image of himself. He doesn't understand that God really is and that God has specific designs and that some of the great philosophers and the great religionists and the humble spiritual people have had the same desire that you have: *to search until they find.*

What does it say in the Bible? It says, "Seek, and ye shall find. Knock, and it shall be opened unto you. Ask, and ye shall receive."[57] From whom?

From whom are you going to receive it? From a preacher? Are you going to get it from a preacher? Is he going to give it to you? Are you going to get it from a book?—"Just read this book and you'll be enlightened!" It's all going to happen, just like that!

"In your patience possess ye your souls."[58] Yes, we teach some of the hidden laws of the universe. We unveil the mysteries of God taught by Paul and revealed unto us by the Lord's Spirit; but you don't get it in one night. You don't get it all in one sermon. Even if you understood that sermon and you could condense that sermon till it had every element of perfection from Alpha to Omega in it, you still couldn't get it because you wouldn't be able to retain it.

And even if you put it down on tape and listened to it every day, you still would not have the spiritual experience in your mind that you require, unless you received it through the Comforter, the Holy Spirit.

But it's all up there in your Mighty I AM Presence and in your causal body, and God himself will reveal it to you if you have patience and apply the Teaching. And we're here to help you and to offer to you freely the techniques Jesus has given to us for your blessing.

But you have to see beyond yourself and recognize that your Holy Christ Self is revealing himself through you in many loving and wise ways. Just like the Father was revealing himself through his Son. But they didn't know it.

And you do the same thing. You say to me, "Show us the Holy Christ Self and it sufficeth us—show us the I AM Presence and we'll believe. Show us Saint Germain and then we'll follow you forever." But it doesn't happen like that. The path to God depends upon *our instrumentation.* In order to see Christ and the Almighty I AM and Saint Germain, you have to become the instrument of all three. Or you need to recognize their Presence in God's little ones as well as in the greatest of his emissaries.

STOP JUDGING PEOPLE!

And so, in order to understand Jesus' Teaching for the Aquarian age that will turn the key in your life, you need to change your vibrations and make attunement with the triune aspects of God—Father, Son, and Holy Spirit—which always agree in one. "For what man knoweth the things of a man, save the spirit of man which is in him? Even so the things of God knoweth no man but the Spirit of God."[59]

You need to go into the marts of life, and you need to meet people and not look at them as though they were some lost cousin of some neighbor of yours, long lost, too. But rather look at them as though they were pilgrims upon the spiritual path.

Look upon them as the same masterful person that you look at yourself as—because, after all, if you don't treat yourself as a masterful person, if you don't hold to the authority of your own divinity, if you do not uphold the Christ within you, you are, in effect, denying God before men.[60]

Because what are we talking about? Are we trying to say that the universe doesn't exist? Are we trying to say that God doesn't exist? Is that what we're trying to say? I don't think so.

So, what we are really trying to say is that God doesn't exist in us. Well, that isn't true either, because God *does* exist in us! But what we are really trying to say, then, is that God doesn't exist in us in a great enough measure to make any significant change in ourselves or our fellowmen.

Well, you see, if you really *aren't* trying to say these things, you are in fact doing so every time you belittle or berate yourself—every time you say, "I can't," or stamp your feet and fold your arms and say, "I won't." And when you so limit yourself, because you are actually denying the power of God in your life, then people look at you and they consider you from the standpoint of mediocrity and they say, "Oh, that person—he doesn't amount to much."

Well, who are we or they to be able to say that the

Son of God doesn't amount to much? I say, ye are sons of God and daughters of God. And I say to you all, in the name of Christ, recognize who and what *you* are—and act the part!

It isn't just a matter of words. We know words may seem easy to come by, but in reality if those words are based upon a spiritual utterance, an utterance that speaks of the elements of Truth within our life, then they are not so easy to come by because they are of the risen Christ, the Christ that is raised up within us as the rising sign of our divinity—not just someone's opinion of us.

"Henceforth know we no man—*no man*—after the flesh," not even Christ, says Paul.[61] That's one of the first lessons you have to learn. Stop judging people. To judge is to attempt to mentally control another by putting him in a box of your human opinion. People who are chronically judgmental of others are chronically insecure. They only feel secure when they have everybody else neatly labeled and canned.

Don't look at people and decide that this is as far as they go, or that they can only go as far as you can see—that is, as far as you'll let them. I always say, you can't tell how far a flea can jump by lookin' at 'im—and when 'e does, you can't stop 'im and you can't find 'im!

I'd like to tell you a rather interesting little drama that took place back in the heyday of the great Packard motorcar in Milwaukee, Wisconsin. Into a showroom of the Packard Motor Company walked a man in overalls accompanied by another man in overalls. And they went around the car and practically overhauled it with their eyes.

And as they went around the car, they observed that there was a young man, who looked like a very smart and successful salesman, sitting on a little bench. He was sitting down there, where he'd size up his prospects.

These two men in overalls—he looked at them as they looked at him and he decided they didn't have it. And there wasn't any use in his getting up and wasting his time by trying to play with these two farmers. So, he sat there, and even when they asked him questions, he said, "Well, the car's there, you can look it over and see for yourselves."

So, the two men went around and one said, "Well, I rather like this car, methinks. Methinks I like this car." And the other one said, "Methinks I do, too." And the strange speech nearly raised an eyebrow on the young salesman.

And then a little later, they said, "How much is this car, young man?"

He said, "Three thousand dollars" (at a time when a thousand dollars was worth six and a half times what it is now).

And so, the two men in overalls—they looked at one another and they said, "Methinks me likes this car. Methinks me'll take this car, methinks." And so, they finally communicated this to the young man, who then bestirred himself.

He got up and he walked toward them and he said, "Uh, sir, may I have your name on the order blank?"

And the man said, "Oh, my name," he said, "ya, my name is Ole."

He said, "Yes, yes, sir—Ole." He said, "The last name, please."

He said, "Evinrude."

Ole Evinrude—the head of Evinrude Motors that makes all these beautiful outboard motors. And so, of course, he could have bought many car dealerships with just a flick of his finger.

But here the salesman was, talking to the great Ole Evinrude, who was having a great deal of fun traveling incognito and buying his little Packard car.

So, we have to understand that it is wrong for us, even if we've known someone for quite a while, to say, "I've got their number. I know who they are. I know what they are." They did this with Jesus, too, you know. They said, "Well, we know him. He comes from Nazareth—a carpenter's son. He never amounted to very much. He's kind of a rabble-rouser—runs around the country and gathers a bunch of rag-tailed people together, you know—and so, we don't think too much of him. And after all, we know his father and his mother." [62]

"Henceforth know we no man after the flesh."

When you stop this nonsense and you settle down to the serious business of living in a world where souls inhabiting bodies are on a permanent journey, where the merry-go-round isn't going to stop so they can get off—it's going to keep on going and if they want to get off they'll have to tumble off—then you'll realize that you could also fall off, and you'll say to yourself, "Well, I want to stick with Reality. I want to find something I can sink my teeth into." And then you'll look around the world, but you won't find the answer—not in this world, nor in all the philosophy books.

You'll find it in part. You'll know it in part. You'll see some of it in yourself. You're going to find some of it in other people and you're going to find, after a while, that this world's got a lot of magnificent people in it. And when you find the magnificence in people, you're going to find the thread that leads you back to the Cause behind the effect—the magnificence of our heavenly Father shining through the star of each one's causal body.

PEOPLE TRYING TO FIND GOD—HIS WAY

One of the things that I found out myself when we began to put together The Summit Lighthouse and so many beautiful people joined our staff—I realized more and more, when I looked at the staff, just how wonderful they are. We're not dealing with ignorant fishermen—neither in them nor in the apostles. We're not dealing with lost souls, sheep gone astray and easily led into byways of occultism. We're dealing with people who are trying to find God. They're trying to find God, *his way.*

And you would be absolutely amazed at how people change. I said, *people change.* It reminds me of a young man who said that when he was seventeen his father was so terribly, terribly ignorant. And he was absolutely amazed at how much his father had learned in four years!

The concepts we hold of people are so deteriorating that they delay the fruition of the Christ consciousness both in them and in ourselves—simply because we're so busy looking at the drama of human lives.

Why, I took this thing up with Jesus himself one time. I talked with the Lord about this and I asked him point-blank: "What about me? You're asking me to go out and talk about you. Now, how am I going to do that?"

And he gave me the answer I needed to hear: "If I wait for you to become perfect, you may never be able to do it, so you'd better start now." The Master said to me, "You have to have faith. You have to believe in the goodness of yourself, just as you believe in the goodness of God. You have to trust yourself."

You have to realize the power that is available to you through your Higher Self. Now, I'm not talking about this lower self, I'm not talking about that slimy serpent personality that people have, you know. I'm talking about the Real Man, "the inner man," or "the inward man," as Paul identified him.[63] This "hidden man of the heart," as Peter referred to him,[64] is not only the voice of conscience but your Real Self and the intermediary between your evolving soul and your I AM Presence.

"The hidden man of the heart"—isn't that a tremendous concept when you stop and think about it? Well, who is the hidden man of the heart? That's the Christ image. But it has to be adapted. Did you know that? It has to be fit to our capacity to understand it, until the narrow room of our consciousness adapts *to it.*

I mean, at first we have to relate to the Christ image in the best way we know how. And once we let him in, we find that we are the ones who are beginning to adapt—slowly but surely to the T square of the cross and the 360 degrees of the crown. This is the value of the concept of Christ the carpenter. He is continually adapting the Christ image to our need. Jesus is the expert craftsman. He has successfully adapted the Christ image to millions!

But everybody has his little triangle and everybody has his spiritual gifts, you know—tools which the carpenter of Nazareth used to build with. We all have those little building tools, whether we realize it or not. And when we start to use them constructively, the plumb line of our Presence becomes a reality. It comes right down the center of the crystal cord, passing through the Holy Christ Self into the domain of our heart.

And upon our heart's altar where the light of God manifests as the threefold flame of Power, Wisdom and Love—we realize, after all, that *we are all builders* "working in these walls of Time," as Longfellow wrote.[65] It's the plumb line of the Christ consciousness

that reminds us that we, too, "can make our lives sublime, and, departing, leave behind us footprints on the
sands of time." [66]

Well, we can do that. But, you see, some people
say, "All of our righteousness is as filthy rags." [67] Well,
this is true—all of our *human* righteousness. But we
have to understand that God in us, Christ in us, is our
divine righteousness. For this reason he was revealed
to Jeremiah as The LORD *Our* Righteousness. [68]

Christ in us is the standard-bearer, and our attunement through his Mind with the Ascended Masters—
and with the angels and great beings who have evolved
in all of cosmos as extensions of that Mind—does manifest God's righteousness. And we, too, can exercise his
righteousness (*right use* of the Law), just as the immor-
tals have done before us, as we learn our lessons in the
great schoolroom of life from the wise masterbuilders.

This is what is important to us—to learn from
them the wisdom whereby they themselves have
evolved and to put this knowledge into practice, and
to begin to love as God loves and to begin to feel as
God feels and to begin to be a part of the universe of
his Mind. And this is true righteousness—the right
exercise of God's laws. To this end are we the pilgrims
of the eternal song.

Then, you see, singing in the footsteps of the
enlightened ones, we hear the songs of their souls.
By their fiery spirits echoing through our own, we remove the cloud of unknowing (our karma) from our
existence. [69] And our vision itself becomes a vision
of higher dimension—through the eyes of the great
luminaries and beyond we pass through the orbs
of the stars. And, O what a glorious thing it is!—this
universe mine!

But, I'm not just concerned with the great feelings
you get out of it. I'm concerned with the reality of it!

A lot of people say, "Well, I get a good feeling out of this. And I always give to the Salvation Army, because every Christmas when I go by and I drop a dollar or ten dollars in the pot, the universe sends a wave of happiness to me because I've given this money."

Well, this is probably true. I've tried it myself—it works. But the point is we don't do things just for the feeling of goodness, just for the feeling of being happy, you see. We do it because it is reality. It's Christ's and God's reality. And when we get that idea, we become the most exciting person on the face of this earth.

Yes, you! You become exciting because you begin to find that your treasures that you thought were all in heaven are in fact partially distributed to you already right here on earth. And you find out that you're able to polish the gem.

Did you ever see an uncut stone? Some of you are lapidaries or interested in lapidarian work. Well, there is a process involved that is precision work. For the stone is most precious, and if you're not careful you can break the stone in the process of cutting it. But if you don't cut it, it will not properly refract the light through its prismatic quality; and without the light sent back into the eye of the beholder, the inherent beauty will not be perceived and its value will not be full.

You must cut and polish the gem of self, which exists solely as a window upon the reality of your Great God Self. You want people to see in the mirror-like quality of the crystal the actual image of the hidden man of your heart. He will remain hidden until you unveil him through the prism of the soul.

This gem of selfhood has an inherent design, a geometry and a mathematics waiting to be discovered by the lapidary who knows his trade. Someday our Montessori schoolchildren will aspire to learn the rudiments of this art as a practical spiritual exercise in the unlocking of the inner crystal, and some will go on to become experts. And they will learn to exercise great care and patience in the mighty work of the ages—the building of the temple of man.

And now we're talking about the stone that the builders rejected that has become the head of the corner. Well, whose corner? Yours or mine? Ours. Everybody's. Our corner, right where we are. And that is the thing that really brings happiness and peace to people—the realization that they are on the spiritual path and that at last they know who Christ is and can therefore follow him.

You see, it is the real and living Christ Jesus and the Christ Self of everyone whom the priests and rabbis have rejected. This is that Messiah that is become the head of the New Church and the New Age.

There are many mystical organizations in the world, both fraternal and religious. And if you get what you're supposed to get out of them, you can really become a much, much better person. And the gem and the germ of Christ-reality in yourself can be stimulated. And believe me, it will stimulate you!

That's the interesting part about it. Not only will you stimulate your own sense of Christhood, but it will stimulate you, you see. And that's very wonderful because it establishes a principle of radioactivity within you. Through the nucleus of your own Christhood, there follows the spontaneous emission of 'alpha', 'beta', or 'gamma' rays!

Some people say to me, "How much time did you spend in preparing your sermon?" Why, I don't spend any time at all preparing my sermon! I never think of a single idea, because I work strictly with my Holy Christ Self. And my Holy Christ Self knows already what you have need of, what I have need of, what we all have need of—and our need is a togetherness, not a separation.

And so, the whole idea of the spiritual path is one of reintegration with your inherent Reality and the stimulation of the Divine within your evolving soul personality and the scientific release of that Light by the exercise of the sacred heart—and then not being ashamed that you did it.

You remember back forty years ago? Charles Atlas was a really important man. Why, he was more important than Jesus Christ in the eyes of a lot of people. Charles Atlas, "dynamic tension"—very great man, you know—a physical culturist and a nice person. Made a lot of money in it, too. Was quite a success, until he died at about eighty years of age.

Here's a man who ran in the human race. Remember Saint Paul—we touched upon it before: We all run in a race but one receiveth the prize. And this One is Christ in you. The only winner is Christ. Paul was excluding no one. What he was really getting at was that we should run to win. And the one who discovers himself in the Oneness of Christ—not two but One—is always the winner.

The world strives to obtain a corruptible crown, but we are striving for an incorruptible. "I therefore so run, not as uncertainly; so fight I, not as one that beateth the air," *but as one who runs to win.*

THE SPIRITUAL BODY AND BLOOD OF CHRIST

What I really want to see in all of you, what God wants (and that's more important), is that you win in the battle of your own life—that you understand who you really are and that you become what you really should be and who you really are.

Oh, this is so mysterious, so mysterious! It reminds me of the time that Jesus said, "Unless ye eat my flesh and drink my blood, ye have no Life in you."[70] And so, people were sitting around, and they still do, thinking that they had to become cannibals and eat the flesh of Jesus Christ as though they were actually devouring it and drink his blood as though they were devouring that. And so, many people left him right then and there. They just walked off. They said, "That's a hard saying.[71] You can't make a cannibal out of me!"

Some have come to accept the significance of the transubstantiation—the changing of the wafer and the wine into the literal Body and Blood of Christ. They accept that. And some have come to accept it so absolutely that many people today don't even question it.

And I didn't say you should. But I don't think you should feel that you're eating the living flesh of the physical body of Jesus that he wore 2,000 years ago, or that you're drinking his physical blood. I think you should accept transubstantiation as the changing of the sacrament into the *spiritual* Body and the *spiritual* Blood of Christ. Because he said it is the Spirit that giveth Life—the Life that is God in us. And this is the mystical significance of the ritual.

You should understand that just as the cells of Jesus' flesh and blood were carriers, or 'cups', of the Light of Alpha and Omega, so the bread and wine can be filled with or 'charged' with the essence of the Light of Christos, which the Master bore and still does as the Light—the illuminating Presence—in the world.

You should accept the assimilation of the Perfect Design of the Christ image transferred to you through the ritual of the Eucharist. For truly it is the divine intent that you partake of the currents of Alpha, the Father principle, and Omega, the Mother principle, through the wine and the wafer as these are blessed by God through the Son, who confers upon his ministers (through their beloved Christ Self) the blessing of the

Last Supper. "This do in remembrance of me. . . as a memorial to my Word reestablished in you."[72]

Now you understand "Except ye eat the flesh of the son of man [who is the Son of God] and drink his blood, ye have no Life in you"—because the Life-essence is what he was talking about. When you understand that the life that is in the blood is not only the substance of one's physical life, but that it is something greater—that the blood actually carries the essence of one's spirituality—you begin to unravel the Grail mystery: Christ the Chalice. "I AM the Grail." His reason for being that he would make your own, but that you alone can adopt.[73]

Some activities of the Brotherhood have taught that our blood would one day be changed to golden liquid light within our veins. This all sounds very strange and very involved. But, after all, where does the physical leave off and the spiritual begin? And so, what we have come to think of and recognize as material may actually be spiritual, and what we've come to believe as spiritual may actually be physical.

If today we were to leave this domain and find ourselves in a spiritual realm where the great Masters were teaching thousands of students, we might look at their bodies and see that they look just as solid as any earth body. But then, if we were there, we would also have the same kind of bodies they have—or we couldn't see them, could we? And yet, you know something? If they hit you with a giant flyswatter, you'd see how solid you are.

This is what is known as the etheric octave, where Ascended Masters and their unascended students meet on common ground. It's the plane where the Spirit/Matter spheres are visibly one. And there are etheric temples and etheric cities where the golden age is already in progress.

And so, what we need in order to experience the

exalted dimensions of our own being is the Mind of Christ. You've got a lot of air in your physical body just as you've got a lot of air in your mind. There's also a lot of *err-or* in the mind. There's a lot of misconceptions, you know, tragic misconceptions that we have in our minds. It's true. What we need are the spiritual values.

Let *this* Mind be in you which was also in Christ Jesus. [74]

Be ye therefore perfect even as your Father which is in heaven is perfect. [75]

When you come to hear the Teachings taught in this manner, as we are giving them to you, you will always find that you will receive something of value, something of inestimable truth, because it comes from the Masters' domain.

But don't knock yourself. You are the orifice of God—you are the mouth of God. God speaks in you the lost Word. And the recovery of that lost Word by you will assist you in being redeemed with Christ.

There's nothing wrong in esteeming one another. I don't find any fault in learning to love and esteem people, because "inasmuch as ye have done it unto one of the least of these my brethren, ye have done it unto me." [76]

Let us stop and realize that possibility—the possibility of the espousal of Christ through the love of the Friend who lives in all our friends. Then through love and through search, through faith and through the mounting wings of the divine eagle that God gives to us, [77] we shall rise above the mountains until we find at last that our happiness and our success is become—through Christ's love unto all—cosmic, universal.

Fear not. There is no death in God. Death exists only in the physical domain, that the bodies may be broken when they become of too little service to the Creator—that the Master Potter may take back the clay to his own hands, in order that he may later issue it forth once again, more perfectly formed in body, mind, and soul.

One day we shall stand in that perfection which we foreknew in the spiritual domain—before the world was, before we took upon ourselves the garments of personality and the shades that presently conceal the great Light.

Now work in that hope, as Jesus said, "while ye have the Light."

Chapter Four

MOMENTUM

Momentum

THIS year of our Lord, *anno Domini,* 1986 is our moment of challenge. It is our moment—when all of our past and its adventures have fallen with the sand to the bottom of the hourglass; and above, all of our future awaits us as opportunity descending for the renewal of our life's energy.

Our *moment,* our *challenge,* our *renewal.* It's your life and mine and the life of all mankind. And it's our opportunity—what we make of it is our "hourglass decision."

Many are caught in the spider's web. Many are unable to escape. Many do not understand the purposes of life. Many do not perceive the joys that are the potential of life. These are also our brethren.

They exist here in the whole wide earth, and yet we may or may not know them. We may not understand from whence they came or even that they are also chosen. But chosen all were by Life itself to bear witness to its magnificent opportunities, perceived in the doorway of our opportunity—individually.

You and I have a mind that is free to think, a heart that can ponder and love, a being that is motivated and can move in the busy streets of life and learn the control and the self-mastery of the body, the mind, and the form and its dimensions—that we may also master the worlds of the unformed and the formless.

How can we best convey this in a world where tradition has caused life to appear in many trees that are rooted to the soil and cannot move—some that may bear fruit and some that are barren? When I speak of trees, I speak also of religious trees which signify that by their side is a well, either empty or full.

And so we should recognize that religion today, which was intended to be a consecrated altar of worship and contact with the Deity where the vital fires of Reality could become known to each man, has instead become a dead and empty activity. This is true throughout the world and we are able to witness it.

Yet men defend their religions almost with their lives, primarily because they feel that they are their own. They do not seem to understand that religions all point the way, supposedly, toward the same God. In other words, every signpost leads to the same Goal—or so it should.

THE BROTHERHOOD AND THE PATH OF INITIATION

And so, if we know about it, we are compelled to recognize the Brotherhood whose emissaries long ago came to earth from other planets and systems of worlds. These were spiritual beings ordained by God to convey the mysteries of eternal Life to embodied souls. The latter having been assigned to this planet in order that they might learn in its schoolrooms how to master their lives and take dominion over the earth and multiply and replenish it with every good gift— because it was so ordained.[1]

There is a purpose to life. And the Brotherhood of which I speak is, of course, the Great White Brotherhood—the name often being bandied about by people who utter it as though it were not the sacred name that it is.

The Great White Brotherhood is sacred for many reasons. First of all, because it has never been polluted and cannot be polluted. It is impossible for anyone to join it. Only those who are initiated into it can become identified with it.

Individuals often speak about it as though it were a common thing. And we even hear the profane say, "Oh, I'm connected with the Great White Brotherhood, you know." They do not understand the sacredness of the altar of which we speak. "Put off thy shoes from off thy feet, for the place whereon thou standest is holy ground."[2]

Let us understand, then, as we approach the shrine of the Great White Brotherhood, that we are speaking of a bond between the Ascended Masters and their unascended chelas (disciples), of the communion of the saints in heaven with the saints on earth, and of the cooperative adventure of angels, elementals, the Sons of God and mankind.

Yes, we speak of a bond and more than a bond. We speak of that which will lead us through the orderly process of initiation into such a fountain of Light, embracing such dimensions in consciousness as earth has not known since early, pre-Lemurian golden ages.

The term *Great White Brotherhood* is not racial; it refers to the spiritual body of world servers, their auras purified, their garments white, who serve humanity from the level of the Ascended Masters (the same level from which the Ascended Master Jesus Christ functions) and the level of the angelic beings.

Each individual, if he will, may find, then, through the power made manifest in the Great White Brotherhood—its techniques, its mastery of life, its attunement with God, and its function as a link, or mediator, between God and man—the answer to all of his problems.

It is certainly not intended to supplant Christ. It *is* Christ in action. In fact, it is Christ's Mystical Body. Because Christos, the universal emissary of Light, works through the members of the Brotherhood as the bridge connecting embodied mankind with God and the heavenly hosts.

When one is able to gauge the great scope of the Brotherhood and the heavenly order of hierarchy it represents, one arrives at the place where he stands in awe of the initiatory experiences that will bring to man a realization of who and what he really is.

"But," you say, "why haven't the churches discovered this?" Well, why haven't they discovered many things! including the fact that Jesus traveled to the Far East before he was thirty—an idea waiting to be kindled in the hearts of his beloved.[3]

When you have the flint and you have the floss, you need to strike the flint and let the spark leap from the flint into the floss, that a flame may be captured. Without the actual spark itself, the flame is not born— so it is with the churches today.

Each man should understand that every day is intended to be a day of progress, welcoming new experiences of divinity in the unfolding drama of the ages. This drama includes those fiery spirits born into every race, creed, and clime. Through the initiatic process of the Great White Brotherhood, all are able to find the answers to their everyday problems.

These answers do not come tumbling out of space into a hat that we may hold in our hand and say, "I want to catch thee." No. These answers must be sought—and sought diligently—by all who would have the spiritual experiences that precede spiritual mastery.

Unless we are willing to obtain these experiences ourselves by humility and service (the watchwords of our Brotherhood), we may find ourselves outside the pale of it. And so, in this hour of our history, I want to speak to you about momentum.

THE LAW OF ENERGY ALLOTMENTS AND MOMENTUMS

We are all given allotted energy. With this energy we move and think and act. With this energy, in waking and in sleeping hours, the body temple maintains itself. With this energy we do all things; and we are held accountable for its use or misuse, as the case may be.

Just as your gas and electric company installs a gas meter or an electric meter in the line, interrupting the flow from the source to the customer, so, in a like manner, the Godhead vouchsafes a measured amount of energy into the hands and use of each individual. This quota can be increased or decreased through the correct or incorrect use of the Law.

As "the very hairs of your head are all numbered,"⁴ so the energy allotment of mankind is also numbered. Thus, some people have a thick head of hair, some are bald, and some carefully count the number of hairs they have left! Even so, some have a little energy and others have much. Some have no money and others have "money to burn." From this we deduce that there is a law governing the release of energy into our worlds. And this we should study.

The vital fact is that you are at all times, waking or sleeping, receiving energy which, when used by you through either the positive or negative exercise of your free will, is credited to you and you alone. You are charged for it and you are charged by it. You are the recipient of that energy which is God's investment in your creative self—in effect, a measure (talent) of his

Light and Consciousness with which you may secure a momentum.

Now, some people say, "Well, I'm not interested in securing a momentum. I don't even know what a momentum is." Well, a momentum, dear hearts, is anything that you may develop a habit pattern on.

If, for example, you elect to be fat and you want to be fat and you decide you are going to be fat, you will develop a momentum on eating. And you're going to eat until you get fat. And then when you get fat, you're not going to stop eating, because you have developed a momentum on it.

If you decide you are going to be thin and you're going to diet excessively, you may then do so. And as you diet, what will happen is that you will develop a momentum of habit, a habit pattern, which will produce in you an eventual thinness.

Just as people can desire to be fat, so they can desire to be thin. But the habit pattern that they develop that produces these qualities is what I'm talking about: That's a momentum.

Now, we will not only apply this to the physical body, but we will also apply it to the mind. If you decide that you are going to learn French, you will start studying French and you will do so diligently. Every opportunity you get, you're going to be at it.

If you decide to be Hercules, you're going to go out and build your body. You go to your club or your backyard or your garage or anywhere, and you begin lifting weights and you do all kinds of exercises because you want to develop the quality of your muscles. You develop a momentum on it. And by and by, this momentum becomes larger because you keep doing it.

I'm going to give you a law that Jesus gave you, a law that is very important concerning momentums.

And I'm going to show you that momentums are all-important in your life—so important that even if you decide that you're not going to do anything about anything, this law will still be operable in your life. I'm going to show you that no matter what you do or don't do, you are going to come under the law of momentums as Jesus taught.

Let's say you decide you're going to be a vegetable, you're going to draw nutrients out of the soil, out of your environment, you're going to pull energy into yourself and you're going to do what you want—let it be as whimsical as possible, you're just going to do whatever comes into your mind. OK, you will be developing a momentum on that—and that momentum, an intrinsic part of the act itself, is going to affect your life powerfully.

If you do nothing, you'll be developing a momentum on doing nothing. And by and by, this law will come to its own fruition in your world and you will find your cornucopia empty, *empty!* because you have made it so—empty and devoid of consciousness or motivation except to do nothing.

So whether we will or no, all of us are developing momentums. And our momentums determine the kind of person we are as well as the kind of person we will be.

KARMA, PAST LIVES, AND RIGHT CHOICES

We like to look back into the dingy and dim past with what degree of perception we are able to muster to find some record of self-importance. Some people like to sit and speculate on who they might have been in a previous embodiment. Then, if they discover that they were a certain person, they grab all the history books they can find on that person and begin to study their so-called past life.

But after all, stop and think about it: What can you do about a dead momentum? Nothing! Whatever has been in past history, the die is cast and in that life you have fulfilled your momentums. You have out-pictured what they have dictated. But you are the one who created the monster—or the saint, as the case may be. Not heaven, but you.

People like to think that their glory is perhaps in their stars. They like to think that the gods have favored them through their stars and that the Fates have dictated to them a certain personality and for-tune—a standard of life or the lack of it. And so they say, "Well, it's all in our stars, you know," blaming the unfortunate situations on planetary forces beyond their control.

And so people become creatures of superstition instead of being prime movers of their destiny. But, in reality, as Cassius said: Our faults really lie in our-selves, not in our stars.[5] And so we must learn to outwit the dictates of our stars as well as of our past karma that is so clearly inscribed in our astrology, if we know how to read it.

Frequently I hear individuals say, "Well, it's my past karma, you know, and that is my excuse for not doing anything about anything. Just sitting here, I am actually reaping my past karma." Well, quite so. We are all reaping our past karma.[6] There's no question about it.

But we don't have to reap and weep!

Do you understand what I mean? We don't have to reap and weep, because heaven has provided a way of escape. We today can harness our past momentums constructively and still make things right, because we will it so.

Do we dare say that it is God's will that we go *down, down, down* a series of steps? Of course not!

Then, why should we think that our past karma is itself conspiring to cast a net before our pathway to snare us, to trip us up, to make us to stumble? Not so.

Our past karma is our past karma, but it need not be a stumbling block even if it be negative in nature. We can outwit it. We can make it right, just as a man who has gone bankrupt and thoroughly escaped all of his creditors can at any time he so chooses pay up his debts in honor.

Let us understand this law so that we do not become morally and spiritually bankrupt or dependent upon the whimsical side of life to ordain our freedom—*maybe*, if the odds are favorable. But if the universe were run by whimsy, by what case of jackstraws would life then elect to choose this individual above that individual? None, I am sure. Because just as the laws in the universe are ordained by mathematical precision, so that same precision—God's as well as man's—determines what man is going to be and what he is going to do. And this is the mathematical equation of both divine and human free will.

Someone may say, "Well, I have struggled very hard and very long. I have worked diligently to escape from my past karma but it's closing in around me like a net."

We remember the story of the yogic master who was outside his ashram when he met a king cobra in the pathway. And the cobra was coiled, ready to strike. He looked at the cobra and he said, "Cluck-cluck. Come on, Mr. Cobra!" And then he subdued him with rhythmic handclapping and a pure heart.[7]

What else can you say or do if you face a tarantula or a cobra or a mouse that roars at you? You can scream and say, "*Oh!* I'm going to die right now! There's no hope for me!" Or, if you will, you can welcome the return currents of your own squeamish

energies of the past—your momentums that are returning to you now both for redemption and to edu-
cate your soul through the whole process.

The primary purpose of returning karma is the
education of the individual. In examining many records of people's past lives, I have found that the universe does not conspire *against* man; on the contrary,
it conspires *with* him to give him his emancipation—it
being a joy to God to bring liberation to man rather
than to see him in the traitor's toils.

So, let us recognize that in all of these old
momentums that we have created, there is a way of
escape—and that way is through Christ and through
the mystical understanding of universal purpose and
through the violet flame and the dynamic decree of the
Word taught to us by beloved Jesus and the Ascended
Masters of the Great White Brotherhood.

How dare anyone say that we are created to do
our own will in defiance of God's will, just because we
have it! Possessing our own will does not mean that we
are supposed to use it unwisely against the mainstream of universal purpose. The point of free will is
so that the gift of a greater individuality can be bestowed on us because we *do* make the right choices.

If we make the right choices, we'll come out on
top; and if we don't, well sure, there's a big circle to
put your 'x' in and a little circle to put your 'no' in—but
then, after all, the rewards are greatest when we move
with the currents of Life rather than against them.

To tell you the truth, no one can win going against
the currents of Life. All you can get, all I can get, or
any man can get are those obstructive results that frus-
trate our true aims, afford fleeting satisfaction and
deprive us, sometimes for lifetimes, of the real results
we ought to have. It's only when we move *with* the
cosmic stream that our best dreams are fulfilled and

the joy of God is with us. Even the regrets that come from our regressions into past lives teach us the folly of defying the course Love holds for us.

"UNTO HIM THAT HATH A MOMENTUM..."

But there's one particularly sacred statement that Jesus made—that I promised to tell you about. And this has been a great mystery to many believers. Now watch what I'm going to tell you. This has been quoted variously by Matthew, Mark, and Luke, and then again by later translators.

Unto him that hath shall more be added and from him that hath not shall be taken away even that which he hath.[8]

This is a strange and enigmatic statement until understood. Christ spake of momentums.

To him that hath a momentum of constructivism, more of God shall be added. But from him that hath not a constructive momentum shall be taken away even that which he hath.

To him that hath a momentum of constructivism— of working with the cosmic currents, of flowing with the stream, of allowing the divine Tao to flow through his consciousness, of opening himself to God and God alone, willingly and gladly—*more of God shall be added. But from him that hath not a constructive momentum shall be taken away even that which he hath*—because he's got nothing going for him, not even enough momentum to hold on to what he's got, and so even what he has is taken from him.

Stop and think about this—if you don't put the plus factor of God in your life, what are you putting in? If you eliminate the plus factor of the Creator and his purposes and his will from your life, what are you eliminating but the plus factor you need in order to multiply your own momentums? And then you're a have-not and you've got a momentum on being a have-not and every day you have less and less.

And this will continue indefinitely, like a satellite in orbit, until God becomes the motivating momentum of your life, and his Light (as Christ in you) gathers more and more of his purpose and his will unto itself. And every day you have more and more. And you're a have and because you're a have, and have a momentum on being a have, more is added. And it just keeps rolling, like Ol' Man River—"He jus' keeps rollin' along."

It is an utterly bizarre thing for man to think that the Creator of the universe—the one capable of creating a physical body like we have, the one capable of creating a mind like we have, the one capable of creating a spirit like we have with all of the solar powers, or *soul powers,* inherent within man—would then be incapable of correctly directing human life if asked.

But even to ask requires a momentum of will, of desire to have divine direction. And for some people, even life's most blatant purposes have not motivated the inner desire for divine direction. So it seems that in seeking to build our momentums we must begin before the beginning.

Mastering Circumstances through the Will of God

"If you ask your father for bread," Jesus said, "will he give you a stone?"[9] I believe that the will of God may be made known to man. And I believe that when man gets to know the will of God it will be proven to be a comforting and an exhorting will that inspires man to pursue in himself greater examples of Reality.

I believe that those who are endowed with God's

will, as they come more and more to understand that will and its inherent goodwill toward them, will become more complementary to the universe—as the universe in turn will become more complementary to them. There will follow a push-pull action of divine currents flowing into and out of that man or that woman, and they will not be stymied by circumstances but they will rise above circumstances. And they will learn to master circumstances, and they will learn to control themselves and their environment.

If conditions are not to their liking, they will divert conditions—because such a man or woman is able to do just that. And this is true of any one of you— if you will accept it and be free.

Drinking the water of Life freely[10] means just that: to accept it without money and without price[11] because it is the gift of God. And besides, the best things in life are free. So, your momentums, *your God momentums,* are the gifts that—as you accept them and grow in them—will add more of their kind to themselves, and you will become a person of greater and greater spirituality.

And as you grow spiritually, you're going to grow in every way because you cannot experience growth in one aspect of the triune nature of man that will not spill over into the other cups of consciousness. You will always perceive Power, Wisdom, and Love as the axis of man's being.

And so we find the Father, the Son, and the Holy Spirit—the body, the soul, and the mind. We find the triune aspects of God in expression in ourselves. You're not going to find just one idea, you're going to find these three ideas manifesting in and as the three-fold flame within your heart.

You have to have power in order to motivate an idea. Let an idea come into your mind that you want to carry out. Suppose that that idea is very brilliant and clearly defined. If, when your mind perceives it, you lack the power and the love, the wheel of the Law will not turn, because you will not have the will or the desire to give it life.

You cannot turn people on merely by an idea in the mind unless that idea be loved. And why is it loved? Because it is seen and perceived as a potential, as a possibility. People love it because they see that it can work, and so they set about making it work.

But if they don't have the power, they can love the idea to pieces, they can think about the idea until they are blue in the face and nothing is going to happen—until they *are* 'blue in the face'! In other words, we need to be blue with willpower, blue with the determination that something is going to happen because we *are* going to endow our thinking and our loving with decisive action.

So, how about thinking *now* about the idea of momentum? If for one hundred years you were to think about drawing down this divine energy from God into your mind, into your heart, and into your being, and you didn't do anything about it for that one hundred years, you would be spinning your wheels, wouldn't you? As I have said before, the only difference between a rut and a grave is one of depth.

My mother used to say, "God helps those who help themselves." And to some people, this may be a bromide. They've heard it before and they say, "Yes, it's true, but . . ."

And this is perhaps one of the problems of our times and of all time—that once they know a certain thing, people have a tendency to feel more complacent about it. By reason of simply entertaining an idea that they never put to work, of having a seed in their packet that they never put into the ground, they think, "I've done this before, I've heard it before, it's not new."

Well, your pansy seeds were not new last year when you put them into the ground; your 1985 income tax was not new until it finally became due. Everything has to be new in its season and time! We have to take up some things because they are forced upon us, but other things we are not forced to do at all.

One thing we're not forced to do is to love God. We're forced to love our wives, supposedly. We're forced to love our country, supposedly. We're forced to love the systems to which we pay allegiance, supposedly. Practically everything in life is forced upon us—attendance at school; we have to work or we don't eat. All kinds of things are forced upon us. But the one thing that is not forced upon us in life is the greatest thing of all. And that is the gift of God—the *gifts* of God (let's make it multi, because they are multi).

We worry about becoming multimillionaires—and if we did, we'd only increase our responsibility as well as our potential for good. Let's become spiritual millionaires—people that can multiply the gifts of God because we want to!

And so the matter of momentums is the greatest law of life that I can possibly think of, and we create or uncreate momentums every single day.

YOU CREATED IT—YOU UNCREATE IT!

We make New Year's resolutions. We say to ourselves, "Well, this year is going to be different than last year. I didn't get enough exercise last year, so this year I'm going to get me a new machine." Or, "I'm going to a horse ranch. I'm going to ride horseback." Or, "I'm going to join a club and I'm going swimming." Or, "I'm going to start jogging this year and I'm going to jog every day."

And we do, for maybe a week or two, and then all at once something comes up and we're distracted and the chain of our momentum is broken. It was easy to put off the first time. It's easier still the second time. And the longer a person goes along the road of neglect of a particular momentum, the weaker the momentum becomes.

This is why people today don't attend church as much as they should—because they have weakened their resolves. They have allowed themselves to stay away. And by staying away, they develop a momentum on staying away. And the momentum gets bigger and bigger and bigger and bigger. And after a while they are a little guy, shrunk, as it were, to the size of a one-year-old baby, looking up at a giant that's lasted for a year and grown every day accordingly—the giant of their own negative momentums, their neglects.

The pathway to spiritual values is through the development of momentums—and I mean right momentums.

Saint Germain said that his salvation, his ascension whereby he became an Ascended Master, was the result of two million right decisions that he made. Now, if you stop and think about that from a mathematical standpoint, you will see that it would take a man quite a few lifetimes to make two million right decisions. Yet he made those decisions.

So the whole idea is not to get into procrastination, putting off till tomorrow what you can do today. You know this, but unless you do it, you most certainly will not be developing the correct momentums that will carry you along to *your* ascension.

Now, some people used to say (as we run into my little story on the French debtors) in France many, many years ago (actually it was Gaul at that time) as I recall quite well—it was when the doctrine of reembodiment was taught by the Catholic Church, before it was taken out—"Well, Pierre, I do owe you ten francs, but I'm not going to pay you in this lifetime. I'll pay you in my next lifetime." Or, "Pierre, I'm not going to church today because I'll go to church in my next lifetime, and then I'm going to become a saint."

Procrastination is an excuse which we all at one time or another have fallen prey to. But it is an excuse which is lame and halt and blind. And who are the victims of this lameness and haltness and blindness but you and I? *We* are the ones who suffer as a result of it. For whether it be a worldly momentum that leads to worldly success or a spiritual momentum that leads to spiritual success, our momentums (or the breaking of our momentums) are the point that determines whether or not we are going to measure up to what heaven expects of us.

I think you should understand this because so many people don't. They say, "This poor man, he's a sinner. He's been doing wrong things. Every day he does wrong things. He's a butcher and he weighs his thumb on every scale. And he's not good to his family. When he comes home at night, he is cruel to his wife and children and he goes to bed grumpy."

Well, he has a momentum on this. And so you say, "Well, why doesn't heaven break that momentum?" Because he's getting deeper and deeper in debt! You know that old song about the coal miner made famous by Tennessee Ernie Ford: "You load sixteen tons, what do you get? Another day older and deeper in debt. . ."

Well, heaven doesn't break *his* momentum, precisely because *he* created it and only *he* can uncreate it. You have to realize that your threefold flame is the divine spark of God's creative potential in you. It's the authority whereby you act as a freewill agent of the Father, the Son, and the Holy Spirit.

To you, then, is given the power (of the Father) to

create in your world, the wisdom (of the Son) to decide whether or not to preserve your creation, and the love (of the Holy Spirit) to transform or transmute it by the sacred fire.

These three functions of the trinity of Light within us relate to the Eastern understanding of the Persons of the Trinity as (1) the Creator of the creation, (2) the Preserver of the creation, and (3) the Destroyer, or Transformer, of the creation.

As you are destined to become a co-creator with God, you can see why all of heaven respects your free will and the fact that Almighty God gave you that free will to re-create yourself in his likeness. Unless you invoke the intercession of the LORD's hosts, they, in honor, will not interfere with your creative experiments. For they know that the lessons best learned are those of an unimpaired exercise of free will. With it you have the power to do almost anything—and you should take care that whatever you do is within the bounds of God's laws. Because you have accountability.

Spiritually speaking, so many people are getting deeper and deeper in debt every day they live because of their negative momentums. After a while, they begin to love them like a pet chameleon or a goldfish in a bowl. They say, "That is *my* momentum! Don't you meddle with that! You leave that alone! That's mine."

Why, in heaven's name, who in the world would *want* to meddle with it? No one in their right mind really wants it anyway, so why meddle with it?

But those who do try to get us to change are not doing so just for their sake. They're doing so for our sake. So let's learn to recognize the difference between meddling and sincere comfort and consolation and instruction in wisdom from true friends. And the best friends any of us can have are the Ascended Masters; and they're the ones who want you to understand this instruction on momentums.

POSITIVE AND NEGATIVE MOMENTUMS—GOALS AND GENES

You know, while the best things in life are free, some things are very costly. And one thing that is more costly than anything else is to go ahead and waste your time building a negative momentum—which, by the way, doesn't take any effort to build.

You see, a negative momentum is a downhill momentum, and the minute you start to stop, you see—you heard what I said? The minute you start to stop, right away you start rolling back downhill. And so it doesn't take any energy at all to build negative momentums. They just automatically take care of themselves. They're automated.

You go ahead and stop your progress—stop somewhere on the hill and say, "I'm going to rest. Just let me rest awhile, heaven. Just let me stand here a few minutes. I can't keep going!" You're going to find yourself back a few steps, because this is an uphill climb. This is the ascension. This is what's worthwhile in life. Nothing equals the ascension. This is what Jesus Christ demonstrated.

Some in the Christian church demonstrate the *via dolorosa*—the sorrowful way, the way of lamentation. They talk about the Gethsemanes in life. They talk about the suffering and the tortures and the horrors of life and how black it is. They don't seem to understand how *light* it is. "Take and learn of me," the Master said, "for my yoke is easy and my burden *is Light*."[12]

We can learn how to put on the yoke of Christ and we can rejoice in that yoke. And that's not a joke—it's a yoke. And it's true! It's true as steel. And through the process of building momentums we'll be surprised at how much we will develop.

Now, let's take anybody in this room. I would bet you my bottom dollar that if I passed out paper and pencils and asked you to write down what you really want, the bulk of you would put down your spiritual goals because you have recognized that sooner or later in life only the spiritual goals have permanent meaning.

Go ahead and get a million dollars, and you've got trouble—spending it or giving it away or doing whatever you want with it. You can ask old Jean Paul Getty or Howard Hughes. They have more trouble in life than people who are poor.

People may say they want money. But they know very well that they wouldn't need it if they weren't here on this earth. They also know—and they know positively—that they're not going to get out of this world alive, so they won't need the money then. But they need it while they're living. But they don't need a million—they can exist quite comfortably on much less.

So, you would write down, no doubt, permanent goals. Because, if you wrote down worldly, passing goals, you know very well that they'd be fulfilled or not fulfilled.

Supposing you said, "I want to marry the most beautiful woman in the world." Well, that'd be a matter of opinion—and whether she'd have you or not, you just don't know. And, really, such goals are very trite in one way, because if you got all the things you might want as a human being, it wouldn't assure you one iota of happiness. You can't be sure, if you get the goal you think you want, that you're going to be happy after you get it.

Spiritually, whether you're rich or poor, wise or foolish, or whatever you are—if your goals are spiritual, if you put God first, you know that all things will be added unto you. [13] You know that if you lack wisdom, you're going to get it. You know if you lack money, you're going to get that, too. You know if you lack friends, you're going to get friends—because there are spiritual people on this earth just like you.

Oh, you say there are not so many right now. And why is that? Because we live in the age of *Kali Yuga.* The Hindus describe this age as a dark age. It's an age where material concepts are coming to the fore because of man's scientific orientation almost to the exclusion of spiritual reality.

But the greatest scientist of all is the Creator. The Creator is the one who was able to put inside the little DNA chain in microscopic form the most tremendous patterns that anyone could ever envision. Isn't it amazing that these little 'chips' that can only be seen through an electron microscope contain the code of your whole life, genetically speaking, all written down?

Well, if you're not healthy enough when you're born and start out in life, all you have to do is blame your genes, because it's all stamped there. Have you thought about that? The color of your hair and eyes, your hearing, your internal organs, the health of your skin. You look at somebody else and you say, "Gee, they've got wonderful skin. Mine isn't as nice as theirs." Well, it's all the fault of your genes.

But then, how did your genes get that way, huh? How did your genes get this stamp on them? They got that way because of your past karma. So, you see, what you do and what you have done has made an indelible imprint on the genetic pattern which you wear today as your own. "That's my genetic pattern"— but you don't hear people saying that, because everybody wants to change the pattern of their genes.

They're discussing cloning today. They think maybe they want to be duplicated. (For spare parts, you know.) Imagine duplicating yourself in another body! I shudder to think of the responsibilities of this. We have enough to do to take care of our present body without having a whole bunch of us running around!

"Say unto This Momentum, 'Be Thou Removed!'"

And so the process is not a matter of cloning but of keeping our faith in the responsibility of the Deity to help us if we ask. The greatest problem with people is that they don't ask. People have no momentum on asking. A lot of times they don't ask God for anything until they're in trouble.

They get in trouble and they say, "Dear God, there's a cliff. I've got ten feet and I'm skidding. I'm going to go over that cliff. Help me, Lord!" they holler. Because they're in trouble! But if they weren't in trouble, they wouldn't even think of God.

So God becomes a sort of charm bracelet—a charmed-life bracelet they wear on their wrist. It's like Aladdin's magic lamp. They rub it when they're in trouble and the genie appears, and they say, "Do this for me." But they don't understand that they can do everything for themselves that they expect God to do, if they rightly understand life.

Now, isn't that a strange statement to make? I said you can do *everything* for yourself that you expect God to do. This is exactly correct. Because God made man self-sufficient. Each individual monad was built to be able to draw down the power of the universe and make that power go to work for him and do for him whatever he wants done.

Well, why then do we have such a lack of faith? you say. Why do some people have so much faith and others have so little? Jesus said, "If you have faith as a grain of mustard seed, you can say to this mountain, 'Be thou removed,' and it will be so—and nothing shall be impossible to you." [14] There doesn't seem to be very much faith on earth then, does there?—because we don't see many mountains moving.

But we have to understand that just as he was talking in a very symbolical way about the eye of the needle—that "it's easier for a camel to go through the eye of a needle than for a rich man to enter into the kingdom of God" [15]—so the Father also had certain thoughts in mind when he said through Jesus, "Say unto this mountain, 'Be thou removed!' and it shall be done." [16]

He was talking about a mountain of adversity. There is no purpose in going to a physical mountain and saying, "Get off of there! I don't like the spot you're sitting on and I don't like you occupying it!"

People get so ridiculous! The mountains are the mountains of trouble and adversity and confusion, the problems we have—that's what you can talk to and it'll go. I can testify that this will work. But I can't say that I've ever seen a man running around— even Mohammed—moving mountains physically!

Have you ever seen a mountain moving physically (except in earthquakes and the rise and fall of continents)? Did you ever see Jesus move a mountain physically? Did you ever hear anything in Matthew, Mark, Luke, or John about Jesus moving any mountains? There's no recorded history anywhere that says he moved a mountain.

Have you ever heard of any of the great masters over in the Himalayas moving mountains? You hear of them traveling in the mountains, of going here and going there; you hear of them levitating and bilocating and flying around and in between the mountains like the famous yogi Milarepa, but you don't hear of them moving physical mountains.*

So, the Master was not talking about a physical mountain. He was talking about mountains of adversity, mountains of karma, mountains that are problems. And what are they but mounting momentums? You built it!—and you've got to clean it up. That's the Law. And, of course, it's a very unpopular idea.

Everyone in the world today is looking for someone like 'George' to do it for them. Poor George is so overburdened that I can't really understand why anybody wants to name their child George. They say, "Let George do it." They're looking for a messiah, someone to forgive their sins—in fact, someone not only to forgive their sins but to turn around and live their life for them afterward.

A lot of people find the greatest of comfort in going up to Jesus and saying, "You just live my life, Lord. I'll surrender it all to you." And that works very well until the first little crossing. You know what the first crossing is? It's when they come up against something they want to do that they don't think he wants them to do. Then they say, "Well, this doesn't count now, Lord. Don't look." And they go running off to do this thing, you see. "Time out, it doesn't count, the clock isn't running," they say. And they do it!

And right afterwards they want him to come back in, and they say, "Now I'm going to switch the plug back and you can come back in. You can take over my life again, Lord."

And after a while the Lord gets rather confused, so he goes on a vacation because he doesn't believe them anymore. And do you blame him? People don't

*Except, of course, in the epic of Krishna, who, on one occasion, was said not only to have moved Mount Govardhana but to have held it aloft for seven days and seven nights to save his cowherds and their cows from the fierce storm sent by the jealous Indra.

even believe themselves. And that's true. People don't believe themselves, and so they lose faith in everything and everyone—including the Lord; and this is the sad part of it all.

But if they'd start to trust the Divine within themselves and to pay attention to it, if the voice of conscience were not seared with a hot iron, [17] people would actually find that God-guidance is possible.

And I am here to tell you today that God-guidance builds mountains! It builds momentums. That's what a spiritual mountain is. It's a momentum mountain—a mountain that moves. It has power and it generates the power to do things that ought to be done!

I was just talking to a gentleman who is of Arab descent. We were talking about the momentums that some of the Arab peoples have, where they don't get along with each other and they're not really unified. And the question came up, "Do you think these people are ever going to get together?" And I said, "No, not under the present circumstances. The way they're behaving, it would take a miracle!" And that isn't just the Moslems, it's the Irish, too. It's a lot of people.

Somehow or other, people have a way of finding fault with each other—and so many times the fault they find is really in themselves. They have eyes and they cover those eyes with their glasses and the glasses are colored a certain way. They're polarized so that when they look at things, they don't see them as they are but they see them as they want to see them.

Yes, I think there's a real problem in getting people together. And I'll tell you why. How are you going to get them together? How do you create unity? The only way that you can create unity is by having faithful stewards to carry on your word and your work.

Christ had twelve apostles. Those apostles were specifically endowed by him with power from on high.

He told them that. He said, "I'm going to endow you with power from on high. I'm going to anoint you."[18] And the only way that you could ever unify people today would be through a spiritual power—a power greater than any one individual.

MASTERS AND MOMENTUMS ON MIRACLES

When Mary appeared near Cairo over the Coptic church,[19] do you think, for example, that that galvanized all of Egypt into a sudden desire to love each other? Those who saw her, those who were in the church—they were moved by it. Those who were healed were moved.

But, after all, this, too, was an act of karma. They deserved to be there and they were, because they had built a momentum of devotion that brought them to the church. They had made themselves receptive to the power of vision.

It's people themselves and their negative or positive momentums that make the determination as to what is going to act. It's not really their genes at all. Because the power of the genes can be changed.

What are you going to do when I tell you that your genetic patterns can be erased right while you're alive? What are you going to do when I tell you that you can change your own genes so that they are not negative anymore, when they were negative to start with?

Are you going to call me a liar? It's alright if you do. I know that I have personally, by the power of God, changed the genes that are in my own body many times. Some people look at me one day and they see me one way and then again they see me another way. And so I demonstrate to people that they can look this way and that way, because the power to change, the potential to change, is in everybody.

You don't have to be insipid. You don't have to feel helpless. You don't have to be physically weak. You don't have to be spiritually weak. You don't have to be anything you don't want to be! I didn't say that you're going to be able to do it like Aladdin—just snap your fingers and it happens. But some can. Some have a momentum on that, too. And it can be done.

I have seen healings that occurred in the twinkling of an eye. One time there was a young man sitting in my audience who had cataracts on his eyes at the age of about twenty-seven. The cataracts cleared right up during a dictation and he was completely healed!

That's an instantaneous type of healing. It happens occasionally. But there's such a thing as a slower type healing. One of the people we talked to who saw the appearance of Mother Mary in Cairo had had leukemia. She went home and the next day it was a little less and in a few days it was a little less; and two or three weeks were required before she was actually healed. We saw the same thing in the time of Christ. There are fast and slow healings. It's like what Brother William said to me one time when I was on a fast. He said, "What are you on—a fast fast or a slow fast?"

Well, it's rather interesting, all the little things— and the momentous things—that can happen in life. This keeps life interesting. It makes it worth living. But if you have an idea that the apostles and the early prophets—and even the later prophets—didn't really have any fun in life, disabuse yourself of that.

Just imagine that prophet going along on his ass and all of a sudden it turns into Francis the talking mule![20] And the ass looks at him and he says, "What are you beating me for, Balaam?" He had beaten her three times because she refused to go. You see, she had seen the LORD's angel standing in front of her, sword drawn. So she stopped dead in her tracks as any normal, intelligent ass would do!

It actually happened. It happened before Francis the talking mule, of course, or before talking pictures. And, you know, that reprobate prophet didn't think anything of it at all! He thought it was perfectly natural for the ass to talk. And that, to me, was the strangest thing of all! He started talking back to the talking ass! He was so angry that he just answered her right back and said, "I beat you because you mocked me, and if I had a sword in my hand I would kill you right now!"

Well, along about that time the LORD opened Balaam's eyes, and when he saw the angel he was so startled, he bowed his head and fell flat on his face. Needless to say, the angel extolled the virtues of the ass, whose halting, the angel said, had saved Balaam's life lest for his perverseness he should have been slain at the hand of the angel.[21]

Well, what we've got to do is to realize a little bit of the drama of life that we can bring into our ordinary and drab existence. Just like Balaam and his ass, who were quite ordinary before the hand of the LORD came upon them, we don't have to carry on with our humdrum existence if we don't want to.

I think people are fascinating—and angels and elementals, too, for that matter! Just stop and think about all the people you meet that have different ideas. When you get them together, you find out that they're all authorities. They're all authorities on something—if on nothing else but themselves! And they'll tell you all their troubles, if you'll sit and listen to them.

And the first thing you know, you'll find you have a tin ear. So you say to yourself, "Well, where can I go? How can I escape? I'm overwhelmed by this person's troubles. If this keeps up, I'm going to be washed away from the very face of the earth by the sea of troubles that is come upon me!"

And the other person that's telling you about them—he feels so good because he's getting rid of all his troubles. So life is really very interesting if you understand how to read and run. (Now, that's not a pun!)

So, coming back to the subject of momentums . . . Don't lose sight of this Teaching, now! This is the most important Teaching from Jesus you can ever hear because on it hinges your own future development in every way! . . . There's *nothing* more important than your understanding of your own momentums and their power play in your life.

Because there's great power in the proper use of your momentums. The Ascended Master Saint Germain, the great Master of Freedom—he was the prophet Samuel as well as Joseph, the husband of Mary. Later he embodied as Christopher Columbus and Francis Bacon. Well, he returned to earth after he ascended, some say reembodying as the son of Prince Rakoczy II, and he appeared throughout Europe as "the Wonderman." And he worked all kinds of miracles because he had a momentum on it.

He called himself le Comte de Saint Germain and he went around the courts of Europe for at least a hundred years in the eighteenth and nineteenth centuries performing all sorts of feats to get their attention, you see. But his main purpose was to advise the kings and queens and prevent the bloodshed of the French Revolution in particular, his great dream being the founding of a United States of Europe.

And he never aged. One of the ladies at the court of Louis XVI said that his face hadn't changed in twenty years, while hers had become covered with wrinkles and furrows. That's what you get when you have a momentum on seventh-ray alchemy!

The story is told that he was once seated midst a gathering of men who wanted to see if he could demonstrate his power to them. So on that particular occasion—it was in Paris, you remember—he decided he would demonstrate his power. Oh yes.

So he waved his hand, and the next thing you know, the table and all the chairs were hanging out over the street in Paris, several stories up in the air. They were all sitting out there in thin air! And there they were. And they looked at him and they blinked and they looked down—and what could they do? They were there and they were seated. So pretty soon he waved his hand and they came back in the room and the chairs were all in their places again.

All this he did and more. Do you know that Saint Germain could take a gemstone like this one? He'd hold it up before his eye like this, and if it had a flaw in it, he'd look at it and he would see no flaw. He'd unsee it. Then he'd take the stone away with him and bring it back days later and the flaw would be gone!

All these things Saint Germain did.²² Jesus did all kinds of miracles. Mother Mary can do miracles. I know this from a personal standpoint. I've seen her do it. In fact, you might be surprised—Paolo Veronese, now the Ascended Master Paul the Venetian, he can do miracles, too. And what's more, *you* can do miracles!—but you don't even know it. They had a momentum, you see.

THE EVIL EYE, JEALOUSY, AND WITCHCRAFT

I think sometimes it's very good that people who are living objectively in physical bodies don't know too much about what they can do, because if they did, they might create chaos for each other. Because you find that most of the time people in this world are not stable in their emotions.

It's almost like that program "Bewitched" on television. If the girl doesn't like what someone does, she twitches her nose and the next thing you know, the guy's got horns growing on his head, or anything else. This is what you see in "Bewitched." You'll see all kinds of things happening. Why? Because it's supposed to be witchcraft.

We don't believe in practicing witchcraft. We're not interested in that. But you should know what it is and guard against it. Because people are, in effect, practicing witchcraft on each other. Take, for instance, the situation where someone brags about their children (I learned this in the Middle East), and then somebody puts what they call the evil eye on their children; and the children get sick and they die. In Cairo, they definitely believe in what they call the evil eye.[23]

Well, whether you know it or not, the evil eye is simply people using the power of vision for evil. And this is what black magic is all about. So what actually happens is somebody comes along and says, "Gee, I've got a wonderful business. I've got a beautiful home. I've got a beautiful wife. My kids are pretty. Everything's going great for me. I'll become a millionaire in another year." And then somebody else says, "Aha! Think so?" And then he proceeds to tear down the other person in his mind's eye. And his feelings of jealousy intensify to a point of vicious intent until they are released through the power of the 'evil eye'!

It's like the time we sent out one of our pamphlets with the heading "The Summit Lighthouse, a World Pillar." We sent it all over the country and one guy wrote back, "You say you're a world pillar. Well, I say you're not a world pillar." He said he was this high mucky muck from some big planet up there. (He actually wrote us this letter.) And then he said, "I've met with people in spaceships up in New York and they say you *were* a world pillar, but you'll never be a world pillar again!"

The point is, there's always somebody that's jealous of you. So don't be so foolish as to tell people all your wonderful things—what you can do or what you have done or how happy you are. There are people that are jealous of your happiness. Be smart and be silent. For silence is golden. Silence is golden because it will avoid the mass mind closing in on you.

There're many of you who are not aware of the evil power that can be directed through human eyes—not evil eyes from the standpoint of witchcraft or some spooky thing, but human beings that may be a white-haired old lady or a young gal that looks like a saint. You can't tell. Anybody can have an evil eye in the sense that they willfully use the power of their vision for evil.

And if they have it, whoever they are, it's because they have a momentum on the misuse of God's power through the eye. Now, this momentum carries over from one embodiment to the next. And it is used like a curse because it is always condemnatory in nature.

You see, people use the imaginations of their hearts and the power of vision to visualize sudden destruction upon others. When this is charged with intense feelings, it can deliver a wallop on the unsuspecting. And so it is, as the Bible says, that the wickedness of man was great in the earth, and that every imagination—i.e., the 'eye magic', or the 'eye imaging'—of his heart was only evil continually.[24]

Unless they are quickened by Christ, people are often jealous of the light and joy of others. And jealousy is what creates losses. People's jealousy directed at one another can cause calamity in their lives. People see someone and someone sees them, and then one person decides that he doesn't like it because the other person is successful. So he thinks inside, "I wish something would happen to him."

A lot of times it's a subconscious thought. Did you know that? It doesn't have to be a conscious thought. It can just be a subconscious feeling of "Well, I'm not that way. Why should he be that way? I don't have talent, good looks, money, success, and happiness, so why should he!"

RESPONSIBILITY: YOU PAY AS YOU GO

People forget that every thought that they think is their responsibility. They forget that if someone dies because they think a bad thought, they're accountable for that person's death—karmically accountable. And the Law will see to it that they pay back every jot and tittle.

People do not understand responsibility. They think they can get away with something in this universe. We get away with nothing! We're just kidding ourselves if we think we do. In reality, you pay as you go. Life is a cash-and-carry affair.

So go out and build constructive momentums instead of destructive momentums. And keep silent before people.

Some people say, "Well, I'm always out trying to talk about the Masters because I think that by talking about the Masters I'm going to build up the work"— you know, the movement.

Don't worry. Just lift up the Christ in your life. If you lift up the Christ in your life, you are going to draw all men to the Light.[25] Why, you can draw just as much with silence as you can with noise. Speaking doesn't mean anything. Speaking sometimes can detract.

You've heard the story about the man who was all ready to marry a gal until she opened her mouth.

And after she opened her mouth, he didn't want anything more to do with her; because, you know, we often show our ignorance by opening our mouth.

So what we want to do is develop silence and harmony and gratitude. You be grateful to God and you watch how you'll grow! One of the most neglected things in this world is being grateful for what heaven gives you. You just sit and be grateful sometimes. Try sitting for five or ten minutes and just thanking God for all the blessings he's poured out on your life. Try it sometime. Watch the change in your thoughts and the vibratory quality of your mind.

Well, for heaven's sake, the first thing that happens is you begin to realize that by thinking the wrong things most of the day, you're building wrong momentums. Build a wrong momentum and reap the rewards, which are certainly negative. Build a right momentum and reap the positive rewards: *To him that hath shall more be added. And from him that hath not shall be taken away even that which he hath.*

You say, "What an unfair thing!" My mother used to hear those words of Jesus and she used to say, "That's such a strange statement." And so many other people in the Christian church today have heard that statement and wondered about it.

Well, it's very simple when you view it as a momentum. "To him that hath a momentum..." In other words, if you start a momentum and you get a momentum going of doing anything, maybe for sixty days—in sixty days, then, you'll have a momentum and more will be added. Because the momentum itself will generate more of its kind. But supposing you don't ever start it—well, then you're going to have a sixty-day momentum on not starting. And you're going to have taken away the blessings you already have. And that's exactly what the teaching means.

So I think that some of us better start building momentums correctly, because they are the key that will make us masters of ourselves and our worlds. We can be like Saint Germain. We can be like Mother Mary. You can be anybody that you want to be and be like them, because you will see them as they are.[26]

Do you know that a lot of people look at God the wrong way? It's really frightening sometimes to think that human beings can look at God the way they look at him.

God is not a dictator. He doesn't sit up there on his throne and polish his halo. He's not a god sitting in an antiseptic corner of the universe saying, "I am holy. I am sprayed with chlorophyll," you know. "And all you people down there, you'd better get on the ball, or else!" He's not like Nero, fiddling while Rome burns.

God is God of all mercy and all justice. And he's got a representative right in your city—you! You're his emissary. You can communicate with him. You can talk to him. The channels of communication are open. Try it!

He says, "Bring ye all the tithes into the store-house . . . and prove me now herewith, saith the LORD of hosts, if I will not open you the windows of heaven and pour you out a blessing that there shall not be room enough to receive it."[27] God has said that. And that is a promise.

And so our failures to realize that promise come about because we lack the faith to accept it. And the lack of faith is the lack of momentum, because a momentum *is always* a momentum of faith. You believe in what you're doing and that's why you do it—or you accept your parents' or your teachers' or your employers' belief that what they are telling you to do will produce results. And by obedience you build a momentum. So it is when we follow the sound advice of the Ascended Masters.

Sometimes people look at our decree books and they say, "Those people—they sit there and they decree and they decree and they decree." Well, that's our momentum. We have a momentum on decreeing and we use it for positive world good. And it works. [28]

But I've seen people who have developed a decree momentum use it for negativity as well as positivity. You may be surprised when I say that.

In Wanamaker's department store in Philadelphia, a woman who had been decreeing for about thirty years became irritated with a salesclerk because she asked her to sign the same slip three or four times. The woman got irritated because she was almost going blind from diabetes. When she wrote her name down, she signed it in the wrong place. And the diabetes and the insistency of the salesclerk and the whole situation finally threw her and triggered in her an absolute tirade of anger, or what we would call a riptide.

And she took her fist and she raised it up with all of her thirty years' momentum of decreeing, and she slammed it down on the counter and she yelled out in Wanamaker's department store at the salesgirl. And the people that were in there thought a bomb had gone off because of the power that that woman had when she channeled her decree energy into anger. Do you see what I mean?

So you have to be very careful with the responsibility you have when you decree and pray a lot. Because when you decree and pray a lot, you have a more than ordinary contact with heaven—and if you turn around and say something to somebody, your words may come true so quick, you'll be really surprised.

So you be careful with the power you develop in decrees. You be careful with the powers of your spiritual momentums, because spiritual momentums can be used wrongly. And when they are, it becomes tantamount to black magic.

I want you to understand this law. Paul taught us the teaching of Jesus Christ, "Let not the sun go down upon your wrath," and you should obey it because it is for the protection of your soul.

You see, the Master Jesus was familiar with what the ancient Egyptians called the *ka,* the ka being that part of you which can go out of the physical body at night. It is sometimes referred to as the "astral body." And if you go to sleep at night and you retain in your consciousness a measure of anger against someone, the ka, ungoverned by the conscious discriminating Christ mind, can go out like a ghost of yourself, charged with feelings of anger or jealousy or even a murderous intent—a death wish on someone, either conscious or unconscious—and it will travel to the target and without restraint dump the entire load of hatred, as your momentum unchecked, on the doorstep of another's world.

I am telling you now that that anger can gather such a momentum of negative energy that it can be responsible for the death of another individual against whom you have directed that anger. And I'm telling you that to warn you *not* to do it. Because if you do it, you really will have to clean it up. Because you can cause people to have sickness, heart failure, and all kinds of problems—just because you hate them.

If you hate them in waking consciousness, when you're asleep the 'blind' ka—as the carrier of your desire momentum—will go out and do whatever the conscious mind willed it to do.

That's why Paul wrote to the faithful at Ephesus: "Let not the sun go down upon your wrath; neither give place to the devil." As translated in the Jerusalem

Bible, this reads: "Even if you are angry, you must not
sin: never let the sun set on your anger or else you will
give the devil a foothold [i.e., do not harbor the hatred
of the devil in your desire body or in the conscious or
subconscious planes of your being]."

The concept of the sun "going down" upon your
wrath is metaphorical. Not only does the sun go down
as you go into the realm of sleep and your wrath goes
out on the prowl, but also the Son, or the Light, 'goes
down' because it is eclipsed by your own negative
momentum consciously willed in life.

This teaching is further amplified:

"And grieve not the holy Spirit of God whereby ye
are sealed unto the day of redemption. Let all bitterness and wrath and anger and clamor and evil speaking
be put away from you, with all malice: And be ye kind
one to another, tenderhearted, forgiving one another,
even as God for Christ's sake hath forgiven you."[29]

And so we must learn to interpret the scriptures
and understand the scriptures as vital and living.
We're dealing with tremendous cosmic laws and principles. And when we use these principles correctly, we
will find out that no one is responsible for our rise or
fall except ourselves. Heaven has already willed it so—
that we shall be free. But it's up to us to make it a
determinate fact by building a spiritual momentum.

FAITH BUILDS MOMENTUMS

Why, a momentum is the most wonderful thing
in the world when correctly used. Your momentum is
what will bring ya. You know what I mean? That's
what brung ya, and it'll bring ya a long way, too! But
without it, I have very little hope for anyone.

Why, we could bring thousands of people into a
hall or a tent or a cathedral and talk to them about the
Teachings of the Ascended Masters. But if they don't

have a proper spiritual momentum, those people are going to go out and they're going to lose their souls and, in many cases, become castaways.[30]

It's like the parable of the sower—only those with good ground and grounding in the practice of precepts learned, having a fallow field of consciousness and a lightful heart, do hear and receive and bring forth the fruit of the Word.[31]

There are many reasons why you need to master the art of completion—the fulfillment of a cycle from the beginning of Alpha to the ending of Omega. And "train up a child in the way he should go"—to always finish what he starts, taking care to start only those projects which are practical for him to finish—"and when he is old, he will not depart from it."[32]

Children and new souls on the path of discipleship need practical experience in the art and science of momentum building. This is why the Guru/chela relationship under the Great White Brotherhood is action/performance oriented. Can the individual cut through consistently with constancy in fine or foul weather, through the ups and downs of karmic and emotional upheaval?

If he has a momentum on striving, he will. But if his mentors or he himself has allowed his life to be a series of starts and stops, erratic schedules and doing exactly what he feels like doing whenever he feels like it—this person will simply not have the momentum of will, desire, wisdom or love to keep on keeping on when the going gets tough.

The successful disciple must bring to the altar a successfully internalized momentum of self-discipline that is the cumulative virtue of centuries of overcoming the many obstacles to Divine Selfhood—else he must apprentice himself to a wise masterbuilder who has such a momentum and learn from him just what temple building is all about.

Now we begin to see that spiritual momentums must be garnered ahead of time—before the Lord comes suddenly into his temple—your temple.[33] The momentum is the greatest thing you can build, because whatever you want—I don't care what it is—you can get it with a momentum.

It's like the old story from Tolstoy.[34] It seems there was a bishop who sailed out to a little island where there lived three old hermits. Their sole prayer was: "Thou art Three; we are three—have mercy on us!" And oh how happy they were to see him. At last they were visited by a real live bishop.

And so he had come to teach them more acceptable prayers, explaining that theirs was not customary in that it suggested a coequality with the Trinity. Through one whole day of practice and repetition, he at last taught them to recite the Lord's Prayer. Finally, as it was getting dark, he took his leave and sailed in a little boat to the ship that was waiting for him.

Long after the hermits and their island had disappeared over the horizon, as he was sitting alone at the stern, the bishop saw a radiant light following the ship. And he couldn't imagine what in the world it was—not a boat or a bird or a fish or a man. But as it came closer he recognized three little figures moving toward him. It was the hermits, all gleaming white, running hand in hand across the water!

When they reached the ship, they began to say with one voice: "We have forgotten your teaching, servant of God. As soon as we stopped repeating it, it was gone from us. Teach us again."

The bishop crossed himself and said, "Bless you, my children. Go back to your island. Your own prayer will reach the Lord. It is not for me to teach you. Pray for us sinners." And so they glided back across the sea to their island.

They were walking on the water!

By developing the correct momentum, we won't need anything else. The correct momentum can work through your present prayers, by the way. Your methodology doesn't have to be according to our tradition. It can be according to your own church's traditions. It can be according to *your* traditions. It can be according to *no* traditions. It doesn't matter. If it works, if it is a momentum that is constructive and will draw forth the hoped-for response from heaven, why worry?

Archangel Michael tells the story. . . and I'd like to have "The Navy Hymn" played that they sing at Annapolis—"Eternal Father, Strong to Save." I'm going to ask Archangel Michael to charge this hymn with his radiation. Of course, it's already there but I'm still going to ask it of him so that you'll get a special blessing from this captain of the LORD's host who, you remember, appeared to Joshua.[35] I want you to hear the moving strains of the melody and then I'm going to tell you the story about it.

Go ahead. "Let 'er rip!"

You know where I got that, don't you? It was over in Soldier's Field in Chicago. They had the place just jammed for a great big ecumenical conference, and they'd asked the Methodist bishop to stand up in this tower which was high above the field. And the people looked like ants from that tower. And he was up in there, and he had a red and a green light. And they told him, "As soon as the green light comes on, you start to pray."

So the red light was on and, of course, the green light didn't come on. And he sat there, and they pushed the button for the green light but it never activated it. So he sat there and sat there and sat there till he was almost beside himself looking at the people, and they were all looking up at him. And no prayer.

So finally, he saw one little figure like an ant going across the field, and this little figure kept getting closer. And the guy got to the bottom of the tower, and he couldn't communicate by telephone—all systems had failed and the red light was still on. And so he yells, "Bishop," he says, "Let 'er rip!"

So, let 'er rip!

[Pianist begins playing "The Navy Hymn" and Mark stops her at the beginning of the fourth verse.]

You got that charge at that one point there, didn't you? That's why I stopped you. Because I saw it come down.

But, then, you have to understand that you're dealing now with a hymn that Archangel Michael was given by the LORD to infire him with the faith to overcome in his darkest hour of trial.

Do you know what an archangel is? Well, it was just last week that Archangel Michael told me what he was. He told me, "We are architects." That's what the word *arc* means: it's speaking of the seven archangels arcing the Light from God to man through their pure hearts. See? They're architects whom God uses in the drafting of plans for various projects in the universe—arcing God's Light to outline the blueprint for God's will, which we then may choose by our free will to follow.

People think that angels and archangels don't do much, you know. They think they're just functionaries, like a plenipotentiary. Well, what really takes place is that in addition to all their other duties initiating souls on the path of personal Christhood on the seven rays, they work as architects. And being universal architects is a full-time job in itself, I can assure you! An architect is a tremendous individual. Did you know that? Do you realize what an architect is on a big project?

An architect's a very important, key person. He's responsible for putting everything together. So an architect or an archangel or an archeia (feminine complement of an archangel) is a very important being, you see.

Now, Archangel Michael was not always an archangel. Millions of years ago he was only an elemental, a nature spirit. And after he became an elemental, he accomplished one of those unusual feats described in a book, supposedly by Saint Germain, in which the Master explains how the elementals can bridge the gap and come through the human kingdom into the angelic kingdom.

So Archangel Michael made it. He not only got to be embodied in human form like we are, but he also climbed up the ladder of hierarchical initiation into the angelic realm. And there he got promoted, reached the rank of captain, finally became an archangel, and was made that great prince of the archangels who confronted Daniel the prophet. [36]

Now, a lot of people think that these great beings just happened, that God—out of the whimsy of his mind—suddenly sat there and said, "I'll make me an archangel." So he says, "Alright, boom!" One of these flowers or a snowflake or something turns into an archangel.

Well, it doesn't work that way. Those people— I'm speaking about the archangels (in one respect they are just like people—after all, Joshua saw Archangel Michael as a man in the same way Daniel saw Archangel Gabriel [37])—they start out on the bottom rung of the ladder and they just keep on; and the members of the angelic realm are promoted, too, just like we are.

And that's why the universe is so big. That's why we have the 'borders' of infinity—it just keeps on going. Everybody is intended to find his place in the sun. People are supposed to go up higher and higher and higher and higher spiritually. They're not supposed to stop.

Wouldn't life be terribly uninteresting if we had no challenges? My present challenge is here in Colorado Springs, but I don't expect to be forever in Colorado Springs. I don't expect to be forever here in this world. Do you? 'Be kind of silly! It'd really be kind of silly because there are so many more wonderful places in the universe—beautiful places—and there are greater opportunities.

So, Archangel Michael was on another world before he ever was an archangel and he was winning his victory. And during the period when he was being absolutely sawn asunder by events—he just couldn't hardly live—when he was face to face with the greatest, most crucial trial of his entire career and winning his victory, this melody came to him: [Mark hums the melody of "The Navy Hymn."]

When you hear it, you begin to feel that tremendous power in the universe! There's a current of power in that song. Do you realize it? It's got *power* in it that overcomes, you see. It's faith—is what it is. That song is a song of faith. And through that great song of faith, the radiation of Archangel Michael is anchored into a person.

So you sing that song and you get that feeling and you really grow. And it's faith that will enable you to build a momentum.

I wanted you to have this Lost Teaching of beloved Jesus. I wanted you to understand it, because it'll make you a different person. It's faith that overcometh all things. But faith is developed by momentum.

Layer upon layer upon layer upon layer,
The giant redwood trees grow and grow and grow.
With the cycles of the years
And the passage of time,
We can all master events and circumstances
And make our lives sublime.

So let's do it!

Chapter Five

KAL-DESH:
THE INTERMINGLING
OF TIME AND SPACE

Kal-Desh:
The Intermingling of Time and Space

WE would speak about time, *kala* in the Sanskrit, and space, *desha* in the Sanskrit,[1] and of the intermingling of time and space. And we would speak of it in terms of past history and the future, or that which is to be, and the fulfillment of the cycles of life.

EVERY ONE OF US A TEACHER

For, not too long ago we were sitting in a high chair, drooling out our oatmeal upon our chin. And now we are here, quite a ways from that particular sorry state, and we are supposed to have a greater knowledge and a higher concept of what life is all about so that we can teach our children—as that old song goes, "Mother, teach thy children. . ."

Every one of us is a teacher. But we sometimes forget that we have this role to play. We sometimes think of ourselves as someone who is the victim of tyrants—as though life itself were a tyrant, as though our teachers were tyrants, as though everywhere we turned everything were in a tyrannical state and we ought to rebel against it.[2]

Then we suddenly stop, and we begin to realize what I began to realize long ago: that the meanest teacher I ever had in school—my Latin teacher—was, in reality, the one who taught me the most.

We ought to ask ourselves this question: Do we really want a sweet and beautiful personality that will pat us on the back and say, "Yes, you have learned all your lessons, Johnny. Mary, you know everything. You're just wonderful!" when in reality we're down in the D class? Is that what we want?

Shouldn't we look up to those who may seem to us to be tyrants by reason of their diligence and desire to chasten our souls, as God himself does? Shouldn't we look up to them as our most dedicated instructors, who teach us the very best of life that's free but whose precepts are meaningless to us unless we accept them?

And so we rebel no more, but we welcome the chastening rod that speaks in the Lord's name and says to us, "Whom I love, I chasten."[3]

THINKING IN TERMS OF THE HEAD AND THE HEART

Let us stop for a moment, and let us begin to think in terms of thought. Yes, think in terms of thought. What is thought? We have heard of the ancient Thoth, the Atlantean, the great master Thoth.[4] And we come to realize, if we pause to think upon the relationship of words, that *thought* and *Thoth* are perhaps one— that the word *thought* may even have sprung from his name. But whether or not it did is not so important as the fact that we are endowed with the capacity to think.

Yet, this great think tank that we have here [pointing to the brain] and this great think tank that we have here [pointing to the heart] are not always functioning together as they are supposed to. For, you see, man is supposed to think both with his head and his heart. And what happens is that he separates the heart and the head, and we find that the heart, expressing the feelings of man, leads the head.

And so, in almost every case where you are dealing with motivation—for example, in the field of salesmanship—and you want to sell someone something, you appeal to their head and you say, "Well, this particular product is going to do you a lot of good," but you don't get very enthusiastic about it. And you cite some facts and figures and graphs, and everyone looks unimpressed as though nothing has happened, and really nothing has.

And then, after a while you begin to get the idea. You get the message of the heart. You begin to wax enthusiastic. And in your enthusiasm you are creating an infectious feeling which is easily picked up at the emotional level by anyone.

And what is emotion? It is E—*energy*—in motion. You have created a feeling. And wherever there is a feeling created, good or bad, the feeling will lead the head—and, in most people, it will win every time.

So, if the husband is thinking with his head and the wife is feeling with her heart, the wife will have her way. But if the reverse is true, strange as it may seem, he will have his way. And this is always the case. It's the heart that leads.

But, in reality, it is not intended to be just that way. We are supposed to learn to think with our heart and govern our feelings so that we are not always carried away by the tides of emotion. But when we are able to feel with our head and think with our heart and do both in both places, then we have a great duality going for us and a masterful situation where we, if we will it so, can be in total command of ourselves.

We are our own man or our own woman. We are able to think the way God wants us to think—to think with our head, to think with our heart, to feel with our head and to feel with our heart. For we can learn to do this, as difficult as it may seem.

THE FIVE SENSES AND SEVEN CHAKRAS REVEAL REALITY

Now, in connection with thought, I am going to ask you to think with me as we begin to explore the great sphere of reality that is made known to us through the avenues of our five senses.

Our five senses telegraph to our inner self what is taking place. They reveal the world to us, but they reveal only a part of it. Therefore, unless we have the endowment of the quickened capacities of the higher senses, we cannot penetrate the totality of the world within.

And so we come to the place where we are going to climb the thirty-three steps of the spinal ladder to the place of the skull, Golgotha, where the Christ is crucified between the two malefactors[5]—the anterior and posterior lobes of the pituitary gland.

Now, you think about that for a moment. And if you *can't* solve the mystery of it, then decide that you're going to search further until you *can* solve the mystery of it, because it is filled with significance for each individual. And it correlates to the blossoming of the spiritual flowers on the spinal stalk. These are the great spiritual centers (chakras) culminating in the thousand-petaled lotus of light, right here at the crown of the head where the pulsation of the crystal cord can be observed in the newborn babe.

When the thousand-petaled lotus of light opens up, it reveals the whole universe to man. There is absolutely nothing hidden from one's eyes when the crown chakra is opened, but only the full penetration of the inward man reaching out and perceiving all things in the light of just what those things in actuality are.

Now, fortunately or unfortunately, many people like to be very pragmatic. They like to think in terms of results right now. And this, of course, can be very good. It has its value. But sometimes it does not give a clear picture of what has just happened to us or what is about to happen to us. We're interested not in a bubble that's floating in a level that is almost infinite in its horizontal plane, but we want to know the relationship of this bubble to the plane, to the surface whose incline we are measuring.[6]

Similarly, unless we have some arbitrary markings upon the scale of our judgments, our values will be warped because either we will see through the eyes of contemporary society or we will read—and read as other people read—but never read to think beyond what other people are thinking. We will be achieving what is known as mediocrity.

I cannot believe that it is God's will that man, endowed with his image, is intended to think in terms of mediocrity. We are intended to think big!—to think gigantic thoughts but to tether it all to reality. And this reality has already been established for us. We are not in a world where reality does not exist.

There are those who have come to this planet and who have had the oatmeal drooling down their chins just as we did, who today are spiritual Masters—masters of themselves and of their destiny. Once they walked amongst us and today they are still in contact with us.

If your spiritual centers are whirling with light— those little transformers (seven chakras) that God has all wrapped up inside of you—you may feel the cosmic energy flowing through you when in the presence of one of the Masters or while listening to their dictations on tape. It will pass through you and you'll know it.

If your centers are closed, you may not feel the Master Jesus' vibration, but you'll still hear his words and benefit from his instruction. And you'll understand some of it, I hope, and the great significance of his Lost Teaching brought to our remembrance in these times of testing.

LIVING IN THE MIST AND IN THE CRYSTAL

So now we come to the point of time, which we will deal with first, this *kal*—this infinite calculation of the finite.

Because, you see, all we can ever do with a piece of string that represents all known history is break it up into segments. We call them years. We take this piece of string and we arbitrarily make our mark on it. We say this is such and such a year, and this is such and such a year. Two thousand years ago, Christ was born. We put that on the string and we call it A.D., the year of our Lord.

Well, when we come to the end of the string, we come to the end of history today; then we take another string. We don't tie them together. We just stretch this one out in a line continuing in the same direction because it's forward moving. Our history has met our present, and the future is unknown.

Now we realize that we really don't know just what is going to happen because, as Kahlil Gibran in his book *The Prophet* says, "Life, and all that lives, is conceived in the mist and not in the crystal. And who knows but a crystal is mist in decay?"[7]

So then, you see, there are some people who have this little idea in their brains. They say to themselves, "Well, what I *think* is not so important, it's what I *do* that counts." But I'm going to tell you that what you think *is* important, and what you do is also important. And I'm going to show it to you by Kahlil Gibran's statement.

Let us take the man who thinks the evil thought of adultery. According to the scriptures, a man who looks at a woman with lust in his heart has already committed adultery.[8] Remember this now. Jesus said it: if he thinks it in his heart, he has already committed the act—that is to say, in his heart.

So, a man said to me one day, "Well, it doesn't make any difference if I commit adultery, because I've already thought it and therefore I'm committed to it." I wish to prove to you that this is where the man is wrong in his thinking.

We live in the mist and we live in the crystal. The mist is the state of thought wherein we begin the thought processes that may or may not eventuate in the crystal. When Judas Iscariot was thinking that he was going to betray Christ, it was still in the mist. But the Master read his thought and said to him, "That which thou doest, do quickly."[9] And having received the sop, he went out immediately and betrayed him.

Now, when he betrayed him, that was crystallization. The mist of thought had crystallized and it could not be changed. It was the unalterable act. His fantasy had become fact. It was a fait accompli. The moment the deed was done, it was history. Thought had passed through the nexus and by the lever of the will became the action indelibly stamped on akasha. Karma.

No matter what deed you contemplate, as long as it is not crystallized into action, there is still hope that you will avoid the karma of deeds that will accrue to your life record *only* when the act is committed.

Wise is the man who does not allow himself to fall into the pit of wrong thought in the first place. But if he find himself in wrong thought, wise is he who will quickly correct himself before it becomes a recorded deed in the second place. As the Master said, "You can't help it if a bird lands on your head, but you don't have to let him build a nest in your hair!"

And that's the whole idea for all of us. To exercise control over ourselves is to realize that we live in the mist of thought, which we must tether to Truth and Righteousness before a momentum becomes "bigger than both of us" and topples the energies of both thought and feeling into words and deeds we later regret.

When we come to the realm of thought crystallization, it is far better to watch our thoughts before they manifest in the arena of action, because the karma (consequences) of thought is still not as great as the karma (consequences) of deeds. For the karma of deeds affects the lives of other people more physically and therefore often irrevocably; whereas with the karma of thought, though the effect may be more psychological, it can be healed and sealed and the damage undone "before it is too late," as they say—before the die is cast.

The fact is that transmutation is as a rule easier on the mental plane than on the physical—but not always, as in the case of mental cruelty and emotional abuse. But then, these are also the result of acts.

As long as we are dealing with just our own private thought—although it still may be error, often carrying a 'thought karma' proportionate to its duration—it can be pulled back, our desire purified, and the plot sequence taken out of consciousness by our own free will and the correct application of cosmic law.

Now, it's a wonderful thing that there is hope for people after they've erred. And it's a wonderful thing that there's hope for people before they've erred. But I still think that an ounce of prevention, as my mother told me, is worth a pound of cure. Don't you?

LEARNING THE LESSONS OF OUR PAST HISTORY

Now then, enough with the ordinary human consciousness of just doing things. Let's look backwards and forwards in history and go to the very foundations of our own soul's evolution. We can go back to the hanging gardens of Babylon. We can see the great tower of Babel. We can still perceive, in thought, Sodom and Gomorrah.

We can experience the past, as Risë Stevens did in the old amphitheater in Athens. While she was singing Orpheo's aria of lamentation at the foot of the Acropolis, the scene bathed in moonlight, she "lost all touch with reality" and felt herself in ancient Greece, "mentally and physically" living a former life in which she had acted on that very stage. Later she wrote about the incident, saying she finished the aria as in a trance and "fell prostrate on the body of Euridice." It took five minutes of thunderous applause to bring her back to the present. [10]

We *have* lived in the past and we *have* lived in the present. And we *have* also lived in the future that has become our past and our present. But our tomorrows cannot be any better for us than our todays and our yesterdays unless we transcend both and become the masters of our fate.

Since we have made our home in the past, the past has its effect upon our lives. In fact, unless we learn the alchemy of change, our past becomes our present *and* our future! And we may be its prisoner, and all we will have to look forward to in life are the replays which we ourselves project upon the screen of life—when we ought to cast ourselves in new and futuristic roles.

Thus, the present and the future can only be a clean white page if we clear our world of the causes we ourselves set in motion yesterday. If we don't, as sure as God made green apples, they will come home to roost as today's or tomorrow's "Surprise!"

Yes, yesterday's karmic involvements produce sideshows and side effects that have a magnetism all their own. Their force, or forcefield, can be felt; they have both weight and gravity. Call it astrology or fate or what you will, the fact remains that all too often we allow the effects of causes we and we alone created (and which we therefore are obliged to uncreate) to deter us from center stage and the spotlight of our own I AM Presence, who expects us to perform well—both in the mist and in the crystal.

Most of us like to think only in terms of this particular embodiment, this life. We like to think of our mother and our father and the old homestead and the good old days. Some people in this room go back to the horse-and-buggy days, and some remember the Model T and some the Model A. Some, of course, have a little different background—they only remember television! But we find in the record and the memory of the psyche that all of us go back somewhere into the distant past.

And some of us can go back farther than others. We can go back to the ruins and the records of the Sumerian civilization beyond the pale of current Mideast crises. We can go back to the building of the ancient pyramids and to the moment of the carving of the Sphinx.

We can go back through our soul memories to many countries and many climes; and the recordings stored in the unconscious, written in our "inward parts,"[11] as Jeremiah tells us, reveal to us many things.

And so, we can read and learn the lessons of our own past history and see to it, if we will it so, that our history does not repeat itself by our neglectfulness in studying the chemistry of our hearts and the elements that make up our actions, reactions, and the unfortunate distractions that impel us by the karma of desire from the highway of our God.

Some of us walked where Jesus walked. Some of us can literally remember Golgotha. Some of us can remember other times and other places. We have participated in various enterprises throughout history. Some people here were in the War of the Roses. Some remember King Henry VIII. Some sailed the seas with Christopher Columbus. Others, of course, have been paupers. Some have been princes. And some have really been kings and queens.

WE ARE THE SOLE AUTHORS OF OUR DESTINY

We have been many things. And we have not always been on top of the heap, nor have we always been at the bottom. Sometimes we've been in the middle. And sometimes we've been caught in between. We've been through lots of different situations in our past lives. And our future will be exactly what we make it. In fact, the script is already written. Only we can unwrite it, for we are the sole authors of our destiny.

This is why the Masters are so interested in our state of consciousness. They want us to be able to probe all of the past, to learn its lessons dispassionately, and then to look to the future with hope and joy born of the idea that God has placed the pen in our hands: We can rewrite the past upon the pages of the future!

I think it's a great tragedy that most of us just live from day to day. I mean, we get up each day and we say, "I wonder just what this day is going to bring forth, in time, for me. What is it going to bring forth?"

"Well," we say, "I don't know."

Isn't it a tragedy that we have so little governing power over our lives that we say we don't know? Especially when at subconscious levels we know the end from the beginning, because we've seen it all before—before we ever took embodiment in this life.

Don't you think that when God said to man, "Be fruitful and multiply and replenish the earth and subdue it, take dominion over the creatures of the sea, the air, and the earth!"—in other words, "Rule the earth!"—don't you think he intended him to exercise control over himself and his environment through careful planning and conscientious striving—even probing the mysteries of self and science?

It's a great travesty of the Law that we have not availed ourselves of the promises of self-mastery foreordained in the covenants and commandments of God. Why, we are not even masters enough of the fates to know, to be, and to determine what is going to happen to us in a single day, any day, of our lives! Instead of making things happen, we just sit back and let the future decide itself—instead of realizing that we *are* our past, our present, and our future.

Therefore, no matter what we do, we are deciding to be, to remain as we were, to appear, and to appear to change but to change not at all—to seem to be, but to be not—to feel, taste, smell, and still to see or not to see. Alas, the choices are infinite, but we are still finite and can only outpicture a few. Let them be wise in the mist so we will not have to undo the crystal—molecule by molecule.

WE CAN PROBE THE MYSTERY OF SELF

Must we forever think the future is a great mystery and that we can never pierce the veil and divest the mystery of its mystery? Dear hearts, the future will only be the mystery *we* make it or the mystery *we* unveil.

Well, we can probe the mystery of self, if we want to. Through the Masters' Teachings, through spiritual insight, we can look ahead. And not only can we look ahead, but we can plan ahead. We can make things happen.

There are two kinds of people: the kind who make things happen and the kind who watch them happen. Now, we're interested in being able to make things happen. Is this wrong? Does God blame us for making things happen? On the contrary, he blames us for just watching them happen. Because when we watch them happen, we are not participating at all in the constructivism that lies as a coiled spring within ourselves.

Oh, you say, you don't have any power within yourself. Well, I'm here to assure you that if you follow the true Teachings of Jesus taught by the Ascended Masters, and if you follow them long enough, the Teachings themselves will prove to you beyond question that you do have the power *and the ultimate power* to make things happen in your world. And when you prove to yourself that you can do it, why then you will see that you can govern your life from now on. And your future can be tailor-made just the way you want it!

But, of course, people will always come up with this question: "Well, how will I want it? And how will I know how I want it? I don't even know how I want my life to be today, let alone tomorrow and the next day and the next."

But, you see, dear heart, you have already created your yesterdays, your todays, and your tomorrows. And unless and until you get in the driver's seat and become the charioteer in your own race against karma, you are not going to be first at the finish line. Your own human creation may very well beat you to the punch!

THE PROBLEM OF DESIRE

Well, let's talk about giving someone a million dollars. You give them a million dollars and they're overwhelmed with the gift, but they don't know what to do with it. Of course, everybody says, "Well, I know what I'd do if I had a million dollars." And they can think of all kinds of things they would do with that money. But, you see, it isn't quite that easy.

Now, I can't speak from the experience of having had someone give me a million dollars, but I have had people give me gifts in the course of my life. And I have had the experience of walking into stores and really not knowing just how to spend a certain amount of money that I had in my pocket that I thought I ought to spend.

But you know what the biggest problem was? It was the problem of so many wants, so many desires that it became a question of: "What shall I select that I can buy with this amount of money, because I don't have enough to buy everything I see? What will I pick out? What can I buy?"

And the ideas would come so thick and fast, it was like a blizzard. You know, you're in a snowstorm and you're batted from one side of the store to the other. And in the end you go home with the money in your pocket—yet it was burning a hole in your pocket when you came into the store—and you say, "Well, I guess I'd rather have the money than anything," because you can't settle on any one thing that you really want.

This shows that man has a real problem. His real problem is that he needs to learn to school his desire, to master this chaotic condition of the mind where he cannot settle upon one particular thing that he feels is most important in his life.

I think, then, that all of us should stop for a while this business of just thinking randomly in what we will call the stream of consciousness. Most people think in the stream-of-consciousness mode. And do you know that the planetary stream of consciousness is muddied from the refuse of human thought and feeling that has been dumped into it from all over the world?

Because of this pollution we have to learn to protect our aura and our astral body against the impinging negative thoughts of the world—those "arrows of outrageous fortune" that beset Hamlet. We have to learn to upraise the shield of the mind in order to shut them out of our consciousness so that we can build great positive passions for what God wants us to have for ourselves.

Otherwise, you see, we cannot even receive the gifts that God has to give to us. He's got all kinds of gifts to give to us and he's right ready to hand them to us now. But we can't receive them until we have purified our desires. Do you understand this?

The desire is important. But, you see, desire is a key which may be understood through the esoteric interpretation of the two syllables of the word: *desire*. *De* stands for your divinity—the *De*ity of your selfhood—in other words, your Mighty I AM Presence. And what is *sire?* It means lord, the term whereby we address the Son of God. Put them together and you get God and the Son of God:* *Desire*.

Another way of looking at this word and the cocreative power it conveys is to realize that *Deity sires*— begets or brings into being—the Son of God out of the depths of his own desiring.

And if you want to understand the science of Being, you should know that your I AM Presence through the "Sire"—your own beloved Christ Self— bestows upon you through the power of the spoken Word the same power to re-create yourself in the image of Higher Consciousness by which you came forth from Elohim in the beginning!

*or the Mighty I AM Presence and the Holy Christ Self

"Let there be Light!" [12]
This is the original fiat
   of the LORD who made heaven and earth.
"Let there be Light!"
Say it now with determination.
With the deep desiring of your heart.
With the Peace-commanding presence
   of your Christ Self.

"Let there be Light!"
Say it into the teeth of every problem
   and temptation.
Say it in your mind and in the most secret secrets
   of your heart.
Say it in your desires and in the musings
   of your soul.

"Let there be Light!"
Say it for loved ones.
Use this divine decree to heal the sick—
   to challenge evildoers and to bring order
   out of the chaos of global crisis.
Speak it in the eye of God's whirlwind
   and in the center of his fury and
   when elemental forces rampage in fire and flood.
Speak it on the shores of life,
   to your beloved and your children
   when they are happy and carefree
   and when they are bowed down
   by the void of noncaring, noncreativity.
And when Darkness covers the land
   and the face of the earth is consumed
   with war and plague and famine and death,
   say to the whole earth and to the Sun:
   Let there be Light!

"Let there be Light!"
Speak it in the dark night of despair
   and in the morning's light of joy.

Speak it to thy God who loves thee
   and shall love thee evermore,
   who says to thee even in this moment of eternity:
   "Let there be Light!"

Give answer, O my soul.
Tell Him thou hast heard.
He longeth for thy confirmation...
   "And there was Light!"

Yes, it was desire and the spoken Word that struck the first note of cosmos, and it will be your desire as God's desire in you yoked with the command to Light that will strike the true chord of your identity.

So, what have we got to do? We have got to learn that we are acting creatively as God acts creatively, that we are co-creators with him of our destiny and that by purifying our thoughts—the offspring of our minds—we will be siring a true and noble lineage made in the image of our Christ. And then we will actually produce in our world what we want to produce.

Yes, the thought that you create is the offspring of your mind. And the way you create it is the same way that Leonardo da Vinci created. You have got to learn how to create. And this requires the purification of both the mind and the heart.

But first we must bring our desire and our desire body into alignment with the desire of God. We must study what Deity sires, what the Creator creates, and then pattern our designs after the heavenly patterns. We must study the lost Word and pattern our speech after his speech, as it is written: "The heavens declare the glory of God; and the firmament sheweth his handywork. Day unto day uttereth speech, and night unto night sheweth knowledge."*

---

*"The heavens declare the glory of God, the vault of heaven proclaims his handiwork; day discourses of it to day, night to night hands on the knowledge." Ps. 19:1, 2, Jerusalem Bible translation.

De-signs are the Deity's signature on every component of his creation—every leaf, flower and star. And, do you know something? You also sign your name to your creations—just like a famous designer—because every thought and feeling, motive and momentum contains the microscopic signet of your molecular and electronic blueprint. You can never deny your creations, whether human or divine, just as you cannot stamp out your etchings in the crystal unless you learn the alchemy of change.

THE VIOLET FIRE AND THE CREATIVE FIAT

It's the violet fire! You've got to get the violet fire—both to create what you want and to uncreate what you don't want. And that's what Jesus and Saint Germain and El Morya sent us here to do. To teach you how to use the violet fire. And that's exactly what we're going to do.

But don't skip over first principles: The body should be kept clean, because a clean body breeds clean thought. Whatever you feed the mind should be glorious, should be miraculous, should be beautiful, should be wise, should be comforting to humanity, should, as with scientific precision, produce something good in the world.

Do you see how important it is that you grasp this thought? Because through this thought you can purify your own concepts and then, you see, this world of time becomes a world where you can step from the present into the space of the past.

And soon you can learn to move through the realm of ideation where ideas are being born and then conveyed along the corridor of the mind, where they take on thought and feeling modes just before they thread the needle of the drive and the shuttle of action.

You can learn the laws of spiritual alchemy to transmute by violet fire the base metals of your human consciousness into the refined gold of the divine.

Well, you may think that you can't change the past. Because it's the crystal. So, for the time being step over here into the mist and experiment with the laws of change that can change the future.

It doesn't matter what you have been in the past—how weak or worrisome you've been, how you've frittered and failed, or what you have or haven't discovered. I'm interested in awakening within you the realization that the power of God in yourself has every answer that you need for every human problem.

I don't care what that problem is! God has the answer. And the answer, of course, can best be conveyed if we go back to what Jesus actually taught and said to the inner circle of his disciples and what he's saying to us today. For example, we have illustrated here in symbolic form the violet transmuting flame [pointing to the violet flame surrounding the lower figure in the Chart; see Chapter 13] and soon we're going to be giving creative fiats called decrees with that violet flame.

If you can understand the Chart of Your Real Self, you can understand the Almighty One individualized and personified in your Beloved I AM Presence. You can understand its relationship to the Christ of your being, the one anointed with the Light of the Son of God. And you can understand the relationship of your soul (which, while in embodiment, occupies the relative position of the lower figure) to your Higher Self and the I AM THAT I AM.

So I'm just about ready to give you as complete and thorough an understanding of that whole kingdom of God within you as you'll get anywhere. And when I do you'll be as thrilled as the day you were born in God. Because it'll put you in that go position to be what you were and what you still are: a co-creator with God.

So hang on to your hats because the mysteries of God are so wonderful they'll just blow away all your old thinking caps—and not only you, but your mind and your thought/feeling modes will be truly born again in the encounter with the Universal Christ.

THE HUMAN ANIMAL RE-CREATES HIMSELF

Robert Louis Stevenson said, "The world is so full of a number of things, I'm sure we should all be as happy as kings." [13] But we aren't, are we?

Look around you on the street as people walk up and down. Park your car sometime—or park your carcass in your car—and as you sit there, just look at the people's faces. And tell me if you don't think that's entertaining.

Why, I remember that in Sutton, Nebraska, one time during World War II, I went down to the main street of the town, and as I walked down the street in my military uniform, everybody in town who happened to be parked along the street was looking at me. Now, I wasn't just embarrassed or self-conscious—they actually were looking.

So I decided to get into one of the cars and sit there, too. And so I sat there, and as I was sitting in one of these cars looking at the people, I took note of the faces of the people coming by. And I realized that this was really a very entertaining situation. It was a substitute for going to the movies. I could study the lines and expressions of their faces, read the records of their past lives—and of this life—and learn why people do the things they do.

Then after a while, the lookers-on went into the restaurant. They had a cup of coffee and some sandwiches, and they relaxed a little bit after they'd had their entertainment.

Well, it's really interesting when you stop and think of just how people function. The human animal has become just that—an animal in the zoo on exhibit. Because no higher image has been set before him as a goal or standard. So he unknowingly re-creates himself daily after the image of the earthly creature.

I cannot believe that Almighty God, who framed this universe and made this beautiful earth and all the stars and planets out in space, ever intended the creation that he put here to take dominion over this planet to function the way they are functioning today. In fact, I don't guess at it: I know that they're not supposed to be the kind of people they are today.

We're not supposed to have war. We're not supposed to have human greed. We're not supposed to have unkindness between people. We're not supposed to have bad motives, we're supposed to have good motives. And we're supposed to have good movies instead of bad ones coming out of Hollywood.

But in many cases we don't have either good motives or good movies! And as a result, we often don't have either good messages or good momentums in the media as a positive creative force in society. And this, too, is our responsibility. For the mist and the crystal are all right there on film passing to the frames of consciousness that then frame the actions of our lives.

Wherever man is, man creates. And the manifestation is the projection of someone's self upon the minds of other 'selfs'—or elfs, as the case may be. And failure is everywhere around us, but the trick is we must much more abound and surround our defeats

with the good feats of our faith and the feets of
Victory's legions marching!

Of course, many more people love the Beatles
than love Christ—so the Beatles tell us. But somehow
or other, I don't believe that. Because I know I don't
love the Beatles. I may love their souls, but I certainly
don't love the Beatles. Nor do I love their phonograph
records.

And I don't love to stick a hypodermic needle in
my arm in order to give me a kick! In fact, all I have to
do is look up and I already have my kick for the day
and for all the days to come. Because if you look up at
your Presence—once you've learned to look up to your
God Presence—and realize that that is the only part of
yourself that is absolutely real, then you're going to
look back and you're going to say, "Well, I guess when
I was a baby I hadn't yet realized all that God wanted
me to be"—that oatmeal again and the toodle that
comes toddling along.

By gosh, we needed some support in those days or
we fell flat on our faces! And then we had to learn to
take our little hands and put them on the desk and
take our little fingers and learn to hold a pencil and
write. Then we had to take the beatings in the school-
yard that many of the children take. Then we had to go
through the fear of a beating at home if the report card
wasn't up to the standards that Father and Mother
thought it should be! And all kinds of experiences.

We were exposed to theft, where people tried to
induce us to steal in the dime stores. We were exposed
to pornographic pictures and drug paraphernalia.
We've had all kinds of struggles toward morality,
toward decency, toward God. We live in a time when
everybody's pulled this way and then they're pulled
that way. And sometimes people don't know which
way to go.

Some people have had no experience in the Church. Some people have had no experience with God. Other people have had a lot of interesting experiences with God—enough so that they're turned off by the Church or else they've been burned off. And they don't exactly like the idea of some of the pastors trying to tell them if they don't be good, they're going to go to Hades and burn forever on some kind of a spit—roasted like a turkey on Thanksgiving Day!

I can't accept this idea because I know that God doesn't intend to do this to anybody—simply because, as a father, I wouldn't do it to my own children.[14] And I'm sure that I'm not better than God, you see.

The Second Coming of Christ

We've talked a little about time and the stream of time and ourselves floating down the stream, like the bright colored leaves of autumn, coursing through our destiny. And we have said that we are moved by a power higher than our own that we can harness to chart our own compass in life and be the captains of our ships—instead of chips of wood floating as flotsam and jetsam eventually to be submerged by the stream of our own karmic crystals.

Now, I'd like to talk briefly about space. We always think of space in terms of the great vastness that rolls before the eye in the mountains or at the seashore or on the open plains of the West. If you take a trip across America by car, you'll have some idea of just how big this country is. And then, if you go across it in a jet—from New York to California—you'll seem to be annihilating space by speed.

And when you annihilate space by speed, you also experience the annihilation of time. This is quite an experience in physics and mathematics. If we were to take off in a spaceship from planet earth and go to some star so many light-years away in such and such a period of time, transcending the speed of light and then come back—even though, let's say, only five years had elapsed for us, by the time we got back to earth, all the people we had ever known would be dead, because a hundred years would have passed.

This is a bit of a ridiculous picture, but nevertheless a true one, which gives us something to think about in terms of the Second Coming of Christ. People say, "Well, Christ is coming back to this earth again." Well, I hope so. But they think of it in this way: They say that a cloud is coming, and it's coming out of the East. But they don't even know what the cloud is or what the East is.

But they say it's coming out of the East and it's going to be somewhere up in the Eastern sky and Christ is coming in that cloud. And then all the people in the world that are now alive are going to be able to see him.[15] But if you know anything about logistics and the cramming of people into space, you know that if you were standing on top of the Washington Monument and you had all the people who live in the District of Columbia gathered around you on the ground, they couldn't see you from the periphery of that group nor could they see you from below. They wouldn't see you and you wouldn't see them.

So you have to begin to understand that many of the scriptural references are significant only in terms of the individual—you and I and our personal relationship with God and his Christ. It's a matter of our realization of what we read and what we run with— what we know and what we are.

Do you think for one minute that if you had ascended with Jesus from Bethany's hill (if you'd been standing right beside him and you'd both gone up together) that you'd be dead now? Of course not! And neither is he. And if you had been standing there and he had ascended and you didn't, he'd still be alive, the Ascended Master, and you'd still be alive, the unascended disciple—wondering why you didn't make it when he did. And so here you are two thousand years later determined to find out how he did it so you can do it, too. Well, I'm here to tell you tonight that you've come to the right place.

Jesus said, "I am alive forevermore, and have the keys of hell and of death."[16] The Master is here to give you the keys to time and space and to eternal Life.

We have to understand, then, that the Second Coming of Christ does not have to occur in the physical sense of him floating in on a big white cloud—and everybody down here looks up and they see him like they would the Hindenburg dirigible floating through space.

We have to understand that the Second Coming of Christ is the specific event that occurs because the hearts of men have prepared themselves to receive him in all generations—not only in this one but in all generations. Otherwise the Everlasting Gospel could not be preached. Because Christ must first come in your hearts. Because if Christ had not first come in your heart—and this is the real Second Coming—then you could not understand the Everlasting Gospel even if you heard it preached.[17]

How could he preach to you the Everlasting Gospel if he'd come a hundred years ago and we were living now? If Christ had come a hundred years ago in time and we're living now, where would we stand then—if he'd come and gone? Or if he was still here ruling everything, supposedly, as they sometimes think of it? Well then, of course people wouldn't have any free will, would they—if he ruled it all? If he made them do exactly what he wanted them to do, he would be taking their free will away from them.

The solution to all of this is the Truth that the First Coming of Christ is in the exemplar, the son of man Jesus, who fully expressed the Light and was the Word incarnate, and that the Second Coming is in you. This glorious event takes place when the Son of God comes to live and reign in your heart and mind and soul and temple—because you have prepared him room.

When this planet achieves its immortal perfection, it will be because man has accepted the fiat of Almighty God, because man has recognized the great creative potential that is inside of him and is beginning to exercise it. As he begins to exercise that spiritual prerogative, then, you see, he achieves greatness.

And in that state of mind or frame of reference, he sees Christ within him, Christ above him and Christ all around him. And he experiences the Second Coming of Christ into his temple—the First Coming, of course, being his original creation in the beginning when Christ was formed in him and he was formed in Christ.

But that doesn't mean the Bible prophecies won't come true. The prophecies are, in fact, just like Jesus himself—"the same yesterday and today and forever."[18] They are coming true in the Eternal Now—whenever you are ready. For you are also the creator of your own time and space.

And when you look at your beloved Christ Self depicted on the Chart, if you so desire you'll also see him in your mind's eye as he is—coming into your heart and mind in the clouds of heavenly consciousness. And when you experience this mystery in your being, your heart and mind will feel and know at once his power and great glory. (The Second Coming of Jesus Christ is likewise glorified in the coming of the Ascended Master Jesus Christ as he delivers his Everlasting Gospel in the full power of the spoken Word through his Messengers.)

Well, once you experience his Second Coming in

this manner and you meet me somewhere on the highway of Life between time and space and eternity, and I ask you when is Christ's Second Coming, do you know what your answer will be? Why, you'll say to me, "He never ever went away and he never came back—he's always been—the same Christ with me—yesterday, today, and forever. It is I who went away and I who have come back."

And then you'll realize what you just said and you'll know that even so, your own comings and goings in and out of God's kingdom and in and out of embodiment have also been relative—only real in time and space. And when the eternal Mind within you gets through devouring your karmic cycles in time and space, why then you'll know that the Real You never left Home!

But don't get ahead of yourself on this evolutionary string. Because before you realize all of this you're going to have to thread the eye of the needle with that Gemini mind of God which Morya speaks about to his chelas, and which the Master, bless his heart, has through many lifetimes truly become.

This is the mind that leads to that spiritual greatness which, because it is true mastery, is outpictured through and tethered to the physical form and consciousness. This type of greatness that is not of this world, but comes from above and blesses that which is beneath, is brought forth from previous lives and other spheres of soul experience.

Now, Rabindranath Tagore achieved a certain greatness in the field of poetry. We have had many great poets in the world. We've had many great sculptors. We've had great teachers. We've had great doctors. We've had great avatars. Mighty souls have brought Truth to humanity and awakened the people. But, my goodness, none of them have been able to save the world.

Tagore can't save the world. I can't save the world. You can't save the world. In the end, each individual— and I'm saying this to the little children who are here— has to take the gift that God has given us (the gift of Life, first of all) and reach out in time and space and realize that we're natives of eternity, that we're here in this universe, we're in this mighty soundless sound stream—for a reason.

We're in it, and we've got to listen to it and vibrate with the cosmic sound. We've got to vibrate with the Cosmic Logos, the lost Word. We've got to let the Word begin to move in our lives.

And when that Word moves, we will be moved by God's intent. And when we are, we will learn how to control our thoughts. Because *the* controlling *thought* of the Mind of God will be our example. But it will be neither the controller nor the comptroller, because we will be in command of our thought by free will and by our individual exercise of some facet of the Great Thought of God, where all the desiring and the siring of the creation began.

Because, in the final analysis it's the God-control *we* allow in *our* lives that is going to save the world— one times one times the One. In *kal/desh* it is the individual and his individualization of the God flame that provides the only key to unlock our eternity. The flame, the One, the God-control and *you.*

THE ANCIENT BROTHERHOODS AND THE FIAT OF ORDER

If you can't control your thoughts, if your thoughts are wandering around like will-o'-the-wisps on a swamp wherever they happen to go, nothing will really be happening at all except chaos. And chaos is the illusion that something is happening, when actually nothing is happening that's real in the Mind of God.

So when you think something's happening when it's not—like on a psychedelic trip into the astral plane—you are also a part of that illusion which is the definition of chaos. 'Tis then that Tiamat, the great dragon of chaos,[19] is eating us up, devouring us.

Unless we're devouring God—assimilating his Thought and his Mind as Jesus taught, "Except ye eat the flesh of the son of man [who is the Son of God incarnate] and drink his blood, ye have no life in you"[20]— we ourselves will be eaten up by forces of the anti-Self beyond our control, that is, our control of *kal* and *desh*.

And God is not glorified in the Tiamat scenario because he cannot be glorified in chaos. Because God is order. And man is order. And the twain are made one in the glory of the universal Order of Light's perfection.

This is why the ancient Brotherhoods established the fiat of order. They established the fiat of order because only by obedience to the Law of the One and by order and by a quickening in consciousness can man achieve the brilliance of the Mind of God in his own mind. And when he does, there are changes that he will work in the world—both in and through and beyond time and space.

This is the sacred fire that has been forever and forever central to the th-r-r-one of God. And I said it purposely like the old Scotsman, th-r-r-one, because I wanted to illustrate the three-in-one of the threefold flame—of Power, Wisdom, and Love in man: the three-in-one consisting of the Father, the Son, and the Holy Spirit, you see, focusing through the body, the mind, and the soul.

When we understand these parallel triune aspects according to the law of the equilateral triangle and we put our understanding into practice by obedience to God's laws, we can see that by visualizing ourselves working with the great hierarchies of Light—angels,

archangels, Elohim and elemental builders of form
(whose offices of cosmic service were established long
before we ever knew who we were)—we are going to
have extraordinary experiences like the ancient Masters used to have.

We will not be just ordinary people. We will be the
sort of people—believe this or not—that could stand
here and disappear right in front of our eyes. We'll be
people that, in the body or out of the body, could go to
the ancient temples—in Egypt and in the fastnesses of
the Himalayas, beneath the seas and under the polar
caps or in the center of the earth, wherever there are
retreats of the Great White Brotherhood—and hear the
great mystic songs of the Masters and the music of the
spheres. We will be able to absorb the Light of eternity
right here in time.

And we will be able to enjoy ourselves a thousand
times more, a million times more, infinitely more than
we ever possibly could in this rat race we call human
life, which has been made a rat race because everybody is trying to rush around in their horseless char-
iots. Running around with, hopefully, two lights and a
taillight on—maybe two taillights—and a little aerial
sticking up, listening to some radio station that's putting out acid rock or classical rock or punk rock or
country Western rock or just plain old rock 'n' roll.

It's all the same because it all takes you to the same
place—the place where you really don't want to go if
you know what's good for you. But then, in time and
space where everything's relative, or so they say, most
people don't know what's good for them. And they don't
know because their teachers haven't taught them.

The preachers haven't opened their understanding to the true meaning of the scriptures of Life written
in our hearts and in our memories and in the akashic
records that reveal Christ and his disciples conversing

with the adepts in the Himalayas, both listening and demonstrating the Word, that reveal the ancient Masters and their circles of devotees sitting beneath the Tree of Life in the Garden of God. And thus the shepherds in every field have not fed their sheep with sufficient Christ-love to satiate their spirits and melt their self-images of worthlessness frozen in time and space.

And you go down the street and you see the boys and girls with long hair or shaved heads or astral cuts and colors, mohawks and spikes, and chains around their arms and legs and necks that look like they just stepped out of some Atlantean time warp. And they're bobbing along, bouncing up and down—probably injected with acid—LSD, STP, and God only knows what else. And they're going down the street, not knowing where they're going, and sometimes they bump into people. But then, that happens to the sane element of our society, too, doesn't it? They bump into people, too.

So, you see, I won't be able tonight to give you very much more than I've already given you because, for goodness' sake! it's ten after nine and I'm supposed to quit at nine o'clock. So, I've gone ten minutes over what I'm supposed to. I've bumped into the cudgel of time and my space is no longer.

You see, no matter what we know, as long as we're in the world we're still subject to *kal/desh.* So about all I can do is tell you that I hope you will have success in getting rid of this great dragon Tiamat—that right now is devouring my tale!—and learn to bring order out of your lives. And I can promise you that you can learn a great deal about how Jesus conquered *kal/desh* from the Ascended Masters of the Great White Brotherhood, if you want to.

So make the most of your opportunity in *kal/desh* to weave the fabric of eternity.

I'll see you in my next chapter!

Chapter Six

THE CHART OF
THE I AM PRESENCE

The Chart of the I AM Presence

Let's talk about the Chart of the I AM Presence and you. It is a form-presentation of your electronic reality. This Chart can be very beneficial to you personally if, through the understanding of it, you can learn to think of yourself as you really are and forget yourself as you are not.

Now, the self that is not was revealed to John by one of the seven angels as "the beast that was, and is not, and yet is."[1] This is the synthetic self made out of the synthetic image. Down deep in our hearts, we all know that this is the self we allow to get in our way a lot of the time. That is, the human gets in God's way, when, in fact, our souls are really created in the Divine Image.

You see, the Chart helps you to realize the Reality of yourself. And when you know the meaning of it, you will never again be alone—not if you practice the great truth embodied in it.

Now, if you didn't have an eye picture of yourself at all, if you had never seen yourself in a mirror or in a photograph, it would be somewhat difficult for you to actually know yourself—to understand who you really are. The same principle applies to the knowledge of the Presence.

Here we are dealing with something that is invisible to our physical senses but visible to our cosmic senses—the senses of the soul. This 'eye picture' of the Chart has brought that magnificent, invisible but all-powerful Electronic Presence of ourselves before our gaze for one purpose: to inform us as to the Reality of ourselves.

Consequently, our ability to respond to the ancient maxim inscribed on the temples of Atlantis and later in the temple of Apollo at Delphi—"Man, Know Thyself"—is aided magnificently by the Chart.

This Chart is valuable. It is perhaps the most valuable possession you can have outside of the Reality for which it is a symbol. And it has a purpose—and that is to quicken in our consciousness the advent of the Presence in our lives, of the Holy Christ Self, the violet fire, and the tube of light.

You may not see your Presence—but you do see this Chart. And that's the important thing, because the Chart is a scientific explanation of your Reality, *your Divine Reality*. It shows you your own relationship to God.

If, early in this century, this Chart could have been in the hands of the Christian churches, accepted by their pastors, taught to their parishioners, and understood and practiced by millions of people, we would have an entirely different world today.

You wouldn't have your global problems of Communism, juvenile delinquency, crime, drugs, the manipulation of our money and energy by the international bankers and big oil, and many other serious conditions—because eye contact with the visual image awakens the soul's memory of preexistence and independence from the time/space continuum.

Just seeing the Chart reconnects the soul to the inner knowledge of its tie to the Source of universal Light, Love, Energy, and Consciousness. And this awareness of one's individual relationship to God alone produces miracles of expanded potential and joy and soul satisfaction!

The Chart is self-knowledge—Self-knowledge! And this is power. Translated into action, it is your ultimate power to work the works of God on earth [2] and ascend to his throne at the conclusion of this life.

BEING A MANIFESTATION OF GOD

Quite a few years ago I heard someone say to another person, "Who in the world do you think you are? Do you think you're God or something?" No doubt you have heard people say such things to one another. Is that bad? Is it bad to equate one's potential with God's?

Well, it must be terrible, because Jesus was thrown out of his hometown and practically pushed headlong over the brow of a hill because he presented himself in the synagogue of Nazareth as the Anointed One of Isaiah's prophecy. [3] And later, because he said, "I AM the Son of God," they would have stoned him and taken him but he escaped out of their hands. [4]

People are very touchy about their gods, whether they have just one or many; and they don't like anyone to claim that they are God, i.e., a manifestation of God— even though Jesus taught them by example that it was not robbery for the Son of God to make himself equal with God, [5] admonished them to be perfect as their heavenly Father was perfect, [6] and showed Paul how to embody the same mind (of God) that was in himself. [7]

Well, being a manifestation of God simply means that the stream is the issue of the Source. After all, if the stream of your consciousness comes from God— directly from your I AM Presence, as it is illustrated in this Chart—then isn't that stream *of* God? Isn't it actually God?

When we say you are a "lifestream," we mean you are a "stream of Life"—of the Life that is God; for the terms *Life* and *God* are synonymous. Often the Ascended Masters address us affectionately as "precious lifestreams," in the same way they would say "dear hearts" or "beloved ones." And this is because they know us as the Light-emanation, or *Light-stream*— a ray of Light from God's heart.

Jesus taught that the stream cannot be any different than the source—as his brother James said: Does a fountain send forth at the same place sweet water and bitter? Can a fig tree bear olive berries or a vine figs? So no fountain can give forth salt water and fresh.[8] Thus we are the fruit of God's Tree of Life—the thought-emanation of his Mind bearing the seed of the Christ potential. We are God's, fully his—spirits of his very Spirit.

One of the tricks of the evil forces on this planet is what is known as intimidation. That's why you have to know who you are in relationship to God and your Beloved I AM Presence. Because they intimidate you through inferiority; they try to make you feel so small and so insignificant and so little that you figure, "Well, I haven't got a chance to run in this race anyway. I might as well quit before I start."

The Chart is the most immaculate proof of the fact that you *do* have a chance, because there isn't a man or a woman or a child that God created on this or any other planet who does not have this exact relationship to him. Because you are a lifestream of God, you can walk the earth as a joint-heir with Christ Jesus. This means that you stand to inherit the same Christhood, the same Sonship which Jesus had and demonstrated.

And this is the true teaching of the apostle Paul. If you don't believe me, then read Romans 8:14–17 and tell me what it means. And I'll tell you that this

Chart is an illustration of the teaching which the Ascended Master Jesus Christ gave directly to Paul:

> For as many as are led by the Spirit of God [*the 'Presence' of God, whose name is I AM*], they are the sons [*suns*] of God [*they are the Light-emanations of God*].
>
> For ye have not received the spirit of bondage again to fear [*bondage to the law of karma, without grace*]; but ye have received the Spirit of adoption, whereby we cry, Abba, Father. [*As we have been adopted by the Cosmic Christ, who is personified in our Christ Self, we may now call in his name directly to the Mighty I AM Presence.*]
>
> The Spirit [*of the I AM Presence*] itself beareth witness with our spirit [*through our divine spark, our threefold flame, and our souls*] that we are the children of God:
>
> And if children, then heirs; heirs of God and joint-heirs with Christ [*every child of God stands to inherit the full potential of the Universal Christ, or Light (of the only begotten Son of God), individualized in his Beloved Christ Self*]; if so be that we suffer with him [*if we bear our own burden, or karma, as well as his burden of Light*] that we may be also glorified together.

This teaching does not deny the divinity of Jesus; it affirms him, and the Godhead dwelling in him, bodily.⁹ It also affirms Jesus, as well as the Christ that he incarnated, as being within your range. It makes it possible for you to reach up and touch the hem of his garment. It shows you how and why you can have an intimate relationship with him—and, through him, with God.

Jesus himself taught us so simply the requirements that must be met in order for us to enjoy the

Presence of the Father and the Son indwelling with us—precisely as illustrated in this Chart: "If a man love me, he will keep my words; and my Father will love him, and we will come unto him and make our abode with him." [10]

This contact with your Lord and Saviour may be very different from what you realize at this point. In the case of beloved Paul, the Lord not only converted him in the divine encounter on the Damascus way, but he personally overshadowed his ministry and tutored his soul in the mysteries of God *every step of the way.*

And the Lord will do it for you through your own I AM Presence and Holy Christ Self, if you just make the call and lovingly obey the answer.

Now, let us examine that Chart very closely, because it is the key to your discipleship under the Lord Jesus Christ.

DIAGRAM OF GOD'S KINGDOM WITHIN YOU

Here is the threefold flame in your heart. Here is the silver cord connecting you to your Mighty I AM Presence. Here is your Holy Christ Self—your Real Self, who is sometimes called your Higher Consciousness or Higher Mental Body—standing between you and your God Presence. And, of course, this is the tube of light, sealing you in the white light, and the blue flame reinforcing its protection, called up all around you through that great defender of your faith, Archangel Michael.

This is your causal body surrounding the One whose name is I AM THAT I AM. These bands contain the treasures of heaven; together they comprise your causal body and focus the Cosmic Christ Consciousness of your Higher Self.

Here we have illustrated the dove of the Holy Spirit descending from the Father upon the Christ

Self that signifies the baptism of the Holy Spirit. It is the Paraclete, whose love passes through the silver cord to fill the heart and soul and mind of your lower self until that self becomes *wholly* the vessel of the Light, truly the temple of the *Holy* Ghost.

Then you have the love radiance of the Christ in this beautiful expanding heart of your Holy Christ Self, the golden flame of illumination identifying him as the Tutor of your soul and the Healer.

Here you have a lighthouse, its great beams sweeping out over the sea of humanity's consciousness symbolizing the All-Seeing Eye of God, the Watchman of the night illumining the Homeward path.

Here (all around you inside your tube of light) you have the violet flame, in one way the most important part of the revelation of the Chart because it's the key to transmutation—the washing of your being with the sacred fire.

THE VIOLET FLAME AND THE LAW OF RECOMPENSE

As I have told you before, there're two things that are sure: death and taxes. So goes the saying of Ben Franklin.[11] And you'll never get out of this world alive except through the ascension. And the only way you can really make your ascension is through the violet flame.

There is no person who has ever made his ascension who hasn't had the violet flame given to him some way or another. All may not have had the formula written down. All may not have addressed the LORD, "Beloved mighty victorious Presence of God, I AM in me . . .," etc., as we are taught to do when we invoke the violet flame from God's altar, but in some way, perhaps on the inner planes, they had to have reached the state of consciousness of the seventh ray where they could call forth the violet flame to consume their human creation.

Because if you don't consume your human creation, dear hearts, you are never going to be able to win the battle of life—because if you don't master your human creation, your human creation will master you, rest assured of it.

There's no two ways about a thing like this. We like to think that there's two ways; but this is only the human, and the human consciousness is constantly changing its mind. One minute he's running hot and the next minute he's running cold. The human is the most unpredictable despot of our natures.

Don't let it fool you; it will try. It will tell you that God isn't going to do anything about it anyway, that he's not concerned with you because you are so little. Well, Jesus said, "One jot or one tittle shall in no wise pass from the law [i.e., the law of Moses and the law of Christ, both being reflective of the responsibilities of karma] till all be fulfilled." [12]

Now, a jot and a tittle are pretty small portions on the karmic scales. But if it gives you any consolation, your enemies will suffer to the uttermost for the things they do to you. And, consequently, you will suffer just as much, in fact more so—because you know better!—for anything you do to them.

So the safest thing to do is to forget vengeance and forget and forgive immediately, because it just doesn't pay to carry it out to the last farthing and seek your pound of flesh, "Shylock," because when you get your pound of flesh, it is an empty victory. And a vendetta is never a happy circumstance.

There is a moment of triumph when the enemy lies bleeding on the ground before you—he the vanquished, you the victor. But this is soon replaced by the remorse of the spirit when the pangs of guilt give you pause to wonder if, in depriving another of life, liberty, and happiness, you will ever sleep again the sleep of beatitude in God.

So forget and forsake the idea of vengeance in any matter. You have the promise of your Creator— "Vengeance is mine; I will repay, saith the LORD"[13]— and he will keep his promise if you don't interfere and try to take matters into your own hands.

Defend yourself if you have to. I don't think any one of you should give up your life to just anyone because they want to take it. I don't say you shouldn't protect yourself. But, by the grace of God, you should also protect yourself against yourself—because it's alright to protect yourself at any given moment.

But don't carry that too far and "let the sun go down upon your wrath"[14] and then find out that while you were sound asleep, the force of your human mind went out and created something that caused someone else to suffer or to die.

Remember, as we have said, there's a part of your psyche that—if you go to bed harboring anger against another in your heart or in your mind—could go out and actually cause that one to die. A lot of people don't know this. And the next day might come and you'd hear, "Oh, they passed away." And then you'd say, "Well, good enough, they deserved it! They hurt me and I'm pretty important. That's what they got. They got it. They deserved it."

Well, what happens when the Lords of Karma confront you with the record of your energy sent forth as a poisoned arrow and say, "You did this"? So it's best that people "put it into the flame," as we say— the all-consuming violet flame. Forget—forget every wrong as soon as it happens. If you will only do that, you will not be engaging in karma-making action.

And then the violet flame that you use with the

plus factor of your Christ Self will be able to remove some of that crusty old karma that's down inside your four lower bodies somewhere lurking—and it needs to be scraped off just like you scrape the barnacles off the bottom of a ship. You need more than a spring housecleaning. Your hull needs a complete overhaul by violet flame!

But if you're so busy creating more human nonsense—and I know of some people (I'd rather not mention them by name) who used to have a violet-flame service, and then they'd have a good fight outside the sanctuary right afterward, the idea being that they'd invoke the violet flame to pay their anticipated debts, you see, and build up their credit in advance—well, this doesn't work because the record is clear:

The purpose of the violet flame is to shed mercy upon the earth. And if people are going to have mercy, they've got to be merciful. And if they're going to think that they can use the violet flame just to make themselves feel good and clean up their human creation—the worst of the scum off the surface so that their pores can breathe for a while—and then they are going to start in with their old hate and hate creations and their fighting and wrangling and human viciousness and discord and keep saying to the Law, "We won't pay! Let the violet flame pay for all our transgressions, for we are above the Law . . . ," let them know that sooner or later the Great Law will make them pay.

And the first thing they know, the violet flame will not be working for them the way it should, because they'll get so clogged up that the Lords of Karma will come down and say, "Wait a minute. You haven't paid your debt and we're turning off your light and power. We're not going to give you any more violet flame!"

Now, I am saying this in a jovial sort of way but,

believe you me, there is an inner law that's involved in this, and this could happen. It could happen that you would lose your efficacy in the use of the violet flame by abusing it. So, let's hold on to the violet flame by using common sense and not go out wasting our energy and creating more karma just because we've now balanced a little and we "feel so good."

The last word on the subject of new-age truth is that no matter how much you think you know or how much of an adept you think you are, you are never above the Law. In fact, you are always under the rod of Christ and the commandments of Moses.

Those who invoke the violet flame, therefore, must know that they must operate under the laws governing its use, beginning with faith, hope, and charity toward all—faith in God, hope in his Christ for every man, and charity toward the evolving soul.

WHERE IS GOD?

Let us understand that man has been confused by the time-spatial relationship of himself to Himself. How many angels can dance on the head of a pin? The answer is an infinite number, because angels do not displace time and space.

When it comes to spatial relationships, we believe that two people can't occupy the same square foot at the same time. We say it's just not possible. If we get into a revolving door and there's someone else in there with us, somebody might get hurt! Somehow we can't get it through our heads that maybe, if we knew how, we could walk right through that revolving door—or one another!

So, because of our concrete conceptions, we have a little difficulty in fixing in our mind's eye just where God is. "Well, where is God?"

Where is he? Where indeed! He's everywhere.

Well, this doesn't quite satisfy a child. And somehow even child-man is not quite satisfied with it. We always have the idea that God should be somewhere and that maybe if we knew just where to look for him, we could go and find him.

That's why Jesus warned there would arise false Christs and false prophets proclaiming a flesh-and-blood messiah that could be located in time and space, saying: "Look, here is Christ!" or "Look, he is there!" But the Master said, "Believe not, go not, for the kingdom of God is *within you*." [15] Now, let us see what he meant.

Past, present, and future, the kingdom of God is within you. Well, what is God's kingdom? It is his realm—the realm of his habitation and the realm of his Mind. It would be the dwelling place of his Spirit—and the farthest reaching out of his consciousness. From the point of center where he declares, "I AM...," to the bounds of beingness where the Word "... THAT I AM" resounds, the name of God defines his infinite awareness of himself. Indeed HE IS WHERE HE IS!

Jesus the Christ, God's son who knew his Father well, told you and me that God's kingdom—not part of it, but the whole infinitude of his universal Mind—is inside of us. He meant that within every one of you God's kingdom already is: it always has been and it always will be so for every son and daughter of God.

This Chart is a diagram of God's kingdom within you. In his Teaching on the kingdom within, Jesus also taught by example that it is not blasphemy for you as a son of God to think of yourself as being made in the image and likeness of God, because God created all of his sons in his image and his likeness. So what's wrong with thinking that you *are* this image!

Paul even said we all are changed into the image

of the glory of the LORD.[16] And the glory of the LORD, the Shekinah, is the Word, the Light, or Christ, of the I AM Presence. Indeed, we shall bear the "image of the heavenly"[17] Self—our Real Self, who is Christ.

Yes, Christ is the image of the invisible God. And this Christ is the firstborn of each of us. Christ is our original Self. This Self we now see as the Mediator between the soul (the lower figure in the Chart) and the immortal Spirit of the I AM (the upper figure). Your beloved Christ Self in whose image you were made is shown as the middle figure who stands between heaven and earth as your open door to the glory of the LORD above (some witnesses of the Light call the I AM Presence "Jehovah").

Physically speaking, your body may not look just like God, but you're not your body any more than you are your dress or your suit of clothes or your overcoat. Your body is something you wear. It may fit you like a glove, or you may think it does; but you may find out that it doesn't fit you so well, when you find out what you really look like. So let's take a look at who is God where you are, and who you look like at inner levels.

YOUR BELOVED I AM PRESENCE

The upper figure in the Chart is the individualized God Presence of each one of us. This which is called your Mighty I AM Presence, and the Light-manifestation thereof—who is called your Holy Christ Self—is representative of your true Being.

Your I AM Presence is your electronic body of Light. This electronic body of Light is the actual image of God; and every person has the image of God individualized for him. It is an exact replica of the Electronic Presence of God in what is called the Great Central Sun, or the Hub. This is the core of cosmos whence, through the Logos of Alpha and Omega, all of the star systems emanate and the physical creation sprang forth as the counterpart of the spiritual.

Everything in the material universe comes forth from this great center of Light—which itself is the nexus, or go-between, between Spirit and Matter. The Great Central Sun is the focus of the Cosmic Christ consciousness of all life. It contains the image, or divine pattern, for the whole of creation just as your Christ Self contains the image of your soul and your divine plan.

And so this ray of light above the Presence at the very top of the Chart symbolizes the continuation of the crystal cord that connects your heart, through your Christ Self, through your I AM Presence, to the Heart of the Cosmic Christ in the Great Central Sun—and to the Sun behind the sun, the spiritual First Cause behind the material center: the One Supreme God, the Almighty.

Thus, you are very well connected! And every soul who has come from God has an individual I AM Presence, which is an extension of the being of God individualized for him.

The knowledge of the image and likeness of God with you brings you closer to God than you have ever been before. This Presence is actually 'in the air' above your physical body right now and it always has been. Many people have seen this Presence when they were a child and they thought that it was an angel, a beautiful angel hovering over them. But it was the Divine Presence.

Remember John's description of the "mighty angel come down from heaven"? He saw him clothed with a cloud and a rainbow on his head, his face brilliant like the sun and his feet as pillars of fire. [18] Now, that's as apt a description of your own Mighty I AM Presence as you'll get anywhere.

Moses also described the 'Presence' of Yahweh as "the angel of the LORD" who appeared in a flame. Next thing you know, it's the LORD himself who calls Moses out of the midst of the burning bush. [19]

The fact is that that which the prophets and patriarchs interpreted as the LORD's angel was the LORD himself, who would *personify* himself before man, whether through the I AM Presence or one of the Archangels or through the Christic manifestation of the Mighty I AM Presence, whom the prophets addressed as the Ancient of Days [20] or the LORD of hosts.

You see, the I AM Presence is an individualized and very personalized expression of our God, who is Spirit, who is living Truth, who is Mind, who is Principle—as some of our Christian Science and Unity friends like to think of the Presence of Divine Love.

Therefore, for the purposes of intimate communion and verbal one-on-one communication with man (the manifestation of himself), God may assume the form of the man he made so that man will recognize God as his Creator. And this apparition is in the pure likeness of the Son of God, the middle figure in the Chart.

Doesn't that make sense? Don't your children recognize you because you are like them and they are like you?

We are dealing, then, with the One Supreme God—the Almighty, the Maker of heaven and earth—who is one Spirit everywhere present, who sends comfort to his offspring by sending to each one the greatest gift and the only gift that could totally comfort his sons and daughters when they are journeying in that far country—the Matter cosmos. He sends the gift of his Presence, his Electronic Presence individualized for each and every one of his children.

When your children are away from home, aren't

they comforted to have a photograph of you as a remembrance? Well, our loving Father, who knows our hearts and how much we miss him and need to feel his nearness, took a photograph of himself and duplicated it for every one of us! And because he is the God of very gods, that photo contains the full momentum of himself—it's just like having the Godhead dwelling with us bodily.

In fact it is, because, you see, this "photograph" is not made of paper and chemicals; it's made of Light. Why, it's made of the very same substance he's made of—or it wouldn't be a duplicate, would it?

Jesus revealed the Almighty to John the Beloved in this wise: "I AM Alpha and Omega, the beginning and the ending which is and which was and which is to come. . . ."[21] Therefore we know that the beginning and the ending of every man and of all creation is God.

Now, this God, who admittedly is everywhere yet centers his 'Beingness' in the heart of the Great Central Sun, has the power to duplicate his image and make as many luminous presences (focuses) of himself as he wishes.

Just like a woman with a lump of dough. She rolls it out with a rolling pin and she gets out a cookie cutter that looks like a little gingerbread man. She can stamp out as many cookies as she wants to and they all look alike. So don't expect you're going to find anything different about your I AM Presence and mine.

Jesus' I AM Presence looks just like yours. This is the common denominator. This is the coequality of the sons and daughters of God. He created you equal in the sense that he gave you an I AM Presence—he gave you a Divine Self.

"Hear, O Israel: The LORD our God is one LORD!"[22]

When we pray "Our Father. . . ," inherent in that address is the acknowledgment by each one of us that our Father belongs to each one of us somehow uniquely.

He may be *your* Father, but he's also *my* Father. We share him but when we're alone with him, he's all ours. We feel complete in him and we feel his very personal caring for us alone.

It's like a family of five children. They share their parents, but each one senses a very private and personal relationship with Daddy and Mommy—or should, if the parents truly understand their role and their children's need to feel very special in those moments of being supremely loved for their intrinsic worth, rather than as part of the group.

So when you realize that your Beloved I AM Presence is in fact the omnipresence of the Father made very tangible right where you are, when you realize that it is both the privilege and the power of the Father to so identify himself to each of his children, when you realize that he is one God, he is the Almighty, and he can do anything—including give you an exclusive Mighty I AM Presence that is yours alone—then you will really know just how much God loves you!

And then you will know that this love is available to you—ever flowing like a mountain stream that never runs dry because it is fed from snowy heights—and that it is yours to give to everybody you know or don't know.

Your Father has given to you, because you are his very own, a limitless Source of light, love, wisdom, joy, peace, and healing power—vested in the Mighty I AM Presence. And all you have to do is call it forth in his name, and it will pour through you to his other children until they, too, learn to depend on their own God Source.

DRAW NIGH UNTO ME AND I WILL DRAW NIGH UNTO YOU

This Divine Presence abides in the atmosphere from seven to seventy feet or more above your head, and it varies in its locale. One minute it may be up seventy or eighty feet, and then again it's down to twenty feet. And what governs it is this covenant of your Maker: "Draw nigh unto me and I will draw nigh unto you," saith the LORD.[23]

When you draw nigh to God and your thoughts are high and kind, the Presence will drop down around you. When you're engaged in vicious human activities of criticism and gossip or doing the things that consume your energy in the wrong way, the Presence pulls away from you because your discord and dishonesty with your True Self actually repels the LORD.

Think of it—your vibration can be a repellent to the Godhead. Maybe now you understand why God doesn't always seem to be there when you need him. (Discord of any kind puts a wedge of darkness between your soul and your Highest and most Perfect Love. Then you hear the unbearable words spoken to Eli, "Be ye far from me."[24])

When we lose touch with our Presence, we also lose the protection of the 'angel of the LORD'. And that's why we need the tube of light and why we need to learn how to call it forth by Christ command from the heart of the I AM Presence.

You understand that when you gaze at a blinding light, no matter how bright it gets, as long as it's blinding, you can't see it anyway. So there has to be a contrast. And that's the beauty of heaven, because I think God puts us down here on earth so that by becoming acquainted with all the vibratory actions that occur down here, we can really learn to appreciate heaven.

It's like someone knocking their head against a cement wall. They say it feels so good when they quit! And that's the truth of it—because after you get socked by your own karma and a few other people's karma, you get to the point where you don't know which way is up and which way is down. Why, then you're ready for heaven—we hope!

It reminds me of the story of the young enlisted man who was very nervous about going overseas. And he was so nervous and shaking all over that he was actually breaking out in a cold sweat. And so his friend came up to him to comfort him and he said, "Well, I tell you, my buddy, I wouldn't worry too much about that—there's always a possibility that you won't pass your physical."

"Well," the soldier said, "that's true."

"And there're two chances for you right there," he said. "You either pass your physical or you don't, and then," he said, "if you should pass your physical, you may go overseas and you may not. They may decide to use you in the States."

He replied, "That's true. I do have two chances."

So he said, "Well, another thing, too, when you get overseas, you may be sent into battle and you may not be sent into battle. So, you see, you'll have two chances." Then he said, "And if you get sent into battle, you may get killed and you may not get killed, and," he said, "even if you get killed, you still have two chances!"

So that's a very down-to-earth way of looking at the calculated risk each of us takes every day of our lives. When John Kennedy was asked not long before his death if he feared an assassination attempt, he said, "To get out of bed each day is a calculated risk." Each day as we get back into the four lower bodies that comprise the lower figure in the Chart—the outer man—we are taking our chances with the risky business of earthly living.

I don't want two chances, do you? I'd rather take the one chance. This is the greatest chance that you can take—the chance of a lifetime to identify with God through your own Beloved I AM Presence. So, identify with God. It's your guarantee of 100-percent success— not necessarily down here through the lower figure, but up here through your Christ Self.

But you have to bring your Higher Self down here to your lower self and superimpose the 'Big Me' over the 'little me'. Then you take charge and, as a wise parent, you control that little "so and so," and you don't let him get in the way of your Great God Reality.

YOUR FINITE SELF AND YOUR FOUR LOWER BODIES

Now, natural science, divine science, is magnificent to behold and nowhere more so than in our own body—and ultimately in the seven bodies of man—a cosmos 'all inside' patterned after the seven creative forces of Elohim.

The lower figure in the Chart is symbolical of your finite self, your soul lodged in a human form. I don't like to compare you to a piece of bologna, but it's useful to do so for a moment's digression. Bologna actually has a skin around it and you cram the meat down in there, and it's in its skin, you see. Well, that's the way we are. We're crammed down into this body and we're in our skin, aren't we? Whether we like it or not, or are comfortable or not, we are there.

This human figure down here in the Chart is symbolical of the little man that's down here in his skin—having all told, uppers and lowers, seven bodies, of course. (The I AM Presence, Causal Body, and Holy Christ Self are considered to be the three upper bodies.)

The four lower bodies of man, vehicles of vibration and consciousness in the Matter universe, are his "coats of skins," [25] as the Bible calls them. It is said that the material body is made of the earth element "from dust to dust."[26] Though an earthen vessel, it is composed of more of Light's energy than most people realize; and therefore, the physical envelope is the focus of integration in the physical octave of the other three bodies.

The mental, or air, body—the vessel of cognition, thought processes, reason, logic, and concentration for decisive and discriminatory action—is just beneath the etheric in vibratory rate. When it is purified holy, it becomes the pure vessel of the Christ Mind, and the etheric and mental bodies are fused as one.

The desire, or water, body—the vessel where the feelings and emotions undulate with the currents of desire stimulated by memory, mind, will, or external causation—is larger and more dominant than the more concentrated mental body. Whereas the Christ Mind ought to dominate both mind and emotions, if the desire body is not disciplined and under the control of the Holy Spirit through the Higher Self, it can cause shipwreck to the soul's evolution lifetime after lifetime.

The physical body is the focus of integration for the evolving soul, which must gain its freedom and self-mastery in the physical octave. The etheric chakras, the seven major with the eighth, are anchored in the three lower bodies; these—including the threefold flame in the secret chamber of the heart and the seed atom as well as the Kundalini (the Life-force) at the base-of-the-spine chakra[27]—are the centers for the spiritual fire and the interchange of the higher and lower energies for the purpose of spiritualization, transmutation and the emission of Light, or the Christ consciousness, to the planetary body.

While each of the four lower bodies has many levels of awareness (conscious, subconscious, and superconscious), "the form of the fourth is like the Son of God,"[28] as the astonished Nebuchadnezzar observed. The etheric body, most like the Christ Self, is mirrored in the physical. But the image is not always clear, as it is troubled and murky with the record and karma of the mental and feeling (astral) bodies. These intercept the pure polarity of the fire and earth elements held naturally between the etheric blueprint and the physical form.

Thus, you can see why the highest vibrating of the four lower bodies is the etheric (the memory, or fire) body. It contains the records both of your soul's preexistence in heaven above (stored in your causal body and Christ Mind) and of your soul's experiences in physical embodiment here below (stored in your subconscious, the astral sheath and lower electronic belt[29]).

Whatever the plane of your activities, the memory body contains the Tablets of *Mem*—the electronic, computerized recordings of all vibrations and energy impulses you have ever sent forth through your soul and its higher and lower vehicles. This life record is written on innumerable discs of light which comprise the changing, evolving identity pattern of the soul merging with the Spirit. It is this life record (the L-field) which determines the patterns which will be outpictured in the three lower vehicles—the mental body, the desire body, and the physical body. (Only the violet flame can permanently alter the effect by thoroughly transmuting the cause.)

ETHERIC OCTAVE—THRESHOLD OF THE SECOND COMING

The etheric body of man the microcosm—as well as the etheric body of planet earth, the macrocosm—is perceived as the heaven-world. It is recorded that Enoch was taken up to the ten heavens.[30] These are distinct planes of consciousness through which the soul evolves in its ascent to God. What we call the etheric octave is the plane to which the Lord Jesus Christ descends (from the highest heaven where he is seated "on the right hand of God"[31]) in his 'Second Coming'.

Paul described his coming as "with a shout, with the voice of the archangel, and with the trump of God."[32] He said that those who are one in Christ's consciousness (those in physical embodiment as well as those who have passed on and are in the etheric plane) shall be caught up together in the clouds (the etheric octave) to meet the Lord in the air (in the plane of the Christ Mind).

By the Lord's descending grace and our willing ascent on the path of attainment, we will meet in the etheric octave of the heaven-world and from there we will follow in the footsteps of Enoch, who by faith "was translated that he should not see death, and was not found because God had translated him: for before his translation he had this testimony, that he pleased God."

And we will mount with Enoch the planes of heaven above, viewing their respective hierarchical orders. These include the plane of Jesus Christ's habitation ("In my Father's house are many mansions. . . . I go to prepare a place for you. . . that where 'I AM', there ye may be also"[33]), the Ascended Master octaves of light, the realms of archangels, Elohim, and so on, all leading, spiral upon spiral of infinity, to the throne of the Most High God.

Thus, the etheric body and plane is the meeting ground of heaven and earth where, one by one, souls advancing up the mountain experience the Second Advent of Christ, the rapture, and the resurrection.

The Ascended Masters teach that the Second Coming of Jesus (descending in clouds of glory, as depicted in the Chart) is the descent of the Lord to quicken our soul's consciousness of "his" Christ as "our" Christ—the Universal One, the Only Begotten of the Father. This is the common loaf, or Light, we share and identify as our own Real Self.

Their message is that those who are caught up in the Spirit of Christ through their fiery hearts and the purified etheric vessel (waiting in this earthly life or in the next world) will see Jesus Christ descending, and through him know the image of the Son of God as the God Reality to which they, too, shall indeed ascend.

The author of Hebrews saw that "it was therefore necessary that the patterns of things in the heavens should be purified" in order that Christ Jesus, our High Priest, who comes to us through the person of our Christ Self, might enter our etheric abode, thence to appear for us in the I AM Presence of God.[34]

Because we have altered the heavenly, or etheric, patterns of our lifestream (reflected in the DNA chain as our precise genetic code), we must purify these by the violet flame (the blood, or essence, of Christ) so that the lower mind, the desire body, and physical body might also be remade after Christ's image and the fourfold vessel become the temple of the God who would take up his abode with us.

All of us have an inner awareness of our Christ image, both by self-knowledge and through the auric emanations of our own Christ Self-awareness. By the many layers of consciousness both higher and lower which play upon the 'plastic' substance of these four sheaths, the human personality is formed. The first sheath (the etheric) is incorporeal, for it is impressed with sacred fire; the mental and emotional bodies are subject to certain disintegration factors, but not entirely—the physical, of course, being subject to total dissolution.

The identity patterns of the mental and emotional bodies together with their 'nucleus' are retained from one embodiment to the next as an electronic matrix in the etheric sheath. These records are reproduced lifetime after lifetime on vessels fashioned of earth's frequencies for another round of the soul's self-discovery and self-mastery in the physical plane.

Thus, the reincarnation of the soul in new coats of skins that are most compatible and well suited to her evolution is by a mathematical formula made to order by one's own self-creating actions and thought/feeling impulses which continually mold and shape the outer man.

Though we do not always see "in the flesh" of one another the reflected image of the Anointed One, we may commune with heart and soul and mind of dearest friend and see beyond the veils of skins the Son of man in all his splendor. It is this man we love so dearly—in the plane of reality where our friendships are sealed, our true loves revealed.

It was his hope in the Universal Christ image that led Job to exclaim, "Yet in my flesh [in my genetic code outpictured in my flesh and blood] shall I *see* God!"[35]

The path of the foursquare gospel made plain in the Teachings of the Ascended Masters is the means whereby the soul wed to Christ takes dominion over the four lower bodies and the four planes of Matter simultaneously.

Through the joyous process of soul-purification—transmutation—the earthly patterns are transformed by the heavenly, and the goal of the ascension is attained when the seven bodies of man, as Above so below, are become as one: the soul united with the I AM Presence through the Christ Self now occupying the totality of Being. This, then, is the likeness of the Son of God who dwells forevermore as the One. In all seven planes of Being he is the Ascended Master.

Even so, Ascended Master Jesus Christ, come into my temple—Come into the seven planes of my being!—and dwell with me, my Lord, forevermore.

THE SILVER CORD

Now, the flow of light between the Spirit of the living God and your soul is over the silver cord. It is the thread of light and the thread of contact, not only with God but also with all souls ascended in the white light who comprise the Great White Brotherhood. (The terms *silver cord* and *crystal cord* are synonymous, being descriptive of men's perceptions of the 'umbilical cord' of the soul, tied to and fed by the Spirit.)

The silver cord originates in the Godhead in the Great Central Sun. You can visualize it as a ribbon of light descending down infinity to your Mighty I AM Presence, passing through your Christ Self to nourish your soul and your four lower bodies. Everyone who is of God has the magnificent 'crystal' cord connecting all planes of his being—heart to heart—to the Sun.

The forgiveness that pours through this crystal cord is absolutely unbelievable! You are dealing with what Saint John saw as the River of Life.[36] The River of Life is crystal. It is radiant. It is bubbling. It is effervescent. And it is individualized for you and for me. All children of the Light have it. It will make you truly, divinely happy.

You don't need any champagne if you can put yourself in God's campaign! Because you have everything you need in the heart of the Presence and it's delivered to your doorstep over this iridescent crystal flowing Life-stream.

The silver cord enters the four lower bodies through the crown; its pulsations can be seen physically by observing the soft spot on a baby's head. Once the silver cord stabilizes the breath and the heartbeat at birth, and the threefold flame is rekindled in the "secret chamber of the heart"[37] and the child begins to "wax strong in spirit,"[38] the soft spot begins to close over. By the time the child is about two years old, it is no longer visible.

While in the womb, the baby lives by the heart flame and crystal cord of the mother. The moment of the cutting of the umbilical cord—when the Holy Spirit has breathed the breath of Life into the form—is the symbolical moment (and sometimes the actual moment, depending on the correct timing of the cutting of the cord) of the descent of the baby's own silver cord from the Beloved I AM Presence. The baby's first cry or sound is often indicative of its sudden recognition of the burst of flame in the heart, of the sacred breath infilling the lungs, and of the bodily sensations now keenly felt.

A long time ago, back in the old Methodist church way out in the country, to the music of a little old organ they used to sing, "When breaks Life's Golden Bowl, / Or the Pitcher at the Fount, / Or the silver cord be loosed, / Then upward shall I mount / Fling wide the pearly gates. . ."[39] You see, they talked about it as it was spoken of by the preacher Ecclesiastes.

Clairvoyants way back in the 1800s reported standing over dying people and watching the loosening of the silver cord. Spiritualist mediums observed when attending departing souls at their deathbed that something silvery seemed to disconnect from their body and float up into the air. They described it as a beautiful silver ribbon they could see with their inner sight.[40]

In his autobiography, Charles Lindbergh tells of an experience he had during the twenty-second hour of his transatlantic flight in the *Spirit of St. Louis* when he sensed a "tenuous strand" connected to his body:

"I had been without sleep for nearly two days and two nights. My conscious mind had lost control of its body. My movements were made by instinct, not by will." Then he became aware of what he called "phantoms" grouped in the fuselage behind him.

"Gradually, the apparent difference between self and phantoms faded and I, too, existed independently of time and matter. I felt myself departing from my body as I imagine a spirit would depart—emanating into the cockpit, extending through the fuselage as though no frame or fabric walls were there, angling upward, outward, until I re-formed in an awareness far distant from the human form I left in a fast-flying transatlantic plane. But I remained connected to my body through a long-extended strand, a strand related to the form of man, a strand so tenuous that it could have been severed by a breath, an ethereal breath unrelated to the propeller's wash.

"Then I re-formed slowly as a man again, returning from spatial distances to my plane and body, condensing and collapsing into earthly qualities."[41]

Thus, a man of our time, an aviator, one not in the religious field, saw the silver cord as the lifeline connecting his spirit to his body and experienced his soul's independence from the human form. This is exactly what the Chart depicts.

We learn that the actual cause of death is the cutting of this silver cord (an act of God), which causes the threefold flame to "go out" in the physical body. And this is the accurate and true meaning of Ecclesiastes 12:6–7, which reads: ". . . or ever the silver cord be loosed, or the golden bowl be broken, or the pitcher be broken at the fountain, or the wheel broken at the cistern [metaphor for the withdrawal of the silver cord and the simultaneous withdrawal of the threefold flame—i.e., the 'breaking' of the heart, the going out of the breath of Life and with it the soul, and the taking up of the light from the chakras—'wheels']. Then shall the dust return to the earth as it was, and the spirit shall return unto God who gave it."

When the silver cord and threefold flame (the 'spirit' or 'spirit spark') are withdrawn from the lower vehicles, the physical heart stops beating and the life-force and breath which animated the form return to the heart of the Christ Self and the etheric plane. The soul of Light also rises—with the accumulated light of the chakras which has been woven into the wedding garment—to the etheric plane where it abides 'dressed' in the etheric sheath until its next incarnation, when the three lower vehicles are remagnetized by the inner blueprint during gestation in the womb.

If the soul is dark, destructive, and given to the passions and possessiveness of this world, it gravitates to the astral planes of the lower vehicles to the hellish existence of its own making and liking. Reincarnating in the lower order of things, the soul experiences the replay of the cycles of death and mortality in and out of the body until the awakening to Christ and the desire to be free sets the soul on the path of self-liberation under the disciplines of so-called spirit guides, some of whom are really the angels and Ascended Masters.

THE KARMIC BOARD REDUCES THE SILVER CORD

Going back into past ages, we see, as the Ascended Master who is called the Great Divine Director* points out in his series of Pearls of Wisdom entitled "The Mechanization Concept," that this silver cord was as large in diameter as the tube of light, and the stream of energy from your Presence was just magnificent. It came down all around you. You didn't have to invoke

---

*also known as the Master R, who founded the House of Rakoczy and the retreat of the Great White Brotherhood in Transylvania and is the teacher and sponsor of Saint Germain

the tube of light because that was flowing naturally from the fount of the Godhead day and night.

Men lived to be eight and nine hundred years old [42] because, you see, this vital shower, like a Niagara Falls, was pouring Life and Life's essence into their physical forms. It kept out imperfection. It kept out disease. It maintained their souls' contact with God.

Then mankind began to abuse the Law. And so, by divine decree reflected in an edict of the Karmic Board, set forth in order to prevent mankind from misusing greater and greater quantities of God's energy (because we are all accountable for how much energy we use or misuse), God took away this tremendous shower of energy and reduced the silver cord to its present size.

That you may profit from the Great Divine Director's own words, I shall read them to you at this time:

> Some of the students are aware that when it became necessary to restrict mankind because of his viciousness and bestiality, the Lords of Karma did cut the allotment of cosmic energy for many lifestreams upon the planet until the stream of Life flowing into the body of man at the top of the head (which had once been the size of the tube of light) became a very narrow cord of silvery light-substance through which a relatively minute portion of energy could flow.
>
> Because there is a relationship between the apportioned size of the lifestream, or silver cord, and the spectrum of consciousness upon which man's awareness vibrates, the reduction in the actual size of the cord caused a corresponding decrease in the number of years of the allotted life span of mankind as well as a gradual shrinking of the spectrum of consciousness.
>
> You will recall that in the days of Methuselah

men did live to be many hundreds of years old. Then the shrinking of the rate of descending energy was reflected in a shrinking of the life span, together with the aforementioned spectrum of consciousness.

In a practical manner, this meant that the vibratory peaks of happiness which could be experienced by man and those of consciousness and of awareness were also diminished. And while, through the power of various spiritual exercises, mankind have been able to expand their consciousness, the physical vessel of man and his brain structure have continually impeded the flow of the vital essences because of the shrinking of the cup of consciousness. [43]

We see that the function of the silver cord is of ultimate importance, because the silver cord is the lifeline to our Presence. And, as the Great Divine Director teaches, for those willing to make the calls the lifeline can be expanded.

But bear in mind, dear hearts, that all of us are responsible for the energy we draw down from our Presence. Therefore, we must ask that we may receive the Light of the Christ consciousness and use that energy constructively always. [44] And this is the prerogative of every soul, whether you're in a male or female body—to magnetize the Christ and thereby become one with the Eternal Bridegroom. [45]

I've seen nervous people—like you see sometimes at some of these jazz places, where boys and girls are chewing gum and diddling with one foot and they just don't know what to do with themselves. They're just bouncing with energy.

Just think of all that nervous energy, all sent out in undisciplined thought and feeling. Is it any wonder they're nervous? Now, bring that energy under control and use it to heal the cells of the body. Bring that energy under control and use it to make the mind still. And the mind, then, becomes a clear pool, and in that clear pool the reflection of your Real Self can shine.

You see, as long as you have a choppy surface, you don't know whether you look like Fatty Arbuckle or Slim Jim. You don't know who you look like! If you look in the water, one minute you look fat and the next you look thin, and the image is shaking like a leaf. But still that pool, and you see a true reflection of yourself.

And if you can avoid the sin of Narcissus, you beautiful ladies and good-looking men, I mean—if you can resist falling in love with your own image (in the egocentrism of the human consciousness) and then falling in and drowning in the pool of self, you will behold instead your beloved Christ Self, whose loving face will rekindle in you the desire to be wed spiritually to the Divine Spouse.

THE THREEFOLD FLAME OF LIFE

In this little circle down here, shown in the center of the chest of the lower figure of yourself, is what is known as the threefold flame of Life. That flame of Life is one-sixteenth of an inch high inside of your physical heart.

You may say, "Well, if it's there, why hasn't medical science discovered it?" Well, the minute they get into it, you are no longer living and the flame is gone out. But that flame is there. And that flame is the flame of your life.

The threefold flame has three plumes—a blue plume, a yellow plume, and a pink plume. This may sound very strange to you, but it is true, and these three plumes form the pattern of the fleur-de-lis.

Most of you are familiar with this French lily which is a very beautiful motif—the emblem of the House of Bourbon.

Truly, the threefold flame is the divine right of every son of God. It is the seat of his conscious divinity. Through this tiny spark the identity of God can be known and contemplated. It is the sacred fire of creation, the preserver of Life, and the all-consuming Presence of Love.

Also called the holy Christ-flame and the threefold flame of liberty, this flame flower of the heart increases the divinity of the soul while blessing its humanity. It traces the inner blueprint on the parchment of Life. It shapes the soul's destiny in earth and fire, endows it with air and water, aerating the mind, washing the desire. It generates life and warmth, friendship and peace, kindling the noblest aspirations toward heaven, enlivening the earth with happiness and love of Home.

Consider, then, the three plumes that make up this tripartite light. The blue plume is the anchor point in your world for the will of God the Father; it sparks your willpower, your faith, and your God-determination to outpicture your divine plan through the four lower bodies. The golden yellow plume anchors the discriminating intelligence, the wisdom, the illumination, and the mind of God in Christ. The pink plume anchors the love, compassion, mercy, tenderness, and the grace of God, the Holy Spirit, together with the practical know-how to put the divine plan into action.

Saint Germain taught us about the threefold flame in a heart-to-heart Valentine message. His teaching is yours to contemplate:

Your heart is indeed one of the choicest gifts of God. Within it there is a central chamber surrounded by a forcefield of such light and protection that we call it a "cosmic interval."

It is a chamber separated from Matter and no probing could ever discover it. It occupies simultaneously not only the third and fourth dimensions but also other dimensions unknown to man.

This central chamber, called the altar of the heart, is thus the connecting point of the mighty silver cord of light that descends from your God Presence to sustain the beating of your physical heart, giving you life, purpose, and cosmic integration.

I urge all men to treasure this point of contact that they have with Life by giving conscious recognition to it. You do not need to understand by sophisticated language or scientific postulation the how, why, and wherefore of this activity.

Be content to know that God is there and that within you there is a point of contact with the Divine, a spark of fire from the Creator's own heart called the threefold flame of Life. There it burns as the triune essence of Love, Wisdom, and Power.

Each acknowledgment paid daily to the flame within your heart will amplify the power and illumination of Love within your being. Each such attention will produce a new sense of dimension for you, if not outwardly apparent then subconsciously manifest within the folds of your inner thoughts.

Neglect not, then, your heart as the altar of God. Neglect it not as the sun of your manifest being. Draw from God the power of Love and amplify it within your heart. Then send it out into the world at large as the bulwark of that

which shall overcome the darkness of the planet,
saying:

> I AM the Light of the Heart
> Shining in the darkness of being
> And changing all into the golden treasury
> Of the Mind of Christ.

> I AM projecting my Love
> Out into the world
> To erase all errors
> And to break down all barriers.

> I AM the power of infinite Love,
> Amplifying itself
> Until it is victorious,
> World without end![46]

This precious prayer of Saint Germain is more
powerful than you realize. It draws the holy angels—
Faith, Hope and Charity, who bear the Light of the
Trinity to your heart, fanning the fires of this little
sixteenth-inch-high flame, which is your signet of
eternal Life.

As the flame of your Holy Christ Self, it is truly
"the ornament of a meek and quiet spirit,"[47] as Peter
said. Burning on the heart's altar as the votive light of
the Father—tended by the hidden, or inner, man of
the heart,[48] whose image of the Only Begotten of the
Father is clearly outlined within its self-enveloping
flames—this threefold light is the replica in sacred fire
of the Holy Trinity.

Without this holiness unto the LORD,[49] beloved,
this spark of the Divine, you would be as beasts of
the field. Not particularly evil, but not particularly
good either, you would lack the free will to choose
to transcend the genetic patterns of the species
and the potential to become divine. Without this

endowment, you would exercise no choice of right or wrong, feel no conscience, desire no betterment of self, share no co-creative powers with Elohim through the spoken Word, and know not the all-encompassing Love of the Master-disciple (Guru-chela) relationship.

All the evildoers in whom the divine spark has grown cold (by their own willful neglect and blasphemy against the Godhead) have lost forever their original capacity to seek and find the Source of the creative fires. They have sunk below the level of the beasts; for they have sinned against the Holy Ghost, would not repent, and are hollow even of the hope of spiritual evolution through the sons of God—which even the blessed elementals yet retain.

Truly, with all thy getting, get the dominion over thy human self, by this flame of thy Divine Self.

Ask Saint Germain to help you. He will.

Use his mantra affirming the "I AM" as the Light of your heart. It contains his momentum of devotion to the sacred fire whereby he has demonstrated the spirit's mastery over the elements by the alchemy of the threefold flame.[50]

THE ONLY BEGOTTEN SON OF THE FATHER— YOUR HOLY CHRIST SELF

The Holy Christ Self is the Mediator between God and man. God in the absolute sense of Spirit is wholly perfect. He is not even aware of what we call sin or iniquity or any evil vibration. Of him the prophet declared, "Thou art of purer eyes than to behold evil and canst not look on iniquity . . ."[51] Therefore, he created the "Christ Mind"—which descended to the midpoint (the etheric octave) between our highest and lowest self-expression.

This replica of the only begotten Son of the Father, full of grace and truth, serves as the Mediator of each lifestream before the throne of God. He is the Advocate before the Father, The LORD Our Righteousness whose coming was foretold by the prophet Jeremiah. [52]

This Son (or Light) of the Presence came forth to do the will of God as the Father's own representative at your side. His is the still small voice of 'conscience' you hear whenever you are willing to listen.

Jesus was both the actual and symbolical representative of this Christ Self. Jesus was the example, the one who self-realized the Christ Mind and was at one with it at all times. Jesus himself was not the only begotten Son of the Father. The Christ of him was and is the only begotten Son of the Father; and Jesus was the pure vessel of that Universal One. He was the One Sent, chosen from among the Sons of heaven to embody the Christ on earth as the avatar, the exemplar for all to follow for the two-thousand-year Piscean cycle.

When the soul of Jesus became one with the Christ, the son of man was called and he called himself the Son of God. This is the selfsame office to which you can aspire through the path of your personal Christhood on behalf of your family, community, nation, and even world.

Jesus was the embodiment of the Sun, or Light, of God on behalf of the *man*ifestation of earth's evolution. He was the Keeper of the Flame—of the threefold flame of Life—on our behalf until by our own devotion to the Source, we, too, might magnetize a sufficiency of the Sun Presence to intensify our own divinity and hold the balance for others until they, too, are able. Thus, teaching us how to be "my brother's keeper" is one of the fundamental purposes of the Great White Brotherhood.

Beloved Jesus' Christhood was both an office that he filled and a mantle that he bore. And before our very eyes the son of man became both the office and the mantle—which in turn shaped the very nature of his individual Sonship and mission. Jesus was uniquely the Christ and the Christ was uniquely Jesus. And this is the way it is intended to be for all of us—each one showing forth a very precious profile of the Universal One. And the ray of his divinity shone upon him and merged with his humanity. And this consummation of Love's Presence both with and in you will happen to you.

Jesus came to teach us by his example that every child of God has a Holy Christ Self and that the Holy Christ Self is the means to our individualization of the God flame according to the divine plan and free will of our lifestream. The Christ Self is the expression of the absolute love of God for each of his children, the very same love bestowed upon Jesus. Otherwise, God would have had a favorite son, Jesus, and all the rest of us would have been defrauded of our sovereign right to his kingdom.

I don't believe God did this, and I know you don't either.

We wouldn't have stood a ghost of a chance of getting anywhere with God except perhaps in the outer court. As it is now, we have the chance to sit, as it were, on the throne of our own divinity. We can be rulers over many things in the four planes of Matter by being faithful in a few things of the Spirit.[53] All things are possible with God, and this includes the raising of every lifestream that he ever created into his divine inheritance.

I used to wonder, as a child, how it could be that God only created Jesus, who I was taught was the only son that was really 'begotten' of God. Then Jesus revealed to me the truth. Your Holy Christ Self is begotten of your own I AM Presence in order to mediate between the human and the divine—for the express purpose of showing the soul how to correct its human faults. Your beloved Christ Self is your Teacher who inspires you through the intelligence of God's Mind and shows you how your lifestream down here can ascend back to your God Source up there, as Jesus did.

The Chart, then, illustrates to you that day by day you may put on the identity of the Son of God. As you live in a Christlike way, your Christ Self descends closer and closer to you until, by kind words and thoughts and pure feelings and actions motivated by goodwill, you and your blessed Christ Self become one.

It's like some Christians say they're being "partners with God." God will act through you through the Son of his heart. Through the threefold flame—that spark divine—you know Christ and in him you know your Father. Your soul and body temple, your mind and heart become illumined and radiant by the presence with you of this Emmanuel. And your light shines because you are anointed with the Light of your Christ Self. So you become like your elder brother Jesus, who was the "Anointed One"—Jesus, "the Christ."

This is the original meaning of the word *Christ.* One who is Christ is anointed with the Son-Light of God, one who becomes the very embodiment of that Light. Jesus is described as one in whom the Godhead dwelt bodily.

If you are to ascend to the heart of God, you must do so by first ascending to the level of your Christ Self. For only the Son of God who came down from heaven can ascend to the plane of the I AM Presence.[54] All in whom the Spirit of the LORD dwells can claim their present sonship as heirs of the promise. But only by becoming fully integrated with your Christ Self, body and soul, can you affirm in the physical plane, "I AM *the* Son of God"—i.e., the Christ of God incarnate.

Nonetheless, you can affirm right now that your Real Self is the Son of God and that, by right, you are a disciple of Jesus Christ on the path of becoming one with the Son of God. This is the goal of your life which God has ordained for you, as for Jesus. And when you attain it, you will know it and no one will need to tell you, and no one will be able to deny it.

You may walk the earth for many a decade or for centuries bearing the burden of the LORD's Light dwelling in you bodily, until one day the Father calls you Home and your soul, hid with Christ in God,[55] ascends to the I AM THAT I AM to go out no more. "For in him dwelleth all the fullness of the Godhead bodily. And ye are complete in him, which is the head of all principality and power."[56]

When Jesus was taken up "in a cloud" of infinite energy from Bethany's hill, two angels who looked like "men in white apparel" said to the disciples: "Ye men of Galilee, why stand ye gazing up into heaven? This same Jesus, which is taken up from you into heaven, shall so come in like manner as ye have seen him go into heaven."[57]

Even so, from the day of your ascension, my beloved, or even from states of attainment of God-mastery before the ascension, you may also come in like manner, stepping through the veil as the saints do at times to appear to those loved ones on earth, bearing witness to them of their God-potential in all the glory and radiance of the great Light you shall have become in Jesus' name and power.

The descent of the Ascended Master Jesus Christ into your world is most likely to occur through the consciousness of your own Christ Self. Those who saw him ascend were in the Christ consciousness, else they would not have witnessed the angels as well; and those who see him descending day by day are also witnesses of Christ in their own temples, by the same Spirit of the LORD.

BALANCE THE THREEFOLD FLAME

Now, I want to explain that most of you do not have a balanced threefold flame. Some of you—we can see it—do have a lot of power and a lot of faith and your blue plume is big.

But some of you have very, very little love. Some of you have a lot of love. You're just so loving, you could just love the whole world! So you're a third-ray type. You've got a great big pink plume but a very tiny plume of illumination—you don't have a lot of real understanding yet.

Some of you have a great big plume of gold. You have all kinds of understanding, like the second-ray people, but you don't have much faith; and therefore, you don't put it to work. Or you don't have much love for people—just for yourself.

Now, what the Christ wants us to do is to *balance the threefold flame.* If we're a person with great faith and great power, we're a first-ray person. He wants us to learn to love one another. He wants us to obtain wisdom. With all thy getting get understanding.[58]

If we have a lot of worldly wisdom but very little love for the world, very little faith in the purposes of Life, he wants us to gain these other two legs of the tripod of being.

This is what all of you have to understand: our duty on earth is to first balance our threefold flame, and then expand the three plumes together—not just one aspect of being but all three of them. It is only by balancing all of the elements of the Trinity in our lives that we can actually attain the fullness of our Christ-perfection.

This is a decree you can give for this purpose. It's called "Balance the Threefold Flame in Me!"

In the name of the beloved mighty victorious Presence of God, I AM in me, and my very own beloved Holy Christ Self, I call to beloved Helios and Vesta and the threefold flame of Love, Wisdom, and Power in the heart of the Great Central Sun, to beloved Morya El, beloved Lanto, beloved Paul the Venetian, beloved Mighty Victory, beloved Goddess of Liberty, the seven mighty Elohim, beloved Lanello, the entire Spirit of the Great White Brotherhood and the World Mother, Elemental Life—Fire, Air, Water, and Earth!

To balance, blaze, and expand the threefold flame within my heart until I AM manifesting all of thee and naught of the human remains.

Take complete dominion and control over my four lower bodies and raise me and all life by the power of the three-times-three into the glorious resurrection and ascension in the Light!

In the name of the Father, the Mother, the Son, and the Holy Spirit, I decree:

Balance the threefold flame in me! (3x)
    Beloved I AM!
Balance the threefold flame in me! (3x)
    Take thy command!
Balance the threefold flame in me! (3x)
    Magnify it each hour!
Balance the threefold flame in me! (3x)
    Love, Wisdom, and Power!

And in full Faith I consciously accept this manifest, manifest, manifest! (3x) right here and now with full Power, eternally sustained, all-powerfully active, ever expanding, and world enfolding until all are wholly ascended in the Light and free!

Beloved I AM! Beloved I AM! Beloved I AM!

Note: Use the word "Blaze" and then "Expand" in place of "Balance" for two alternate decrees once you have developed a momentum on "Balance."

YOUR CAUSAL BODY

Now we will discuss the point at which people begin to differ in the Divine Self. You have an I AM Presence and it looks just like everybody else's. It looks just like God's.

I always learned that if you put one and one together, you got two—that's all there is to it. You can't change mathematics. And therefore, you can't say that God is more God than himself, or that man is more or less God than God. Because if God created man in his own image, then he made him in his own image, period! There is no difference between the image of God and its manifestation in man! Man is not more or less the image of God; in his natural spiritual state he is simply the image—pure and undefiled.

We have to understand this in order to understand the Chart, because we've got to change our thinking. We can't keep thinking that we're just nothing, because nothing could not possibly come forth from nothing, and nothing could not possibly come forth from something, could it? Therefore, something comes forth from something; and what came forth, of course, is the Divine Man, *the divine manifestation.*

Oh, he doesn't look very divine now, does he?—when you see him lying drunk in the gutter, when you

see him out here misbehaving and doing all kinds of
unruly things. He doesn't look very divine, but up-
stairs he is. Up here, everybody who came forth from
God is divine. There is absolutely no difference between your I AM Presence and my I AM Presence—
because, as we have said, the Presence is the replica of
God. And there is only one God.

But here's where the difference comes in. This is
important. In the Bible it says, "For one star differeth
from another star in glory. So also is the resurrection
of the dead." [59] This means that people have causal
bodies of varying size and magnitude. These circles of
color bands are spherical bodies. They're not flat as
they're painted on the Chart with pigment; these are
spheres of energy, pulsating energy, permanent energy, eternal energy. They're spiritual Light energy
radiating the color of their frequency and vibration.

Your causal body is shaped like a globe; the
white fire core is in the very center enfolding the I AM
Presence in its central sun of purity's Power and Light.
This is the first, or primordial, sphere. The yellow
sphere which surrounds it is the primal radiation of
the Mind of God; and it contains the record and the
momentum of all the intelligence, divinely illumined
action, self-knowledge and wisdom that you have ever
externalized from God. It is the second sphere.

And here is the pink, the core of love—the third
sphere—and then mercy and the violet transmuting
flame, the fourth. And then the purple-and-gold band
of justice and the ritual of the Law outpictured as your
service to life is the fifth sphere. And then the green,
the healing and supply in your life, the abundance of
Life, the sixth. And all of these are sealed in a magnificent blue-flame sphere, the seventh, of protection,
perfection, fiery faith, and God's own goodwill.

You see, every time that you do a good deed on

earth, the angels of record build up the size of your electronic body. The good deed is, in effect, a cause you set in motion, which multiplies its vibration around the world, begetting more of its kind as it ripples out to bless many more than the one who was first the recipient of your graciousness.

The light of virtuous acts automatically ascends to the corresponding ring of your causal body. Multiplied by your Christ Self, it returns again and again to increase the good of your divine potential. Therefore, when you need more light to accomplish more good works, you can draw forth from your causal body the 'treasures of heaven' you have stored there as your reserves.

For example, the white has all the colors of the rainbow in it; it's a symbol of purity. Every time that you permit purity to function in your world, every time you perform any soul-purifying ablution—you better believe that that is adding to the size of that band of white.

And every single thing that you do for yourself to keep yourself pure—beginning with your pure perception of all life, the immaculate concept of what is really real—is yours forever. You can never lose what you spiritually gain. And as you gain spiritually, you gain physically, mentally, emotionally, and etherically.

Everything you do out of *pure* love, *pure* truth, *pure* devotion, service for the sake of service and not self-gain adds to the size of the central white sphere—and the bigger it gets, the more purity-power you have in your world. And that's why one star differs from another star in glory.

"In glory"—this means in its glorying in God or in its glorification or magnification of the Word of God. So, the one catch about building your causal body rings is that whatever you do in your use (or

glorification) of the seven rays, it must be "to the glory of God" [60] and in the service of some part or every part of his Life expressed in his children.

So if you do what you do to the glory of your ego and its self-serving ends, it doesn't count. *It doesn't count for grace.* You may get what you want—a glorified ego, fat with the riches and successes of this world, and a developed and even powerful personality down here—but you won't be storing up treasure in heaven.

None of that goes to build your causal body; instead it accumulates as the momentum of the lower electronic belt. This is the memorabilia of your human karma, which one day, piece by piece, you will want to put into the violet flame—because you won't need it anymore. Once transmuted, this energy, after having been reconsecrated by you in the building of the patterns of perfection on earth, will ascend to your causal body.

Now, let's take a look at that yellow sphere again. Every time you pick up the scriptures, the holy books of East and West, and you read and you run with the Word, or every time you study and demonstrate your mastery of the learning process of anything constructive—if it's to the joy of God's flame in you, you add to your storehouse of knowledge, and that adds to the size of the golden sphere of illumination. This is how you lay up for yourselves treasures in heaven where, Jesus said, "neither moth nor rust doth corrupt, and where thieves do not break through nor steal." [61]

Everything that you do where God works through you—of purity, of learning, or of expressing love, as in this pink band—every time you're loving and kind to any human being, immutably, it registers up there by God's I AM THAT I AM. The Law demands it!

So whatever you do of good down here in the

human end (the lower figure in the Chart) is registered up there. That's why you never lose it. You can lose your body, you can even lose your mind, but you will never, never, never lose your causal body. It's there forever. Your soul came forth from it, and it will return to it. It is the place prepared in heaven by God and by your good works on earth.

What's this violet band here? Well, that's the quality of mercy that is not strained—"It droppeth as the gentle rain from heaven upon the place beneath. It is twice blest; it blesseth him that gives and him that takes."[62] That's mercy and forgiveness and the alchemy of transmutation, ritual and diplomacy—take note of that.

And here, in the fiery blue-purple adorned with pure gold, is the path of Christ's ministration and service which you outpicture daily as you minister to all life, serving to set God's life free on earth.

And here is the green folding stuff you carry in your wallet; it's also chlorophyll—symbol of health and the abundant life, your physical/spiritual wholeness and supply. It's the ray you use for precipitation in conjunction with the alchemy of the seventh ray. It's the green of nature, the healing power of the universe. It's a combination of the yellow and the blue, isn't it?

It's the wisdom and the power to produce good health and honest wealth. That's in the green sphere. That's why many of your physicians today are using green in their operating rooms. Because that color is health, chlorophyll—the imprisoned Life-splendor of the sun.

It's also the light of Truth as science that sets you free from drudgery. It's spiritual Truth as the *true* Teachings of Christ and not the false. And it's the all-seeing, all-knowing eye of God that will act through you, through your Christ Self.

And what's that blue sphere? That's power. That's the first ray. That's the will of God. That's faith. Every time you have faith in divine things, you add to the size of that. It is the envelope of protection and power vouchsafed to you through your obedience to the will of God. Without love of the Father and submission to his goodwill for you and your loved ones, you cannot retain the power to act. Isn't that a beautiful sphere of radiant blue light!

Do you see how the Law works? You draw forth protection through your calls to God and Archangel Michael, and you seal yourself below as you are sealed above in this wonderful emanation of your causal body that protects you always.

ACCESSING YOUR COSMIC BANK ACCOUNT

This is why the woman followed Jesus everywhere and came trembling to get ahold of his garment. Because she had so much blue ray, so much faith up in her causal body, that she knew if she could just touch the hem of his garment, she'd be healed—and she did and she was healed.

But did you take note of what happened? What did he say? He said, "Who touched me?"

Peter said, "Master, how can you say, Who touched me, when the whole multitude are pressing around you on every side?"

He said, "Nay, somebody has touched me, for I perceive that virtue is gone out of me." [63]

Take note of that. Out of his causal body, the virtue of God descended down the silver cord and came through his chakras, through his flesh form and went out through the hem of his garment. This is the energy of God, and it's also yours to conserve and to command. And when you are one with your Christ Self, you will also feel it pass through you and out of you.

So this is your causal body, or your heavenly storehouse; it's your cosmic bank. And every single one of you in this room has a different size causal body with different size spheres within it.

Now, if you're real wise, if you're really smart, you have a lot of intelligence vibrating in the yellow band of your causal body. If you're really full of power and you've got a lot of faith, you know—you've got a lot of blue energy up there. If you're in the healing arts or you're a banker—you've probably got a lot of green. And here, of course, you may be a very merciful person—you've got a lot of pink in your aura (Mary Magdalene had a lot of that)—you're a person of great love.

And that's why some of you people who are so little down here in the human—some of the little women we have here—you have an aura that is so big that it really belies your size. You are not limited by your physical envelope in these matters. You can be a spiritual giant and have a small physical form. Or you can be as big as I am and have a puny little aura, you know. So don't be fooled.

Now, how does the energy of the causal body, which is your cosmic bank, get down here into the physical plane so it's available to you to use at will for more good works in the name of the LORD?

The answer is very simple. It comes down through this silver cord; and it will intensify and accelerate in answer to your call. By your dynamic decrees and "good credit"—showing your wise investment of the light/ energy/consciousness entrusted to your use from this cosmic bank account—you can access more and more of God's infinite resources day by day.

I have told the story about the little girl who had a balloon filled with helium so that the balloon always stayed up, and she held it on a string. And like Mary who had a little lamb that followed her wherever she went, the balloon followed the little girl wherever she went.

As long as you live, wherever you walk, just like the little girl running through the park with a big balloon and a string going up, you are right below your own causal body and your own I AM Presence, dangling on the end of the string. Except the string is a silver cord running down through your head, right down to your heart, and that's what beats your heart. And it goes with you everywhere you go, just like Mary's little lamb.

If you walk three steps to the right or to the left, your God Presence moves with you. How could it be otherwise? "Have not I commanded thee? Be strong and of a good courage. Be not afraid, neither be thou dismayed, for the LORD thy God is with thee whithersoever thou goest." [64]

So the Presence is never very far from any of you wherever you are. That's why the psalmist said, "If I ascend up into heaven, thou art there. If I make my bed in hell, behold, thou art there. If I take the wings of the morning and dwell in the uttermost parts of the sea, even there shall thy hand lead me and thy right hand shall hold me." [65] It's because God goes with you—specifically, God individualized in your I AM Presence.

Now, can't you better imagine your Presence (the angel of his Presence) with you in hell than the Almighty God himself stepping down from his throne to follow you into hell? It makes perfect sense, you see, for God to create this blessed expression of himself to interact with you from day to day. For while his eye beholds you as "the apple of his eye," [66] at the same time he is beholding the All-in-all of Cosmos so that it too, like your eternal Spirit, will be eternally sustained.

YOUR TUBE OF LIGHT

The power of the Divine Presence was with Moses and the children of Israel as the LORD, the beloved Mighty I AM Presence, "went before them by day in a pillar of a cloud to lead them the way, and by night in a pillar of fire to give them light to go by day and night. He took not away the pillar of the cloud by day nor the pillar of fire by night from before the people." [67]

Your Mighty I AM Presence has existed from the moment God thought of it and it will exist forever as the thoughtform of his Mind for your perfection and protection. The rays of light from your Presence signify that your God Presence can reach any corner of the universe instantly with the speed of light. Therefore, you really have something omnipotent here, don't you? Omniscient—yes! Omnipresent because it's the Presence—that's right.

Remember the angel of God which went before the camp of Israel? [68] Well this 'angel' is the messenger of your I AM Presence. Why does your I AM Presence need a messenger? Because, as we have just said, your Presence is ever beholding God Good—creating, preserving, and sustaining worlds of perfection for your soul to inhabit.

Because the Divine Presence does not behold iniquity, the LORD's angel in the person of Archangel Michael as well as your own Christ Self does go before and behind your camp; and wherever the Christ Self is, there is the pillar of the cloud: before, behind, and in the midst of his chosen people is the Spirit of the Great White Brotherhood.

Now, here you are down here in a physical form. You make a call up through "the angel of the LORD," one of the archangels or angelic messengers, by your Holy Christ Self, to your Presence. And the immaculate, all-pure, all-powerful eye of your Presence answers you through the discriminating, all-seeing, all-knowing eye of your Christ Self and sends down the energy as the Light, Life, and Love of the Godhead. And the tube of light—the pillar of cloud by day and the pillar of fire by night—is created in answer to your call.

The call compels the answer and down comes the tube of light from the Presence. It drops like a curtain all around you and protects you against the harmful effects of the mass consciousness because it stops human creation from coming through.

Did you know that the vision of your Holy Christ Self, your seven chakras, the transmutation of karma, and the Chart of your Mighty I AM Presence was given to Joshua the high priest about five hundred years before Jesus Christ was born? Well, listen to this reading.

After the LORD chose to forgive and transmute Joshua's iniquity (sin, karma) and to change his garments—from filthy to the raiment and mitre of the high priest before the altar of God, standing in the office and the stead of the Holy Christ Self on behalf of the people—the LORD said to him:

> Hear now, O Joshua the high priest, thou and thy fellows that sit before thee, for they are men wondered at: for, behold, I will bring forth my servant the BRANCH.
>
> For behold the stone that I have laid before Joshua; upon one stone shall be seven eyes. Behold, I will engrave the graving thereof, saith the LORD of hosts, and I will remove the iniquity of that land in one day.
>
> In that day, saith the LORD of hosts, shall ye call every man his neighbour under the vine and under the fig tree. [69]

And this is the interpretation: My servant the BRANCH is the Person who embodies the Righteousness of God, who comes to replace the self-righteousness of the human. This Person, whom Jeremiah called The LORD Our Righteousness, as we have said, is your own beloved Holy Christ Self.

The BRANCH endows the individual soul with the capacity to be conscious of himself within Christ and to be conscious of Christ within himself. The stone is the unquickened, unredeemed, unanointed who shall receive through the BRANCH the consciousness of God focused in the seven chakras.

Micah says, "Every man shall sit under his own vine and fig tree."[70] The Vine is the beloved Christ Self, the fig tree is the I AM Presence and the causal body bearing the fruits of God consciousness in good works. The LORD is the Mighty I AM Presence, who is represented in the Christ Self.

In the coming kingdom, the reign of God's consciousness on earth, the people will no longer preach the LORD, every man to his neighbor, for they shall all know their Mighty I AM Presence and Christ Self.[71] And "my servant the BRANCH," the Righteousness of God with and in each soul, will serve as high priest at the altar of the living God.

Through Zechariah, the LORD prophesied to Joshua: your office foreshadows the coming of Christ incarnate in Jesus, the Lord; and then, in the fullness of the time ordained, it shall reveal that Christ as the Person, *Pure Son,* of each one's own divinity. This is the path of the return to Eden and the lost estate of God-dominion for every son of God.

Let's seal this revelation of your God Reality through and through with our "Violet Fire and Tube of Light Decree," dictated to me for you by the beloved Ascended Master Saint Germain.

Wherever you are in this glorious universe God made, in whatever plane of heaven or earth, won't you pause with me in the oneness of our communion in the Holy Spirit and send forth this call spoken aloud to God through your Beloved I AM Presence.

O my constant, loving I AM Presence, thou Light of God above me whose radiance forms a circle of fire before me to light my way:

I AM faithfully calling to thee to place a great pillar of Light from my own Mighty I AM God Presence all around me right now today! Keep it intact through every passing moment, manifesting as a shimmering shower of God's beautiful Light through which nothing human can ever pass. Into this beautiful electric circle of divinely charged energy direct a swift upsurge of the violet fire of Freedom's forgiving, transmuting flame!

Cause the ever expanding energy of this flame projected downward into the forcefield of my human energies to completely change every negative condition into the positive polarity of my own Great God Self! Let the magic of its mercy so purify my world with Light that all whom I contact shall always be blessed with the fragrance of violets from God's own heart in memory of the blessed dawning day when all discord—cause, effect, record, and memory—is forever changed into the Victory of Light and the peace of the ascended Jesus Christ.

I AM now constantly accepting the full power and manifestation of this fiat of Light and calling it into instantaneous action by my own God-given free will and the power to accelerate without limit this sacred release of assistance from God's own heart until all men are ascended and God-free in the Light that never, never, never fails!

Thus it is written, and thus the LORD, the Mighty I AM Presence (YAHWEH), has sealed his promise by his 'angel'—by the "man with a measuring line in his hand," who now stands before you as the eternal Messiah, the same yesterday and today and forever, even your own beloved Christ Self. He has promised unto you, the living soul, the daughter of Zion, who has gone forth from his Spirit:

I, saith the LORD, will be unto her a wall of fire round about, and will be the glory in the midst of her. . . .

Sing and rejoice, O daughter of Zion; for, lo, I come, and I will dwell in the midst of thee, saith the LORD.

And many nations shall be joined to the LORD in that day, and shall be my people. And I will dwell in the midst of thee, and thou shalt know that the LORD of hosts hath sent me unto thee.[72]

Peace be unto you, beloved, in the name I AM THAT I AM.

YOUR DIVINE SELF

THE ASCENDED MASTER JESUS CHRIST

THE ASCENDED MASTER SAINT GERMAIN

SEVEN CHAKRAS IN THE BODY OF MAN

SEAT OF THE SOUL
CHAKRA

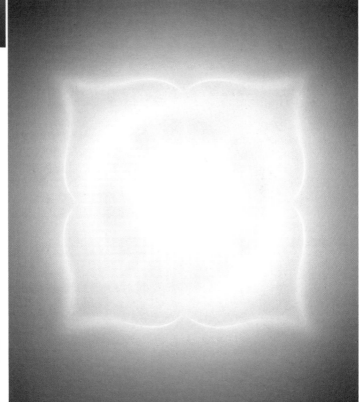

BASE OF THE SPINE
CHAKRA

THROAT
CHAKRA

SOLAR PLEXUS
CHAKRA

HEART CHAKRA

CROWN
CHAKRA

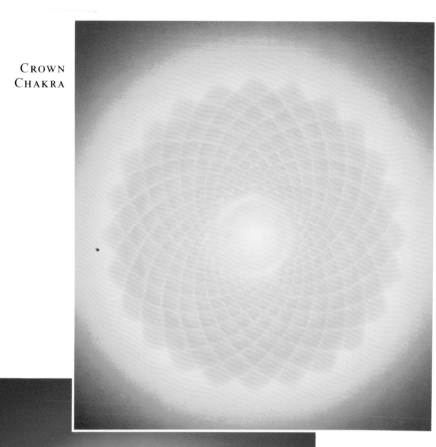

THIRD EYE
CHAKRA

Chapter Seven

THE INTEGRATION OF THE CHAKRAS

The Integration of the Chakras

"THE Fitness Craze," "Body Beautiful," "America in Training." How many headlines have you read about the benefits of physical exercise?

The current trends would have you believe that almost any problem you can think of can be cured through some sort of workout program. Books, magazines, and television shows abound, touting everything from aerobics to racquetball as the ultimate remedy for a wide range of maladies from simple stress to heart disease.

Health, as we all know, is a product of proper diet, positive mental attitude, enough sleep, and physical exercise—right? Well, maybe . . .

THE MISSING DIMENSION IN PHYSICAL FITNESS

While such activities are definitely valid, there has been a consistent omission of a very important element. The missing dimension in physical fitness has nothing to do with what we normally think of as health-promoting factors.

What we are talking about are centers of energy flow within your body that you cannot see or touch but that are as important to isolate and condition as your triceps. These centers are called *chakras*—the Sanskrit word meaning "wheel" or "disc." There are seven major chakras within your body.

You're probably wondering how in the world something you can't even see, let alone exercise, can be so important to fitness! Well, you *can* exercise your chakras. And even if you can't see them, you can feel them. More on this later.

To begin with, the physical body of an athlete is only one-quarter of the whole person. You also have your mental body (your thoughts and cognitive mind), your emotional body (feelings and desires), and your etheric body (your memory, containing layers of the subconscious and the superconscious mind as well as the blueprint of life) to train for the optimum performance in any situation—be it track, court, or gridiron.

These three other 'bodies' fulfill a very important role in any athletic training program. It is these which support the physical body and give it that extra determination to push through, to work those muscles, even when—and especially when—you feel that "burn" that lets you know you are making progress.

As anyone familiar with the world of physical fitness can testify, workouts are grueling and painful and exact a heavy toll on the body. Except for a possible endorphin-induced high, there is little immediate physical gratification. (Endorphins are chemicals produced by the body during periods of intense exertion that mimic the effects of opium on the brain. They contribute largely, along with pain-blocking enkephalins, to the phenomenon known as "runner's high.")

Another phenomenon known to many runners is the "wall." This is the point at which the body has used up all of its available glycogen and has no more energy to give to the muscles. Usually this is after twenty miles or so, when the body is physically exhausted. Sometimes drinking sugar water during the run will combat this problem. Most people, however, will get "exhausted" long before the wall is reached.

For those who do not run regularly, to actually go twenty miles would be impossible without risking serious injury.

The point I am making here is that there are many who could run the twenty miles but stop at six or ten because they *think* or *feel* that they can't do it. If those people would get their mental and emotional bodies working with their physical, they would excel. This is only common sense.

Any gratification achieved through a fitness program is delayed. Be it drinking a glass of apple juice and taking a cool shower after the evening's program or long-term muscular gain, the joy of a workout is not the workout itself.

Consequently, unless you are someone who enjoys pain, there must be other factors driving you to put your body through its paces. These could be your *memories* of how good you felt last time you 'pumped iron', your *mental* determination to excel, or the desire to attain the *emotional* control that comes with the true mastery of any sport or martial art.

Take, for example, the case of John McEnroe, the tennis pro who plays a very good game but has been known to throw his racquet and berate the judges. His actions reveal a temporary absence of emotional control for which he receives no small amount of bad publicity.

In the Davis Cup tournament held in Buenos Aires, McEnroe was badly beaten. This was due in large part to the clay courts on which the games were played. Sullen and dejected, McEnroe broke his routine by remaining unusually quiet for the duration of the competition.

But even this despondency is a lack of emotional control. If McEnroe had really wanted to win that tournament, he would have had to maintain a positive attitude while at the same time keeping his lid on. This is the middle path of the Buddha—just enough of the right qualities at the right time, without ever losing control. In any event, he could probably play a much better game, as well as increase his popularity immensely, if he would integrate his "emotional body" with his physical.

Tennis, or even racquetball, requires a great deal of memory in addition to emotional control. Just think of the countless hours of practice McEnroe has spent. Not only must he have developed his forearm and trained his eye, but also he must remember with intimate detail which type of shot to use on what occasion and the exact angle of incidence and reflection of every ball that screams over the net and into his court. Once memorized in every cell, these responses must then become automated—like a bio-electric formula invoked and executed faster than the 'mind' can think.

As far as mental attitude is concerned, this is mainly being "psyched up" for the game. No matter how skilled your opponent, or what the playing surface is composed of, you must know you have the ability and determination to win.

Alright, you say, what does all of this have to do with your chakras? Thought you'd never ask!

Each body is separate and distinct—sharing, or intersecting through, the common coordinates of the seven chakras. In the physical, they are specifically attached through the central nervous and endocrine systems. The chakras are the central vehicles for the flow of light from your soul to your four bodies.

In order to maximize your potential, you must have a clear passage for the light and energy you receive from the Life Source each day to move freely through all of your bodies. If any chakra is clogged, it can throw one or more of your four bodies out of alignment. If one of the four lower bodies is out of alignment, you can't make the most of any of them.

All the push-ups in the world won't mean a thing if you are still fighting your own sense of limitation. Therefore, it behooves anyone who is really serious about fitness and well-being to study and know the chakras and their effects on training as well as all aspects of everyday life.

THE THREEFOLD FLAME OF THE HEART

The central and most important organ of your body is your heart. Likewise, the central and most important chakra is the heart chakra, which contains the threefold flame. The threefold flame is the blossoming of light within your heart, anchored there through the descent of the crystal cord. It is not really a flame like a candle, but we can think of it more in terms of the bush that burned with fire and was not consumed.[1] The crystal cord is the thread of light which descends from your "I AM Presence," another name for your God Self.

Why is the flame in your heart called "three-fold"? Because it embodies the three God-qualities of Power, Wisdom, and Love, also personified in the Trinity. Ideally, these are kept in balance. But few have the mastery to do this. Instead, people fill their hearts with hatred, fear, and malice, which on the spiritual level resemble lead or asphalt. (Heart disease, though on the decline, remains the biggest killer in the country. Small wonder.)

One of the most important parts of keeping fit is cleaning up and balancing the heart chakra. Just as the brain and organs depend on blood flow, so all other chakras depend on energy flow from the heart. Thus, when the heart is clogged through selfishness and possessiveness, which block this flow, all of the chakras suffer.

Secondly, after the threefold flame is balanced, it must then be expanded. Before the proverbial Fall of man, the threefold flame surrounded the body completely and reached a height of five to seven feet. At that time, the crystal cord was over nine feet in diameter, channeling tremendous amounts of divine energy into the heart chakra of man. This increased his longevity—hence the extraordinarily long life spans, earlier noted, of such antediluvian figures as Methuselah and Noah—and enabled him to perform what would now be considered as superhuman feats.

Finally, the heart chakra must be protected. It is extremely sensitive to all types of vibrations, both good and bad. This sensitivity must be guarded. Negative frequencies impinging upon the heart can cause heart attacks. Most dangerous are hatred, mental criticism, hardness of heart, envy, and even the death wish, which amounts to witchcraft. By failing to groom their thoughts and feelings with love, people actually engage in mental and emotional malpractice against one another on a day-to-day basis.

LIGHT MANTRAS FOR THE HEART

Saint Germain, the Master who is the keystone in the arch of the Aquarian age, has given us a mantra for the cleansing of our chakras. This mantra can be used in conjunction with all of the other mantras contained in this chapter. It is very simple and easy to remember and can be given aloud or under your breath any time things aren't going well or you feel a heaviness in your body or a burden on your heart.

I AM a being of violet fire,
I AM the purity God desires!

Similar in quality to the threefold flame in the heart, the violet fire, or violet flame, is specifically for the transmutation of negative karma, records of nonfulfillment in this or past lives, or negativity in any form. It is the flame of freedom and of the Holy Spirit which forgives sin by dissolving its cause, effect, record, and memory. It is the God-energy that frees the atoms, cells, and electrons in your four lower bodies to sing the song of their fiery destiny. And it will liberate all who use it—mentally, psychologically, and spiritually.

Saint Germain's mantra for the Aquarian age can be adapted for use with all chakras as follows:

My heart is a chakra of violet fire,
My heart is the purity God desires!

My throat chakra is a wheel of violet fire,
My throat chakra is the purity God desires!

My solar plexus is a sun of violet fire,
My solar plexus is the purity God desires!

My third eye is a center of violet fire,
My third eye is the purity God desires!

My soul chakra is a sphere of violet fire,
My soul is the purity God desires!

My crown chakra is a lotus of violet fire,
My crown chakra is the purity God desires!

My base chakra is a fount of violet fire,
My base chakra is the purity God desires!

Simply give the mantra corresponding to the specific chakra you feel needs cleansing, and give it until you feel a release from your tension, anxiety, or whatever problem you may have. Try it! It works.

For the purposes of visualization, the heart chakra,

when at its optimum, emits a white fire clothed with shades of pink, rose, and ruby—depending on the intensity and purity of the love expressed. This rose of the heart has twelve petals. It is visualized over the place of the physical heart, although in the perfected state, it and its physical counterpart would be in the center of the chest.

See the threefold flame within it, with its three plumes of Power, Wisdom, and Love as flames of blue, gold, and pink respectively. As an added protection against world weight, you can see in your mind's eye a spinning disc of white light in front of the heart. For a real clearing action, give the "I AM Light" mantra.

When you say the mantra aloud, you are setting up a forcefield of light around your heart. This forcefield will keep away the 'bad vibes' and other assorted negative energies that tend at times to make things go wrong.

This is one of many practical applications of the science of the spoken Word. Through the correct use of the throat chakra in decrees such as this one, we become effectively co-creators with our Higher Consciousness. As spoken of in the Book of Job, "The Almighty shall be thy defence. . . . Thou shalt make thy prayer unto him, and he shall hear thee . . . . Thou shalt also decree a thing, and it shall be established unto thee: and the light shall shine upon thy ways."[2]

"I AM" is the name of God as spoken to Moses: Tell them, 'I AM' hath sent me unto you. This is my name for ever.[3] Therefore, when we affirm "I AM," we are affirming *"God in me is"* or *"God in me is the action of. . ."* Whatever follows—whether it be speech, prayer, mantra, or decree—it is self-realized because it is the power of God's name and his Be-ness that works creative change in our lives.

I AM Light

I AM Light, glowing Light,
Radiating Light, intensified Light.
God consumes my darkness,
Transmuting it into Light.

This day I AM a focus of the Central Sun.
Flowing through me is a crystal river,
A living fountain of Light
That can never be qualified
By human thought and feeling.
I AM an outpost of the Divine.
Such darkness as has used me is swallowed up
By the mighty river of Light which I AM.

I AM, I AM, I AM Light;
I live, I live, I live in Light.
I AM Light's fullest dimension;
I AM Light's purest intention.
I AM Light, Light, Light
Flooding the world everywhere I move,
Blessing, strengthening, and conveying
The purpose of the kingdom of heaven.

By meditating on the white fire surrounding the threefold flame in the secret chamber of your heart and giving the "I AM Light" mantra by Saint Francis (known today as the Ascended Master Kuthumi) for the protection of the heart chakra, you are really benefiting all of your chakras. As you know, oxygenated blood from the lungs must first pass through the heart before it can nourish the rest of the body. Similarly, the light from your I AM Presence must also pass through the heart. Whatever the heart contains is then carried to all the other chakras.

Indeed, the energy of the Life Source is the only real 'fountain of youth' in existence. (Ironically, Ponce

de Leon and countless others have spent a major portion of their lives chasing that flaming youth which
was really in their heart.)

As a result of the misuse of this energy, the crystal
cord is today a mere thread, and the threefold flame
measures an average height of one-sixteenth of an
inch. If we are ever to regain our former power and
vitality, we must prove ourselves the master over what
we now have.

VITALITY AND PRANA

As for vitality, it is the endless pursuit of this
elusive quality which drives many fitness devotees to
their efforts.

Why is running a natural high? Why do you feel
so invigorated after a brisk walk or a good hard workout? What is it that makes you think more clearly and
feel like you're really alive?

Prana. The Sanskrit word for "breath" or "breath
of life." But it is much more than what we think of as
breath. Prana is the life energy that vitalizes all living
things and controls all activities in the body—physical
and spiritual, mental and sensory. Without it, blood
won't circulate, organs won't function, and the brain
won't do its job.

The concept of a universal energy force has been
taught for many centuries and in many cultures. The
Sanskrit term *prana* has been compared to the *mana*
of the Polynesians, to the Chinese *ch'i,* energy which
circulates through the meridians detailed in the ancient science of acupuncture, to the Hebrew *ruach*
("spirit of life"), and to what scientists have in recent
times called "bioplasma."

Prana is most easily absorbed into the body
through the air, where it is found in its freest state. As

you exercise—especially in fresh air and sunshine—you are inhaling, with each breath, air charged with this dynamic force. Like an electric current, it courses through an intricate system of nerve passages in the etheric body and is carried to every organ and part of the system, giving renewed strength and vigor.

Prana has its greatest concentration in the seven chakras, which serve as generating centers and focal points for this energy. The chakras regulate specific bodily functions, and at each of these energy centers the prana is collected and distributed to its destination.

Every activity—from muscle movement, to digestion, to thought itself—utilizes prana, and the supply needs to be constantly replenished to sustain good health. Unless enough fresh air reaches the lungs, for example, the venous blood (which accumulates waste from all parts of the body) cannot be purified or renewed with life. This poisonous waste matter, instead of being expelled, is then circulated through the body and poor health or disease ensues.

In fact, it is said that disease is due to an imbalance of prana. And some proponents of yoga believe that all sickness can be controlled when the proper flow of prana is restored. Along the same lines, in the West jogging has been used successfully as preventive medicine and even as therapeutic treatment for patients with heart problems. However, some practitioners believe jogging is harmful to the organs, the spine and sacrum.

Because all of the four lower bodies are interrelated, causes set into motion by prana are not limited to physical effects. A lack of prana can influence the mind and the emotions as well. Clinical tests have shown that there is a relationship between poor breathing and low IQ in children. And it's not hard to see how being confined to a stuffy room for too long can produce moodiness, depression, or apathy—instead of the buoyancy that an energy boost of fresh air and prana will provide.

Prana comes from God through many channels. The most reliable source of prana is clean air near moving water, charged with sunlight.

It can be postulated that the amount of prana in the air is a direct function of the concentration of negatively charged ions. (A negatively charged ion is an air molecule that is carrying one or more extra electrons. Similarly, a positively charged ion has been stripped of one or more electrons.)

I would not go so far as to say that prana *is* negatively charged ions, but let's just say that when the concentration of negative ions is naturally high, you can be reasonably sure there is some prana around.

Many studies have proven that the ion concentration in the air has a profound effect on the body. In working environments in the cities, positive ions which are detrimental to health are generated in quantity by central air-conditioning systems, pollution, and automobiles. On the other hand, rain and lightning storms generate negative ions which benefit the body. The ocean, rivers, streams, and all types of vegetation also contribute to the negative ionization of the air.

When you run along the beach on a clear day, you are doing far more to revitalize your physical temple than if you were to jog for twice the time through the back streets of Los Angeles. Once you take into consideration environmental factors, the where and when becomes as important as the how and for how long.

Since most of us do live in the city, it's important to find the time to go elsewhere—into nature to clear out our physical bodies of pollution and processed food, cleanse our chakras through fasting, meditation, and mantras, and bring the other three bodies into alignment.

THE POWERFUL THROAT CENTER

The next center we should be concerned with is the throat chakra. It is located over the physical throat, has sixteen petals, and is blue in color. It is the power chakra, and through the gift of speech unique to man, it can release large quantities of energy, both good and bad.

Through the disciplined use of the spoken word, we can make great progress in the toning of all of our chakras. With misuse—such as cursing in the name of God or Jesus Christ, gossip, criticism, sarcasm, angry words, or "unseemly conversation"—we do ourselves great harm as well as increase the planetary level of human effluvia.

Even irritation toward others and the voicing of that irritation causes imbalance within all of the chakras, because the throat is the command center through which our creative forces flow to all life, establishing the tenor of our aura and our person.

This concept is not new. Jesus admonished us, "Let your communication be, Yea, yea; Nay, nay: for whatsoever is more than these cometh of evil."[4] This was not meant to exclude necessary communication between persons but was a reminder to us of the seriousness of the misuse of the word; it also revealed his awareness of the power of the spoken word to affirm Truth.

Through the affirmation of Truth—"Yea, yea"—we channel it into action in our lives, and by denying error—"Nay, nay"—we cast out error's effects in our lives.

He also warned that "every idle word that men shall speak, they shall give account thereof in the day of judgment. For by thy words thou shalt be justified, and by thy words thou shalt be condemned."[5]

This shows that Jesus believed words were as

important as actions, and that both would be weighed in the ultimate evaluation of the soul. It's also important to realize that idle chatter (like idle sex) drains you of the energy you need to focus for maximum performance. Too much talk and not enough action, like any other indulgence, squanders the life-force and reveals an absence of control and personal integration.

Despite its enormous significance in human relations, our society has deemphasized the word to such a degree that cynicism and incisiveness have become more important than true communication.

Now, as we all know, music is the barometer of society, and as the Scottish patriot Andrew Fletcher of Saltoun so aptly commented, "If a man were permitted to make all the ballads, he need not care who should make the laws of a nation."

Just tune in your radio to any popular station. Tell me if you can find four songs in a row where some aspect of life isn't being degraded. Everything is made common. Every action has a hidden motive. People are painted as having no sincerity in word or in deed. Even words themselves cease to have meaning in the minds of many. People can lie, curse, gossip, and it's all justified matter-of-factly with "It's just words."

Take, for example, the hit by the group Missing Persons. It speaks for itself. The lyricist is obviously following the current trends of musical cynicism, but he ends up making quite an accurate social comment. This is not to say that the words of the song really meant any more to him than to his imaginary listener.

"Words"
by Terry Bozzio & Warren Cuccurullo

Do you hear me
Do you care
Do you hear me
Do you care

My lips are moving and the
   sound's coming out
The words are audible but
   I have my doubts
That you realize what has been said

You look at me as if you're in a daze
It's like the feeling at the
   end of the page
When you realize you don't
   know what you just read

What are words for
When no one listens any more
What are words for
When no one listens
   what are words for
When no one listens there's
   no use talking at all

I might as well go up and
   talk to a wall
'Cause all the words are
   having no effect at all
It's a funny thing am I all alone

Something has to happen to
   change the direction
What little filters through is
   giving you the wrong impression
   it's a sorry state... [6]

Sorry, indeed. The sad part is that, to many, words
have become empty—something to use to manipulate
others or to express anger. Even though the song is not
taken seriously by the majority of those who hear it, it
is a most apt description for the way many people
communicate.

Much of social interaction today is governed by
the 'cocktail party' mentality of one-upmanship—

along with the couching of every aggressive statement in terms of some sort of joke or good humor so as to be able to hurt another deeply without "ruffling anyone's feathers." And heaven forbid that the poor guy should take anyone seriously, lest he be greeted with more hoots of laughter and shouts of "Paranoid?" and "Can't take a joke?"

Generally, the way this is dealt with is that these 'sophisticates' develop a razor-sharp tongue, ready to counter each rapier thrust of caustic wit with an even more incisive jab. Then everyone laughs and supposedly none are the worse for the wear.

But are they? What about the deep-seated scars that this inflicts on the unsuspecting and sensitive individual? What about the sincere seeker whose nature will not allow him to participate in this type of game? Is he to be cast out of society, branded a simpleton?

Certainly all of this is not what the throat chakra is meant for. When an individual is accustomed to hearing mostly innuendo and sarcasm from everyone around him, who should be surprised that he "doesn't listen any more"?

In our society, more than anything else we need to realize the importance of the word. Now that communication has become all but automated, and computers 'talk' to each other faster and more accurately than people, we think of technology as the cure for all of our ills. Just look at the word *technology.* It comes from the Greek *techne,* meaning "art" or "craft," and *logos,* meaning "word." So here we are, in the *age of the art of the word,* and communication between individuals is one of our biggest problems!

David's prayer ought to become our own: "Let the words of my mouth and the meditation of my heart be acceptable in thy sight, O LORD, my strength and my redeemer."[7]

If we all thought about what we said each time we said it as if we were speaking to or in front of God, our conversations would be quite different. This, then, is the first step to the clearing of the throat chakra: to purify our speech.

The very strength of God's will we misuse in this center can become the power to engage the cosmic law in our life. Try this mantra of Christ's victory in you:

> Not my will,
> Not my will,
> Not my will,
> But Thine be done!

Mentally or verbally affirmed, it can even be used to maintain the rhythm of your exercise. Visualize the blue flame of Life's blueprint working through your throat chakra and spoken word to charge your body with the integrating will of the universe.

THE PLACE OF THE SUN

Complementing the throat, below the heart, is the solar-plexus chakra. It is located at the navel and corresponds to the nerve center there. It has ten petals and its colors are a combination of rich purple and metallic gold. When you become agitated and feel that familiar discomfort "in the pit of your stomach," you know that it is your solar plexus that has been affected.

This energy is usually released through the throat in the form of disruptive verbiage. The solar plexus and the throat are corresponding chakras, and when in harmony, the energies of both converge in the heart for peaceful and loving communication. When one or the other is in disharmony, both chakras are involved.

Many of our emotions are expressed through these two chakras. You will notice that under normal circumstances, when people are expressing feelings of love, kindness, or any other positive emotion, they usually speak in a quiet and resonant tone of voice. As soon as the solar plexus is agitated, however, the pitch and the volume go up. This is most noticeable when the person is in a state of anger or anxiety.

Mastering the solar plexus requires the mastery of our emotions by harnessing ourselves to the divine will—by the sacred fire of the heart. When they are controlled, we can begin the purification of this chakra through meditation and dynamic decrees.

While visualizing the chakra as shown, give "The Balm of Gilead." This prayer will help calm your emotions (your *energies in motion*) whenever you feel agitated or ill at ease.

> O Love of God, immortal Love,
> Enfold all in thy ray:
> Send compassion from above
> To raise them all today!
> In the fullness of thy power,
> Shed thy glorious beams
> Upon the earth and all thereon
> Where life in shadow seems!
> Let the Light of God blaze forth
> To cut men free from pain:
> Raise them up and clothe them, God,
> With thy mighty I AM name!

The solar plexus is very much linked to the soul. Therefore, if this chakra is kept pure, you will be more in touch with your true feelings and self. Our emotions, magnifying the pure desire of the Higher Self, are intended to amplify the soul and the potential of the soul.

THE INNER EYE

Ascending once again above the heart, we find the third-eye chakra. This center is just as important to keep free of human debris as any of the other six—even more so, because it is the orifice of spiritual vision.

Jesus, our beloved World Teacher, was speaking of this 'eye' when he said, "The light of the body is the eye. If therefore thine eye be single, thy whole body shall be full of light."[8]

Located at the center of the brow, it is emerald green when purified and has ninety-six petals (sometimes represented as two, as in the winged caduceus). Ideally, through the third eye, we should be able to anchor the vision of God, the vision of perfection.

Today, we live in a world of relativity and do not see or outpicture the absolute perfection of the God Self. When man was first created, before the descent of the soul into the planes of illusion (the Fall), he had the single-eyed vision of his original perfection in the third eye.

At the time of the Fall, when he partook of the fruit of the tree of the knowledge of relative good and evil, he fell into a state of duality. This is the propensity to see good and evil as relative qualities.

At the lowest point of the planetary evolution, some had lost the divine spark and walked the earth as animals. (It seems that Darwin was really a latecomer!) In actuality, mankind did not start as cavemen but descended to that state through neglect of devotion to the sacred fire of the heart and the misuse of the throat chakra and the third eye.

Since then, man has not been able to regain the fullness of his former faculties, although he may make great strides through the *exercise* of the heart chakra in devotion and meditation, the *exercise* of the throat chakra in the scientific use of the mantra or the dynamic decree of the Word, and the *exercise* of his spiritual vision by seeing the good (God) in friend and foe alike.

The very fact that America has enjoyed such prosperity over the last two centuries has to do with the fact that its people have had the third-eye vision of a higher standard of excellence to make things happen. Not only have we built a mighty nation of our own, but we have exported money and technology to almost every other nation on earth.

"Yes," you say, "but what about our economy? What about all of the unemployment?" Well, some of the nation's poor are those who have misused their chakras in the past, causing great harm to others, and are now experiencing the effects of causes they set in motion. And some of the rich have taken unfair advantage of the rest of us (through no fault of our own)—and that's their karma, too, which they will surely reap. And some of them already are—having returned in this life as the nation's debtors who cry the loudest for welfare payments and food stamps, now that the shoe is on the other foot. But even this can be undone by the violet flame.

Karma, after all, until submitted to Mercy's grace, is the iron law of cause and effect, more binding and all-encompassing than any earthly statute. That's why Jesus said, "The poor you have with you always."[9] You see, there's always someone at the bottom of the socio-economic ladder. This is not to disallow the negative and even diabolical influence that our past and present leaders have had on the economy and employment picture.

Small comfort to the little people, the working people and the low-income brackets. But then, too, there is the karma of neglect where you fail to champion your economic rights or to challenge the power elite's international cartel who exercise control of the money, the banks, trade, and the economies of the nations. If the people don't stop complaining and start stumping for the Coming Revolution in Higher Consciousness, they may be lost before they are found centered in Saint Germain's fires of freedom.

It's a fact. The high and the mighty, the captains and kingmakers have interfered with the free market by monopoly capitalism, federal regulation and bureaucratic red tape for the small businessman, which has hurt a lot of good people who are the backbone of America. And, as we have said, they shall not escape their recompense. However, technically, there is no injustice in the universe. Everyone must face the reaper in the form of his own personal karma. Everyone must ultimately pay the price for the misuse of the light of God—the oppressors as well as the oppressed. There are no exceptions.

Now, getting back to the clearing of the third eye, this can be accomplished through meditation on perfect geometric forms, as well as through the raising of the energies of the lower chakras to the level of the third eye. "Behold the Good!" is truly the motto to espouse for strength of vision through this instrument of God's all-seeing eye.

To begin, visualize a disc of light superimposed over your forehead, like a miner's light, only brighter. See it spinning and filling your vision center with light, flushing out the misqualified substance of the ages from your chakra, cleansing it until it is a brilliant emerald green.

As you are holding this picture in your mind's eye, give the following mantra of the science of the Word:

O disc of Light from heaven's height,
Descend with all your perfection!
Make our auras bright with freedom's Light
And the Master's love and protection!

Then call to your Christ Self and affirm:

I AM, I AM beholding All,
Mine eye is single as I call;
Raise me now and set me free,
Thy holy image now to be.

Clearing the third eye is a very important step in soul evolution, as it is directly correlated to the soul chakra. Whatever is seen through the third eye is also mirrored in the soul.

As a practical measure, third-eye vision can be improved through the cleansing of the blood, the colon and the physical body in general. Toxins accumulated in the blood and fatty tissue as well as in the colon are a direct hindrance to that vision. A balanced program of fasting on fresh vegetable or fruit juices, as well as distilled water and herb teas, is a good place to start.

THE CHAKRA OF FREEDOM

All the images seen with the third eye are re-flected in the soul. The soul is anchored to the physical body through the seat-of-the-soul chakra, halfway between the navel and the base of the spine. This chakra governs the genetic code, heredity, and the manufacture of the seed and the egg. The seat of the soul has six petals and is violet in color.

Because of the very close relation between the soul and the third eye, the soul is easily damaged by impure and imperfect thoughtforms and images. This is especially true with some of today's art.

Color is especially important. Pastel light-emitting hues are better than loud or muddier shades, which are detrimental—as are amorphous shapes. The pat-tern of Christ in the individual contains the geometry of the cosmos. Any dissonant or jagged art form is destructive to this geometry—disturbing to its reflection, from the eye image to every cell.

Long ago, advanced civilizations on the continent of Africa were brought down by perverted art and music, which eventually led to all forms of black magic and witchcraft being practiced there.

This has continued up to the present with voodoo, ritual murder, and sacrifice. These are extreme examples of the destruction of the soul chakra. Misuse of this and other chakras has caused vast devastation and, more than once, brought down a civilization or a continent.

The seat of the soul is the chakra of freedom. The movement toward 'artistic freedom' in many cases actually accomplished the reverse. Because some modern art forms pervert the inner symmetrical blueprint of the soul chakra, they take away from the freedom of the soul. For what the eye sees is instantly mirrored in the four lower bodies. Dissonance in art and music is without doubt self-disintegrating to those who give their attention and allegiance to it. Fohat follows the imaged key.

Parents with young children should be especially careful of what they allow their children to look upon and listen to. Some children today have never seen thoughtforms of perfection nor heard a chord of classical music. For them harmony has no definition.

It is vital that children have established within them certain archetypes, such as the Madonna and Child, the father figure in saints and heroes, flowers, and internally harmonious objects taken from nature in her unpolluted state. Through the very mathematics of the molecular structure of things, there is instilled in them the aspiration toward a path of self-discipline that can be won by striving for excellence in all of the four lower bodies.

Man is not unique in the possession of chakras. States and nations also have spiritual centers—highly concentrated energy focuses which govern the inter-action of their people, their destiny and their vibra-tions, personal characteristics, language, accents, customs, and mannerisms. People who have a certain karma to work out through the lessons and self-mastery imposed by the disciplines of a certain chakra will gravitate toward the corresponding city or state within their nation.

Los Angeles, the soul chakra of California as well as America, is the place of the greatest perver-sion of the freedom flame through the entertainment industry. (Does anyone really consider the *Texas Chainsaw Massacre* or *Scanners* to be worthwhile art?) This perversion causes a distortion of the soul chakra of all the youth who view these and other similar motion pictures.

Since the soul chakra is the creative center, what-ever is created by those affected may then also be distorted. As these youth grow up to be tomorrow's parents, educators, civic leaders, and film producers, it becomes a self-fulfilling prophecy. They look upon a distorted creation and then create more distortion in every field (even in the fertile field of consciousness of their own children). This, in turn, is looked upon by others and distorted further.

Indeed, you can see how each year the movies are more violent, delve deeper into the collective un-conscious, and portray more hopelessness to an ever younger age group. The only cure for this is for people who really care to begin purifying their soul chakras through meditation on images of beauty, symmetry, and Higher Consciousness. This is the first step.

Next, we must hold the visualization of the whirl-ing sun disc, as with all of the other chakras, to flush out the substance that has built up with years of misuse of this vital center. Use of the violet flame is essential, especially in this mechanistic society which is in large measure devoid of the pure thoughtforms and images necessary to maintain soul (solar) consciousness.

The mantra for use with this chakra is very short, but when repeated—and accompanied by visualization and the violet flame—it will have an extremely beneficial effect. Remember, "I AM" means "God in me is."

> Light expand, Light expand,
> Light expand, expand, expand!
> Light I AM, Light I AM,
> Light I AM, I AM, I AM!

THE THOUSAND-PETALED LOTUS

The crown chakra is the chakra of illumination which regulates the mental faculties and memory. It is located at the top of the head and has 972 petals, which has gained it the name of the "thousand-petaled lotus." Yellow in color, the crown is the center through which we must attain God consciousness (the awareness of yourself as a part of God). A clogged crown chakra can ruin your memory just as surely as drug abuse. In fact, the taking of drugs is one of the primary factors that leads to the polluting of this chakra.

Mental density, the lack of a "clear head" when you need it most, "spacing out"—these are the effects of misqualified energy in the crown chakra.

On the opposite end of the scale are those who pervert the crown chakra by overuse of their mental faculties. There is nothing wrong, and in fact everything right, with having brain power. What we are concerned with here are the 'eggheads'—people who believe that the only pursuits that matter are intellectual ones and who believe that those who are ignorant of the 'higher' knowledge which they possess are naïve and should have no say in the affairs of the world.

There are many in our universities and in our government and political arena today, as well as in top positions in major corporations, who fit into this category. It is they who feel that we need to be controlled for our own good—that the little people of this world lack the ability to govern themselves. It is they who try to calm us with facts and figures, while they slip their chains of control around our economy, our government, our educational system and our entire lives.

These individuals, the mentalists, instead of developing an attunement with the higher mind through the crown chakra, are constantly releasing the poison of their lies and half-truths which stem from a corresponding relative perspective of good and evil in the misused third eye.

This comes out of the aura in the form of a violent orange/black/silver astral discharge which is wont to intimidate anyone of "lesser sophistication." It seems that they are able, through the sheer force of their highly developed and highly manipulative mental bodies, to dupe the vast majority of the public.

If you are like most people in America, you have the earnest desire to see this country make it out of its current slump—to regain the lost glory and fervor of patriotism that has carried it through revolution, civil war, and global conflict. Most of us sincerely want to improve ourselves as well as our surroundings. In this case, a little violet flame coupled with the following mantra will go a long way.

> O Flame of Light bright and gold,
> O Flame most wondrous to behold,
> I AM in every brain cell shining,
> I AM Light's wisdom all divining.
> Ceaseless, flowing fount
> Of Illumination flaming,
> I AM, I AM, I AM Illumination.

THE BASE-OF-THE-SPINE CHAKRA

The final chakra we are concerned with is the Mother chakra. This is the base-of-the-spine chakra, referred to simply as the "base chakra." It derives its name from its location at the base of the spine. But it is also the base of our physical (and spiritual) temple. The God-quality of this chakra is purity. Its color is white and it has four petals, forming the foundation of the pyramid of being.

The life-force of the base chakra is intended to be raised to the crown and the third eye by meditation on the I AM Presence. This will magnetize the energy upward. As the life-force, or Kundalini as it is called in the East, passes up through the channel connecting the chakras, it nourishes each one with the purity of the Mother light.

When the life-force is perverted or abused, it contaminates all other chakras. Or, if it is spent entirely, there is nothing left to rise to activate the polarity of light in the other chakras. Disease, disintegration, decay, old age, and death are the price mankind pay for the misuse of the energies of the base-of-the-spine chakra. In our society, this is the chakra which has been most flagrantly abused through impurity in all forms. Those who conserve the Mother light are the best performers and the most creative individuals in every field. The mantra that will help rid your four lower bodies of impurity is called "I AM Pure":

> By God's desire from on high,
> Accepted now as I draw nigh,
> Like falling snow with star-fire glow,
> Thy blessed Purity does bestow
> Its gift of Love to me.
>
> I AM pure, pure, pure
> By God's own word.
> I AM pure, pure, pure,

O fiery sword.
I AM pure, pure, pure,
Truth is adored.

Descend and make me Whole,
Blessed Eucharist, fill my soul.
I AM thy Law, I AM thy Light,
O mold me in thy form so bright!

Beloved I AM, Beloved I AM,
Beloved I AM.

Now that you have cleared all of your chakras, go out and run! Go out and work that body until it won't work any more! You will feel an exhilaration you have never felt before, because now you have a complete program. Many professional athletes have discovered that they cannot survive in their training without the benefit of spiritual assistance.

Take, for example, the case of Toshihiko Seko, the winner of the Fukoka Marathon for three consecutive years. His entire life consists of training, both physically and spiritually. He is a devotee of Zen and, thanks to his trainer Kiyoshi Nakamura, he has developed "Zensoho"—running with Zen.

According to Nakamura, "The idea is to clear your mind of everything and to let your body function naturally, undisturbed by thoughts." Nakamura has studied all of the world's religions for over forty years. "You can learn from them all, just like everything in life," he explains. "We must study the Bible, scriptures, and all famous works. We must study nature—mountains, rivers, the stars, the sun and moon. All of them are our teachers."

Nakamura also subscribes to the belief that "physical training is only ten percent of the total preparation, the other ninety percent is mental."

In conclusion, many have come up with philosophies of training two or more of the four lower bodies while incorporating spiritual teachings from the world's religions. Seko is obviously utilizing a brand of this philosophy, with great results.

Why not take it a step further, then, and train all four of your bodies? Integrate them, clear out your chakras, breathe the prana of life, and gain maximum mastery over your total being.

I only hope that all who are aware of this teaching use it to its fullest. It is only through dedicated application of the law that change can be effected. Just as the weekend or occasional runner will never make it to the marathon, so the dabbler in this science of the chakras will never make it to the spiritual Olympics.

Chapter Eight

THE ETERNAL VERITIES

The Eternal Verities

LET us be aware of the eternal verities.

The world, the individual, and everything around us are cloaked with obscurity whenever the eternal verities do not manifest in our consciousness.

Whenever we are lost in a world of darkness and suspicion—of mistrust of the plans of the Infinite—whenever we are confused by the chaos at the crossroads of life, whenever we are uncertain of the way in which we ought to go—it is a matter of obscurity being cast across our pathway.

This obscurity does not come from God, nor does it derive from his goodness. It comes from the human realm, from the cocoon of mortal ignorance. It comes from a lack of knowledge of what life really is.

What, then, is the reality of life?

THE SENSE OF SELFHOOD

Life is not darkness. Life is not chaos or confusion. Life is not an uncertain probing. Life is magnificent—even biologically.

The construction of the body is beautiful: our flesh and bones are intricately and wonderfully formed! And the brain—itself a recipient of the impulses of the eternal Mind—is a magnificent switchboard and a storehouse of infinite Truth.

Just pause and think, then, not only of the flesh and blood but of the consciousness which rests in the chalice of identity and gives identity to the chalice!

We are aware of a power outside of ourselves that at the same time is identifiable as the power within. This power defines right and wrong when all moral codes fall short of the mark. This power derives from the Real Self. And this is the beginning of the sense of self.

There is an innate sense of justice that is inside of us, superior in all of its rights and ramifications to all codes of justice that man through the years has manufactured—sometimes out of great wisdom and then again out of the complexity of word knowledge, a mere assimilation of facts and figures thrown together without rhyme or reason. Because these codifications of law have been accepted by humankind, precedence is established whether or not justice is served by it.

And these are not necessarily the eternal verities.

Today the whole human race needs to lean not upon the arm of flesh,[1] not upon the classification of mere human knowledge, but upon spiritual treasures of that wisdom which is to be found within the heart.

Such treasures of the gnosis of God are indeed within the heart, and they can be drawn forth to illumine the mind, even as they cast the light of Truth upon the screen of the mind and, in so doing, change our whole viewpoint.

And these are of necessity the eternal verities.

The majority of humankind are governed by their emotional energies, moving as they do according to acquired sensibilities and ideas that all of us have held, not always wise but ofttimes central to our ego. And this ebb and tide of the emotions is for the most part unreal, a chimera of the not-self—persistent yet persistently unreal.

What, then, is the reality of the Self?

In and through and out of all of this, we ourselves have an identity—an *id-entity*—a central focus of awareness. We call it "my self." Within this self we have an awareness of the I—of me, myself, and mine (id-entity extending to the periphery of the sense of the possessive self and beyond).

This self is in a state of becoming and it always will be—for such is the nature of an active Be-ness. The unwinding of the inner coils of this potential is an infinite process because the nucleus of Life is the infinite Light.

Because it has already been demonstrated to us that change is being wrought from day to day, we know that the 'I' of today is not the 'I' of yesterday; nor will it be the 'I' of tomorrow.

By a like token, the consciousness of today is not the consciousness of yesterday, and hopefully it will be better tomorrow. It will either move forward or backward. And if it moves forward on the crest of the forward movement of cosmic cycles, then certainly the self will take on new meaning, new relevance, and a new momentum.

This new phase of our *id-entity* can be cast in the light of the personal ego—where the struggle for recognition is ongoing—or it can be cast in the illuminating Presence of our God-identity.

And, if we permit it, the God-identity will engulf the human. And when it does, we shall no longer be compelled by the same transient desires. Little by little, they will fade away. They will lose their meaning as we take on in our consciousness new desires of the Spirit.

THE GOOD SAMARITAN

We read the story of the Good Samaritan who came upon the wayfarer lying by the side of the road, bruised and beaten by thieves and left half dead, a man he knew not, a man for whom he had formed no attachments, a man who could not reward him—just a man lying there, on whom the priests had cast a disdainful eye and passed by.

What did he do? In his richness of spirit, his strength, and his solid sense of knowing who he was, he could step out from himself to serve the ends of someone he did not know. He bound up his wounds, took him upon his horse, carried him to an inn and paid the fee for his lodging so he could have a comfortable bed in which to rest.[2]

This was an act outside of the self—yet at the same time it was supremely within the security of a healthy self-completeness. It was a concern other than the immediate concern of his own needs. It was reflective of his recognition of the soul's need to serve others—and not for the glorification of the ego, not to be identified with some great movement. It was a surge of the flame of charity, not necessarily Christlike, but an urge simply to act on behalf of a fellow human being who was in need.

And by his act, he identified more closely with the goodness of God than those who, even then, made religion their business but not their life. This God whom he served, deliberately or not, had already stated through Christ that it is sometimes wise to leave the ninety and nine who are securely within the sheepfold and go in search of that which is lost[3]—the little wandering lamb caught in the brambles who is not only without comfort but also without apparent worth to the total picture.

Truly, the ability to save that which is lost, that which has strayed from the centrality of Life—to save to the uttermost—reveals the levels of one's own wholeness, a wholeness that is nourished by the Greater Whole and therefore always has something to give to another's sense of incompleteness. Whenever you behold the Good Samaritan, say to yourself, "There goes one destined to become the Good Shepherd."[4]

We are aware of the fact that when we deal with the Spirit and when we deal with God, we are dealing with an infinite power that has awareness of us whether or not we have awareness of him. He is aware of us not as insignificant, not as dispensable to his design (as one of the herd or the so-called mindless Atlantean masses that can be mechanically replaced and never missed).

No, he seeks to convey to us a higher, a holier, a purer sense, a more beautiful consciousness, emphatically *because* we have an identity *in him* that is not only supremely significant to his own, but one which is indispensable and would be sorely missed—simply because he loves us as his own and as his own individed Self. We are his, fully, freely, forever.

LOVE DEFINED

Let us then ask ourselves what motivates the action of the Good Samaritan.

Love.

But love has been defined so many times, and so many times selfishly. Here is love without expectation. We do not even find record that the Good Samaritan thought that he was going to receive some reward for his deed in the hereafter. He simply acted out of the compulsion of the needs of another soul with whom he identified, perhaps saying to himself, "There but for the grace of God lay I, the hapless victim of robbers, naked and wounded. I will do what I can for him."

Love to be truly Love must begin with the love of self in the sense of self-appreciation. One must have the sense that one is of some worth and therefore worthy to be loved. If one judges oneself unworthy, of no value to God or man, then the self-love that ought to be will turn to self-hatred.

Only if a man can love himself, can he love his neighbor. Only if he can love his neighbor, can he love his God. And if a man hate himself, he will hate both his neighbor and his God. Therefore Jesus said, "Love thy neighbor as thyself"[5]—i.e., as though he were *thy self* and as though he were *thy Real Self.*

The Master also revealed the great truth that we already treat our neighbors with the same contemptuous or possessive love with which we treat ourselves *(our souls)*—and, for that matter, our Real Self, the inner Christ. If you would have immediate and keen insight into your personal psychology, just analyze for a moment how you treat your neighbor and you will know how you feel about yourself and your God.

Let us realize, then, that we must always search our hearts for the motives of our actions. And ever strive for the purer reason. But if we find there a selfish motive, if we see clearly that we are attempting to underwrite ourselves in our charities and kindnesses, we should first understand that, in any case, it is neither healthy nor proper to condemn ourselves. Because, if I act selfishly to serve the needs of another, it is still a higher purpose than if I act selfishly to serve only the needs of myself.

It should also be remembered that to take to oneself today in order to give of oneself tomorrow is always better than to act from the amoral premise of: "Never mind what happens to anybody else—what will *I* get out of it? I want to know what's in it for *me!*"

If we act entirely selfishly, you see, just serving what we think will produce something for ourselves, both in the immediate and the long-term goals of our lives, then we are not very high at all on the spiritual ladder. And all of this striving of the self *for* the self may well smack of a pseudorighteousness, a self-assertiveness that is formulated by what *we* do or what *we* think, as if we of ourselves could make ourselves to be 'good gods'. (Ye gods!)

So, we understand that there are times when one has to think in terms of a 'selfishness' that must be exercised so that later one may be generous.

Now, this may not always be the highest form of devotion or the highest form of self-sacrificing love. But it may very well be a legitimate step on the path leading to the highest Love—when the Christ in us declares, "Take, eat, this is my Body which is broken for you. . ."[6]—and the soul, fully integrated with the Light, no longer feels its sense of self threatened by such a statement of self-givingness.

For the soul has attained sufficient identity in God to give away part or all of its 'corpus' and yet remain centered in the flaming vortex of self-declared Being: "I AM WHO I AM."[7]

And so, as we live our lives, we may observe that we are motivated by this selfishness that may subsequently become generous, even magnanimous; and this of itself may include the desire to love because we desire to be loved. When one loves, one is often loved—although there are many cases of unrequited love.

We see that when that love-exchange emanates from the Real Self, it is true and blessed because it does not come forth from beneath, but it is magnetized from on high. And thus it fulfills one's reason for being in the ultimate self-givingness—the reciprocal love of God in man and man in God.

When love does not emanate from the God Source, by and by it becomes apparent that something is missing, and the soul waits for the real thing—*someone who is Real!*—while the heart languishes for the ever more perfect union through the highest and truest Love.

These steps and stages of love are not self-contradictory. On the contrary, each step is taken through an unfolding awareness of individuality, an individuality that must first exist in order to love—and then must love in order to exist.

Individuality may become selfish when, self-satisfied, it sits on a rung of the ladder to bask in the light of its own achievement, failing to recognize that as the seasons pass, the tree of self must share its fruit with those who must needs taste of another's selflessness in order to attain their own.

Such a self-satisfaction robs us of the joy of self-givingness and deprives us of the need to feel self-emptied so that we may strive again to be filled—so that we may live again another day to give again.

SELF-WORTH AND SELF-NEEDS

Man climbs the stairway to Reality—not in one giant leap, but up he goes, step by step. He may skip a step here or there but he will continue to climb if he maintains his interest in doing so.

Thus, motivation from within is essential if one is to consciously climb. And that motivation can only derive from the mantra of the true disciple's heart: "Lord, I AM worthy. Make me worthier still." Try whispering it in your heart—to him. It affirms a healthy sense of well-being—I am worthy *because* God, the "I AM" in me, is worthy. But it also acknowledges the *need* to strive and the *need* for help.

If you think you have no needs, if you are highly self-satisfied, you, then, have no need to climb. Only the dead have no self-worth and no needs. The quick have both self-worth and self-needs. Therefore, in true Love they speak to their Christ—"Lord, I AM worthy. And because you made me worthy, Lord, make me worthier still."

Did you know that some people have so little self-worth that they don't even think they're good enough to talk to Christ? If that's so, then you can't even say the Lord's Prayer or make this simple declaration: "Lord, I AM worthy. Make me worthier still."

By God, if you are going anywhere in life, you have got to know that God in you is worthy! And, if you don't, stop right now and ask him to show you that *he* is, and that because he is, *you* are!

No greater insult to the Godhead could be muttered than the cowardly confession "I have no worth." For in this the coward declares, "My God has no worth."

"O thou ungrateful wretch, knowest thou not that he that made thee is worthy, and that thou art in his image worthy, if thou wilt rise up and be all that he made thee to be?"

Indeed, there is no greater wretchedness that can come to the human soul than the denial of self-worth. Such a state of mind is suicidal—killing both soul and Spirit in man. For the denial of the Creator cancels out the creature (as effect cannot be sustained without Cause), while the denial of the creature obliterates the omnipotence of the Creator.

Life is a polarity, "as Above so below"—as in heaven so on earth, as in Spirit so in Matter. Each side confirms the other and so the worlds are sustained. Self-denial in either sphere cuts the spinal cord, and God is dead in man and man is dead in God.

The greatest need of real people is to find their self-worth in God.

Most people today, because they don't like themselves, seek to climb socially. They seek to climb financially. They seek to climb the ladder of fame and fortune that will lead them to a position where they can receive the adulation of others. Their sense of self wants to be honored.

Actually, they do it because they don't like their Real Self and they like their unreal self too much—but even this 'self-like' is the other side of self-dislike and a self-destruct drive that turns to self-hatred.

Beware the man who hates himself, for he is the most dangerous man on the face of the earth. Beware the man who has no capacity for self-love, for in him the divine spark has gone out.

But there is a self-love that, in the extreme, is self-hatred. Beware of it also, for all the works of that man are evil—verily the self-canceling energy veil of hatred—and "his days are as grass," as it is written of the flesh that is without the spirit, "for the wind passeth over it and it is gone, and the place thereof shall know it no more."[8]

O God, how shall I escape to the eternal verities!

THE WICK OF SELF

Only *perfect* Love will cast out that fear[9] which leads to the death of the soul through the blind pursuits of a blind self-hatred. Let us renew our sense of self and be renewed thereby...

But this self is only the wick. And the wick stands there in the tallow of matter, yet it is meaningless until kindled by the flame of God's grace. A thousand wicks standing side by side in a sameness that reveals no separate identity—until one wick says, "I desire the quickening, I elect to glow, I desire to light a world that it might see—and that I might see 'face to face' the reflected light of a million souls."

When the grace of God as his holy purpose enfolds the soul, when there is a pulsation of infinite reality that descends and fills the consciousness with the beautiful Spirit of God—when all of that surrounds one and one feels it (if the spiritual senses and the chakras are activated), then you know that the flame of God's grace has kindled the wick of identity.

The wick is only a structure. It is that *somethingness,* rather than that *nothingness,* which alone is ours to offer—in order that Life might burst forth in all its vibrant reality where we are. The wick is the means whereby these noble aspirations we feel of wanting to be a good person—"good and kind"—may be quickened by the flame of higher purpose.

You see, the goodness and kindness must start with the human wick, consuming and being consumed (i.e., self-purifying) by human virtue and meritorious deeds. But, by and by, in the self-burning (i.e., the self-refinement), the divine alchemy is activated by the heat of spiritual desire, and the striving spirit becomes one with the sacred fire itself—of our own *Christ* goodness and *Christ* kindness.[10]

Without the enkindling flame, human goodness dies and is not reborn. But with the flame and a wick to ignite—a wick whose self-determination is that free-will creativity which burns with a self-consuming compassion for life—by and by the Spirit comes to dwell with us and illumines the whole house. One candle sets the soul of a universe aglow.

The wick of self is not a God Self-awareness until it exercises its *potential* to be. In so doing, it must muster the courage to be (by the very process) self-consumed. And here our case must rest in the faith that the all-consuming flame will deliver to us a permanent Selfhood—one that we cannot now see or hear or taste or touch.

We must believe that that Self exists as Cause behind effect of lesser self we now know. We must believe in the flame as we believe in God. We must believe that God loves us. And that his purpose for us is that we may live forever with him as individed flames of his kindling Reality.

If we have not personally experienced God's quickening Love—the kindling of the sacred fire on the altar of being—then it is a unique and glorious experience that awaits us. For his Love is truly all-consuming. It consumes all within our human loves that remains unlike the divine and transforms our paltry motives of self-gain into our highest expression of Selfhood, one to which we ourselves could not attain . . . without his flame.

The Spirit of the Most High God comes into our temple for the kindling of the wick. And we are made aware that this flame now burning within is not something that we created, nor indeed could, but a Thing-In-Itself (the *Ding an sich*).

It is the Self-created. Formulated not from the dust—as "dust thou art, to dust shalt thou return" [11]—but of and from the Beyond. (We cannot control It; but It controls us. We cannot subdue It; but It subdues us.) Nor did It spring forth from the tallow at the moment of the kindling.

Yet the flame was there, inherently within us. It preexisted us, etched the crystal, fired the clay and kept the midnight watch of our gestation, self-creation in the womb of time . . . It was always there—anywhere and everywhere our love should suddenly spring forth to greet the fiery purpose of his own—there, there the flame that always was!

OUR IDENTITY A CONTINUUM IN CHRIST

Our minds possess the capacity to be stirred. And our emotions as well. Our beings can be shaken to the roots by unreality as well as by Reality. Too many times have we responded to the vibrations of the spoilers who have told us: "You don't have a chance. Only *the* Son of God has a chance. And you're not *a* son of God, 'cause *there's only one Son of God!*"

Falser words were never spoken. Our Father has told us that he created us in his own image.[12] Is there a higher image than the image of God? No. And the image of God is Christ—the Light-emanation of the Logos.

So then, we perceive that long ago where the mists of time and space disappear in the eternality of the Great God Self—back, back on the belt of our soul's eternal evolution, the self-evident Truth is known: "Before Abraham was, I AM."[13]

These were the words of the World Teacher Jesus Christ, the Anointed One, cupbearer of the LORD's Light—the Son of God who knew his identity to be a continuum in Christ.

Now *we* see, now *we* say: Before Abraham was, I AM—I EXIST in God's consciousness in the image of Christ. 'My' Christ is the same as 'his' Christ—the One (sun/sphere of radiant Being) whose many reflective fragments establish Be-ness not only in Jesus, 'my Lord', but in every soul that has ever received the gift of Life as self-awareness through the Son, back to the first fiery breath of creation.

And it was a creation of and by and in that same Logos that, in order to create 'me', placed a portion of himself within me. For without his essence inbreathing in me the sacred fire breath, without *himself,* was not anything made that was made—including me! For, as our Lord revealed it unto his beloved disciple, "That was the true Light which lighteth every man that cometh into the world."[14]

We were all there—if we have a soul, if we have a spark of God inside of us. We were there at the supreme moment when the first monadic expression was created, when the first manifestation sprang forth. We were there then. And we are there now.

Oh yes, we were—*and are*—spiritual! We didn't have these 'coats of skins'[15]—these four lower bodies we now need to navigate the denser spheres. The memory of that moment may not be thoroughly enlivened within us. Some of us may say with Saint Paul:

> For we know in part and we prophesy in part, but when that which is perfect is come, then that which is in part shall be done away. . . .
> For now we see through a glass, darkly; but then face to face. Now I know in part, but then shall I know even as also I AM known [as the 'I AM' in me is known and confirmed by the voice of the Spirit above and my soul's reflection below].[16]

We can dispense with all our disorderliness, our untidiness of consciousness—and the soot that has marred the expression of the divine image. We can dispense with it all. We can cast aside purse and scrip.[17] We can cast aside our hungers and our desires. We can part with them all—once we are engulfed with the divine intent.

We can do this because he speaks to us and says, "I AM come that you might have Life and that you might have it more abundantly. I AM the Christ of you speaking from the innermost recesses of your creative Being. I AM the Good Shepherd. I give my Life, the essence of my Light, so that you, my soul, may live."[18]

When the abundant Life begins to express itself within us, the moment that pulsation engulfs us we are changed from glory to Glory—from the glory of this world to the Glory of the next.

With our faces unveiled, we behold in the mirror of God our true image in Christ, and by the flame— *The Flame* of Holy Spirit—the appearance of a man or a woman is changed into the selfsame image of Christ into which beloved Jesus was changed, from the lesser glory of the son of man to the greater Glory of the Son of God, even as by the Spirit of the LORD. [19]

No sudden inspiration carries us from the first to the thirty-third step, but without the first step none other can be taken. The taking of the first step of initiation is an act which may not even be preceded by any spiritual awareness at all, but may come suddenly, as with the rushing of a mighty wind [20] we are "face to face" in the encounter with our Lord.

For the first time, our eyes are opened and we know him. We see that he *is there*. We see that the Spirit *is there*—a living symbol and more!—the magnificence of the Person of Reality in whose face *we see* ourselves as the creation of the first begotten.

We are also the issue of the Only Begotten of the Father, full of grace and truth. [21] We are the offspring of the Eternal Mind and joint-heirs [22] with all who have issued forth from the same Fount!

Descending from the Cosmic Christ image, the great glyph of the I AM Presence which is above us all, the symbol of our 'Personhood' becomes clothed upon with the reality of the personal Christ. And the Anointed One steps forth in our consciousness. The Son has returned.

Suddenly the Lord has returned to his temple, [23] and just as suddenly *we know* that through the long dark night of our sense of mortality he has never really been away. With Martha we say:

"Yea, Lord: I believe that thou art the Christ, the Son of God, which should come into the world." [24]

And we are truly born again.

With him we are alive forevermore.

With him we shout unto the stars: "Behold! I AM everywhere in the consciousness of God."

We have taken the first step on the path of Christic initiation unto Personhood in God.

But where did it all start—this fantastic, fabricated, celebrated sense of selfhood outside of God which we now starkly see face to face—mask to mask—and desire to discard? Where indeed.

WHY DO WE ENDOW OURSELVES WITH MORTALITY?

You see, only we ourselves could have endowed ourselves with mortal consciousness. In the mists of an antiquity older than old, we captured the historical stream of monadic man, mortal man, whose prehistoric image resembled not at all the original. Yet we entered that primitive form. How could we forget!

While all of these wounded ones, golemlike,[25] haunt the dark centuries of mankind's infancy when the creation had not yet identified itself with the living Word, child-man sleeps in embryonic twilight, and the long night of the womb is the void of a spiritual creation yet to be—becoming. . . waiting to appear.

At one point there was a turning into the Dark, and the ones darkened by their dark decision to turn away from the Light and live in their own self-created shames and shadows, in their turn manufactured other dark ones—and the counterfeit race of mechanization man was spawned in a coil of self-doubt and dubious nondecision.

These bodies, vacant and vacated, yet roam the planet infested with howling demons who clamor for more and more noise, dreading the echo of their own godlessness in the empty chambers of a house neither occupied nor enlightened by the Word.

In ages past, before the dawn of recorded history, the real manifestation of God stood forth in the ancient temples and the Masters walked the earth and discoursed with the Children of the One on the mysteries of creation.

And they spoke not of Darkness but of Light—not of Antichrist but of Christ. They spoke of the radiating power of Light, the energy of Light, the freedom of Light, and the capacity of man, as the manifestation of Elohim, to express the goodness of God, the desires of God, and even the magical principles of dominion over the elements of his world.

"Take dominion over the earth!" This was the command of the Divine Us.[26] And this we once knew and obeyed.

But today, every man sits under his own separate vine and his own separate fig tree.[27] But what does this independence profit the soul if he knows not the universal schemata of the interdependence of souls through each one's I AM Presence, as the Tree of Life,[28] and each one's beloved Christ Self, as the Vine[29] with whose righteous Branch[30] he must, in all his *in-dependent self,* equate?

Instead of kinship with the Life that is God, man today drifts further and further from being a part of the reality of God. He is estranged, as one floating at sea upon a raft is separated from the mainstream of life.

He may feel a physical, sympathetic kinship with the frequenters of the barrooms of the world. He may have a sort of psychic empathy with their pseudo, surface self through their raucous revelry and noisy sounds and rhythms, vainly music.

He may feel for their untidy desires of human creation that are never satisfied because they come from "beneath," from a bottomless pit which demands more and more satisfaction but can never get it: Because the Light that would satisfy the soul is devoured by the 'black hole' of the not-self, which, as a consequence thereof, always feels empty and never has anything to give except its own emptiness. And the vacuous ones congregate because they alone understand each other's existential existence.

THE ANSWER LIES IN THE MYSTERY SCHOOLS

What, then, is the answer? The answer lies in the Teachings of the Ascended Masters restored in the mystery schools—not in the soul-damning indictments of the churches of today whose impotent messages, mind you, are broadcast to the world as preachments that distort and contort the original comfort of the Word to His own.

Ever since their expulsion from the heavenly courts and councils, the fallen angels, embodied among men (mortal yet influential beyond the run-of-the-mill Homo sapiens), have substituted social reform for the everlasting gospel of Truth[31] alive and vibrant within you, an endowment from your Father.

Why, all man's needs, artificially met by social-istic schemes, would come to him automatically—and scientifically!—once he had received the kindling Light and the immersion of his soul in the grace of God, and the Lord had entered his temple because he himself had kept the flame of Love.

Like the Good Samaritan, he couldn't help but go out and do good and create just laws to serve his fellowmen—*if* he were filled with the Spirit, *if* he were remade in the image of God. Because he would simply *be* true to his own nature.

Many of the restraining laws of today are of no more benefit than the leash that restrains the dog from escaping his master! Today many are breaking the leash. They refuse to be bound. And this is not necessarily a positive sign.

In the case of the Ascended Masters, they have not demonstrated that they themselves are anything else but men on a leash—willingly tied and obedient to the laws of God.

But in the case of the laws of control, the leash is the headlong desire of the fallen ones for domination over humanity.[32] They, the reprobate angels who were cast out of the higher octaves of light, want to control the people—their human procreation and their divinely co-creative Real Self, both coexisting within the individual. Furthermore, they want to be thought wise. Oh, how they want to be thought wise!

And they create movements and they create unrest to control the restless masses—without ever *truly* understanding or *truly* giving allegiance to the *intent* of God and the *reality* of God or the mystery schools hidden in the everlasting hills. They don't admit to understanding the mystic brotherhoods and they don't admit to understanding their power.

Yet the Great White Brotherhood and the power of the Ascended Masters is active and felt today throughout the whole fabric of civilization. And through their Messengers they gather their own in the Mystery School as in the last days of Atlantis and Lemuria[33] to teach them the power of the Word by which their souls and the worlds were framed.

The fallen angels in embodiment seem not to take note of the historical fact that they will lose their temporal life. Most certainly they will. And if, during the course of that temporal life, they do not achieve some Reality, some sense of the power of God that is within them, and begin to exercise it, they will indeed be cast into the 'outer darkness'[34] of their own creation.

And if they have not made contact with the Brotherhood or sustained in honor the thread of contact they once had with the Ascended Masters, they will have no one to fetch them out of that darkness. Furthermore, if, having heard the Word of Truth, these rebellious angels do not repent of their evildoings and bow before the Universal Christ, "there remaineth," according to the doctrine of Christ recorded in Hebrews, "no more sacrifice for sins, but a certain fearful looking for of judgment and fiery indignation, which shall devour the adversaries." [35]

Thus suspended in limbo during the period awaiting rebirth, they will in all likelihood glean very little or nothing at all from the universe. Waiting for the next opportunity either to "make things right" and "set the record straight" or to squander what little they have left in the cup, they will be in a spiritually embryonic state in the incubator of life. This semi-awareness is in no way conducive to the kindling within them of the realities of the Spirit, which must be enlivened and quickened by a conscious acceptance (whether in the body or out) of the Christic Initiator.

This is the meaning of "the quick and the dead." [36] Both are here amongst us. There are very few who are quick, and there are many who are dead: some who were once alive and have chosen to be dead, and others who have never lived and cannot die except they first be quickened, then exercise the conscious choice to be or not to be. And the Christ, whose flame burns brightly in each of us, is ordained of God to be their judge and ours.

We have, then, a responsibility toward our Creator and toward the Lord of all to seek out the Mystery School sponsored by the Great White Brotherhood. Only by attunement with the World Teachers and with the cosmic reality of the message of Jesus Christ can man today derive the satisfactions and the instructions that will show him in due course of time (if he patiently wait for it[37]) the true path of his own resurrection unto his highest Self.

It does take time—and space. You can't turn the tide of centuries of the karma of self-delusion in one moment, but you can start. And that's why God gave us the good earth and another day to seek and find him. It does take the turning of cycles. And your allotted span remaining in this life is the most precious gift you have. For out of it you can forge and win true Selfhood.

So, you see, you need all of that instruction that is vouchsafed to you by the Holy Spirit through your own beloved Christ Self as you sit at the feet of the Master Jesus and the saints with him who teach and initiate your soul at the Place Prepared.

For in the failure to heed the Master's voice, many who have rejected his Path have found that when the sands in the hourglass have run out they have gone the way of the wandering stars to whom was reserved the mists of darkness forever.[38]

YOU'RE NOT SINNERS. YOU SIMPLY ARE NOT AWAKE!

Without the enlightenment of the Holy Spirit taught to us by the Ascended Masters, who are our elder brothers and sisters on the path of Life, our consciousness may be nothing more than a tramp consciousness that goes from haven to haven or place to place without ever gleaning any sense of its purpose or any understanding of what actually is the intrinsic worth of the soul that cannot be weighed by human scales.

You can have the ageless Teaching of the Truth of your being—the eternal verities. It's here for the asking. I will not beg you—nor will any Ascended Master anywhere in the universe beg you. We are not going to beg you to accept our offering, like a beggar with a begging bowl in reverse.

This is not a matter of a sawdust trail where you come to the altar and get down on your knees and beat your breast and say, "O Lord, be merciful unto me, a sinner."

You're not sinners. You simply are not awake!

I don't say it to all. I say it to many in the world, because it is so. And I, too, was a part of that impoverished sense of selfhood passed on to me by the false pastors. And by His grace I was healed of it. And I walked, step by step, up those stairs.

I have not reached the top of the ladder. Nor have any that I know reached the top of the ladder, but all are struggling toward the top—moving toward it. The word perhaps should not be "struggle" in one sense, but still there is always the struggle between the flesh and the Spirit. And anyone who denies it has not walked the way of the real overcomers, the revolutionaries of the Spirit who have won against the odds of their personal and planetary karma.

And so our friends the Ascended Masters, as graduates cum laude of the Mystery School, definitely have something to offer us. In traveling all over the world to the farthest reaches of the globe, I have not found anything quite like the Teachings of the Great White Brotherhood.

I have never found such instruction as we have been given from the Masters of Wisdom—so pure in its form, so magnificent in its outreach, so unselfish, so completely beautiful, and so demonstrable. You can demonstrate it in your life. And it *will* change your world—and not for the worse but for the better.

That great exponent of freedom, Saint Germain—whose bobtail biography appears in *Encyclopaedia Britannica*[39] in some stance of error—is himself a great

Western adept, known also as a prince of the House of Rakoczy (descended from the royal house of Hungary, his retreat having once been in Transylvania, now remapped as Romania).

Today Saint Germain is the greatest defender of real freedom to humanity that you will ever find on this planet. Jesus Christ and Saint Germain working together are architects of this age. And they are lovingly, willingly, joyously extending their help to humanity. But the Law says: Call unto me and I will answer you.[40]

We don't ask you to make a public display of yourself. You can call in your own heart to God, and no one need know it. And in answer to your call, God will send his servant-Sons, the Ascended Masters, to teach you. They have promised to do his will by helping those of us who are here on earth earnestly involved in the process of winning our ascension.

We have seen the results of their service in a fiery demonstration of joy and happiness and wisdom and an influx of beauty into the lives of our students.

And all that we have we offer to the world without money and without price.[41]

PROLOGUE
TO THE FUTURE

Prologue to the Future

ONCE again, imagine you are a detective.

You finish scanning the last line of the file, lean back in your chair and let out a sigh. You've been hunched over your desk too long.

You wonder how long it's been since the rain stopped. The fire's died down to embers and you're tired. But you're elated.

Could this be the end of the case? The uncrackable case?

Maybe. But your mind is still racing with unanswered questions.

How can you prove this is the Lost Teaching? How can any twentieth-century man, or woman, however inspired, claim to have discovered it? You can almost hear that old police sergeant saying: Where are the facts?

Well, you admit, it's true. You could never prove it. Nothing that would stand up in any court of law.

You get up and stir the embers, put another log on, and begin to pace.

It's a fact that this file *does* explain many of the enigmatic and cryptic sayings of Jesus and Paul. And several parables too.

"Unto him that hath *a momentum . . .*" "And they shall not escape *their karma.*"

And what about the mystery of the body of Christ and all of us being part of that body through the Holy Christ Self? Of putting on the incorruptible, and the portent of "Before Abraham was, I AM"? And the great mystery of which he spoke that was so misunderstood by his disciples—the kingdom of God within you?

There were even things from the Old Testament—Genesis' "coats of skins" and every man sitting "under his vine and under his fig tree."

You go through the chapters again in your mind. And it begins to dawn upon you how much of the Bible is really in there.

Jesus' Lost Teachings must have been along these lines. They must have included an understanding of his life and revolutionary message later taken out of context by only God knows who—causing endless confusion. And many of the keys in this file weren't even hinted at in the Bible. But they very well could have been part of Christ's hidden wisdom.

Since the Lord's teaching in its entirety is most likely forever lost to this world, you muse (barring some archaeological discovery which even then couldn't uncover what was never recorded), it is up to us who live in the present to discover it wherever we can.

Besides, the file did fill in a lot of your unanswered questions about Christianity.

Like, did I have to become a cannibal and literally eat his flesh and drink his blood in order to have his life in me. Or how some people could say they were good Christians and deny the Good Shepherd's injunction: "Be ye therefore perfect, even as your Father which is in heaven is perfect."

You'd wondered how God could consign the soul of a baby who'd died a few days after it was born to limbo or a worse fate just because it hadn't been baptized. And how if you merely confessed Jesus as the

Son of God, you could be saved and all your sins would be forgiven.

Or how a man could reap everything he'd sown in one life! How did 'only one life' stand up so long in light of the obvious mathematics of the equation: threescore and ten, more or less, and so much to do and undo!

Karma and reincarnation—now that was a major part of the Lost Teachings. A real missing link. Something you'd always suspected even before you discovered Jesus had gone to India and the Far East. You don't know whether you actually *believe* you lived before. But it's as logical as any other explanation of the afterlife, and the 'before life'—even more so in the broader perspective of Jesus' teaching. In fact, it's *the* missing link—answering many questions that for scholars and the faithful alike have ended at the proverbial brick wall.

What I'd like to have done, you say, walking into the kitchen and plugging in the coffee pot, is to have lived maybe in old London. It would've been fun to have pounded the waterfront with Sherlock Holmes.

Wait a minute, you stop.

He was fictional. Maybe you're getting a bit carried away. What you need, you tell yourself, walking back to the fire, is a day or two off. You lean against the mantle and stare into the flames.

But have you really discovered anything? Ineluctable logic notwithstanding, can you *convince* anybody?

You can almost hear your devout maiden aunt saying, "Just because the file purports to contain what Jesus might have taught doesn't make it so!" You wrestle with that one a minute. Then you say, Hey. Why is the burden of proof on me?

The burden of proof is on modern Christianity as a whole, you say, recalling your earlier research. It's missing more pieces than the butler's alibi in your last case. For two thousand years Christians have been playing with half a deck. Maybe less.

How are the Christians. . . or anyone. . . ever going to prove that *they* have all the essentials of Jesus' teaching? Or that your file (you glance over at it) *doesn't* contain the Lost Teachings of Jesus?

Even if you could never prove conclusively that you *had* uncovered the Lost Teachings, no one could prove you hadn't. And they were going to have to come up with some pretty fancy explanations about how they could have the whole Truth (and nothing but the Truth) when half of it was missing.

Half of it *was* missing. You'd done enough leg work to prove that conclusively.

So in the final analysis, you've proven that something was lost and you've discovered something that could be it. Now, you say, the controversy will rage in the realm of belief. But isn't that what religion is all about? Conviction. Whether or not *you* can accept a certain tenet. That's what determines *your* faith. It's your own witness that counts for you.

So what's to stop somebody—yes, a twentieth-century man—from having a revelation that Christ did and taught much more than what was recorded? And what's to stop people from believing he's right—based on the file of their own research with the *Ascended Master* Jesus Christ?

After all, whatever Jesus did and taught back then is what Christianity was based on. (Or so they say. But after reading the file, you're not so sure.)

You recall once more that Christ did say he'd send another Comforter to bring all things to our remembrance—"whatsoever I have said unto you." The prophecy of the Comforter was hardly the promise of a rabbi who believed his teachings would remain intact for two thousand years.

. . . I would bet, you start to say and then catch yourself. On most cases you'd bet. But this one? Well, *if* you were betting on this case, you'd say that the odds are good that some people will *believe* that what's in your file *is* the Lost Teachings.

That file makes a lot of sense. Something about it rings true, you decide, and you've seen enough phonies in your day to tell the difference. You recall that last femme fatale you unmasked. The one you'd rather not recall.

You begin pacing back and forth again. Alright, so you're not a theologian. A rabbi, a priest or an Indian chief—or guru. Maybe you're not qualified to judge. But your intuition—heart, you say, remembering a line from the file—tells you you're dealing with something sincere. You get up and walk into the kitchen and start rummaging in the refrigerator for last week's bagel.

There were many more mysteries explained in this file, you're thinking, pouring yourself some coffee: dying daily; obtaining a better resurrection; how there could be only one Son of God when Melchizedek had also been made in his likeness and John had written, "for now are we the sons of God"; Christ being formed in you; and even the secret teaching behind Martha's exclamation: "Yea, Lord, I believe that thou art the Christ, the Son of God which should come into the world."

It's something you can sink your teeth into, you say, washing down a bite of bagel with a swig of coffee.

Now you're onto something. Something that would mean a lot to all those people who'd wondered what Jesus really said and did.

Some would agree you'd found the missing pieces and some—those who had the most to lose—would never agree. Everyone would have to be their own judge and jury—let the chips fall where they may.

And somehow, you say, going back to your desk and sitting down, the jury that really counted—the one Jesus had been speaking to all along—would believe you had cracked the case.

The phone rings. You decide to let it ring. It's either that old gang of yours sitting around playing poker or it's a wrong number. Either way, you'll have plenty to say to them in a while.

You set your coffee cup down on an invitation to last month's policemen's ball. Of course, the file didn't explain *every* teaching Jesus gave. A few of the mysteries it brought up were only touched upon. Like the violet flame. Or climbing the thirty-three steps of the spinal ladder. And chakras. Mustn't forget chakras. And all kinds of other things you'd like to hear more about. Chapter 8 hinted at some of them—golem, fallen angels, outer darkness, the quick and the dead, Atlantis and Lemuria. You pick up the file and move it aside, heading for your letter opener. You stop.

Atlantis and Lemuria? Lost teachings from lost continents? Taught by Jesus? Where does that connect? Rummaging for the letter opener, you push aside yesterday's *Daily News,* three-quarters of a chocolate bar and some black-and-white prints that should have been filed. Where is that thing, you say, as a pile of neglected folders falls to the floor.

You reach over to pick them up when a familiar-looking folder, lying innocently among them, catches your eye. That old thrill runs up your spine. You can make out the words *Teachings* and *II.* With fingers that would be trembling if you'd let them, you pick it up. There've been a lot of strange coincidences in this case.

The Lost Teachings of Jesus II? I suppose I should have anticipated it, you say to yourself. There were too many loose ends, too many unanswered questions.

Suddenly you realize there's a lot you are missing. "You don't get it all in one sermon," you can hear Mark saying. And I suppose he would have said, "You don't get it all in one file."

You sink back into your chair and stifle a yawn. A wave of fatigue settles over you. The fire has burned down again. The coffee didn't help much, either. And this new file is even thicker than the last one, you say, laying it down next to file I. A lot thicker.

You open it and read a few pages. You start to get excited, like a hound scenting the hunt. But there've been too many hunts lately.

Another yawn. And there is no stifling this one.

Tomorrow, you tell yourself.

You look up. The sky is flushed with the first faint plumes of dawn.

Yes, tomorrow, you say, as you get up and wander down the hall to get a few hours' sleep . . . knowing it has already arrived.

Our detective doesn't yet know the half of the mysteries to come in Volume II. As our saga continues (we just couldn't fit it all between two covers), you'll discover much more that is essential to your spiritual survival in this age.

We'll explore together the many mansions Jesus promised, the etheric retreats of the Brotherhood, and you'll meet some of your elder brothers and sisters— yes, the Ascended Masters who *do* stand preeminently with Christ, ready to initiate you into his Everlasting Gospel through the nine gifts of the Holy Spirit.

Continuing where we left off in Chapter 8, we'll share with you those mysteries the Lord is bringing to our remembrance—things taught to us at the time of his earthly mission and ever since, in past lives and the present. Seeds buried in the memory of the soul that need only to be awakened by the Sun of Righteousness.

You'll also study the lives of some of the 'unascended' Masters who have gone before you and see how they received the revelation of the Holy Ghost as well.

You'll learn about the continuing warfare waged by the forces of Darkness against the shining ones, the hosts of Light, how free will fits in, where the fallen angels are today, and the tools Jesus has given us for our spiritual self-defense. We'll continue our revelations on the origin and nature of Absolute Evil begun in this and earlier exegeses, *The Forbidden Mysteries of Enoch* and *Mysteries of the Holy Grail.*

We'll examine some of the puzzling questions of the creation, where exactly Atlantis and Lemuria came in, what the fallen angels were doing back then, and other records which have been expunged from our history by the corrosion of kal-desh and the rise and fall of continents. We'll trace the telltale signatures of those who succeeded (almost, but not quite) in erasing their untenable tracks. Records that are vital to our decision-making process in this day of space travel, international terrorism, and genetic engineering.

You'll read about the Romanization of Christianity and those who effectively secularized Jesus' message concerning the path of personal Christhood.

More of the ancient wisdom: the violet flame in greater detail as alchemy, as the new light and dispensation of Aquarius, as the 'universal solvent'; the science of mantra and of the spoken Word; karma and reincarnation further explained; the twelve gates to the city; Jesus' working of miracles, and how Christ in you can work marvelous works too; the explanation of the warring in the members, and how you can win!

And the meaning of the Final Judgment and the Day of Vengeance of our God.

You'll find keys to the mystery of becoming Christ's vessel, of feeding my sheep, and of the marriage of the Lamb—the rite of the ascension through which Jesus passed in order to prepare the way for his brothers and sisters—"I go to prepare a place for you...that where 'I AM', there ye may be also."

And so, beloved friends of Light, with these words we send you our missive as an arrow shot from the taut and taught bow of our communion with the Mind of God. That it might find lodging in the hearts of Keepers of the Flame the world around is our prayer.

We wait, as the poet waited, for our arrow to return to us in the song of your soul's rejoicing upon finding again that which was never really lost, only forgotten, as an angel once told me, "but for a little while."

Acknowledgments

I gratefully acknowledge the diligent review and lively comments generously given on "The Past Is Prologue" by John C. Trever, director of the Dead Sea Scrolls Project of the School of Theology at Claremont, California, and Marvin W. Meyer, professor of religion and New Testament studies at Chapman College.

Their learned perspective aided greatly in the assessment of my thesis midst the current as well as historical debate that surrounds the life and teachings of Jesus. And their scholarly disagreement as well as consensus on various points has enriched my understanding, as I know it will the reader's. For their spirit of fellowship and support for my humble endeavor, I thank them fondly.

Notes

Epigraph facing page 1

1. I Cor. 2:10–13, Jerusalem Bible. **The Jerusalem Bible** is a Roman Catholic translation of the Bible originally done in French at the Dominican Biblical School in Jerusalem (1956). The English equivalent (1966) was translated directly from ancient Hebrew and Greek texts and compared with the French translation, using recent research in archaeology, history, and literary criticism. The Jerusalem Bible uses more colloquial language than older translations of the Bible and is considered an accurate and scholarly work.

THE PAST IS PROLOGUE

1. John 21:25.*
2. Mark 6:35.
3. Luke 9:11.
4. Luke 24:27, Jerusalem Bible.
5. Matt. 9:10, 13; Mark 2:15, 17; Luke 5:29, 32.
6. Luke 10:39.
7. **Passages in the Gospels which show Jesus teaching but do not record his words:** Matt. 9:35 (Mark 6:6); Matt. 13:54 (Mark 6:2); Matt. 16:21 (Mark 8:31); Mark 1:21 (Luke 4:31); Mark 1:39 (Luke 4:44); Mark 2:2 (Luke 5:17); Mark 2:13; Luke 2:46, 47; 4:15; 5:3; 6:6; John 4:40–42.
8. **Passages in the Gospels which recount some of Jesus' words but imply that not all of what he said is recorded:** Matt. 4:17 (Mark 1:14, 15); Matt. 4:23ff.; 10:27; 21:23ff. (Luke 20:1ff.); Mark 4:33, 34; 10:1ff.; Luke 13:10–21; 13:22–35; John 7:14ff.; 8:2ff.

*Bible references are to the King James Version (KJV) unless otherwise noted.

9. John 7:14. **The historical reliability of the Gospel of John:** It has been argued that the Gospel of John is a theological work with little historical value. In his *Introduction to the New Testament,* Werner Kümmel points out that "D. F. Strauss in his *Life of Jesus* (1835/36) sought to show that in John was presented a more developed form of 'myth' compared to the Synoptics, so that the question of John as a historical source was not to be considered. . . . Though it was widely perceived as negative, Strauss's criticism was made methodologically certain by F. C. Baur's *Kritische Untersuchungen über die kanonischen Evv.* (1847), in which he maintained that John . . . contained no historically valuable tradition."

Those influenced by Rudolf Bultmann, one of the leading practitioners of the "form-critical" school of New Testament criticism, and a wide range of other scholars are among those who still maintain this position. Form criticism proceeds from the premise that the individual units or "forms" of the Gospels must be studied in terms of their development in relation to the *Sitz im Leben,* or situation in life—that is, the dynamic social forces present in the early Christian communities. Bultmann and Martin Dibelius, another form critic, agreed, says Schuyler Brown, "that a 'form' is neither something accidental nor the result of the literary genius of an individual. Rather, it is the spontaneous creation of a community and grows out of a typical, recurring situation in the life of the community, such as preaching, teaching, or controversy with outsiders." (For a further discussion of form criticism and its weaknesses, see pp. 340 n. 44, 344 n. 47.)

Not all scholars agree that John has no historical value—a position which was once treated almost as a "critical dogma." According to Schuyler Brown, "because of its developed christology, the Fourth Gospel has been generally neglected in life of Jesus studies, a curious example of scholarly illogicality." "Today there is a growing tendency to take very seriously the historical, social, and geographical details peculiar to narratives found only in the Fourth Gospel," points out Raymond Brown in his introduction to the Gospel of John in *The Anchor Bible.* "Modern investigations of antiquity, especially through archaeology, have verified many of these details." These include: "John's references to the Samaritans, their theology, their practice of worshiping on Gerizim, and the location of Jacob's well" (ch. 4); "the very precise information about the pool of Bethesda is perfectly accurate as to name, location, and construction" (ch. 5); "the theological themes brought up in relation to Passover and the Feast of Tabernacles reflect an accurate knowledge of the festal ceremonies and of the synagogue readings associated with the feasts" (chs. 6–8); and "details about Jerusalem seem to be accurate, for example, the references to the pool of Siloam, to Solomon's Portico as a shelter in winter time, and to the stone pavement of Pilate's Praetorium" (chs. 9:7; 10:22, 23; 19:13).

Furthermore, Brown, in a well-reasoned answer to form-critical thinking, asserts that "the tradition of Jesus' works and words that underlies John . . . resembles the traditions behind the Synoptic Gospels. . . . In comparing John and the Synoptics, we find that sometimes the material underlying John's account seems to be more primitive than the material underlying the Synoptic account(s)." (Morton Smith argues that both Mark and John were based on an early Aramaic gospel that was translated twice into Greek; one translation was used by Mark, the other by John.) Given the currently available texts and critical techniques, it is not possible to precisely reconstruct the process of Gospel formation. Yet in answer to the argument that John is purely a theological rather than a historical document, Brown says that "John is deeply historical—historical in the sense in which history is concerned not only with what happened but also with the deepest meaning of what happened."

In an effort to determine the author of the Fourth Gospel, Brown argues persuasively that "when all is said and done, the combination of external and internal evidence associating the Fourth Gospel with John son of Zebedee [one of Jesus' twelve disciples] makes this the strongest hypothesis, if one is prepared to give credence to the Gospel's claim of an eyewitness source."

In assessing the Johannine writings, it is important to keep in mind that the ancient concept of "author" differs considerably from our own. "In the terminology of modern literary criticism 'author' and 'writer' are often synonymous terms," says Brown. "Antiquity did not share this fine sense of proper credits. . . . Therefore, in considering biblical books, many times we have to distinguish between the *author* whose ideas the book expresses and the *writer*. The writers run the gamut from recording secretaries who slavishly copied down the author's dictation to highly independent collaborators who, working from a sketch of the author's ideas, gave their own literary style to the final work. That some distinction between author and writer may be helpful in considering the Fourth Gospel is suggested by the existence of several NT Johannine works which betray differences in style. . . . The necessity of positing different writers for John and Revelation is indeed obvious."

Thus, Brown theorizes that John, son of Zebedee, an eyewitness, was the source of the underlying historical tradition which was fashioned into a coherent Gospel by one of his principle disciples. It was later edited by a secondary disciple, who inserted additional material "stemming from the preaching days of the evangelist himself." Finally, in discussing ancient methods of composition in relation to **John's authorship of the Book of Revelation,** Brown says that "Revelation is the work that is most directly John's. . . . Indeed, even the Greek of Revelation could have come from John, for it is far more primitive and Semitic than the more polished style of the Epistles and Gospel."

Whoever wrote down the Gospel, epistles, and Revelation of John—and we believe that John the beloved disciple of Christ or his scribes did so—we are convinced that these documents are a human transparency for the Divine Love, human concern, and living spirit of Jesus Christ. Only one so close to his heart could have received these teachings and prophecies on the initiatic path of the soul which portend the mystical intimations that are to be bestowed by grace upon the bride (initiate) of Christ.

See Werner Georg Kümmel, *Introduction to the New Testament,* rev. ed., trans. Howard Clark Kee (Nashville: Abingdon Press, 1975), p. 197; Schuyler Brown, *The Origins of Christianity: A Historical Introduction to the New Testament* (Oxford and New York: Oxford University Press, 1984), pp. 35, 37; George Eldon Ladd, *The New Testament and Criticism* (London: Hodder & Stoughton, 1967), p. 161; Raymond E. Brown, trans., *The Gospel According to John (I–XII),* vol. 29 of *The Anchor Bible* (Garden City, N.Y.: Doubleday & Company, 1966), pp. xxxvi–xxxvii, xlii, xlviii, xlix, lxxxvii, xcviii, c, cii; Morton Smith, "Clement of Alexandria and Secret Mark: The Score at the End of the First Decade," *Harvard Theological Review,* 75 (October 1982): 452.

10. Matt. 10:27, Revised Standard Version. **The Revised Standard Version** (RSV) of the Bible (New Testament 1946, Old Testament 1952) is a revision of the American Standard Version (1901), which was a revision of the King James Version (1611). The RSV was the work of 32 scholars from 20 theological seminaries and universities who took into account modern scholarship and additional knowledge of biblical texts. Much of the language was updated for comprehension, but traditional passages from the King James Version that had a special literary or devotional value were retained. Since its publication the RSV has been adopted by many Protestant churches and has become the most popular translation in the United States.
11. Matt. 10:7.
12. Luke 2; 3:21–23; Matt. 2.
13. **Forty days:** Acts 1:3 is the one place in the New Testament where the length of Jesus' post-resurrection ministry is mentioned: "He had shown himself alive to them after his Passion by many demonstrations: for forty days he had continued to appear to them and tell them about the kingdom of God" (Jerusalem Bible). It is generally agreed, however, that forty is a sacred and symbolic number rather than an exact figure. Traditions regarding the length of time between the resurrection and the ascension vary considerably. Matthew and John do not mention the ascension and suggest only a short post-resurrection ministry (Matt. 28; John 20). Chapter 16 of the Gospel of Mark, the closing verses of which (16:9–20) are taken by most scholars to be a later addition by another author, mentions both the resurrection and ascension. Again, the author implies but a brief period of activity after the resurrection. In Luke "there is nothing to indicate," as G. H. C. Macgregor points out, "that the Ascension did not take place on the same day as the Resurrection—a view perhaps shared by Paul who seems to regard the two as synonymous. The acceptance of the longer period by church tradition was probably due to the desire to make room for the imparting of secret instruction to the inner circle of his disciples by the risen Jesus, in particular concerning the kingdom of God."

There were traditions in the late first to third centuries of a much longer interval between the resurrection and the ascension. Church Father Irenaeus wrote (c. A.D. 180) that Jesus lived at least ten to twenty years after the crucifixion and "still fulfilled the office of a Teacher, even as the Gospel and all the elders testify; those who were conversant in Asia with John, the disciple of the Lord, [affirming] that John conveyed to them that information." A number of Gnostic texts also bear witness to a long interval between the resurrection and the ascension. *Pistis Sophia,* for instance, says that after Jesus had risen from the dead, "he passed eleven years discoursing with his disciples and instructing them."

See G. H. C. Macgregor in *The Interpreter's Bible,* 12 vols. (Nashville: Abingdon Press, 1982), 9:26–27; Elizabeth Clare Prophet, *The Lost Years of Jesus* (Los Angeles: Summit University Press, 1984), pp. 4–5, 382–83; Irenaeus, *Against Heresies* 2.22.5, in Alexander Roberts and James Donaldson, eds., *The Ante-Nicene Fathers,* American reprint of the Edinburgh ed., 9 vols. (Grand Rapids, Mich.: Wm. B. Eerdmans Publishing Co., 1981), 1:391–92; G. R. S. Mead, trans., *Pistis Sophia,* rev. ed. (London: John M. Watkins, 1921), p. 1.

14. Acts 1:3.
15. Acts 1:9.
16. Rev. 1:1. **John's authorship of the Book of Revelation:** see p. 334 n. 9.
17. I Cor. 9:1; 15:8. Many scholars believe that in both verses Paul is referring to the moment of his conversion and that these references do not imply further meetings.
18. II Cor. 12:1, Jerusalem Bible. Paul's statement in II Cor. 12:2, 4 that he knows "a man in Christ who, fourteen years ago," was "caught up into paradise and heard things which must not and cannot be put into human language" is generally regarded as a reference to himself, as II Cor. 12:7 makes clear: "In view of the extraordinary nature of these revelations, to stop me from getting too proud I was given a thorn in the flesh. . . . "
19. II Cor. 12:7–9, Jerusalem Bible.
20. Acts 18:9, 10.
21. Acts 22:17–21.
22. Acts 16:7, Jerusalem Bible.
23. I Cor. 7:10; 11:23; Jerusalem Bible.
24. Gal. 1:11, 12, Jerusalem Bible; Gal. 1:20, King James Version.
25. Gal. 1:17, Jerusalem Bible.
26. II Cor. 12:4.
27. **Paul's lost letters:** It is generally agreed that a number of Paul's letters have been lost, although fragments of some of the letters may be embedded in his epistles. I Corinthians 5:9

contains a clear reference to a now lost letter: "I wrote unto you in an epistle not to company with fornicators."

28. **Sources for the Gospel of John**: Rudolf Bultmann has theorized that the Gospel of John, which differs in many respects from Matthew, Mark, and Luke, may have used three distinct sources for its material: a "Sign Source" for its seven miracles (some of which are not paralleled in the other three Gospels); a "Revelatory Discourse Source" for Jesus' discourses, which Bultmann says are stylistically similar to Gnostic writings; and possibly a passion narrative that was separate from the material used in the other three Gospels. See Rudolf Bultmann, *The Gospel of John: A Commentary,* trans. G. R. Beasley-Murray, R. W. N. Hoare, and J. K. Riches (Philadelphia: Westminster Press, 1971).

29. Robert M. Grant with David Noel Freedman, *The Secret Sayings of Jesus* (Garden City, N. Y.: Doubleday & Company, 1960), p. 25.

30. **Synoptic Gospels:** Three of the four Gospels—Matthew, Mark, and Luke—are so strikingly similar in language, sequence of events, and point of view that they have been called "synoptic," which means "seen together," since they are "viewing together" episodes in the life of Jesus Christ. Extensive parallels in content and structure in these three Gospels make it possible to arrange their verses side by side in parallel columns so they can be read together. The Gospel of John, the "spiritual Gospel," differs markedly from the other three.

31. Matt. 5:3–7:27; Luke 6:20–49; Matt. 6:9–13; Luke 11:2–4.

32. **Canon:** an authoritative list of books accepted as Holy Scripture.

33. Grant and Freedman, *The Secret Sayings of Jesus,* p. 29.

34. **Aristion:** the reputed author of verses 9–20 of the last chapter of Mark, according to a tenth-century Armenian manuscript.

35. Eusebius, *The History of the Church from Christ to Constantine* 3.39 (trans. G. A. Williamson, p. 150).

36. Ibid., p. 152.

37. Morton Smith, *The Secret Gospel: The Discovery and Interpretation of the Secret Gospel According to Mark* (Clearlake, Calif.: The Dawn Horse Press, 1982), p. 131.

38. **Authors of the New Testament:** It was particularly important in the early life of the church to associate sacred writings with the apostles. "All twenty-seven books of the New Testament were connected by the early church with 'the apostles,'" notes Schuyler Brown (*The Origins of Christianity,* p. 10). He

goes on to say, however, that "modern critical scholarship
has cast doubt on the traditional authorship of all the New
Testament writings, with the exception of seven Pauline letters (Rom., 1–2 Cor., Gal., Phil., 1 Thess., Philem.). All the
other books may be either anonymous or pseudonymous."
That is not to say that almost every conceivable position
hasn't found support. In his *Introduction to the New Testament,* Werner Georg Kümmel provides a valuable summary
of the history of the various theories regarding the author,
time and place of composition, and literary character and
theological aim of each of the New Testament writings.

39. Smith, *The Secret Gospel,* p. 131.
40. S. G. F. Brandon, *The Fall of Jerusalem and the Christian
Church: A Study of the Effects of the Jewish Overthrow of
A.D. 70 on Christianity* (London: S.P.C.K., 1957), p. 9.
41. **"Based on their understanding of Jewish eschatology, some
scholars believe that Jesus would have thought it unnecessary
to write down his teaching"**: According to *The Universal
Jewish Encyclopedia* (s.v. "Eschatology"), the Jewish conception of the end times during the post-Exilic period (c. 538
B.C.–A.D. 1) was as follows: "The state of the world will
become progressively worse as time goes on, culminating in
great wars . . . and in pestilence, famine and earthquakes.
Then God will intervene, either in person, or through the
Messiah (sometimes there are two Messiahs, the first of
whom will die), and there will be a great battle in which the
wicked nations will be destroyed. All mankind will perish;
but then will come the resurrection of the dead, and all will
be summoned before the throne of God for judgment."

Some scholars say that if Jesus thought his Messiahship
was the fulfillment of these hopes, then he must have thought
the world would soon end. Clarence Tucker Craig (*The Interpreter's Bible,* 7:149) says Jesus' hope of the kingdom was "a
profound conviction that the righteous God of history was
about to assert his full sovereignty." This belief is predicated
upon a literal interpretation of Jesus' statements concerning
the kingdom of God, such as "The kingdom of God is at
hand: repent ye" (Mark 1:15); "There be some standing
here, which shall not taste of death till they see the kingdom
of God" (Luke 9:27); "Thou art not far from the kingdom of
God" (Mark 12:34). If the kingdom of God is seen as a one-
time outer occurrence to be experienced simultaneously by

all, these statements interpreted literally would suggest that Jesus expected it imminently.

In his discussion of the eschatology of Luke, E. Earle Ellis says that "the limited amount of hard, factual evidence and the literary character of the evidence we do possess gives to [any] evaluation a considerable measure of subjectivity." It is made even more subjective by the fact that the phrase "the kingdom of God" is not defined in the Gospels. "The eschatology of the historical Jesus," says Marvin Meyer, "is something that is extremely difficult, maybe impossible, to capture." See E. Earle Ellis, *Eschatology in Luke* (Philadelphia: Fortress Press, 1972), p. 4; Personal interview with Marvin Meyer, 27 May 1986.

Jesus' teaching to us reveals the *kingdom* of God as the *consciousness* of God experienced individually as its mysteries unfold through Christic initiation and the baptism by sacred fire. As one puts on and dwells in this state of God's consciousness, i.e., God's kingdom, the elements (karma) of the 'anti-kingdom' come to naught. These are recorded in the subconscious (as well as in the collective unconscious of the race as world karma) and are described by John in Revelation as the challenge to be met on the battlefield of the psyche by every living soul.

42. **The story of the woman taken in adultery,** John 8:1–11, does not appear in any Greek manuscripts of the Bible earlier than the sixth century, including Codex Sinaiticus and Codex Vaticanus, and does not appear in any of the writings of the Church Fathers before a Latin translation of Irenaeus dated as late as the fourth century. Thus, scholars have concluded that it was not in John's original Gospel. This fact, however, does not establish an absence of authenticity. Some have suggested the story was at one time part of Luke, as it uses words only he would use and contains many expressions John never used. In fact, one group of manuscripts places it not in John but after Luke 21:38. Others have speculated that it may have been removed from Luke for its seeming leniency towards sinners. A reference in Eusebius indicates that this story is ancient, perhaps part of oral tradition. He writes in his *History of the Church* (3.39, trans. Williamson, p. 153) that Papias "reproduces a story about a woman falsely accused before the Lord of many sins." Despite the incident's doubtful placement in John, the editors of the

Revised Standard Version Catholic Edition say that it "is regarded as inspired and canonical by the church."

See Merrill C. Tenney, commentary on the Gospel of John, in *The Expositor's Bible Commentary,* 12 vols. (Grand Rapids, Mich.: Zondervan Publishing House, 1981), 9:91; J. C. Fenton, commentary in *The Gospel According to John in the Revised Standard Version* (London: Oxford University Press, 1970), p. 213.

43. Luke 4:21. RSV renders "the acceptable year of the Lord" (Luke 4:19) as "the year of the Lord's favor."

44. **Scholars have long debated whether or not Jesus believed himself the Messiah**, as his reading from Isaiah in Luke 4:21 implies. Debate has primarily focused upon the question of why Jesus acted so unmessianic if he thought he was the Messiah. Why did he allow himself to be executed? Why did he not proclaim himself more openly? A number of explanations have been offered, which are dependent upon various definitions of the Messiah.

The explanation offered in the *Catholic Biblical Encyclopedia* is that Jesus was, and believed he was, the Messiah prophesied in Psalms, Daniel, Isaiah, Jeremiah, and other books who would inaugurate "an eternal Messianic Kingdom" where he would "rule in peace with justice and judgment" and would be a priest, prophet, shepherd and king. But he also saw himself as the fulfillment of Isaiah 50–53, which describe a suffering servant.

For many Christians, the "Suffering Servant" concept explains why the all-powerful Messiah voluntarily accepted a criminal's death. Isaiah says that the servant "was wounded for our transgressions, he was bruised for our iniquities. . . . He was cut off out of the land of the living: for the transgression of my people was he stricken. . . . Therefore will I divide him a portion with the great, and he shall divide the spoil with the strong" (Isa. 53:5, 8, 12). In determining that Jesus was the Suffering Servant, Christians reconcile his seemingly dual nature. But with the advent of critical studies of the Bible, this explanation was increasingly questioned.

One theory is that he *never* thought of himself as the Messiah but his disciples gave him the title posthumously. German scholar Hermann Samuel Reimarus (1694–1768) was one of the first to take this position, reflecting the rationalistic influence of German scholars who became renowned for their radical biblical criticism. Raymond F. Collins in his *Introduction to the New Testament* summarizes Reimarus' scenario: "Jesus preached a political kingdom of God. The apostles overcame their frustration at the death of Jesus by falling back upon a second Jewish eschatological schema. Then, gathering followers who shared their expectation of a second coming of Jesus the Messiah, they created a different Jesus from the fabric of various historical assumptions. In effect, the apostles perpetrated a deception for their own materialistic reasons."

The form critics expanded upon this notion. Form criticism is the analysis of material which began as oral tradition by dividing it into units and classifying them in various categories or forms which can then be studied. "Form critics analyzed the Gospels," writes scholar George Eldon Ladd, "in order to recover the process by which the original, purely historical tradition was transformed into [what they believed was] the supernaturally colored tradition as it is embodied in the written Gospels which we have today."

In arguing that Jesus did not proclaim himself the Messiah, critics assume that every pre-Easter mention of Jesus as Christ, Messiah, or Son of God was an invention of the community of the first Christians. Thus, they would classify as an invention Jesus' confirmation to the woman of Samaria that he is Messias, "which is called Christ" (John 4:25, 26). They say that "the post-Easter Church was incapable of thinking back to the historical Jesus," who had become so obscured by theology after his death that it would have been impossible for the author of John to have written about him.

In Mark 8:29–30, Jesus elicits from Peter the confession that he is the Christ and then bids his disciples to "tell no man of him." The Church uses this episode to explain why Jesus did not proclaim his Messiahship more openly—he wanted to keep it a secret. Early twentieth-century form critic W. Wrede maintained that Jesus did not reveal his Messiahship until the resurrection, thus Mark's "Messianic Secret" account was not historical.

Though popular at its inception, this type of analysis was increasingly challenged. Biblical scholar Morton Smith recently articulated some of the criticisms. Questions such as whether or not portions of the Bible are additions, he said, "often come down to matters of feeling. Consequently much that passes as form criticism and the like is actually auto-biography—'How I feel about this text.' Hence the welter of contradictions these schools have produced." Summing up his analysis of the form critics' contentions, scholar Schuyler Brown says, "When neither the content nor the context indicates a situation after Easter, the inauthenticity of sayings attributed to Jesus in the gospels must be proved, not assumed. To operate on any other basis would restrict the historian's use of material in a way which no sound methodology can justify."

German scholar Johannes Weiss and his student Albert Schweitzer believed eschatology (see p. 338 n. 41) was the important factor in Jesus' Messianic consciousness. Jesus believed he was the Messiah of Jewish expectation who would inaugurate the kingdom of God, Schweitzer said, and knew it from the moment of baptism. This was not a spiritualized view of the kingdom, he wrote, as "the ancient world, Jewish, Greek and Roman, would have had no point of contact with such an announcement," but necessarily a physical one.

Jesus must have believed the kingdom he would inaugurate would be the same as that which the Jews expected. "If Jesus thinks like his contemporaries about the world and what happens in it," says Schweitzer, "then his view of the coming of the Kingdom of God must resemble that of later Judaism." However, he says Jesus turned out to be wrong, both about the kingdom and about his imminent return. But this does not destroy Schweitzer's faith. "The fact that he [Jesus] shared the outlook of an age long past, which is to us mistaken and unacceptable," should not deter our belief in Jesus as "the supreme revealer of religious and spiritual truth," he wrote. Schweitzer says that the Church's spiritualizing of the kingdom and conferring of divinity upon Jesus was its way of accounting for the nonfulfillment of his word.

Biblical scholar Hugh J. Schonfield, in his book *The Passover Plot,* adopts a similar view, but suggests Jesus had a different conception of the Messiah. Christians contend that the Jews were expecting a Warrior Messiah and rejected Jesus because he preached love and peace. Although the peasantry may have expected a warrior, this was hardly the state of theology in Jesus' day, Schonfield says. Based especially on his study of the Dead Sea Scrolls, he says that the more pious Jews expected a holy and just Messiah of righteousness, who would live in close communion with God, be obedient to his will and defeat his adversaries by the word of truth. Furthermore, Jesus lived in northern Palestine in a spiritual atmosphere marked by less Judean domination and the presence of small, sectarian communities, such as the Essenes. "In the north," writes Schonfield, "the messianic doctrine of the Righteous King could join hands with the idea of a Suffering Just One and the conception of the Messiah as the ideal Israelite, the Son of Man." This belief would explain the seeming dual nature of Jesus' Messiahship.

In fact, Schonfield points out, the Essenes preached a doctrine of their leaders atoning for sin "by the practice of justice and by suffering the sorrows of affliction.... And they shall be an agreeable offering, atoning for the land and determining the judgment of wickedness." It was only a short step, he says, to apply this belief to the Messiah. "It was wholly in keeping with the testimony of the Scriptures that persecution and even death was the likely lot of those who followed the way of the Lord faithfully." Jesus believed he was the Messiah, Schonfield concludes, consciously set out to fulfill the prophecies about himself, and planned the events of the Passion Week right down to his execution.

So we see that the theories as to what Jesus thought range wide. Even though it is undeniable that editing and theologization of the Gospels took place, it seems unlikely that all references to the Messiah were post-Resurrection inventions, as some form critics say (see p. 344 n. 47). But even those who accept that Jesus believed he was the Messiah have not been able to satisfactorily explain just what he thought that meant and why, if he was, two thousand years later the world is still waiting to be "saved." Perhaps the problem lies in a fundamental misunderstanding of his message, something which we are attempting to set straight in this volume.

See John E. Steinmueller and Kathryn Sullivan, *Catholic Biblical Encyclopedia: Old Testament* (New York: Joseph F. Wagner, 1956), pp. 706–9; Raymond F. Collins, *Introduction to the New Testament* (Garden City, N.Y.: Doubleday & Company, 1983), p. 47; Ladd, *The New Testament and Criticism*, p. 144; George A. Riggan, *Messianic Theology and Christian Faith* (Philadelphia: Westminster Press, 1967), pp. 149–55; Donald Guthrie, *New Testament Introduction,* rev. ed. (London: Tyndale Press, 1970), pp. 189, 327; Morton Smith, "Clement of Alexandria and Secret Mark: The Score at the End of the First Decade," *Harvard Theological Review,* 75 (October 1982): 456; Brown, *The Origins of Christianity,* pp. 15, 48; E. N. Mozley, *The Theology of Albert Schweitzer: For Christian Inquirers* (New York: Macmillan Company, 1951), pp. 15–16, 112–15; Hugh J. Schonfield, *The Passover Plot: New Light on the History of Jesus* (New York: Bantam Books, 1965), pp. 28, 32, 207.

45. Luke 4:22.
46. Mark 16:14; Luke 24:45.
47. Some scholars have seriously questioned the **authenticity of Jesus' words and the historicity of the events of his life as recorded in the Gospels** and consider that at least some of what is attributed to the Master may never have been said by Jesus himself. This view has been espoused by some of the scholars who use form criticism to study the New Testament (see pp. 332 n. 9, 340 n. 44).

"According to the more skeptical of the form critics," writes C. E. B. Cranfield, "much of the narrative material which Mark received was legend and ideal construction, and many of the sayings ascribed to Jesus were similarly the creation of the primitive [Christian] community. The tradition, according to them, is evidence of the faith and the interests of the early church . . . and tells us what Jesus had become for Christian faith, not what he actually had been in his historical life. Some have even gone so far as to assert that of the historical Jesus we can now know next to nothing. But there are many considerations to be set over against this radical skepticism, considerations which have led other scholars to believe that there was preserved through the oral-tradition period a substantially reliable picture of the historical Jesus."

Among the factors Cranfield cites are: the survival of eyewitnesses who would have limited any attempts to invent or embellish; the early community's sense of obligation to accurately transmit the Lord's words, reflected in the prominence in the New Testament of the words "witness" and "bear witness" and in Paul's care in distinguishing in I Cor. 7 between what is and is not a commandment of the Lord; the respect that later Evangelists had for the earliest Gospel,

Mark; and "the fact that the church grew up within the Jewish community, a community with a long-established and highly revered oral tradition of its own."

Alfred M. Perry observes that in Matthew the "striking series of Old Testament citations introduced with the formula, 'This was done that it might be fulfilled which was spoken by the prophet, saying, . . .' (Matt. 2:15, 17; etc.)" could have been drawn from one of the "proof texts," or testimonies, in circulation among early Christians. "The Christians and the Qumran community both appear to have made 'testimonia'—a term borrowed from the third-century writer Cyprian for collections of texts which were particularly useful in 'proving' the claims of the community in controversy with other groups," says Schuyler Brown. But this is not to say that these testimonies were not based on what actually happened and what Jesus actually said. "Because of the conviction that there was a continuity between the Old and New [Testaments]," explains Donald Guthrie, "the early Christians sought out the incidents which emphasized fulfilment" of Old Testament prophecy. "The Old Testament Scriptures took on a new meaning because of the close connection between event and fulfilment."

One of the chief proponents of the view that a strong and dependable oral tradition existed is Birger Gerhardsson, who, says Guthrie, "considers that the Evangelists 'worked on a basis of a fixed, distinct tradition from, and about, Jesus—a tradition which was partly memorized and partly written down in notebooks and private scrolls, but invariably isolated from the teachings of other doctrinal authorities.'" Gerhardsson writes in *The Origins of the Gospel Traditions* that his chief objection to the form-critical scholars is that "their work is not sufficiently *historical.* They do not show sufficient energy in anchoring the question of the origin of the Gospel tradition within the framework of the question how holy, authoritative tradition was transmitted in the Jewish milieu of Palestine and elsewhere at the time of the New Testament."

Guthrie further argues that "the words of Jesus would be regarded as sacred and committed to memory because of their intrinsic worth and because of the regard in which the Christians held their Lord. This surpassed any rabbinical teacher-pupil relationship. They recognized His divine nature which invested His words with such authority that every effort would be made to retain as far as possible the very words in which He taught. This accounts for the significant fact that fewer deviations occur in parallel accounts of His sayings than in the narratives of His doings. When it is remembered that Jesus was acknowledged as Lord, it is difficult to conceive that the primitive communities would have 'created' in His honour Gospel material which could be placed on a level with His own authentic teaching. This would appear to make the Christians as great or greater than Christ Himself, a presupposition which is impossible. Oral tradition for this reason could never run riot. Moreover, as men of the Spirit the Gospel writers were sensitive to the quality of the tradition, a fact to which the more extreme form critics have paid no attention."

See C. E. B. Cranfield in *The Interpreter's Dictionary of the Bible*, s.v. "Mark, Gospel of," p. 271; Alfred M. Perry, "The Growth of the Gospels," in *The Interpreter's Bible*, 7:66; Brown, *The Origins of Christianity*, p. 31; Guthrie, *New Testament Introduction*, pp. 224–25; Birger Gerhardsson, *The Origins of the Gospel Traditions* (Philadelphia: Fortress Press. 1979), pp. 8–9.

48. James I. Packer, Merrill C. Tenney, and William White, Jr., eds., *The Bible Almanac* (Carmel, N.Y.: Thomas Nelson Publishers, Guideposts edition, 1980), p. 358.
49. Deut. 6:13, 14, 16; 8:3; 10:20; Matt. 4:4, 7, 10.
50. See Mark 7:5, 10, King James Version; Mark 7:13, Jerusalem Bible; Exod. 20:12; 21:17.
51. Matt. 22:23–32; Exod. 3:6.
52. John 10:33, 34; Ps. 82:6.
53. Matt. 19:16–19; Exod. 20:12–16; Lev. 19:18.
54. **Language from the Old Testament in Matt. 24:** *Eerdmans' Handbook to the Bible* notes that "the words of only three verses [Matt. 24:29–31] draw on no less than seven Old Testament passages"; see Isa. 13:10; 34:4; Dan. 7:13; Zech. 12:12; Isa. 27:13; Deut. 30:4; Zech. 2:6. David Alexander and Pat Alexander, eds., *Eerdmans' Handbook to the Bible* (Grand Rapids, Michigan: William B. Eerdmans Publishing Company, 1973), p. 39.
55. Matt. 27:46. In Luke 23:46, Jesus' last words on the cross are "Father, into thy hands I commend my spirit," from Ps. 31:5.
56. Luke 11:49.

57. S. MacLean Gilmour writes in his exegesis on Luke in *The Interpreter's Bible* (8:218) that **"The Wisdom of God"** is "possibly some lost Jewish apocryphal book from which the quotation [in Luke 11:49] is taken. Cf. Jer. 7:25–26. Others prefer to translate, 'God, in his wisdom, said, . . .' Jesus himself is the speaker in Matthew, and the statement becomes a prediction."

58. See Frederick C. Grant, Exegesis on Mark, in *The Interpreter's Bible,* 7:779. Other exegetes say "as it is written of him" refers to Jezebel's persecution of Elijah (Elias), I Kings 19:2, 10.

59. Matt. 5:17, 18.

60. Luke 22:37.

61. Mal. 3:1.

62. Mark 9:12.

63. John 15:24, 25; Pss. 35:19; 69:4.

64. Luke 24:27.

65. Luke 24:44.

66. Matt. 24:35.

67. John 14:10, 24, Jerusalem Bible.

68. Eusebius, *The History of the Church* 6.25, in *The Interpreter's Bible,* 11:581.

69. *The Interpreter's Bible,* 11:590.

70. Eusebius, *The History of the Church* 6.25 (trans. Williamson, p. 266).

71. Hugh Montefiore, *A Commentary on the Epistle to the Hebrews* (New York: Harper & Row, 1964), p. 3.

72. Heb. 7:3; 6:20.

73. Smith, *The Secret Gospel,* p. 131.

74. Mark 4:10–12.

75. Matt. 13:10–23; Luke 8:9–15.

76. Matt. 13:17.

77. Mark 4:34.

78. Mark 4:9.

79. Matt. 16:6, 7, see King James Version and Jerusalem Bible.

80. Phil. 2:12.

81. Heb. 5:12–14.

82. Jerome, *Praef. in Hom. Orig. in Ezech.* (Lommatzch XIV 4), in G. W. Butterworth trans., *Origen on First Principles* (Gloucester, Mass.: Peter Smith, 1973), p. xxiii; Butterworth, *Origen on First Principles,* p. 2.

83. Morton Smith, *Clement of Alexandria and a Secret Gospel of Mark* (Cambridge, Mass.: Harvard University Press, 1973), p. 24.

84. Matt. 13:38.
85. Mark 4:33.
86. "...**Those who are initiated**": In his exegesis of I Cor. 2:6–9 in *The Interpreter's Bible* (10:36–37), New Testament scholar Clarence Tucker Craig states: "Those who believe that this section is dominated by ideas from the mysteries think that the word [*perfect* (KJV) or *mature* (RSV)] should be rendered 'initiates.' The adjective is built on the noun...'end'; the general meaning therefore is 'brought to completion'.... These people are the opposite of 'the babes' (3:1; 14:20); they are the ones in whom the Spirit has really produced a new life. They are to be identified with the 'spiritual' (vs. 15), and stand in contrast to two other groups: the 'natural' (KJV) or 'unspiritual man' (RSV) and also to the 'carnal' (KJV) or 'men of the flesh' (RSV)."
87. I Cor. 2:6, 7.
88. I Cor. 4:1.
89. Eph. 3:9.
90. Col. 1:26.
91. *The Interpreter's Bible,* 11:180. **Paul's esoteric teaching:** Paul's use of the language of the mystery religions of his time (Eleusinian, Gnostic, etc.), particularly in his correspondence with the Corinthians, has occasioned much discussion over whether Paul really had a secret teaching. Some scholars argue that in Corinthians, Paul is using the language of those with Gnostic proclivities in order to speak to them in their own terms or as a rhetorical device, but not because he has a secret tradition. In I Cor. 1–4 "Paul cleverly takes his opponents' terminology," writes Birger A. Pearson, "and turns it back against them." Not all scholars agree, however.

In the introduction to *The Gnostic Paul,* Elaine Pagels notes that many New Testament scholars take Paul to be an opponent of Gnostic heresy who "writes his letters, especially the Corinthian and Philippian correspondence, to attack gnosticism and to refute the claims of gnostic Christians to 'secret wisdom.'" She also points out that the Gnostics themselves saw Paul in an entirely different light. Rather than regarding Paul as an opponent, "they dare to claim his letters as a primary source of *gnostic* theology. Instead of repudiating Paul as their most obstinate opponent, the Naassenes and Valentinians revere him as the one of the apostles who—above all others—was himself a gnostic initiate."

Furthermore, in light of the discovery of Gnostic texts

at Nag Hammadi Pagels argues that some scholars who hold that Paul is an opponent of the Gnostics, "besides taking *information* from the heresiologists [such as Irenaeus], also have adopted from them certain value judgments and interpretations of the gnostic material." While Pagels does not state explicitly her position on Paul vis à vis the Gnostics, from her introduction to *The Gnostic Paul*, a review of the second-century Gnostic exegesis of the Pauline letters, it is hard to conclude that she finds him an opponent of Gnosticism. See Birger A. Pearson, "Philo, Gnosis and the New Testament," in *The New Testament and Gnosis*, eds. A. H. B. Logan and A. J. M. Wedderburn (Edinburgh: T. & T. Clark, 1983), p. 75; Elaine Hiesey Pagels, *The Gnostic Paul: Gnostic Exegesis of the Pauline Letters* (Philadelphia: Fortress Press, 1975), pp. 1, 3.

Therefore, the case of Paul the anti-Gnostic is by no means closed. Our understanding is that Paul was a direct initiate of the resurrected Christ Jesus and that he was given that gnosis by the Lord wherein he attained to the hidden wisdom of the inner Christ—"Christ in you, the hope of glory" (Col. 1:27)—and that he was capable and ordained to preach both the outer teachings and rituals as well as the inner mysteries and initiations. In fact, in his letter to the Galatians, Paul insists his Gospel "is not a human message that I was given by men, it is something I learned only through a revelation of Jesus Christ" (Gal. 1:11, 12, Jerusalem Bible). Thus, as we have pointed out in the text, when in communication with those who understand his terminology, Paul speaks of "the mysteries," of "initiation" (see p. 348 n. 86) and of imparting "a secret and hidden wisdom of God."

Paul was also well aware that some Gnostics, having not the true inner experience, willfully misinterpreted the mysteries to satisfy their lusts for power and the flesh. Paul was Jesus' two-edged sword who came rightly dividing the word of Truth for both children and the mature sons of God. The spherical body of his work on the applicability of Christ's personal message, both to the initiatic path of the soul and the day-to-day operation of the Church according to a rule of order and love, makes Paul the beloved messenger of Jesus in the wake of whose mantle both fundamentalist and liberal, ecclesiastic and mystic may find the path of the heart that leads to the true Saviour.

92. Smith, *The Secret Gospel,* pp. 81–84.
93. Ibid., pp. 85–86.
94. Ibid., pp. 73–74.
95. Eusebius, *The History of the Church* 2.1 (trans. Williamson, p. 72).
96. **Hierophantic** [from Greek *hieros,* powerful, supernatural, holy, sacred + *phantes,* from *phainein,* to bring to light, reveal, show, make known]: of, relating to, or resembling a hierophant, who in antiquity was an official expounder of sacred mysteries or religious ceremonies, esp. in ancient Greece.
97. Smith, *The Secret Gospel,* p. 15. Note: Words in brackets were added in by Smith for clarity.
98. Ibid., p. 40.
99. Ibid., p. 61.
100. John 11:1–44.
101. Smith, *The Secret Gospel,* pp. 16–17.
102. **"This story, coupled with the very existence of a secret Gospel, strengthens the evidence for secret teachings and initiatic rites":** Some scholars would take exception to this position. But their dissent should be seen in light of the development of the debate that has surrounded the Clement fragment and the secret Gospel of Mark. Initial discussion focused on their authenticity. In 1982, a decade after Morton Smith published a technical analysis of the fragments, *Clement of Alexandria and a Secret Gospel of Mark,* he noted in the *Harvard Theological Review* that the first reports about his work were either neutral or sympathetic, followed by "a swarm of attacks in religious journals, mainly intended to discredit the new gospel material, my theories about it, or both." But by 1982, he reported, "most scholars would attribute the letter to Clement, though a substantial minority are still in doubt."

As for the actual meaning of the fragment, Smith said that "I had shown that the gospel fragments represented Jesus as practicing some sort of initiation." While Smith acknowledged that no one accepted his proposed explanation of the purpose of the initiation, he "was amazed that so many went so far as to concede that Jesus might have had some secret doctrines and initiatory ceremonies." Nevertheless, Smith observed that "serious discussion [of secret Mark] has barely begun."

The lack of such discussion is the starting point for a more recent paper "The Young Man in Canonical and Secret

Mark" by Marvin Meyer, soon to be published in *The Second Century*. "Although the Secret Gospel has been on the lips and in the pens of numerous scholars," Meyer points out, "it seems fair to observe that the text has not achieved any sort of prominence in New Testament discussions." Much of Meyer's paper is a review of the first stirrings of "serious discussion" of secret Mark and includes his own original contribution to the debate. While Meyer assumes "the authenticity of the letter of Clement as an ancient text," he disagrees with Smith about its meaning. Where Smith holds that the "young man" is an actual person participating in an initiatic rite, Meyer and a number of other scholars believe that this is a literary device; the young man in both the canonical (Mark 14:51, 52) and secret Gospels of Mark functions as a "prototype and a symbol of all those who are to be initiated into the higher discipleship of Jesus." Further, he argues, "this story of the young man. . . means to communicate Secret Mark's vision of the life and challenge of discipleship, as that is exemplified in the career of the young man."

See Morton Smith, *Clement of Alexandria and a Secret Gospel of Mark* (Cambridge, Mass.: Harvard University Press, 1973); Morton Smith, *The Secret Gospel: The Discovery and Interpretation of the Secret Gospel According to Mark* (Clearlake, Calif.: The Dawn Horse Press, 1982); Morton Smith, "Clement of Alexandria and Secret Mark: The Score at the End of the First Decade," *Harvard Theological Review,* 75 (October 1982): 449-61.

103. James H. Charlesworth, Foreword to *Secrets of Mount Sinai: The Story of the World's Oldest Bible—Codex Sinaiticus* by James Bentley (Garden City, N. Y.: Doubleday & Company, 1986), p. 5.
104. Personal interview with Marvin Meyer, 30 May 1986.
105. *The Interpreter's Dictionary of the Bible,* s.v. "Text, N.T.," p. 595.
106. **Codex:** The earliest book form. Derived from Latin *codex* or *caudex,* "tree trunk," the term came to be used for wooden leaves or tablets, and eventually for books consisting of leaves laid on one another. Finally, sheets of papyrus or vellum were folded and bound together (*Interpreter's Dictionary of the Bible,* s.v. "Codex"). **Sinaiticus** (most commonly pronounced sign'-eh-it'-uh-kuss or sign'-eye-it'-uh-kuss): from Hebrew *Sinai* + Latin *-iticus.* Of or relating to Mount Sinai or the Sinai peninsula.

107. Bentley, *Secrets of Mount Sinai,* pp. 132–33. Text authorities such as Bruce Metzger also maintain that the omission of this phrase from Matthew was for doctrinal reasons rather than as a result of a scribal error. See Metzger, *The Text of the New Testament: Its Transmission, Corruption, and Restoration* (London: Oxford at the Clarendon Press, 1964), p. 202.

108. Oddly enough, the King James Version of the Bible contains the phrase "neither the son" in Mark 13:32 even though it omits it from Matthew 24:36.

109. Bentley, *Secrets of Mount Sinai,* p. 131.

110. Metzger, *The Text of the New Testament,* p. 47.

111. Bentley, p. 126.

112. Ibid., p. 120.

113. Frank Moore Cross, Jr., *The Ancient Library of Qumran & Modern Biblical Studies,* rev. ed. (Grand Rapids, Mich.: Baker Book House, 1961), p. 201.

114. P. R. Ackroyd and C. F. Evans, eds., *The Cambridge History of the Bible,* vol. 1, "From the Beginnings to Jerome" (Cambridge: Cambridge at the University Press, 1970), p. 284.

115. James M. Robinson, gen. ed., *The Nag Hammadi Library in English* (New York: Harper & Row, 1977), p. 3.

116. Ibid., p. 118.

117. Ibid., p. 117.

118. Ibid.

119. Elaine Pagels, *The Gnostic Gospels* (New York: Random House, 1979), pp. xviii–xix, 142.

120. Ackroyd and Evans, *The Cambridge History of the Bible,* p. 285.

121. Ibid.

122. Gal. 1:12; 2:9; Jerusalem Bible.

123. John 14:26.

124. Rev. 22:18, 19.

Chapter One REMOVING THE MASK

1. Jack Lait, comp., *Will Rogers: Wit and Wisdom* (New York: Frederick A. Stokes Co., 1936), p. 76; Jerry Belcher, "Will Rogers—a Mirror of America," *Los Angeles Times,* 15 August 1985.

2. El Morya, "Let the Twinkle of Mirth Abound on Earth," *Pearls of Wisdom,* vol. 1 (1958), no. 13, November 7, 1958. Since 1958, the Ascended Masters have released their Teachings through the Messengers Mark L. Prophet and Elizabeth Clare Prophet as **Pearls of Wisdom,** weekly letters sent to

their students throughout the world. These letters are the intimate contact, heart to heart, between the Ascended Masters and their disciples. They contain both fundamental and advanced teachings from the saints and spiritual revolutionaries of East and West—more of the lost teachings of Jesus as well as prophecy on current issues—with a practical application of cosmic law to personal and planetary problems. Pearls of Wisdom are sent free weekly to those who support the publishing of the Ascended Masters' Teachings with a minimum yearly love offering of $40—just $10 quarterly. Bound volumes of Pearls of Wisdom available from Summit University Press.

3. Thomas More, *A Dialogue of Comfort*, in *The Complete Works of St. Thomas More*, ed. Louis L. Martz and Frank Manley (New Haven, Conn.: Yale University Press, 1976) 12:155.

4. William Roper, *The Life of Sir Thomas More*, in E. E. Reynolds, *Saint Thomas More* (London: Burns Oates, 1953), p. 358.

5. Reynolds, *Saint Thomas More*, pp. 357–58, 359; John Farrow, *The Story of Thomas More* (London: Collins, 1956), p. 241.

6. From a British army ballad (c. 1915), quoted by Gen. Douglas MacArthur in a speech delivered to a joint session of Congress April 19, 1951, on the occasion of his recall from the Korean battlefield by Pres. Harry S. Truman: "I still remember the refrain of one of the most popular barracks ballads of that day which proclaimed most proudly that old soldiers never die; they just fade away. And like the old soldier of that ballad, I now close my military career and just fade away, an old soldier who tried to do his duty as God gave him the light to see that duty."

7. I Cor. 15:31.

Chapter Two THE POINT OF ORIGIN

1. Gen. 5:2.
2. John 1:14.
3. John 1:1–3.
4. Josh. 10:12–14.
5. Dan. 12:10.
6. Luke 13:32.
7. John 6:29.
8. John 3:17.
9. Matt. 9:13.

10. **"Lost sheep"**: "Lost," from Greek *apollumi,* also meaning "marred."
11. Matt. 15:24.
12. Acts 26:12–14.
13. Joseph Wilson Trigg, *Origen—The Bible and Philosophy in the Third-century Church* (Atlanta: John Knox Press, 1983), pp. 104–5.
14. Origen, "Homily XXVII on Numbers," in *Origen: An Exhortation to Martyrdom, Prayer and Selected Works,* trans. Rowan A. Greer (New York: Paulist Press, 1979), p. 252.
15. Matt. 25:40; I Cor. 15:9; Eph. 3:8.
16. For further teaching from the Ascended Masters and Messengers on the **science of the spoken Word**, see Mark L. Prophet and Elizabeth Clare Prophet, *The Science of the Spoken Word;* Jesus and Kuthumi, *Prayer and Meditation;* Mark and Elizabeth Prophet, *The Science of the Spoken Word: Why and How to Decree Effectively,* 4-cassette album; Elizabeth Clare Prophet, *"I'm Stumping for the Coming Revolution in Higher Consciousness!"* 3-cassette album; *Prayers, Meditations, and Dynamic Decrees for the Coming Revolution in Higher Consciousness,* Sections I, II, and III, looseleaf. See also p. 363 n. 28.
17. **Paraclete:** Holy Spirit, from the Greek *Paraklētos,* lit., "called to one's side"—i.e., "to one's aid"—intercessor, comforter, consoler, fr. *parakalein,* to summon, exhort, comfort, call to help. At one time, a legal assistant in a court of justice; counsel for the defense; an advocate; one who pleads another's cause. In the New Testament, the terms *Comforter* and *advocate* are translated from the original Greek *Paraklētos:* "And I will pray the Father, and he shall give you another *Comforter,* that he may abide with you forever.... It is expedient for you that I go away: for if I go not away, the *Comforter* will not come unto you; but if I depart, I will send him unto you..." (John 14:16; 16:7; see also John 14:26; 15:26). "...And if any man sin, we have an *advocate* with the Father, Jesus Christ the righteous" (I John 2:1).
18. Jesus, March 26, 1978, "As My Father Hath Sent Me, Even So Send I You," *The Second Coming of Christ II,* 6-cassette album, The Summit Lighthouse.
19. Col. 3:14.
20. Job 14:5; Acts 17:26.
21. Isa. 66:1; Acts 7:49.

22. See Morey Bernstein, *The Search for Bridey Murphy* (Garden City, N.Y.: Doubleday & Company, 1956), pp. 103–4; Lama Anagarika Govinda, *The Way of the White Clouds: A Buddhist Pilgrim in Tibet* (Boulder, Colo.: Shambhala Publications, 1966), pp. 141–42; Manly P. Hall, *Reincarnation: The Cycle of Necessity,* 2d ed. (Los Angeles: The Philosophers Press, 1941), pp. 137–42; Ian Stevenson, "The Evidence for Survival from Claimed Memories of Former Incarnations," Part 1, *The Journal of the American Society for Psychical Research* 54 (April 1960): 66–67; Ian Stevenson, *Twenty Cases Suggestive of Reincarnation* (New York: American Society for Psychical Research, 1966), pp. 17, 306–7.

23. H. Spencer Lewis, *Mansions of the Soul: The Cosmic Conception* (San Jose: The Rosicrucian Press, 1954), pp. 24–25.

24. *Origen: On First Principles* 1.5.3, trans. G. W. Butterworth (Gloucester, Mass.: Peter Smith, 1973), p. 47.

25. Gen. 25:21–28; Mal. 1:2, 3; Rom. 9:13.

26. Rom. 9:11, 14.

27. *Origen: On First Principles* 2.9.5–8 (trans. Butterworth, pp. 133–37).

28. See H. N. Banerjee, "Children and Birthmarks," *Reincarnation Report,* no. 1 (July 1982): 10–12; Sybil Leek, *Reincarnation: The Second Chance* (New York: Stein & Day, 1974), pp. 39–40.

29. Matt. 18:3; Mark 10:14, 15.

30. Marguerite Baker, *—And Then the Angels Came to the First Grade Children* (Los Angeles: The Summit Lighthouse, 1975).

31. Matt. 5:8.

32. John 14:16, 17, 26; 15:26, 27; 16:7.

33. II Pet. 1:20.

34. Louis Fischer, ed., *The Essential Gandhi: His Life, Work, and Ideas* (1962; reprint, New York: Vintage Books, 1983), p. 41.

35. Luke 11:52.

36. Matt. 21:12, 13; Mark 11:15–17; Luke 19:45, 46.

37. Rev. 2, 3.

38. In the cover story of the June 30, 1947 issue of *Time* magazine, Mohandas Gandhi was quoted as saying, "If I seem to take part in politics, it is only because politics today encircle us like the coils of a snake from which one cannot get out no matter how one tries. **I wish to wrestle with the snake**. . . . I am trying to introduce religion into politics."

39. II Kings 5:1–16.

40. John 1:11.
41. John 4:24.
42. **Atlantis:** the island continent which existed where the Atlantic Ocean now is and which sank in cataclysm (the Flood of Noah) approximately 11,600 years ago as calculated by James Churchward. Atlantis was vividly depicted by Plato in his dialogues and was 'seen' and described by Edgar Cayce in his readings. See James Churchward, *The Lost Continent of Mu* (1931; reprint, New York: Paperback Library Edition, 1968), p. 226; Otto Muck, *The Secret of Atlantis* (New York: Pocket Books, 1979); Ignatius Donnelly, *Atlantis: The Antediluvian World* (New York: Dover Publications, 1976); Edgar Evans Cayce, *Edgar Cayce on Atlantis* (New York: Warner Books, 1968).
43. Acts 17:28.
44. "And this is the good old Boston, / The home of the bean and the cod, / Where the Lowells talk to the Cabots, / And the Cabots talk only to God." J. C. Bossidy, "On the Aristocracy of Harvard," quoted in *The Home Book of American Quotations,* comp. Bruce Bohle (New York: Dodd, Mead & Company, 1967), p. 66.
45. Matt. 8:5–13; Luke 7:1–10.
46. Rom. 3:29.
47. John 14:12.
48. Rev. 10:7.
49. I Cor. 2:7, 10.
50. Mark 4:33, 34.
51. Mark 4:12.
52. Morton Smith, *The Secret Gospel: The Discovery and Interpretation of the Secret Gospel According to Mark* (Clearlake, Calif.: The Dawn Horse Press, 1982), pp. 85–86. See p. 350 n. 102 in this volume.
53. Isa. 55:1.
54. **"Salem"** (Heb. *shālēm* 'peaceful', 'peace') in Gen. 14:18 is generally regarded by early Jewish commentators and later writers to be a synonym for Jerusalem, which did exist as an important city-state of southern Palestine before the conquest of Canaan by the Israelites under Joshua (it is called *Urusalim* in the Tell el-Amarna letters, 14th century B.C.). This tradition is strengthened by the association of "Salem" in Ps. 76:2 with Zion. Some non-Jewish writers, such as Jerome, have identified Salem with the village of Salumias

and with Salim (see John 3:23). *Shalom* is the traditional Hebrew greeting and farewell meaning "peace."
55. Gen. 14:17–20; Heb. 7:4, Jerusalem Bible.
56. Heb. 7:3.
57. Heb. 5:6; 6:20.
58. Rom. 8:17; Gal. 4:1–7.
59. Gal. 4:19.
60. Col. 1:27.
61. Ps. 17:15.
62. Rev. 1:6.
63. John 3:1–8.
64. Gen. 18:1–16.
65. Gen. 18:17–33.
66. Heb. 7:4.
67. Heb. 7:3, Jerusalem Bible.
68. **The Ascended Master John the Baptist:** On the way down the mount of transfiguration Jesus revealed to his disciples that John the Baptist, baptizer of the Lord in Jordan, was the reincarnated prophet Elijah (Matt. 17:10–13), who had ascended to heaven (II Kings 2:11) and descended again to be Christ's messenger and forerunner. He returned to the ascended state after his beheading by Herod (Matt. 14:10), his mission accomplished—God-victorious. (See also *The Lost Teachings of Jesus,* Volume Two: "Let the Mind of Christ Be in You!" in Chapter 10; "Reincarnation: The Prophecy of Elijah Come Again," in Chapter 11.)
69. See *Saint Germain On Alchemy: For the Adept in the Aquarian Age* (Los Angeles: Summit University Press, 1985).
70. I Cor. 3:12–15.
71. Deut. 4:24; Heb. 12:29.
72. I Cor. 15:31.
73. John 3:30.
74. Rev. 2:17.
75. Rev. 21:19, 20.
76. Rev. 10:7.
77. Gen. 3:5.
78. Rev. 10:9, 10.
79. Gal. 6:7.
80. Matt. 6:22, 23; Luke 11:34–36.
81. Matt. 13:38.
82. "You Are a Child of the Light," song 601, in *The Summit Lighthouse Book of Songs.* Words from "The Hidden Man of

the Heart" by the God Meru, in *Understanding Yourself: A Study in the Psychology of the Soul by the Masters of the Far East* (Los Angeles: Summit University Press, 1982), p. 109.
83. Eph. 5:1, 2, 6–8, 20.

Chapter Three A PERFECT DESIGN

1. **Scriptural names for Christ:** Isa. 9:6; Song of Sol. 2:1; 5:10; John 20:16; 1:1; Ezek. 1:10 (Ezekiel's vision, describing the "four living creatures" who each had four faces—that of a man, a lion, an ox, and an eagle—inspired Aimee Semple McPherson to call the message Jesus commissioned her to preach the "Foursquare Gospel"—the four faces representing Jesus as Saviour, Baptizer, Burden-Bearer or Healer, and Coming King); Rev. 17:14; Exod. 3:14; Rev. 13:8; 19:11, 13. See *Aimee: Life Story of Aimee Semple McPherson* (Los Angeles: Foursquare Publications, 1979), pp. 111–12.
2. **Enoch:** Gen. 5:21–24; Heb. 11:5; Jude 14. **The Elect One:** Enoch 45:3, 4; 50:3, 5; 51:5, 10; 54:5; 60:7, 10–13; 61:1, in Elizabeth Clare Prophet, *Forbidden Mysteries of Enoch: The Untold Story of Men and Angels* (Los Angeles: Summit University Press, 1983), contains all the Enoch texts, including the Book of Enoch and the Book of the Secrets of Enoch.
3. Heb. 3:1; 4:14, 15; 5:10; 6:20; 7:3.
4. John 1:3.
5. **Twin flame:** the spirit's masculine or feminine counterpart conceived out of the same white fire body, the fiery ovoid of the I AM Presence. See Elizabeth Clare Prophet, "Love, Marriage, and Beyond," *Heart: For the Coming Revolution in Higher Consciousness* (Autumn 1983), pp. 29–33, 100–103; "Finding Your Perfect Match," *The Coming Revolution: The Magazine for Higher Consciousness* (Summer 1986), pp. 43–57, 90–95; *Twin Flames in Love I*, 8-cassette album, and *Twin Flames in Love II*, 3-cassette album, Summit University; Jess Stearn, *Soulmates: Perfect Partners Past, Present, and Beyond* (New York: Bantam Books, 1984), pp. 33–50.
6. Heb. 4:16.
7. I Thess. 5:3.
8. Rev. 12:10.
9. II Cor. 6:2.
10. Isa. 1:18.

11. John 10:10.
12. Gen. 14:17–24; Heb. 7:1–5.
13. Gen. 4:9.
14. Rev. 15:1, 6–8; 16; Matt. 24:1–44; Mark 13; Luke 21:5–36; Dan. 12:1.
15. Heb. 11:35.
16. A **cancerous cell** is a defective, nonfunctional cell—one that does not perform a specific function, such as producing blood or building bone. Unlike normal cells, which are controlled and coordinated in their growth, cancer cells are characterized by unlimited, disorganized multiplication. If unchecked, these defective cells can invade neighboring tissues or can spread to other parts of the body through the lymphatic and circulatory systems, giving rise to metastases, or secondary growths. Cancer cells, because of their unlimited growth, kill healthy cells by competing with them for, and eventually depriving them of, nutrition. **Cancer** was given its name by the early Greeks, who used the word (meaning "sea crab" in Greek) to describe breast cancer, which in its advanced stages looks like a crab with claws extending from its body.
17. John 10:11, 15; 15:13; I John 3:16.
18. Matt. 5:18; Luke 16:17.
19. **Kali Yuga:** the last of the four ages, or *yugas,* in Hindu cosmology; called the age of conflicts or the dark age in which strife, discord, and moral deterioration are prevalent. The **four yugas** are Satya or Krita, Tretā, Dvāpara, and Kali; the first age begins in perfection and each succeeding one decreases in length and increases in its degradations. The Hindu scriptures describe the Kali Yuga (the age through which we are presently passing) as characterized by greed, lust, deception, fatal disease and continuous hunger, revolution, war, disrespect for scripture and true sages, and the practice of ritualistic religion rather than true spirituality. Every Kali Yuga, it is believed, lasts 432,000 years and then ends in destruction, after which the entire cycle of the four yugas begins again. For a different calculation of the duration of the yugas which sets the present age 285 years into the Dvāpara Yuga, see Swami Sri Yukteswar, *The Holy Science,* 7th ed. (Los Angeles: Self-Realization Fellowship, 1972), pp. 7–20.
20. Rev. 12:2.

21. John 8:58.
22. Mal. 4:2.
23. John 10:7, 9; Rev. 3:8; John 14:6.
24. Matt. 25:6.
25. Ps. 118:22; Matt. 21:42; Acts 4:11; Eph. 2:20; I Pet. 2:5–7.
26. I Cor. 15:50.
27. Gal. 4:19.
28. John 6:53.
29. Phil. 2:10, 11.
30. I Cor. 15:28.
31. Col. 3:11.
32. Heb. 12:2.
33. Matt. 7:13, 14; Luke 13:24.
34. Luke 17:21.
35. Mark 2:27.
36. Gen. 1:28.
37. Heb. 10:7, 9.
38. Polonius in Shakespeare, *Hamlet,* act 1, sc. 3, lines 78–80.*
39. Ps. 147:3; Isa. 61:1; Luke 4:18.
40. Rev. 19:7–9.
41. Prov. 3:13; 4:7.
42. I Cor. 9:24.
43. Matt. 25:21, 23.
44. Richard Maurice Bucke, *Cosmic Consciousness* (1901; reprint, New York: E. P. Dutton & Company, 1969).
45. See "The Hound of Heaven," a poem by the English poet Francis Thompson (1859–1907).
46. John 8:32.
47. I Cor. 15:41, 42.
48. See "The Soul: A Living Potential," in Mark and Elizabeth Prophet, *Climb the Highest Mountain: The Path of the Higher Self, The Everlasting Gospel,* Book I (Los Angeles: Summit University Press, 1972), chap. 1.
49. *The Confessions of Jacob Boehme,* comp. and ed. W. Scott Palmer (New York: Harper & Brothers, 1954), pp. 79–81.
50. John 14:8–11.
51. John 8:24, 28; 13:19.
52. Matt. 16:19.
53. John 11:25–27.
54. John 15:16, 17.

*All references to Shakespeare's plays are taken from *The Complete Signet Classic Shakespeare* (New York: Harcourt Brace Jovanovich, 1972).

55. Mark 6:5, 6; Matt. 13:58.
56. John 14:12–15.
57. Matt. 7:7; John 16:24.
58. Luke 21:19.
59. I Cor. 2:11.
60. Matt. 10:32, 33; Luke 12:8, 9.
61. II Cor. 5:16.
62. Matt. 13:54–58; Luke 4:22; John 6:42.
63. Rom. 7:22; Eph. 3:16.
64. I Pet. 3:4.
65. Henry Wadsworth Longfellow, "The Builders," stanza 1.
66. Henry Wadsworth Longfellow, "A Psalm of Life," stanza 7.
67. Isa. 64:6.
68. Jer. 23:6; 33:16.
69. *The Cloud of Unknowing* was a book originally written in Middle English by an anonymous fourteenth-century mystic as a practical guide to contemplation. The author writes that all concepts, images, and thoughts must be abandoned "beneath a cloud of forgetting" while a man must "reach out to pierce the darkness above"—the cloud of unknowing that lies "between you and your God." He explains that the cloud must be entered because "by love He may be gotten and holden, but by thought of understanding, never.... Yes, beat upon that thick cloud of unknowing with the dart of your loving desire and do not cease come what may." The author also introduces the science of the sacred word or mantra, advocating the use of a one-syllable word, such as *God* or *Love,* in contemplation to "subdue all distractions." See *The Cloud of Unknowing and the Book of Privy Counseling,* ed. William Johnston (Garden City, N.Y.: Image Books, 1973), pp. 9, 53, 54, 55; Evelyn Underhill, *Mysticism: A Study in the Nature and Development of Man's Spiritual Consciousness* (New York: E. P. Dutton & Company, 1961), pp. 48, 348–49, 466.
70. John 6:53.
71. John 6:60.
72. Luke 22:19; I Cor. 11:24, 25.
73. See Archangel Gabriel, *Mysteries of the Holy Grail* (Los Angeles: Summit University Press, 1983).
74. Phil. 2:5.
75. Matt. 5:48.
76. Matt. 25:40.
77. Isa. 40:31.

Chapter Four MOMENTUM

1. Gen. 1:28.
2. Exod. 3:5; Josh. 5:15; Acts 7:33.
3. According to Tibetan manuscripts and Buddhist traditions, Jesus spent the 17 or so years of his life unaccounted for in the Gospels studying and teaching in the East. For a comprehensive review of what the texts and legends reveal about Jesus' sojourn, see Elizabeth Clare Prophet, *The Lost Years of Jesus* (Los Angeles: Summit University Press, 1984). Includes variant translations of the ancient documents and eyewitness accounts of those who saw and read them, with illustrations, color photos, and maps. See also p. xxx of "The Past Is Prologue" in this volume.
4. Matt. 10:30; Luke 12:7.
5. Cassius, "The fault, dear Brutus, is not in our stars, / But in ourselves, that we are underlings." Shakespeare, *Julius Caesar,* act 1, sc. 2, lines 140-41.
6. Gal. 6:7.
7. See the story of Sri Yukteswar subduing the cobra in Paramahansa Yogananda, *Autobiography of a Yogi* (1946; reprint, Los Angeles: Self-Realization Fellowship, 1974), pp. 131-32.
8. Matt. 13:12; 25:29; Mark 4:25; Luke 8:18; 19:26. "For, anyone who has will be given more, and he will have more than enough; but from anyone who has not, even what he has will be taken away," Matt. 13:12, Jerusalem Bible.
9. Matt. 7:9; Luke 11:11.
10. Rev. 21:6; 22:17.
11. Isa. 55:1.
12. Matt. 11:29, 30.
13. Matt. 6:33; Luke 12:31.
14. Matt. 17:20.
15. Mark 10:25.
16. Matt. 21:21; Mark 11:23.
17. I Tim. 4:2.
18. Luke 24:49.
19. **The Blessed Mother's appearances over the Coptic church:** From April 1968 to early 1971 throngs of thousands gathered nightly outside the Coptic church in Zeitoun (a suburb of Cairo, Egypt, near where the Holy Family is said to have stayed after their flight to Egypt during Herod's persecution) to witness the appearances of the Blessed Mother. Unlike Mary's other apparitions, at Fátima or Lourdes for instance,

everyone in the crowds, of any race and religion, was able to see her. Eyewitnesses said her appearances over the church, which lasted anywhere from a few minutes to several hours, were heralded by flashing lights and the coming of large dovelike birds. On occasion, Jesus and Joseph accompanied the Blessed Mother. Published photographs taken during the apparitions show the figure of the Mother of Christ next to the dome of the church with a luminous bird hovering over her head. During the Zeitoun apparitions, hundreds said they were spontaneously healed, and reports of cures and miracles continued even after the apparitions had ceased. See Thomas F. Brady, "Visions of Virgin Reported in Cairo," *New York Times,* 5 May 1968, p. 71; *Fatima Prophecy: Days of Darkness, Promise of Light* (Austin, Tex.: Association for the Understanding of Man, 1974), pp. 43–50; Jerome Palmer, "The Virgin Mary Appears in Egypt," *Fate,* August 1971, pp. 60–70.

20. **Francis the talking mule**: the hero of a series of motion pictures (1950–56) who continually got his "master" into and then out of comic escapades, outsmarting all the humans around him in the process. Francis was the predecessor of Mister Ed, the talking horse who starred in the popular TV comedy by the same name (1961–66).
21. Num. 22:20–33.
22. See I. Cooper-Oakley, *The Comte de St. Germain: The Secret of Kings* (London: The Theosophical Publishing House Limited, 1912).
23. **Evil eye:** an eye or glance held capable of inflicting harm. *Webster's Ninth New Collegiate Dictionary,* s.v. "evil eye."
24. Gen. 6:5. The concept of **"eye magic"** is explained by Mark and Elizabeth Prophet in "Vestiges of the Synthetic Image Replaced by Real-Eye Magic," *Climb the Highest Mountain: The Path of the Higher Self, The Everlasting Gospel,* Book I (Los Angeles: Summit University Press, 1972), chap. 2.
25. John 12:32.
26. I John 3:2.
27. Mal. 3:10.
28. The **decree** is the most powerful of all applications to the Godhead. It is the "Command ye me" of Isaiah 45:11, the original command to Light, which is the birthright of the sons and daughters of God. The decree is the authoritative Word of God spoken in man in the name of the I AM Presence and

the living Christ to bring about constructive change on earth through the will of God and his consciousness come, on earth as it is in heaven—in manifestation here below as above. It may be short or long and is usually marked by a formal preamble and a closing or acceptance. For further teaching on decrees and the science of the spoken Word, see sources listed on p. 354 n. 16.

29. Eph. 4:30–32.
30. I Cor. 9:27.
31. Matt. 13:3–9, 18–23; Mark 4:3–9, 14–20; Luke 8:5–8, 11–15.
32. Prov. 22:6.
33. Mal. 3:1.
34. See the story of **the three hermits** in Leo Tolstoy, *Russian Stories and Legends* (New York: Pantheon Books, n.d.), pp. 69–77.
35. Josh. 5:13–15.
36. Dan. 10:13, 21; 12:1.
37. Dan. 8:15, 16; 9:21, 22.

Chapter Five KAL-DESH: THE INTERMINGLING
OF TIME AND SPACE

1. When Mark Prophet delivered this lecture, he used the Hindi pronunciation of the words *kal* and *desh* (from the Sanskrit *kala* and *desha*) in which the final *a* of both words is silent. The alternate spelling without the final *a* as written in the title retains this pronunciation and vibration for the reader of the word.

2. **Rebellion,** which often begins to manifest at the age of puberty, is in reality a rebellion against returning karma. In most cases, the individual's karma descends for the first time at age 12 and he is forced to deal with the effects of causes he has set in motion in past lifetimes. The only reprieve in the face of the relentless law of karma that we face from puberty on is the grace of Christ when we receive him as our personal Saviour and Teacher in place of the impersonal Law. The confirmation of the child in the Law of the One at age 12–14 is for the sealing of the soul against the day of reckoning with his karma, and for the anointing of the child with the responsibilities of adulthood. This initiation—commemorating Jesus' coming of age, when he discoursed with the doctors in the temple (his final exam), and his going forth to the East in

preparation for his mission—is for the confirming of the Law by understanding, by teaching, and by action and the dedication of the child as a defender of the faith. By developing a deep commitment to defend the Law, he is thus better prepared to face the onslaught of his own karma and the temptations that come during adolescence—using the pure energies of life flowing through him in devotion to God.

3. Prov. 3:12; 13:24; Heb. 12:6-8; Rev. 3:19.

4. **Thoth:** the Egyptian God, also called Tehuti; the god of wisdom, learning and literature; the inventor of all arts and sciences, including writing, arithmetic, algebra, geometry, theology, political economy, medicine, surgery, music and musical instruments. He is usually depicted as counselor and friend of the Egyptian rulers Osiris and Horus, the scribe of the kingdom and amanuensis of the gods. Succeeding Horus to the throne, Thoth is said to have reigned for over three thousand years as a model ruler, then to have taken his place among the gods as guardian of the moon, patron of history, herald, scribe, and keeper of the divine archives. In addition, he is the recorder of the judgment who weighs the hearts of the deceased and reports the verdict before Osiris. Thoth is often portrayed as an ibis (a bird related to a heron with a long downwardly curved bill) or an ibis-headed man; the exact significance of this symbology has never been discovered.

Archaeologist James Churchward traces Thoth back to the days of Atlantis using information he claims to have deciphered from ancient tablets discovered in India and Mexico, confirmed by more than fifty years of his own research: "The first we hear about the religion of Egypt is where an ancient record states that about 16,000 years ago Thoth, the son of an Atlantian Priest, planted the Egyptian colony at the mouth of the Nile, and at Sais on the banks of the Nile built a temple and taught the Osirian religion. . . . Egypt was a sub-colony of the Motherland [Lemuria] under direct control of the colonial empire—Atlantis" (*The Sacred Symbols of Mu* [1933; Paperback Library, 1968], pp. 197, 199).

The Greeks identified Thoth with their god Hermes (the messenger of the gods, whom the Romans associated with Mercury) and with Hermes Trismegistus (meaning "the thrice greatest Hermes"), author of sacred writings and alchemical and astrological works. On the famous Rosetta stone, inscribed by priests of Ptolemy V (d. 180 B.C.), Hermes is called "the great-great," or "twice great." Hargrave Jennings wrote in his introduction to one of the extant works of Hermes, *The Divine Pymander:* "Hermes was called by the Egyptians TAT, TAUT, THOTH. It is concluded that, because of his learning and address, and in wonder at his profound skill in the arts and sciences, that the people gave him the name of TRISME-GISTUS, or the 'THRICE GREAT.'...Some have been so fanciful as to make him one with ADAM," as well as Enoch, Canaan, and the patriarch Joseph. "Perhaps—in spite of all the foregoing exaggerations, which are always the lot of very great and highly distinguished men, who became deified in after-times—the most probable judgment to be formed concerning him is, that he was some person of superior genius, who, before the time of Moses, had invented useful arts, and taught the first rudiments of science; and who caused his instructions to be engraved in emblematical figures (hieroglyphics), upon tables or columns of stone (obelisks), which he dispersed over the country, for the purpose of enlightening the people, and of fixing the worship of the gods. . . .

"Another Thoth, or Hermes, is said to have lived at a later period. He was equally celebrated with the former, and to him is particularly appropriated, by some, the name of Trismegistus. According to Manetho [an Egyptian priest and historian c. 300 B.C.], he [this second Thoth] translated from engraved tables of stone, which had been buried in the earth, the sacred characters of the first Hermes, and wrote the explanation of them in books, which were deposited in the Egyptian temples. The same author calls him the son of Agathodaemon; and adds that to him are ascribed the restoration of the wisdom taught by the first Hermes, and the revival of geometry, arithmetic and the arts among the Egyptians, after they had been long lost or neglected. . . . He is said to have written a very large number of books, as commentaries upon the tables of the first Hermes, which treated of universal principles, of the nature of the universe, and of the soul of man; of the governing of the world by the movements of the stars (otherwise in astrology); of the Divine Light, and of its shadow. . ." (*The Divine Pymander of Hermes Mercurius Trismegistus,* trans. Dr. Everard [1650; San Diego: Wizards Bookshelf, 1978], pp. iii, iv, v).

Manetho said Hermes wrote 36,525 books and the Neoplatonic philosopher Iamblichus (d. c. 330) sets the number at 20,000. Clement of Alexandria, Greek theologian and a father of the Church (d. c. 215), names 42 "Books of Thoth" dealing with priestly education, temple ritual, geography, astrology, guidance for kings, hymns to the gods, and medicine. These were lost in the burning of Alexandria. Writing of the mystical significance of Thoth, one author states, "In the mystic sense Thoth or the Egyptian Hermes was the symbol of the Divine Mind; he was the incarnated Thought, the living Word—the primitive type of the Logos of Plato and the Word of the Christians" (Artaud, "Hermes Trismegiste," in G. R. S. Mead, *Thrice-Greatest Hermes,* vol. 1 [1906; reprint, London: John M. Watkins, 1949], p. 27).

5. Matt. 27:33, 38; Mark 15:22, 27; Luke 23:32, 33; John 19:17, 18.
6. **Level:** a device for establishing a horizontal line or plane by means of a bubble in a liquid that shows adjustment to the horizontal by movement to the center of a slightly bowed glass tube. *Webster's Ninth New Collegiate Dictionary,* s.v. "level."
7. Kahlil Gibran, *The Prophet* (New York: Alfred A. Knopf, 1969), p. 92.
8. Matt. 5:28.
9. John 13:27.
10. *See* Kyle Crichton, *Subway to the Met: Risë Stevens' Story* (Garden City, N.Y.: Doubleday & Company, 1959), pp. 237–38.
11. Jer. 31:33.
12. Gen. 1:1–3.
13. Robert Louis Stevenson, "Happy Thought," *A Child's Garden of Verses.*
14. Matt. 7:9–11; Luke 11:11–13.
15. Matt. 24:27, 30; Rev. 1:7.
16. Rev. 1:18.
17. Rev. 14:6.
18. Heb. 13:8.
19. In Babylonian mythology, **Tiamat** is the female principle of chaos (represented as the anarchic, tumultuous sea or the powers of salt water) which takes the form of a dragon. She is depicted as the enemy of the gods of light and law. As the story is told in the Babylonian *Epic of the Creation,* Tiamat and her husband, Aspu (the primeval father, a personification of the ocean, the Deep, the powers of the fresh waters), were in existence along with their son, Mummu, before the heavens and earth were created. After a succession of generations of gods came forth from Aspu and Tiamat, Aspu,

angered by these turbulent and boisterous beings who were disturbing his former peace, resolved to be rid of the new gods. One of these, Ea, learned of this and destroyed Aspu before he could implement his plans. The vengeful Tiamat thus became the formidable enemy of the new gods, until she and the forces of chaos (including enormous dragons and serpents which she created as her allies) were at last overcome by Marduk, the great god of Babylon, who then fashioned the heavens and the earth and organized the universe. In another variation of the creation legend, Tiamat represents the subterranean waters of chaos, the elementary principle from which the earth arose in the form of a mountain.

Zecharia Sitchin interprets the creation myth as a tale of the creation of our solar system: In the beginning before the formation of the other planets, there was only Aspu (the Sun), Mummu (Mercury), and Tiamat. Tiamat (the "missing planet") was later split in half when it collided with the satellites of Marduk, a large planet drawn into this solar system by the gravitational pull of Neptune. Tiamat's upper half, along with her chief satellite, became Earth and her moon; her lower half, shattered by Marduk during its second orbit, became the asteroid belt between Mars and Jupiter. Sitchin suggests that in this series of events Marduk transferred the seed of life to Earth, giving her "the biological and complex early forms of life for whose early appearance there is no other explanation." He says that at the time the human species on Earth was just beginning to stir, Marduk had already evolved into a planet with high levels of civilization and technology. According to Sitchin, Marduk is caught in a large elliptical orbit around the Sun and returns to the site of the collision between Jupiter and Mars every 3,600 Earth-years. He calls Marduk "the Twelfth Planet" after the ancient Sumerians' scheme of this solar system, which depicts 12 celestial bodies—the Sun, the moon, and 10 planets. See the following works by Zecharia Sitchin: *The 12th Planet* (New York: Avon Books, 1976), pp. 204, 210–34, 255–56; *The Stairway to Heaven* (New York: St. Martin's Press, 1980), pp. 88–90.

20. John 6:53.

Chapter Six THE CHART OF THE I AM PRESENCE

1. Rev. 17:8, 11.
2. John 9:4.
3. Isa. 61:1, 2; Luke 4:16–30.

4. John 10:22–39.
5. Phil. 2:6.
6. Matt. 5:48.
7. Phil. 2:5.
8. James 3:11, 12.
9. Col. 2:9.
10. John 14:23.
11. "Our Constitution is in actual operation; everything appears to promise that it will last; but in this world nothing is certain but death and taxes." Benjamin Franklin, Letter to Jean Baptiste LeRoy, 13 November 1789.
12. Matt. 5:18.
13. Rom. 12:19.
14. Eph. 4:26.
15. Matt. 24:23–27; Luke 17:20, 21. **"The kingdom of God is within you"** (KJV) has been translated in modern versions of the Bible as "the kingdom of God is in the midst of you" (RSV) or "among you" (Jerusalem Bible). According to G. W. H. Lampe, "in the midst of you" is "improbable as a translation"; three instances in the Old Testament translated into Greek by Symmachus, a second-century translator of the Bible, "are the only real parallel for this meaning of the Greek phrase," he says (*Peake's Commentary on the Bible*, eds. Matthew Black and H. H. Rowley [Walton-on-Thames: Thomas Nelson and Sons, 1962], p. 837). S. MacLean Gilmour notes that "within" does correspond "to the normal Greek use of the word" (*Interpreter's Bible*, 8:300). But scholars have been unable to make sense out of "within you" in the context of Luke's verse because they contend that Jesus would not have answered the Pharisees—who had asked him when the kingdom of God was to come (Luke 17:20)—that the kingdom of God was *within them*.

However, *The Gospel of Thomas*—a collection of sayings which, according to scholar Helmut Koester, "are present in a more primitive form" than parallel sayings in the synoptic Gospels or "are developments of a more primitive form of such sayings"—gives the phrase "the kingdom of God is inside of you" not in the context of a conversation with the Pharisees, but as one of "the secret sayings which the living Jesus spoke": "Jesus said, 'If those who lead you say to you, "See, the Kingdom is in the sky," then the birds of the sky will precede you. If they say to you, "It is in the sea," then the fish will precede you. Rather, the Kingdom is inside of you, and it is outside of you. When you come to know yourselves, then you will become known, and you will realize that it is you who are the sons of the living Father. But if you will not know yourselves, you dwell in poverty and it is you who are that poverty.'" *The Nag Hammadi Library in English*, gen. ed. James M. Robinson (New York: Harper & Row, 1977), pp. 117, 118.

16. II Cor. 3:18.
17. I Cor. 15:49.
18. Rev. 10:1.
19. Exod. 3:2–4.
20. Dan. 7:9, 13, 22.
21. Rev. 1:8, 11; 21:6; 22:13.
22. Deut. 6:4.
23. James 4:8.
24. I Sam. 2:27–36.
25. Gen. 3:21.
26. Gen. 3:19.
27. **Kundalini:** lit. "coiled-up serpent"; coiled energy in latency at the base-of-the-spine chakra; the Life-force; the Mother energy. When the Kundalini is awakened (through specific yogic techniques, postures and bija mantras, spiritual disciplines, or intense love of God) it begins to ascend the spinal column through the channels of the *Ida, Pingala,* and *Sushumna,* penetrating and activating each of the chakras. The raising of the Kundalini before soul purification and the transmutation of negative momentums of past lives have taken place can result in insanity, demon possession, uncontrolled and inordinate sexual desire or a perversion of the Life-force in all the chakras.

The missing link in the Eastern tradition of raising the Kundalini is the use of the dynamic decree in the science of the spoken Word to draw down the Light of the Father from the I AM THAT I AM and causal body and the realization that the Light of the upper chakras is intended to magnetize the Light from the base of the spine to the heart. The descending Light of the Father uniting in the heart with the Light of the Mother raised up from the base of the spine results in the awareness of the sacred heart and the wholeness of Alpha and Omega.

The Blessed Mother has provided the rosary as a safe method of raising the Mother Light by the fervent heat of love and adoration, without a violent eruption of energy. The cleansing of the aura and chakras with the violet flame also enables the Kundalini to rise gradually without danger. When used in conjunction with the violet flame, the bija mantras to the Divine Mother are safe under the sponsorship of Saint Germain, whose East/West experiment in transmutation, combining dynamic decrees with meditation and the recitation of mantras to the feminine deities, provides a path of acceleration for disciples of both traditions. Saint Germain recommends decrees for the tube of light and protection by Archangel Michael as the foundation for these sessions.

    For further teaching from the Ascended Masters and Messengers, see "The Raising-Up of the Energies of the Mother" in Djwal Kul, *Intermediate Studies of the Human Aura,* pp. 78, 95, 108–14; *Pearls of Wisdom,* vol. 26 (1983), no. 38, p. 454 n. 1; Elizabeth Clare Prophet's 1985 European and North American Stump for Saint Germain's Coming Revolution in Higher Consciousness and *Mantras of the Ascended Masters for the Initiation of the Chakras,* 36-page booklet; Mary's Scriptural Rosary for the New Age, in *My Soul Doth Magnify the Lord! New Age Rosary and New Age Teachings of Mother Mary; The Fourteenth Rosary: The Mystery of Surrender,* booklet and 2-cassette album; and *A Child's Rosary to Mother Mary*—15-minute scriptural rosaries for children and adults, four 3-cassette albums. See also Chapter 7.

28. **"The form of the fourth is like the Son of God,"** Dan. 3:25: RSV reads, "the appearance of the fourth is like a son of the gods." The Jerusalem Bible reads, "the fourth looks like a son of the gods." Arthur Jeffery explains (*The Interpreter's Bible,* 6:403) that a son of the gods means "an angel, a celestial being, a divinity, such as were commonly called 'sons of the gods.'" Further evidence that Nebuchadnezzar thought the fourth figure was an angel is found later in the chapter when he says, "Blessed be the God of Shadrach, Meshach, and Abednego, who hath sent his angel, and delivered his servants" (Dan. 3:28).

    Whether the fourth appeared as an angelic being or as the Son of God, the lesson is well taken that the Christic Presence reflects through the etheric body the highest patterns of the heavens that are to be outpictured in the lower three. The story illustrates the personification of the Light descending as the intercessor in the plight of the three Hebrew boys, who symbolize the mental, emotional, and physical bodies of man. The updated translation of RSV and Jerusalem Bible neither diminish nor alter our understanding of the passage.

29. **Electronic belt:** The momentums of untransmuted karma in orbit around the 'nucleus' of the synthetic self (or carnal mind) form what looks like an 'electronic belt' of misqualified energy around the lower portion of man's physical body. Diagrammed at the point of the solar plexus, extending from the waist downward in a negative spiral to below the feet, this conglomerate of human creation forms a dense forcefield resembling the shape of a kettledrum. Referred to as the realm of the subconscious or the unconscious, the electronic belt contains the records of unredeemed karma from all embodiments. Each day, according to the law of cycles, a certain portion of this energy returns to the individual for transmutation. See "Our God Is a Consuming Fire," in Mark and Elizabeth Prophet, *Climb the Highest Mountain: The Path of the Higher Self, The Everlasting Gospel*, Book I (Los Angeles: Summit University Press, 1972), chap. 6, and table, "Flame Color-Qualities of the Seven Rays and Their Perversions"; Elizabeth Clare Prophet, "The Psychology of Wholeness: The Karmic Clock" delivered at *Higher Consciousness: A Conference for Spiritual Freedom,* July 2, 1976.

30. **Enoch taken up to ten heavens:** See Elizabeth Clare Prophet, *Forbidden Mysteries of Enoch: The Untold Story of Men and Angels* (Los Angeles: Summit University Press, 1983), pp. 370–84.

31. Mark 16:19; Col. 3:1; Heb. 10:12.

32. I Thess. 4:16, 17. See Jesus Christ, "The Second Advent: 'The Day of Vengeance of Our God,'" in *Pearls of Wisdom,* vol. 26 (1983), no. 43, pp. 511–19.

33. John 14:2, 3.

34. Heb. 9:23, 24.

35. **". . . Yet in my flesh shall I see God,"** Job 19:26: Controversy surrounds the translation of this verse. Most scholars agree that the Hebrew text of the first half, which the KJV renders "and though after my skin worms destroy this body" and the RSV as "And after my skin has been thus destroyed," is corrupt—i.e., has been distorted from its original meaning

and thus is impossible to translate correctly. They say the second half of the verse is probably better Hebrew, but its meaning remains as elusive as its translation. One source of confusion is the preposition *min,* which can mean "from within" or "from without." Thus the KJV renders the clause "yet *in my flesh* shall I see God" and the RSV "then *without my flesh* I shall see God."

The Jerusalem Bible says in an explanatory note that the entire verse is corrupt and that the various Bible manuscripts differ widely. The Vulgate, a Latin version of the Bible prepared by St. Jerome in the fourth century, gives the verse as "At the last day I shall rise from the earth and be clothed in my skin again; and in my flesh I shall see my God." Perhaps it was inevitable that the Church Fathers would translate this verse in accordance with Christian doctrine. In light of the discrepancies among the manuscripts, the Jerusalem Bible gives the verse as: "After my awaking, he will set me close to him, and from my flesh I shall look on God." "There is no approach to agreement as to the meaning of this verse," says E. F. Sutcliffe, who suggests rearranging the words to get meaning out of them: "Should my skin be flayed from my flesh, even after this I shall see God" (*A Catholic Commentary on Holy Scripture* [New York: Thomas Nelson and Sons, 1953], pp. 431–32).

The difficulty in translation lies in the implication of the phrase "in my flesh." Will Job see God before or after death? If after, in the spirit or in the flesh? Samuel Terrien in *The Interpreter's Bible* (3:1055–56) leans toward translating the crucial phrase as "in my flesh" since "there is no doubt that when used with a verb expressing vision or perception, the same preposition [*min*] refers to the point of vantage, the locale from which or through which the function of sight operates," as in "Yahweh looketh from [*min*] heaven, . . . from [*min*] the place of his habitation (Ps. 33:13, 14)." Terrien goes on to say that this translation possibly infers that Job believed he would in some way receive new flesh after death "for the specific purpose of the divine-human interview."

This verse is meant to tell of Job's hope of incarnating the Universal Christ image. But scholars have been unable to escape orthodox mind-sets and thus have had an ongoing problem in translation. Perhaps the Hebrew was originally corrupted by a manuscript copyist who determined to change it to what he perceived the meaning to be. From Genesis to Revelation, the Bible shows the path of the gradual process of the incarnation of the Word, or the Christ. It was Job's glimpsing of this path that bound him in the faith that one day, in his very flesh, he would realize the Son of God.

36. Rev. 22:1.
37. See Djwal Kul, *Intermediate Studies of the Human Aura* (Los Angeles: Summit University Press, 1976), pp. 38–47.
38. Luke 1:80; 2:40.
39. Aimee Semple McPherson, "Fling Wide the Pearly Gates."
40. Max Heindel takes up the subject of the loosing of the **silver cord** at death in *The Rosicrucian Cosmo-Conception* (1906; reprint, Pasadena, Calif.: Wood and Jones, 1974), pp. 97–102.
41. Charles A. Lindbergh, *Autobiography of Values* (New York: Harcourt Brace Jovanovich, 1978), pp. 394–95.
42. Gen. 5:3–32.
43. The Great Divine Director, "The Mechanization Concept," in *Pearls of Wisdom,* vol. 8 (1965), no. 14 (Los Angeles: Summit University Press, 1980), pp. 72–73.
44. Matt. 7:7, 11; John 15:7, 16; 16:23, 24; I John 3:22; James 4:3.
45. See *Saint John of the Cross on the Living Flame of Love,* for **the alchemical marriage** on earth as in heaven, taught by Mark L. Prophet and Elizabeth Clare Prophet. This 8-cassette album of indispensable teaching on the soul's mystical experience in Christ offers an in-depth study of *Living Flame of Love*—the literary and religious masterpiece penned by Saint John of the Cross in the sixteenth century—with penetrating insights into how to get beyond the burdens of personal karma and psychology in preparation for the Divine Encounter.
46. Saint Germain, *Pearls of Wisdom,* vol. 10 (1967), no. 7; "A Valentine from Saint Germain," in *Saint Germain On Alchemy: For the Adept in the Aquarian Age* (Los Angeles: Summit University Press, 1985), pp. 350–52.
47. I Pet. 3:4.
48. Rom. 7:22; Eph. 3:16; I Pet. 3:4.
49. Exod. 28:36; 39:30; Zech. 14:20, 21.
50. For Saint Germain's teaching on the scientific and controlled release of energy from Spirit to Matter through the thoughtform of the Maltese cross—"a thought and energy matrix whereby the ill effects of personal and planetary

karma can be brought under control"—see "A Trilogy On the
Threefold Flame of Life: **The Alchemy of Power, Wisdom
and Love**" in *Saint Germain On Alchemy: For the Adept in the
Aquarian Age* (Los Angeles: Summit University Press, 1985),
pp. 265–345.
51. Hab. 1:13.
52. Jer. 23:6; 33:16.
53. Matt. 25:21, 23; Luke 19:17–19.
54. John 3:13.
55. Col. 3:3.
56. Col. 2:9, 10.
57. Acts 1:9–11.
58. Prov. 4:7.
59. I Cor. 15:41, 42.
60. I Cor. 10:31. The understanding of the principle of dedicat-
ing one's life and service **"to the glory of God"** and
acknowledging Him as the source ("I can of mine own self
do nothing. . . . The Father that dwelleth in me, he doeth the
works," John 5:30; 14:10) was given to Saint Catherine of
Siena (1347–1380) during the heights of her intimate communion with God, which were epitomized in her great
mystical treatise, the *Dialogue*. This fundamental truth inspired in Catherine the humility and the conviction that
enabled her to confront head-on the forces threatening the
Church in the turbulent fourteenth century, when she acted
as peacemaker and unofficial diplomat, traveling widely and
addressing hundreds of letters to the prelates and sovereigns
of the day.

   In the *Dialogue*—conversations with God the Father
dictated by Catherine to her secretaries during a five-day
state of ecstasy—the Father explained to his "dearest daughter," as he often called her, that "the root of discretion is a
real knowledge of self and of My goodness, by which the
soul immediately, and discreetly, renders to each one his
due. Chiefly to Me in rendering praise and glory to My
Name, and in referring to Me the graces and the gifts which
she sees and knows she has received from Me; and rendering
to herself that which she sees herself to have merited, knowing that she does not even exist of herself, and attributing to
Me, and not to herself, her being, which she knows she has
received by grace from Me, and every other grace which she
has received besides. . . .

"The tree of love feeds itself on humility, bringing forth from its side the off-shoot of true discretion, in the way that I have already told thee, from the heart of the tree, that is the affection of love which is in the soul, and the patience, which proves that I am in the soul and the soul in Me. This tree then, so sweetly planted, produces fragrant blossoms of virtue, with many scents of great variety, inasmuch as the soul renders fruit of grace and of utility to her neighbour, according to the zeal of those who come to receive fruit from My servants; and to Me she renders the sweet odour of glory and praise to My Name, and so fulfils the object of her creation" (Algar Thorold trans., *The Dialogue of the Seraphic Virgin Catherine of Siena* [Rockford, Ill.: Tan Books and Publishers, 1974], pp. 51–52, 54).

Biographer Igino Giordani records that "on another occasion while she was praying—as she herself related to several spiritual advisers—Jesus Christ appeared to her and asked: 'Do you know, daughter, who you are and who I am? If you knew these two things, you would be blessed. You are that which is not; I am He who is. If you have this knowledge in your soul, the enemy can never deceive you; you will escape all his snares; you will never consent to anything contrary to my commandments; and without difficulty you will acquire every grace, every truth, every light.'. . . With that lesson Catherine became fundamentally learned: she was founded upon a rock; there were no more shadows. *I, nothing; God, All. I, nonbeing; God, Being*" (Igino Giordani, *Saint Catherine of Siena—Doctor of the Church*, trans. Thomas J. Tobin [Boston: Daughters of St. Paul, 1980], pp. 35, 36).

61. Matt. 6:20.
62. Portia in Shakespeare, *Merchant of Venice*, act 4, sc. 1, lines 183–86.
63. Luke 8:43–48.
64. Josh. 1:9.
65. Ps. 139:8–10.
66. Zech. 2:8.
67. Exod. 13:21, 22.
68. Exod. 14:19.
69. Zech. 3.
70. Mic. 4:4.
71. Jer. 31:34; Heb. 8:11.
72. Zech. 2:1, 5, 10, 11.

Chapter Seven THE INTEGRATION OF THE CHAKRAS

1. Exod. 3:2.
2. Job 22:25, 27, 28.
3. Exod. 3:14, 15.
4. Matt. 5:37.
5. Matt. 12:36, 37.
6. From *Spring Session M* by Missing Persons. © 1982 Capitol Records, Inc.
7. Ps. 19:14.
8. Matt. 6:22.
9. Matt. 26:11; Mark 14:7; John 12:8.

For further teaching from the Ascended Masters and Messengers on the **chakras,** with color illustrations, visualizations, and meditations, see Djwal Kul, *Intermediate Studies of the Human Aura;* Elizabeth Clare Prophet, *Mother's Chakra Meditations and the Science of the Spoken Word,* 8-cassette album; and Gautama Buddha, "The Prayer Wheel of the Crown Chakra," in *Kuan Yin Opens the Door to the Golden Age: The Path of the Mystics East and West,* Book II, Pearls of Wisdom, vol. 25 (1982), pp. 327–30, also available on *The Seventh Commandment: Thou Shalt Not Commit Adultery,* 2-cassette album.

Chapter Eight THE ETERNAL VERITIES

1. II Chron. 32:7, 8; Jer. 17:5.
2. Luke 10:29–37.
3. Matt. 18:12, 13; Luke 15:4–7.
4. John 10:11–15.
5. Matt. 19:19; Mark 12:31; Luke 10:25–28.
6. I Cor. 11:24.
7. Exod. 3:14.
8. Ps. 103:15, 16.
9. I John 4:18.
10. See Mal. 3.
11. Gen. 3:19; "Life is real! Life is earnest! / And the grave is not its goal; / Dust thou art, to dust returnest, / Was not spoken of the soul," Henry Wadsworth Longfellow, "A Psalm of Life," stanza 2.
12. Gen. 1:26, 27.
13. John 8:58.
14. John 1:9.

15. Gen. 3:21.
16. I Cor. 13:9, 10, 12.
17. Matt. 10:9, 10; Mark 6:8; Luke 9:3; 10:4.
18. John 10:10–18.
19. II Cor. 3:18.
20. Acts 2:2.
21. John 1:14.
22. Acts 17:28, 29; Rom. 8:16, 17; Gal. 4:7.
23. Mal. 3:1.
24. John 11:27.
25. **Golem:** Hebrew for embryonic or incompletely developed substance, shapeless matter (used in the Bible, Ps. 139:16: "Thine eyes did see my *substance, yet being unperfect*"). In Jewish folklore, a robotlike servant made of clay and brought to life by pronouncing the sacred name of God over its form, writing God's name on a piece of paper and putting it in the golem's mouth, or inscribing the word for truth *(emeth)* on its forehead. If the paper or inscription were removed, the golem would be reduced to a pile of clay. In medieval times, the belief in the creation of golems was common and was attributed to various rabbis throughout Europe. In fact, this belief was so strong that Jewish scholar Rabbi Zvi Ashkenazi seriously debated the question of whether or not a golem could be included as part of a minyan (quorum of 10 adult men required to be present for a religious service). Belief in golems was also widespread among the Jews of Eastern Europe during the nineteenth century.
    The golem of the early legends, though unable to speak, was a perfect servant that fulfilled all his master's orders. Starting in the sixteenth century, he was characterized as the protector of persecuted Jews. It was not until the seventeenth century that the Frankensteinlike golem—who in some versions of the tale grew larger in size each day—was portrayed as a physical threat. In some earlier versions of the legend, the golem is seen as dangerous not because of his potential for violence but because he poses the threat of idolatry. For example, in one thirteenth-century legend the golem supposedly created by Jeremiah and Ben Sira, this time endowed with the faculty of speech, warns the two men that their followers may begin to worship them for their seemingly extraordinary powers in bringing the clay man to life. In one variation of this story, the golem himself removes a letter from the words inscribed on his forehead—*YHWH Elohim*

Emeth, or "God is truth"—thereby changing *truth* to the word *dead (meth).* The resulting blasphemy, "God is dead," is a clear message to the golem's creators. As in most of the legends, man triumphs over golem; Jeremiah heeds the warning and destroys his creation.

The most famous golem legend, which has several different variations and has inspired novelists and playwrights, is that of Rabbi Judah Loew (or Löw) of Prague (c. 1520–1609), a historical figure who was a practitioner of the Kabbalah and a Talmudic scholar. He is said to have created a clay man and endowed him with life in order to defend the Jews of Prague from superstitious Christians who accused them of using the blood of Christian babies to bake their matzohs (unleavened bread). The golem served as the rabbi's agent and successfully apprehended those who were spreading the false rumor. He would perform tasks for Rabbi Loew during the week, and every Friday evening the rabbi would turn him back into a heap of clay by removing the inscription from his forehead, because all creatures are supposed to rest on the Sabbath (or, as another version of the legend goes, because the rabbi feared that the golem would profane the Sabbath).

One Friday, however, the rabbi forgot to do this and the golem turned into a dangerous wildman just before the Sabbath began. Rabbi Loew pursued and finally caught up to his golem run amok, tore from his forehead the sacred name of God, and never brought him back to life again. Rabbi Loew's story was the basis for Gustav Meyrink's famous novel *Der Golem* (1915), a German silent film based on Meyrink's novel (1920) which served as an archetype for later films on the *Frankenstein* theme, and the play by H. Leivick, *The Golem: A Dramatic Poem in Eight Scenes* (1921). See Isaac Bashevis Singer, "The Golem Is a Myth for Our Time," *New York Times,* 12 August 1984; Arnold L. Goldsmith, *The Golem Remembered, 1909–1980: Variations of a Jewish Legend* (Detroit: Wayne State University Press, 1981), pp. 15–20; Gershom Scholem, *On the Kabbalah and Its Symbolism,* trans. Ralph Manheim (New York: Schocken Books, 1969), pp. 180, 199, 202–3; *The Universal Jewish Encyclopedia,* s.v. "Golem."

26. **"Divine Us"** refers to the Elohim (plural of Heb. *'Eloah,* God), one of the Hebrew names of God, or of the gods; used in the Old Testament about 2,500 times, meaning "Mighty

One" or "Strong One." *Elohim* is a uniplural noun referring to the twin flames of the Godhead. When speaking specifically of either the masculine or feminine half, the plural form is retained because of the understanding that one half of the Divine Whole contains and is the androgynous Self (the Divine Us). The seven mighty Elohim and their feminine counterparts are the builders of form; hence, Elohim is the name of God used in the first verse of the Bible, "In the beginning God created the heaven and the earth." The Elohim are also "the seven Spirits of God" named in Revelation (1:4; 3:1; 4:5; 5:6), and the "morning stars" which sang together in the beginning, as the LORD revealed to his servant Job (38:7). See *Spoken by Elohim,* Pearls of Wisdom, vol. 21 (Los Angeles: Summit University Press, 1978); *The Seven Elohim in the Power of the Spoken Word,* 4-cassette album, The Summit Lighthouse.

27. I Kings 4:25; Mic. 4:4, 5; Zech. 3:10.
28. Gen. 2:9; 3:22, 24; Rev. 2:7; 22:2, 14.
29. John 15:1, 4, 5.
30. Jer. 23:5; 33:15; Zech. 3:8; 6:12.
31. Rev. 14:6.
32. For further insights into the long-hidden history of these fallen ones, see *The Lost Teachings of Jesus,* Book Two; the Great Divine Director, *The Mechanization Concept: Mysteries of God on the Creation of Mechanized Man,* Pearls of Wisdom, vol. 8 (1965), nos. 3–26 (Los Angeles, Summit University Press, 1980), pp. 9–142; and Elizabeth Clare Prophet, *Forbidden Mysteries of Enoch: The Untold Story of Men and Angels* (Los Angeles: Summit University Press, 1983).
33. **Lemuria:** Mu, the lost continent of the Pacific which, according to the findings of James Churchward, archaeologist and author of *The Lost Continent of Mu,* extended from north of Hawaii three thousand miles south to Easter Island and the Fijis and was made up of three areas of land stretching more than five thousand miles from east to west. He estimates that Mu was destroyed approximately twelve thousand years ago by the collapse of the gas chambers which upheld the continent. See *The Lost Continent of Mu* (1931; reprint, New York: Paperback Library Edition, 1968). **Atlantis:** See p. 356 n. 42.
34. Matt. 8:12; 22:13; 25:30.
35. Heb. 10:26, 27.

36. Acts 10:42; II Tim. 4:1; I Pet. 4:5.
37. Rom. 8:25; II Thess. 3:5.
38. II Pet. 2:17; Jude 13.
39. *Encyclopaedia Britannica,* 11th ed.: **"Saint-Germain, Comte de** (*c.* 1710–*c.* 1780) called *der Wundermann,* a celebrated adventurer who by the assertion of his discovery of some extraordinary secrets of nature exercised considerable influence at several European courts. Of his parentage and place of birth nothing is definitely known; the common version is that he was a Portuguese Jew, but various surmises have been made as to his being of royal birth. It was also stated that he obtained his money, of which he had abundance, from acting as spy to one of the European courts. But this is hard to maintain. He knew nearly all the European languages, and spoke German, English, Italian, French (with a Piedmontese accent), Portuguese and Spanish.

"Grimm affirms him to have been the man of the best parts he had ever known. He was a musical composer and a capable violinist. His knowledge of history was comprehensive, and his accomplishments as a chemist, on which he based his reputation, were in many ways real and considerable. He pretended to have a secret for removing flaws from diamonds, and to be able to transmute metals. The most remarkable of his professed discoveries was of a liquid which could prolong life, and by which he asserted he had himself lived 2000 years.

"After spending some time in Persia, Saint-Germain is mentioned in a letter of Horace Walpole's as being in London about 1743, and as being arrested as a Jacobite spy and released. Walpole says: 'He is called an Italian, a Spaniard, a Pole; a somebody that married a great fortune in Mexico and ran away with her jewels to Constantinople; a priest, a fiddler, a vast nobleman.'

"At the court of Louis XV., where he appeared about 1748, he exercised for a time extraordinary influence and was employed on secret missions by Louis XV.; but, having interfered in the dispute between Austria and France, he was compelled in June 1760, on account of the hostility of the duke of Choiseul, to remove to England.

"He appears to have resided in London for one or two years, but was at St. Petersburg in 1762, and is asserted to have played an important part in connexion with the conspiracy against the Emperor Peter III. in July of that year, a plot which placed Catherine II. on the Russian throne. He then went to Germany, where, according to the *Mémoires authentiques* of Cagliostro, he was the founder of freemasonry, and initiated Cagliostro into that rite.

"He was again in Paris from 1770 to 1774, and after frequenting several of the German courts he took up his residence in Schleswig-Holstein, where he and the Landgrave Charles of Hesse pursued together the study of the 'secret' sciences. He died at Schleswig in or about 1780-1785, although he is said to have been seen in Paris in 1789.

"Andrew Lang in his *Historical Mysteries* (1904) discusses the career of Saint-Germain, and cites the various authorities for it. Saint-Germain figures prominently in the correspondence of Grimm and of Voltaire. See also Oettinger, *Graf Saint-Germain* (1846); F. Bulaü, *Geheime Geschichten und räthselhafte Menschen,* Band i. (1850-1860); Lascelles Wraxall, *Remarkable Adventures* (1863); and U. Birch in the *Nineteenth Century* (January 1908)."

See Elizabeth Clare Prophet, "The Wonderman of Europe," in *Saint Germain On Alchemy: For the Adept in the Aquarian Age* (Los Angeles: Summit University Press, 1985), pp. vii-xxvii; I. Cooper-Oakley, *The Comte de St. Germain: The Secret of Kings* (London: The Theosophical Publishing House Limited, 1912); Irene Tetzlaff, *Unter den Flügeln des Phönix: Der Graf von Saint Germain* (Marshchalkenzimmern, Schwarzwald: Lichthort-Verlag, n.d.).

40. Job 22:27; Ps. 91:15; Isa. 65:24; Jer. 33:3.
41. Isa. 55:1.

Index of Scripture

*References to the Book of Enoch are from *Forbidden Mysteries of Enoch: The Untold Story of Men and Angels* by Elizabeth Clare Prophet (Los Angeles: Summit University Press, 1983), pp. 89–228 (translation by Richard Laurence).

Index

Abhedananda, Swami, *xxx*

Abraham: "Before Abraham was, I AM," 83, 307; and Melchizedek, 58, 60, 61, 76; the three 'men' who talked to, 60

Abundant Life, 76, 308; we can have the, 96

Acceleration, to control your vibrational rate, 100–101

Accountability, for our words and deeds, 78. *See also* Responsibility

Action(s): the elements that make up our, 180; indelibly stamped on akasha, 177. *See also* Deed(s)

Acupuncture, 272

Adultery, the thought of, 176–77

Affinity, as *a fine tie,* 24

Africa, advanced civilizations of, 285

Air: to meet the Lord in the, 227; prana in the, 272–73, 274; in your physical body and in your mind, 119

Air body, as one of the four lower bodies, 225. *See also* Four lower bodies; Mental body

Akasha: action stamped on, 177; a Law written in, 74

Akashic records, 200. *See also* Record(s)

Alchemy: divine, 305; spiritual, 62

All-in-all, God as the, 88

America: has enjoyed prosperity, 282; Los Angeles as the soul chakra of, 286; people in, 288

American Express man, 4

Ancient of Days, 219

Angel(s): "the angel of the LORD," 219, 222, 255; and Balaam, 150; clothed with a cloud and a rainbow on his head, 218; guardian, 13; on the head of a pin, 215; of his Presence, 254; the I AM Presence has sealed his promise by his, 259; pupils reporting visitations of the, 41–43; rebellious, 314; of record, 249; the reprobate, 313; seduction of our souls by reprobate, 74–75; some spirit guides are really, 233; their duties, 164; those who witnessed, 245; when I was four I could see, 41; which went before the camp of Israel, 255; who looked like "men in white apparel," 244; working with, 199–200. *See also* Archangels; Fallen angels

Angelic kingdom, elementals can come through the human kingdom into the, 165

Anger: can be responsible for the death of another, 159; a woman who channeled her decree energy into, 158; if you go to bed harboring, 213. *See also* Wrath

Animal(s): the human, 191; some walked the earth as, 281

209; wondered about Jacob and Esau, 38

Paul the Venetian, 152

Pearls of Wisdom, entitled "The Mechanization Concept," 233. *See also* Teaching(s)

Peck, Gregory, 63

People: are searching for God, 43; change, 111; common, 51; the concepts we hold of, 111; learning to love and esteem, 119; like to laugh at themselves, 7; the little, 282, 288; the magnificence in, 110; sitting in a car looking at, 190; stop judging, 108; today, 191; two kinds of, 183; who have a certain karma to work out, 286; will tell you all their troubles, 150–51. *See also* Man

Perfect: "if I wait for you to become perfect...," 111; the world is already, 90

Perfection: achieved in stages, 29; human, 87; inherent within this universe, 94; original, 281; which we foreknew, 120

Person: to become a real, 51; cutting himself down, 14; a masterful, 107; as *Pure Son*, 257; wanting to be a good, 305. *See also* Man

Personality: any one, in God, 88; a developed and powerful, 250; the human, 228; our outer, 76. *See also* Ego; Self

Petals: the base chakra has four, 289; the crown has 972, 287; the heart has twelve, 270; the seat of the soul has six, 284; the solar plexus has ten, 279; the third eye has ninety-six, 281; the throat chakra has sixteen, 275

Peter, 102; in the secret Gospel of Mark, *xlix*

Phoniness: avoid, 16; people have created, 17; we wish to take off, 14; of the world, 4, 13. *See also* Hypocrisies; Hypocrisy

Photograph, of our loving Father, 220

Physical body: the cleansing of the, 284; is only one-quarter of the whole person, 264; is the focus of integration, 225; the patterns outpictured in the, 226; remade after Christ's image, 228; subject to total dissolution, 228; what causes the threefold flame to "go out" in the, 232. *See also* Body; Four lower bodies; Physical form

Physical form: the polarity between the etheric blueprint and the, 226; a small, 253. *See also* Body; Four lower bodies; Physical body

Pierre, 138–39

Pilgrims, upon the spiritual path, 107

Pink: of the causal body, 248; in your aura, 253

Pink band, of the causal body, 250

Pituitary gland, the lobes of the, 174

Place prepared, 315; in heaven, 251

Plumb line, of our Presence comes down the crystal cord, 112

Plus factor, of God in your life, 133–34

Polarity: between the etheric blueprint and the physical form, 226; life is a, 303

Pollock, Joanna and Jacqueline, 41

Pollution, 274

Ponce de Leon, 271–72

Poor: the nation's, 282; "the poor you have with you always," 282

Possessiveness, 74, 268

Post, Wiley, 6, 7

Potential, to maximize your, 266

Potter, Master, 119–20

Power: of God in yourself, 189; and love, 136; to make things happen, 183; to motivate an idea, 135; in "The Navy Hymn," 166; and the threefold flame, 245; you develop in decrees, 158. *See also* Dominion

Power elite, 282

Powers: psychic, 52; soul, 134

Rays: 'alpha', 'beta' or 'gamma', 115;
of light from your Presence, 255
Reality: reintegration with your,
116; the self must proclaim its
God Reality, 87; we lose touch
with our, 49
Rebels, bearded, 4
Record(s): come full circle, 82; reproduced lifetime after lifetime,
228–29; traumatic, 75; violet fire
to erase, 95–96. *See also* Akashic
records
Reembodiment: the question of, 36–
38; was taught by the Catholic
Church, 138. *See also* Embodiment; Lives; Reincarnation
Refinement, self-refinement, 305
Reflection, of your Real Self, 236
Reincarnation: examples of, 41; is
the means to regain oneness with
God, 40; in new coats of skins,
229; in 1930 three-quarters of
the world's thinking minds accepted, 38; Origen taught, 38–40.
See also Embodiment; Lives;
Reembodiment
Religion(s): all point toward the
same God, 124; all, has had but
one purpose, 32; the bag and baggage of, 33; the blasted, 43; a chart
of all the, 33; an emotional, 47;
has become a dead and empty
activity, 124; I do not see that,
should invade privacy, 14; is
simply our belief in immortality,
36; Jesus', 47; no room for the, of
God, 42; people are born and die
and are buried in one, 35; that
sought to meet the needs of the
people, 32; that stress externals,
13. *See also* Church(es); Doc-
trine(s); Orthodoxy; Theology
Religious organizations, merchandising in men's souls, 45. *See also*
Church(es)
Religious quest, levels and degrees
in the, 93

Resolution, cosmic, 75
Resolutions, New Year's, 137
Responsibility, people do not understand, 155. *See also* Accountability
Resurrection, 99; "a better resurrection," 78; "I AM the Resur-
rection and the Life. . . ," 102;
". . . so also is the resurrection of
the dead," 98; where souls expe-
rience the, 227
Retreat(s): of the Brotherhood, 62;
of the Great White Brotherhood,
200; in Transylvania, 233n, 317
Revelation: the Book of, *xxxi, lxi;*
mysteries described in the Book
of, 64; progressive, *xxxi*
Revolutionaries, of the Spirit, 47
Rich, 282
Righteousness: human and divine,
113; as *right use* of the Law, 113
Rigidity, 9
Riptide, of anger, 158
River, of Life, 230
Rock, listening to, 200. *See also* Music
Roerich, Nicholas, *xxx, following*
p. 68
Rogers, Will, 6–7, 50–51
Roman centurion, whose servant
was healed by Jesus, 53
Ruach, the Hebrew, 272
"Runner's high," 264
Ruthie, from North Carolina, 32

Sacrifice, a God requiring propitiation through human, 83
Saint Germain, 151; a book supposedly by, 165; a great Western
adept, 316–17; has given us a
mantra for the cleansing of our
chakras, 268–69; his ascension
was the result of two million
right decisions, 138; in order to
see, 106; the seventh angel, 64;
study alchemy under, 62; taught
us about the threefold flame,
237–39; the teacher and sponsor
of, 233n; teaches the use of the

painful, 264; after a hard, 272

Works, ". . . and greater works. . . ," 53, 54, 103

World: is already perfect, 90; our own personal, 33; we ourselves go back to the foundation of the, 51; what is going to save the, 198; if you were to create a, 72

Worlds: emissaries from other systems of, 124; other systems of, 98

Worth, self-worth, 302–3

Worthy, "Lord, I AM worthy . . . ," 302–3

Wrath, don't "let the sun go down upon your wrath," 159–60, 213. *See also* Anger

Wretchedness, 303

Writings: of the disciples, *xliii;* Jesus may have quoted, which are now lost, *xxxix–xl;* suppressed, *xliii*

Wrong, forget every, 213

Yahweh, 259; Moses described the 'Presence' of, 219

Yellow: a combination of blue and, 251; of the crown chakra, 287

Yellow band, of the causal body, 253

Yellow sphere, of the causal body, 248, 250

Yoga, 273

Yogic master, who met a king cobra, 131

Yoke, of Christ, 141

Youth, 'fountain of youth', 271–72

Zen, running with, 290

Zensoho, 290

Zero: the violet flame is the, 62; the violet flame reduces your miscreation to, 63

The search goes on . . .

Having written *The Lost Years of Jesus,* it was almost a foregone conclusion that Elizabeth Clare Prophet would follow with something like *The Lost Teachings of Jesus.* In 1984 her *Lost Years* opened to view the unknown life of Christ. Now her *Lost Teachings* takes the logical next step by recovering missing pieces of the World Teacher's message for this age. Together, they do much to reconstruct the life and teachings of the Master.

In *The Lost Years of Jesus* Mrs. Prophet takes you behind the scenes of one of the most intriguing literary controversies and, in a masterpiece of investigative reporting, provides overwhelming evidence to show that Jesus was in India for the better part of the so-called lost years.

The story begins in 1894 when Nicolas Notovitch, a Russian journalist, published the text of ancient Buddhist manuscripts he discovered at Himis monastery in Ladakh which said Jesus spent seventeen years in the East. Mrs. Prophet tells how critics "proved" the documents did not exist, only to have them rediscovered in this century by three distinguished scholars: internationally acclaimed artist-archaeologist Nicholas Roerich, Swami Abhedananda, and educator Dr. Elisabeth Caspari.

Drawing together their eyewitness accounts with variant translations of the text and the oral history of Jesus' sojourn, the author allows the reader to follow Jesus from Jerusalem to the enchanted East—to Tibet, Nepal, Ladakh and India, where he studied, taught and, in what was a dress rehearsal for his Palestinian ministry, challenged a corrupt priest class, healed the sick, and raised the dead.

Continuing right where she left off, Mrs. Prophet draws together in *The Lost Teachings of Jesus* the work on which she collaborated with her late husband Mark L. Prophet.

In this two-volume sequel, we find that Jesus' experiences in the Orient profoundly influenced his teachings—that strains of what are thought to be Eastern beliefs, such as karma and reincarnation, are to be found in the Gospels. First, the Prophets demonstrate that much of Jesus' teaching has been lost—either removed from the Gospels, suppressed, kept secret for those being initiated into the deeper mysteries, or never written down at all. And then, in a modern vernacular, they present the lost teachings Jesus gave his disciples 2,000 years ago—and the very personal instruction he is imparting today to those whose hearts are receptive to Truth. As the pages unfold you will find yourself discovering the key to the sacred mysteries and being quickened to your inner Christhood—a path and a self-knowledge essential to the fulfillment of your destiny on Earth and beyond.

For thirty years Mark and Elizabeth Prophet have been writing down the teachings of the immortal saints and gurus of East and West, setting the highest standard of metaphysical writing and pioneering the new-age movement. They have produced more than fifty books, including such classics of esoteric literature as *Climb the Highest Mountain, Studies of the Human Aura, Saint Germain On Alchemy, The Science of the Spoken Word* and annual volumes of *Pearls of Wisdom* published weekly since 1958. Their works are widely read and used as the authoritative source on the Ascended Masters. Mark L. Prophet passed on in 1973. An international lecturer, Elizabeth Clare Prophet is based at the Royal Teton Ranch in southwestern Montana, a 33,000-acre self-sufficient spiritual community. Here she conducts workshops and retreats on the practical application of Jesus' life and teachings. For further information write Summit University, Box A, Livingston, Montana 59047.

This breakthrough . . .

in modern religious writing documents the loss of the Master's words. And then sets forth the lost teachings Jesus gave to his disciples two millennia ago—and the very personal instruction he is now unfolding to those whose hearts are inclined to Truth.

Here is a work that is at once inspiring yet profound, entertaining (you'll find yourself laughing out loud) yet full of practical spiritual advice you can use to master the circumstances of your life. And work the "greater works" Jesus promised in order to turn back the approaching darkness of the Four Horsemen of the Apocalypse—war, famine, pestilence and death.

The Lost Teachings of Jesus addresses the real issues of life—

from love to war—and comments on everything from how we influence our own genetic makeup to techniques you can use to re-create yourself in the divine image.

Now you can discover the astral causes of cancer, how you are affected by the thoughts and feelings of people all over the world, and how you can use the science of the spoken Word to help yourself and others fulfill the soul's highest potential.

For the first time you can learn the meaning of many of Jesus' sayings that no longer seem to make sense—puzzling aphorisms like "For he that hath, to him shall be given; and he that hath not, from him shall be taken even that which he hath," "Before Abraham was, I AM," and "Behold, the kingdom of God is within you."

The Lost Teachings of Jesus does more than illumine the scriptures. It sets forth the Everlasting Gospel dictated by the Master to his two witnesses for the enlightenment of an age. It is the key to the sacred mysteries essential to the fulfillment of your immortal destiny.

Did you know . . .

. . .that at least sixteen passages in the Gospels say Jesus was teaching but do not record his words?

. . .that Mark wrote in his Gospel that Jesus taught the multitudes only in parables but when he was alone "he expounded all things to his disciples"?

. . .that Clement of Alexandria, an early Church Father, wrote that Jesus had a secret teaching not recorded in the Gospels and that Mark wrote down part of it for those who were "being initiated into the great mysteries"?

. . .that gospels that may have contained Jesus' original teachings were banned and destroyed by the orthodox Church because it disagreed with them?

. . .that Jesus was almost certainly literate? And therefore anything he may have written was either suppressed or attributed to other authors?

The Lost Teachings of Jesus demonstrates that much of Jesus' teaching has been lost, including

- A good portion of what he said in public
- His secret teachings
- The oral tradition that carried Jesus' teaching in the early Church for at least a century
- The source documents used by the Evangelists
- All but a fragment of a recently discovered secret Gospel of Mark

Nevertheless . . .

in *The Lost Teachings of Jesus*
Mark L. Prophet and Elizabeth Clare Prophet have reassembled the heart of Jesus' message.